Using Managing Your Money®

Mark D. Weinberg

With a Foreword by Andrew Tobias

Que™ Corporation
Carmel, Indiana

Using Managing Your Money®

Library of Congress Catalog No.: LC 86-62530
ISBN 0-88022-277-8

91 90 89 88   8 7 6 5

Interpretation of the printing code: the rightmost double-digit number is the year of the book's printing; the rightmost single-digit number, the number of the book's printing. For example, a printing code of 89-4 shows that the fourth printing of the book occurred in 1989.

This book is written for Versions 3.0 and 4.0 of Managing Your Money.

Dedication

To my wife Leslie and
my daughters Talia, Sharon, and Alison

Development Director
David Paul Ewing

Acquisitions Editor
Terrie Lynn Solomon

Product Director
Terrie Lynn Solomon

Managing Editor
Gregory Croy

Editors
Kathie-Jo Arnoff
Gail S. Burlakoff
Rebecca Whitney

Technical Editor
Linda Flanders

Book Design and Production
Dan Armstrong
Jennifer Matthews
Cindy Phipps
Joe Ramon
Dennis Sheehan
Peter Tocco

Composed in Garamond and Que Digital by Que Corporation.

Screens produced with the INSET program from
Inset Systems, Inc.

About the Author

Mark D. Weinberg, a certified public accountant and a member of the New York and New Jersey Bars, currently practices tax law in New Jersey. He received an undergraduate degree in accounting from the University of Michigan's School of Business Administration and a J.D. from the University of California at Berkeley, with his final year at the Harvard Law School. His accounting and legal experience include three years at the accounting firm of Peat, Marwick, Mitchell & Co. and two years as a tax attorney in the New York law firm of Paul, Weiss, Rifkind, Wharton & Garrison. Mr. Weinberg collaborated in the development and marketing of *The Simple Solution to Rubik's Cube*, the best-selling book of 1981, with more than seven million copies in print. He taught a training seminar on the Managing Your Money program in 1985.

Contents at a Glance

Table of Contents

2 Installing and Starting Managing Your Money 35

Foreword

This is the second book I've read about Managing Your Money. It amazes me that the program has grown to the point books would actually be written about it, let alone, in the case of *Using Managing Your Money*, by an author of Mark Weinberg's exceptional credentials and skill. Mark brings to this project years of financial experience as a C.P.A. for one of the Big Eight accounting firms and in the tax department of a top New York law firm. He also is a hands-on instructor of Managing Your Money.

One reason for the books, I think, is our heavy reliance on HELP screens to guide users through the program. The first two versions of the program, in 1984 and 1985, had pint-size manuals. Even the Version 4 manual expects the user to gain much of his or her proficiency with the program simply by using it, and its on-screen tutorial and HELP screens.

If you've gained that proficiency, you probably don't need this book. If you haven't, you may prefer it to our Version 4 manual and HELP screens. My feelings will be hurt, but I will survive.

If you have an older version of the software, a look through this book—perhaps even a glance at the new Main Menu (pictured on page 16)—may encourage you to upgrade to the latest version. It's much, much better than Version 3. (You need not go out and buy it; MECA will upgrade you at a fraction of the cost—355 Riverside Avenue, Westport, CT 06880.)

If you have a pirated copy of the program, return to its Main Menu and press M for a message. Or learn a lesson from Ms. Mabel Partridge of Mapleton, Ohio, who copied the software from a friend ("Who's to know?" she was heard to chirp shortly before the accident) and who two days later choked to death on a peanut butter and jelly sandwich.

Coincidence? You can believe that if you want to. In any event, I want to urge you to let us know who you are—just call (203) 222-9150 with a charge card and MECA will assign you a valid serial number and welcome you to the family. And I want to thank Mark Weinberg for his confidence in Managing Your Money.

Andrew Tobias

Acknowledgment

I would like to thank my brother Paul for his support and encouragement in the early days of this project. Without the initial push he gave me, this book would never have become a reality.

Trademark Acknowledgments

Que Corporation has made every attempt to supply trademarks about company names, products, and services mentioned in this book. Trademarks indicated below were derived from various sources. Que Corporation cannot attest to the accuracy of this information.

1-2-3, Lotus, and Visicalc are registered trademarks of Louts Development Corporation.

Apple and Apple IIc are registered trademarks of Apple Computer, Inc.

Dollars and Sense is a trademark of Monogram, Inc.

Fast-Tax is a registered trademark of Computer Language Research, Inc.

IBM is a registered trademark and IBM PC XT and PCjr are trademarks of International Business Machines Corporation.

Managing Your Money is a registered trademark of Micro Education Corporation of America (MECA).

ProKey is trademark of RoseSoft, Inc.

SideKick is a registered trademark of Borland International, Inc.

SuperCalc is a registered trademark of Computer Associates International, Inc.

TANDY and TRS-80 are registered trademarks of Radio Shack.

Conventions Used in This Book

The following conventions are used in *Using Managing Your Money* to help you learn the program:

The book uses the term *modules* to refer to the program's chapters. In this way, the program's *chapters* are not confused with the book's *chapters*.

Text that the user is supposed to enter appears in **boldfaced** type.

Prompts and screen messages appear in a `special` typeface.

Key combinations, such as Alt-F7, indicate that you hold down the first key while you next press the second key.

References to keys are generally as they appear on the keyboard of the IBM Personal Computer.

Introduction

People fail to manage their money for a variety of reasons. Many merely want to avoid the drudgery and "number crunching" inherent in financial analysis. They avoid making a simple comparison of a stock investment vs. a money market fund investment because the comparison often involves a series of complex and time-consuming rate-of-return calculations. Other people fail to manage their money because they do not have the time and the financial sophistication to calculate the amount of money they must invest today (considering inflation rates) in order to provide, for example, a future college education for a child who is now three years old.

When low-cost personal computers were introduced, people began to realize that they did not have to be financial wizards in order to make important financial calculations. Many learned the hard way, however, that a computer without good software is worth about as much as common stock in a bankrupt company.

Managing Your Money®, an incredibly powerful financial planning tool, is to personal financial planning what 1-2-3® has been to electronic spreadsheets. Spreadsheets existed before 1-2-3, and financial planning software existed before Managing Your Money, but both programs have taken their respective concepts far beyond the capabilities of their competition.

Similar in many ways to the other financial planning programs on the market, Managing Your Money sets itself apart by its ease of use, its speed, and its capability to generate reports that can help you with your financial planning analyses. The program's Version 4.0, which is the focus of this book, provides increased capabilities and addresses the recently enacted tax law changes.

The Managing Your Money program is so easy to use that you literally can be "up and running" in just a few minutes. You can use the program almost immediately to perform the most burdensome task—balancing your checkbook, for example. Be careful, however, that you don't get so wrapped up in your results that you forget to take advantage of the more powerful capabilities of the program.

Using Managing Your Money

Using Managing Your Money is designed to help you take full advantage of the program's capabilities. Study the book's introduction to financial planning and its in-depth tutorial in order to become proficient in the use of the program's intricacies and to gain control of your personal finances. You then should be able to save money and relieve uncertainty about your future financial obligations.

This book and the program will help you develop your personal financial plan, but they should not be used as substitutes for professional advice from either your accountant or your lawyer. Use the book and program instead as additional tools to develop your financial plan and to maintain your financial data. By organizing your own data and developing tentative plans for achieving your financial objectives before you seek professional advice, you will save both time and money. Pay a professional only for advice, not for data organization.

Financial planning within a constantly changing market is a continuing process of assembling and analyzing your income, your expenses, and your future needs and desires. Using this book along with the Managing Your Money program, you can work through the four basic steps of any good financial plan:

1. Collection and assessment of data

2. Identification of financial goals

3. Assessment of soundness of goals

4. Development and implementation of plan to attain goals

Although this book does not provide any hot stock tips, it helps you assess whether your investment portfolio is too heavily weighted toward stocks. Similarly, the book does not tell you when to sell a particular stock in your portfolio, but does alert you ahead of time when a capital gain is due to become long term or when a stock has hit your target price for selling.

Money management takes work and patience. *Using Managing Your Money* helps eliminate tedious tasks and explains concepts in plain English. Use the book and the program one chapter and module at a time. After completing the tutorial, focus first on concepts that interest you most or that are the most difficult. Eventually, you will be able to use the entire program easily to get a firm grasp of your financial situation.

Who Should Use This Book?

The Managing Your Money program and the book are useful regardless of the current condition of your finances. Although many of the program's functions may seem applicable only to the very rich, the principles of money management are the same for everyone.

Do not assume that the information here is too sophisticated for your situation. In fact, if you have trouble making ends meet, if you have no money invested in stocks, bonds, or a money market fund, if your checking account continually is overdrawn, and if you have reached your credit limit on four charge cards, then Managing Your Money certainly can help you. You can focus on the Budget and Checkbook module of the program to determine exactly where your money goes. A graph quickly can alert you that you are spending too much money on lottery tickets. Even if your problems are not this easy to solve, a budget will help. You probably will find expenditures that you can cut, and soon you can make investments and use the Portfolio module of the program as well.

You will be amazed at how quickly you will find yourself using the many features of the program. For me, the program began as a computerized checkbook and has come to serve as an integral part of my personal financial planning. I used Managing Your Money extensively in my analyses of the tax ramifications of investments I made with the profits from the best-selling book *The Simple Solution to Rubik's Cube*, which I helped to develop and market in 1981. As I have become more comfortable with its capabilities, I have used the program more extensively. Also, its capabilities have significantly improved in each successive version that has been released.

You are exposed to risk regardless of the size of your savings and investments. If you take a conservative approach, then you risk stunting the growth of your "nest egg" and being unable to meet your future financial obligations—a new car or house or college for the kids. Worse, if inflation returns (and it inevitably will), your savings could shrink in value. Before the 1970s, comprehending that money earning interest in a bank actually could give you less "buying power" several years later was difficult. Aggressive investing has risks also. By attempting to achieve an above average return on your investments, you risk losing all or a portion of the money you invest.

No investment is perfect. Moreover, today's "perfect" investment can be tomorrow's real loser. During the 1970s, losing money by investing in oil seemed impossible. After all, consumption in the United States and throughout the rest of the world had increased, and OPEC was operating a "well-oiled" machine. If you lost money investing in oil, you are not alone. Many sophisticated investors lost more than a few dollars when the price of oil steeply declined.

You surely did not buy this book, however, just to be told how difficult money management is. This book *does* contain some answers. For example, the book explains how *diversification*, or spreading out your investments, is the key to wise investing. Instead of investing in that "hot stock" your broker advises or in that "can't miss" real estate investment your brother-in-law recommends, first determine your investment goals and then invest a portion of your hard-earned dollars in several areas. A well-balanced portfolio might include a few stocks, some government bonds, a money market fund investment, and some life insurance. The stock market "crash" of October, 1987, points out the advantages of diversifying. Those who had all of their money in stocks were hurt more than those with diversified portfolios. Bond prices actually rose during this period and such gains helped to offset stock losses.

The Managing Your Money program and the book will help you decide whether your investment portfolio is properly diversified. The process begins when you assemble the facts and figures concerning your current position. The process continues as the program helps you track your investment performance during the year and alerts you to both positive and negative trends, in time for you to do something about them. Finally, Managing Your Money allows you to "factor in" the tax ramifications of all your investment decisions, thereby permitting you to keep more of your gains from Uncle Sam.

About This Book

Using Managing Your Money is divided into three major parts. Part I, Chapters 1 through 3, provides an introduction to Managing Your Money and to financial planning. Part II, Chapters 4 through 11, is a comprehensive tutorial. The tutorial, which covers the program's nine modules, gives step-by-step instructions for using each module's features. Part III, Chapters 12 and 13, gives an overview of the program's graph and report capabilities.

Chapter 1, "Getting Started," describes the nine modules and the other major features of the program.

Chapter 2, "Installing and Starting Managing Your Money," covers the process of getting Managing Your Money up and running on your computer. The chapter also discusses caring for your disks, making working copies of your disks, and backing up your data files.

Chapter 3, "An Introduction to Financial Planning," introduces the basics of sound financial planning. Specific financial planning techniques are covered in the tutorials in the chapters that follow.

Chapter 4, "Using the Reminder Pad," tells you how to program appointments, birthdays, anniversaries, or financial reminders to appear on your computer screen a certain number of days before they occur.

Chapter 5, "Using the Budget and Checkbook," discusses the basics of setting up and monitoring a budget. The text encourages you to work through the examples in order to better understand the concepts of classifying income and expense items.

Chapter 6, "Using the Financial Calculator," explains the range of applications available in this module of the program. Examples are used to encourage a "hands-on" approach to learning the program.

Chapter 7, "Using the Insurance Planner," explains the basics of life insurance and shows you how the program can help you decide how much life insurance you need to buy.

Chapter 8, "Using the Portfolio Manager," gives a comprehensive analysis of proper asset management and covers a variety of the analytical tools provided by the program.

Chapter 9, "Analyzing Your Net Worth," describes the concept of net worth and how it is measured.

Chapter 10, "Using the Income Tax Estimator," thoroughly discusses the basic and not-so-basic tax concepts that must be considered in a financial planning analysis. The chapter also contains a section on the recently enacted tax law changes.

Chapter 11, "Using the Card File," explains how to keep records on your business contacts and friends, how to dial telephone numbers automatically, how to locate names in the Card File, and how to print mailing labels.

Chapter 12, "Creating Graphs," lists and displays some of the most useful graphs available in the program.

Chapter 13, "Creating Reports," describes the many reports that can document your analyses of personal record keeping for tax purposes.

The appendix contains menu maps that act as road maps to the various program functions. By following the maps, you should be able to find your way easily into and out of each module.

The glossary highlights some of the important financial terms that you will encounter in the book and provides concise and easy-to-understand definitions.

The book's comprehensive index can help you locate specific topics in the book.

Enjoy the program and the book. You can't help but save time and ultimately money by using the two to become more proficient with your personal financial planning.

## Part I

An Introduction to Managing Your Money and Financial Planning

## Chapter 1

Getting Started

Everyone practices money management to some degree. Some people have a lot of money to manage but are not very good at it, and others have little to manage *because* they are not very good at it. Everyone can use help in the area of money management.

This chapter gives you some background into the development of Managing Your Money as well as a complete overview of the program's modules and special features. You will learn how the program is structured and how to start using the program immediately.

How Managing Your Money Was Developed

The 1977 introduction of the Apple® computer by Steve Wozniak and Steve Job is generally considered to be the advent of personal computers. The Apple was the first personal computer that was sold preassembled. Although only about 500 Apples were ultimately sold, the Apple is still viewed as the forerunner of all personal computers.

Soon after the introduction of the Apple, Radio Shack, a division of the Tandy Corporation, developed the TRS-80®, which also was sold preassembled. Thus the age of personal computers was born.

Computer stores soon began opening nationwide to sell and service the new machines. Business applications for these computers developed, and personal computers began to find their way into businesses. Individuals were slower to recognize the personal computer's capabilities, possibly because software for individual or home use was slower in its development.

The combination of computers and personal financial management was a natural development because of the computer's capability to perform effortlessly the numerous complex calculations inherent in the financial planning process. Despite the obvious advantages of using computers for financial planning, the marriage of the two was fairly slow in coming.

Initially, only the bold attempted to use spreadsheets to help with their financial planning. First came VisiCalc®, then SuperCalc®, and finally Lotus® 1-2-3. These wonderful programs performed the necessary calculations for financial planning, but they provided no help with the concepts that were foreign to most people. In addition, these programs did not provide the graphs and charts that are essential to gaining a clear picture of one's financial health. In short, the spreadsheet software was sorely lacking as a financial planning tool, and only those with strong financial backgrounds were able to use the spreadsheets for financial planning.

In time, Dollars and Sense® by Star Monogram emerged as the first truly comprehensive piece of financial planning software on the market. That program handled all the basics of financial planning—budget management, income tax estimation, basic stock portfolio management, and net worth analysis. Other financial planning programs followed Dollars and Sense into the marketplace, but none has met with the success of Andrew Tobias's Managing Your Money—a program far superior to anything in the $100 to $225 price range on the market today. This superior program is far and away the best-selling program of its type.

Using Managing Your Money

Managing Your Money does everything the other programs can do, but faster and more easily. In addition, the program provides better and more sophisticated graphs and charts for your records. The Budget and Checkbook module allows you to create and monitor a budget. The Portfolio Manager keeps track of your investments, both stocks and bonds, or whatever you choose to invest in or sell, and it even prints schedules that can be attached to your tax returns.

Before reviewing all of the program's features, this chapter shows you how to begin using the program.

Managing Your Money at a Glance

Published by:
  Micro Education Corporation of America (MECA)
  355 Riverside Ave.
  Westport, CT 06880

System requirements:

IBM® PC, XT™, AT, PCjr™, or PC convertible or IBM compatible.

Display: Color or monochrome (80-column).

Memory size: 192K for all but PCjr, which requires 256K.

Disk drive: One double-sided disk drive.

Operating System: DOS 2.0 or later.

Other Hardware: (Optional)
  Color graphics adapter.
  Printer.

List Price: $219.95

Also available for the Apple IIc®.

Using the Modules

The Managing Your Money program is divided into nine modules, which are accessible only through the Main Menu. You may begin by using all nine modules of the program, or you may use only one or two modules at first and later grow into the others. Whatever your reasons for buying the program and whatever your level of knowledge of the program's capabilities, read this section to be sure that you are aware of what the program can do. Someday, you may find yourself needing one of the program's obscure capabilities, and you will remember having read about it in this chapter.

Start up the Managing Your Money program and play around with it. You can't hurt the program or your computer, and you should practice so that you get comfortable moving into, around, and out of the program. If you haven't yet installed Managing Your Money, turn to Chapter 2, "Installing and Starting Managing Your Money."

After you have installed Managing Your Money, you will need to keep your working copies of the program disks available. If you are using a two disk system to run the program, you should always begin by placing your working copy of Disk 1 into drive A and your working copy of Disk 2 into drive B. The program will prompt you to insert your working copies of Disks 3 and 4 if and when they are needed. If you are using a single drive system, begin by inserting your working copy of Disk 1 into drive A, and the program will prompt you to insert your other working copies as they are needed.

Managing Your Money's logical design means that you don't have to learn a whole new set of commands in order to enter or change data each time you use a new module. On the contrary, the program's command structure works the same way in each of the nine modules.

Using the Keyboard

The function keys (F1 through F10 and Alt-F1 through Alt-F7) and the Enter key make Managing Your Money work. You press the function keys to move around within a module, to move into and out of a new module, or to move into and out of the program itself.

You use the Enter key to enter data into the program or to move the cursor to the next data entry position. You also can use the directional arrows (up, down, left, and right) to move the cursor around the screen.

Some of the shortcuts designed for Version 3.0 should be noted. While you are editing text—whether you are in the Reminder Pad, in the Portfolio Manager, or even in the Budget and Checkbook module—you can move instantly to the end of a line by pressing Ctrl-right arrow (press the Ctrl key and hold it down while you next press the right-arrow key). You can move to the beginning of a line by pressing Ctrl-left arrow. You can delete everything to the right of the cursor on a particular line by pressing Ctrl-End, or delete everything to the left of the cursor on a line by pressing Ctrl-Home.

The program has another feature that speeds things up a bit. If you are editing a date or a dollar amount and you want to move the date ahead by one day or increase the dollar amount by one dollar, press Alt-Shift-plus (press and hold down the Alt and Shift keys while you next press the plus key at the top of the keyboard). To increase by more than one day or more than one dollar, hold the keys down until you get to the proper date or amount. To back up the date or decrease a dollar amount, press Alt-minus. Note: Use the plus and minus keys at the top of the keyboard, not the ones on the numeric keypad.

New to Version 4.0 is Speed Scroll. If you are in the Budget and Checkbook module and want to move the cursor to a particular budget category, the cursor will move automatically if you type the first few letters of the item you want. Whenever the cursor is positioned on a scrollable list, the Speed Scroll function will help you to move quickly. This function, which works also in many of the other modules, is available if you see the words Speed Scroll on the screen.

Completing the First Screen

When you first start the program, the Welcome screen is displayed (see fig. 1.1). With this screen displayed, you can do two things. You can adjust the color scheme, if you have a color monitor. And you can set the date.

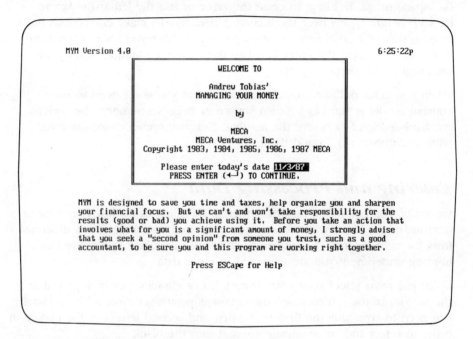

```
MYM Version 4.0                                                    6:25:22p


                        ┌─────────────────────────────────────┐
                        │            WELCOME TO               │
                        │                                     │
                        │          Andrew Tobias'             │
                        │        MANAGING YOUR MONEY          │
                        │                                     │
                        │                by                   │
                        │                                     │
                        │               MECA                  │
                        │         MECA Ventures, Inc.         │
                        │  Copyright 1983, 1984, 1985, 1986, 1987 MECA │
                        │                                     │
                        │   Please enter today's date 11/3/87 │
                        │      PRESS ENTER (◄─┘) TO CONTINUE. │
                        └─────────────────────────────────────┘

        MYM is designed to save you time and taxes, help organize you and sharpen
        your financial focus.  But we can't and won't take responsibility for the
        results (good or bad) you achieve using it.  Before you take an action that
        involves what for you is a significant amount of money, I strongly advise
        that you seek a "second opinion" from someone you trust, such as a good
        accountant, to be sure you and this program are working right together.


                        Press ESCape for Help
```

Fig. 1.1. The Welcome screen, with the date displayed.

Adjusting the Color Scheme

If you have a color monitor attached to your computer, you can change the color scheme of the entire program by pressing the F1 through F10 function keys one at a time. You can access 10 more color schemes by pressing Alt-F1 through Alt-F10. (You hold down the Alt key while you next press the function key.) Decide which colors you like best. If you have a monochrome monitor, then press the F5 key to set the ideal contrast.

Setting the Date

The Welcome screen also sets the current date. If your computer doesn't set the date automatically for you or if the date is wrong, then enter the correct date. The format for the date is month/day/year (MM/DD/YY). You do not need to type the preceding zeros. For example, you can enter February 5,

1986, as 2/5/86 rather than 02/05/86. You do not have to type the year either. Although Managing Your Money will do this for you, you can enter the year if you want. You can type a slash (/) between the month, the day, and the year, or you can type a hyphen (–) or a period (.).

The program is flexible. If you make an error entering the date, use the Backspace or the Del keys to erase the error or use the left-arrow key to back up before typing over the incorrect data. Try to make corrections both ways so that you can find your favorite method. After you have entered the date correctly, press the Enter key. Use these same techniques throughout the program to correct errors.

When you enter dollar amounts, remember that you don't need to use commas or dollar signs ($). When you enter negative numbers, be sure to put a minus sign (–) before the number. Negative numbers are displayed with parentheses ( ) around them.

Entering and Processing Data

Generally, you enter data into the program by filling in blanks. The color or intensity of the blank where the cursor is located on the screen is different from the remainder of the screen. In addition, the cursor is displayed as a blinking underline if you are expected to enter data.

Often you must select your entry from a list of choices that is displayed at the bottom of the screen when the cursor is positioned over a blank. Usually, you need to type only the first or the first and second letters of the choice in order to select and automatically insert it into the blank.

You can process data and move from one module to another in the program by using the function keys (F1-F10). Don't worry, you are not expected to remember the particular function keys that are required to accomplish your objective. At every point in the program, the available options are displayed either in a Mini Menu (see fig. 1.2) or within a rectangular box at the bottom of the screen (see fig. 1.3).

Using the Main Menu

If you have inserted the date and pressed the Enter key, your screen should now display the Main Menu (see fig. 1.4). From the Main Menu, you can access any of the program's nine modules as well as use some of Version 3.0's new functions.

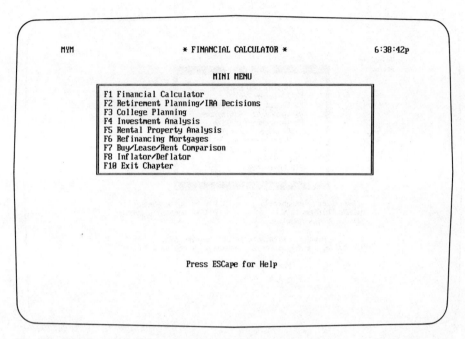

Fig. 1.2. The Financial Calculator's Mini Menu.

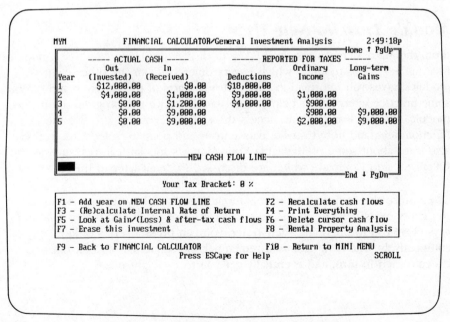

Fig. 1.3. Options displayed in a rectangular box at the bottom of the screen.

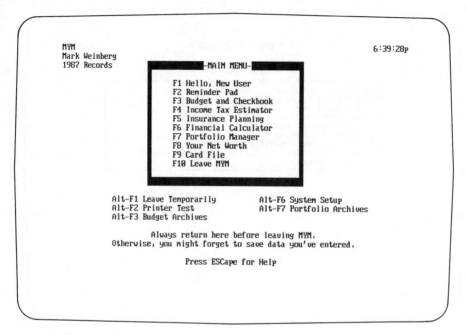

```
MYM                                                          6:39:28p
Mark Weinberg
1987 Records
                         ▓▓▓▓▓▓▓-MAIN MENU-▓▓▓▓▓▓▓
                         ┃                         ┃
                         ┃  F1 Hello, New User     ┃
                         ┃  F2 Reminder Pad        ┃
                         ┃  F3 Budget and Checkbook┃
                         ┃  F4 Income Tax Estimator┃
                         ┃  F5 Insurance Planning  ┃
                         ┃  F6 Financial Calculator┃
                         ┃  F7 Portfolio Manager   ┃
                         ┃  F8 Your Net Worth      ┃
                         ┃  F9 Card File           ┃
                         ┃  F10 Leave MYM          ┃
                         ┃                         ┃
                         ┗━━━━━━━━━━━━━━━━━━━━━━━━━┛

        Alt-F1 Leave Temporarily      Alt-F6 System Setup
        Alt-F2 Printer Test           Alt-F7 Portfolio Archives
        Alt-F3 Budget Archives

               Always return here before leaving MYM.
           Otherwise, you might forget to save data you've entered.

                       Press ESCape for Help
```

Fig. 1.4. The Main Menu.

Module 1: Hello New User

From the Main Menu, press the F1 key to display the Hello New User module (see fig. 1.5). This module, which is very different from the other eight modules, gives you information about various parts of the program and offers some practice exercises to help you get familiar with the program. From this module, you can learn how to access the Help screens, how to use the function keys, and how to make data entries and point to selections. You can also learn about some of Managing Your Money's special features, such as the Calculator and Notepad (which are discussed in detail later in this chapter).

One feature that is described in this module is the ability to type ahead. If you know exactly where in the program you want to go and which function keys (F1–F10) to press and their order, you can press a series of keys consecutively. The computer will remember the sequence of keystrokes, execute each in turn, and eventually get you to the right place.

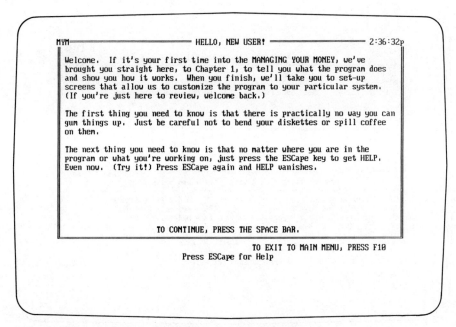

```
MYM══════════════════ HELLO, NEW USER! ═══════════════════ 2:36:32p

  Welcome.  If it's your first time into the MANAGING YOUR MONEY, we've
  brought you straight here, to Chapter 1, to tell you what the program does
  and show you how it works.  When you finish, we'll take you to set-up
  screens that allow us to customize the program to your particular system.
  (If you're just here to review, welcome back.)

  The first thing you need to know is that there is practically no way you can
  gum things up.  Just be careful not to bend your diskettes or spill coffee
  on them.

  The next thing you need to know is that no matter where you are in the
  program or what you're working on, just press the ESCape key to get HELP.
  Even now.  (Try it!) Press ESCape again and HELP vanishes.




                    TO CONTINUE, PRESS THE SPACE BAR.

                                    TO EXIT TO MAIN MENU, PRESS F10
                         Press ESCape for Help
```

Fig. 1.5. The first screen of the Hello New User module.

Module 2: Reminder Pad

You access the Reminder Pad by pressing F2 from the Main Menu. The Reminder Pad (see fig. 1.6) is useful for helping you remember important dates, both business and personal. You can set the Reminder Pad so that it appears on the screen either automatically the first time you start the program each day or only when you request it.

The Reminder Pad offers you many options. You can set a reminder to appear only once on a specific date or monthly, quarterly, or semiannually. You can also specify how many days in advance you want to be alerted to the upcoming reminder. The reminder appears the specified number of days in advance and then each day thereafter until the specified date. This advance notice is important if you need preparation time. For example, if your estimated tax payment is due on June 15, you might need a week or two to transfer the necessary funds from your money market fund or possibly to sell some stock in order to make the payment.

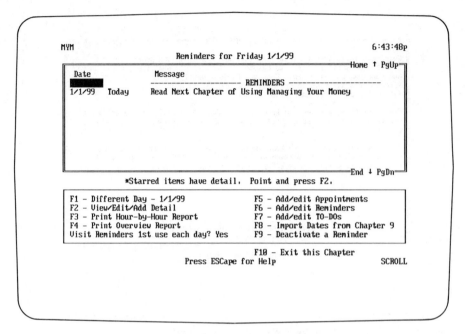

```
MYM                                                              6:43:48p
                          Reminders for Friday 1/1/99
                                                           ┌Home ↑ PgUp┐
 ┌─────────────────────────────────────────────────────────────┐
 │ Date              Message                                      │
 │ ──────────────────────────── REMINDERS ──────────────────── │
 │ 1/1/99    Today   Read Next Chapter of Using Managing Your Money│
 │                                                                │
 │                                                                │
 │                                                                │
 │                                                                │
 │                                                                │
 │                                                                │
 │                                                           ┌End ↓ PgDn┐
 └─────────────────────────────────────────────────────────────┘
              *Starred items have detail.  Point and press F2.
 ┌──────────────────────────────────────────────────────────────┐
 │ F1 - Different Day - 1/1/99         F5 - Add/edit Appointments │
 │ F2 - View/Edit/Add Detail           F6 - Add/edit Reminders    │
 │ F3 - Print Hour-by-Hour Report      F7 - Add/edit TO-DOs       │
 │ F4 - Print Overview Report          F8 - Import Dates from Chapter 9│
 │ Visit Reminders 1st use each day? Yes  F9 - Deactivate a Reminder│
 │                                                                │
 │                                     F10 - Exit this Chapter    │
 └──────────────────────────────────────────────────────────────┘
                   Press ESCape for Help              SCROLL
```

Fig. 1.6. The Reminder Pad.

Module 3: Budget and Checkbook

You can access the Budget and Checkbook module by pressing F3 from the
Main Menu. If you have a two disk system, then your working copy of Disk 3
should already be in drive B. If you have a single disk system, the program
will prompt you to insert your working copy of Disk 3 into drive A (see
fig. 1.7).

```
 ┌──────────────────────────────────────────────────────────────┐
 │ Please put Disk 3 (or disk containing budget.db) in drive A.   │
 │ Adjust the disk and press any key to try again.                │
 │ Press F10 to return to the previous screen.                    │
 └──────────────────────────────────────────────────────────────┘
```

Fig. 1.7. The prompt to insert Disk 3.

Many users spend most of their time in the Budget and Checkbook module (see fig. 1.8). Your needs will determine whether you use all or just a few of the Budget and Checkbook capabilities. Use module 3 to set up budgets, to track your actual expenditures, to print your checks, to reconcile your checkbook, and to perform home banking. Track only certain expenditures, or track every cash, check, or credit card expenditure you make. You can track the transactions in your basic checking account or in your six checking accounts, if that's what you have.

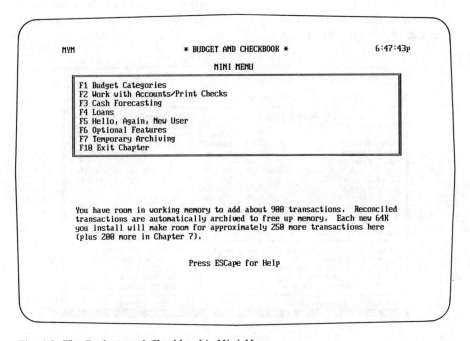

Fig. 1.8. The Budget and Checkbook's Mini Menu.

The information that you enter in this module will find its way into several of the other modules. For example, all the information entered here waits for you in the Income Tax Estimator module when the time comes to prepare your taxes or to turn the information over to your accountant. This integrated system means that information entered in one module and required in order to perform calculations in another module does not have to be reentered. The data automatically finds its own way between areas of the program.

Module 4: Income Tax Estimator

You can access the Income Tax Estimator by pressing F4 from the Main
Menu. If you are using a single or two disk system, the program will prompt
you to insert your working copy of Disk 4 into drive A or drive B.

If you use module 3, the Budget and Checkbook, to keep track of your
inflow and outflow of cash, then that information is waiting to calculate your
taxes for you in the Income Tax Estimator module. You also have the option
of entering information directly into this module. Instead of a Mini Menu, all
functions in this module are accessed through Form 1040, which represents
your tax return (see fig. 1.9).

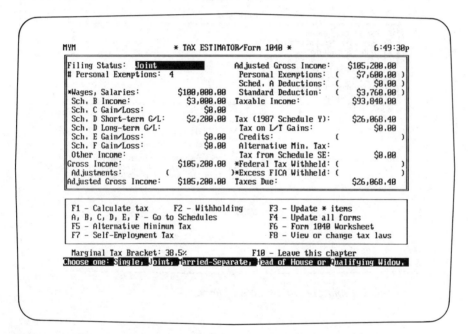

Fig. 1.9. Form 1040.

The powerful Income Tax Estimator allows you to perform "what if"
calculations. What if I defer my bonus to next year? What if I sell my IBM
stock today and recognize a short-term capital gain, or what if I wait until
next month and the gain is long-term? What if the tax laws change, as they
seem to have done almost every year now? How will each one of these
possibilities affect my tax liability?

We all would like our accountants (if we have them) to perform these "what
if" calculations for us. However, the process either becomes prohibitively

expensive, or we or our accountants don't have the time. The Income Tax Estimator allows you to do these things when you do have the time and preferably before the tax year ends and it's too late to make some changes and save some money.

The Income Tax Estimator does not print the actual tax forms that you need to mail to the Internal Revenue Service. The module does, however, print the relevant information for most of the IRS forms. Just review the information and transfer it to the forms.

The Income Tax Estimator is formatted in such a way that, depending on the service used to print your tax forms, you may never have to transfer the information onto paper. So instead of giving your accountant a shoe box full of data that could be lost or improperly treated, you can send instead a disk that contains all the relevant information for the entire year.

Module 5: Insurance Planning

You can access the Insurance Planning module by pressing F5 from the Main Menu. If you are running the program on a single or two disk system, you will be prompted to insert your working copy of Disk 4 into drive A.

When you are ready to start entering your personal financial data, the Insurance Planning module might be a good place to start (see fig. 1.10). Like all the other modules, this small one is easy to follow, and can be entered and exited quickly. If you want to linger in the module, you can experiment by entering various aspects of your lifestyle to see how each one affects your life expectancy.

People seem to be fascinated by this entertaining module's capability to predict life expectancy. Don't be fooled by the fun, though. You can obtain fairly sophisticated information from this module. A financial planner or an insurance consultant would charge you a "pretty penny" to perform an insurance analysis for you, and the results would be similar.

You can use the Insurance Planning module on several levels: to organize and list your various life, health, and other insurance policies; to help you to determine how much life insurance you really need; or to determine the estimated cost of that insurance. Naturally, the results that you obtain here depend to a great degree on the assumptions that you enter into the computer. The same assumptions, however, would be used by a financial planner or an insurance consultant.

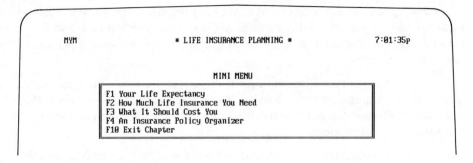

Fig. 1.10. The Life Insurance Planning's Mini Menu.

Module 6: Financial Calculator

Picture one of those fancy Hewlett-Packard pocket calculators that engineers or MBAs carry around: the ones that can calculate present values, future values, internal rates of return, and a whole lot more. On Managing Your Money's equally powerful built-in Financial Calculator (see fig. 1.2 earlier in the chapter), you don't have to read a complicated manual or have an engineering degree just to figure out how to turn on the machine or to figure out why there's no equal sign (=) on the calculator.

You could spend a tremendous amount of time using the Financial Calculator's many features. Because the function key options read as words and not as numbers (see the bottom of fig. 1.3), you don't have to understand the concepts of present and future value that are inherent in many of the calculations, although you surely will understand the results.

You can access the Financial Calculator by pressing F6 from the Main Menu. If you are using a single or two disk system to run the program, you will be prompted to insert your working copy of Disk 2 into drive A.

The Financial Calculator can help you with your retirement planning, with planning for your children's college education, and with various forms of investment analysis. You can analyze the economics of a potential rental property investment or the money you can save by refinancing your home mortgage in order to take advantage of the steep decline of interest rates seen during the past several years. Use the Financial Calculator to help you determine whether you should buy a new car or whether leasing one makes more sense. In short, the Financial Calculator will help you make some of those everyday financial decisions that many people simply are not equipped to make without some help. Managing Your Money provides you with that help.

Review the rest of this chapter to see what it offers. Experiment. Remember: You can't hurt the program. Someday, when you have to make one of these financial decisions, come back and use the Financial Calculator. You will be amazed at how easy it is to use.

Module 7: Portfolio Manager

You can access the Portfolio Manager by pressing F7 from the Main Menu. If you are using a single or two disk system to run the program, you will be prompted to insert your working copy of Disk 4 into drive A.

The Portfolio Manager module (see fig. 1.11) is very helpful if you invest in stocks and bonds. It will not only help you organize your portfolios, but will also enable you to perform time-consuming analyses on your stocks that you might never have taken the time to do.

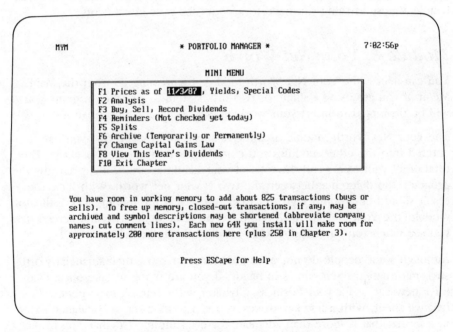

Fig. 1.11. The Portfolio Manager's Mini Menu.

The Portfolio Manager module can organize and analyze the stocks that you hold at Merrill Lynch and at Charles Schwab, and even that tax-exempt portfolio at Citibank. The module can distinguish between taxable and tax-exempt portfolios. In minutes, you can update the prices on your stocks and print out a schedule showing the gain or loss on each stock individually and on the portfolio in the aggregate. Even more important, the schedule tells you which of your gains are long term and which are short term. (This information is relevant in the 1987 tax year, but may no longer be relevant beginning in 1988.) If you hold some shares of the same stock in several different accounts, combine the shares for analysis purposes in order to determine overall how the stock is doing. Without any additional effort, you can see the percentage gain on each of your stocks and be alerted in advance that a stock is about to go long term.

The Portfolio Manager keeps track of your portfolio sales for the year. At the end of the year, without doing any additional work, you can print out a schedule that can be attached to your tax return.

The Portfolio Manager also can handle stock splits, stock dividends, changes in the capital gains laws, the long-term capital gains holding period, and the long-term capital gains exclusion percentage (0 after 1986). The module can handle almost anything you need to account for your investments.

Module 8: Your Net Worth

You can access the Your Net Worth module by pressing F8 from the Main Menu. If you are using a single or two disk system to run the program, you will be prompted to insert your working copy of Disk 3 into drive A.

The Your Net Worth module uses the financial information that you have entered into the other modules and combines it into one neat package. The total of all your assets and the total of your liabilities are brought here by the program; the difference between the two is your net worth. With luck, the result should be a number greater than zero. As in the Income Tax Estimator module, the Your Net Worth Module has no Mini Menu. The first screen that you see when you enter the module is shown in figure 1.12.

Although some people do not need (or want) to know their financial worth, such information often comes in handy. If you are trying to take out a loan for a new car or for your business, a banker will often ask for a personal balance sheet. With a few keystrokes, you can print a personal balance sheet in a format that is more than adequate for even the most demanding banker.

On a more personal level, you can use this module to keep an inventory of the contents of your house or rental property in order to assure that everything is accounted for at the end of the season. Use your imagination and you will surely find other uses for this module as well.

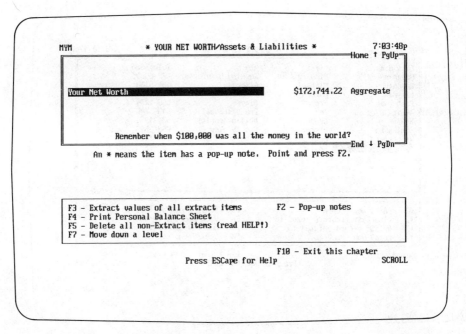

```
MYM              * YOUR NET WORTH/Assets & Liabilities *           7:03:48p
                                                      ═Home ↑ PgUp═╗

     Your Net Worth                          $172,744.22  Aggregate



              Remember when $100,000 was all the money in the world?
                                                      ═End ↓ PgDn═╝
          An * means the item has a pop-up note.  Point and press F2.



     ┌──────────────────────────────────────────────────────────────┐
     │ F3 - Extract values of all extract items    F2 - Pop-up notes  │
     │ F4 - Print Personal Balance Sheet                              │
     │ F5 - Delete all non-Extract items (read HELP!)                 │
     │ F7 - Move down a level                                         │
     └──────────────────────────────────────────────────────────────┘
                                              F10 - Exit this chapter
                              Press ESCape for Help              SCROLL
```

Fig. 1.12. The first Your Net Worth screen.

Module 9: Card File

You can access the Card File by pressing F9 from the Main Menu. The Card
File module might be thought of as a computerized address book, but it is
much more sophisticated than that. The Card File stores names, addresses,
phone numbers, and a great deal more personal information about your
friends and business associates. Moreover, if you have a modem hooked up to
your computer, the module can actually dial the number of any person you
have selected to call. Furthermore, this module can use predetermined
criteria to help you locate someone in your card file. For example, if you
forget the name of the attorney who did some work for you last year, then
your ordinary address book won't be much help. With the Card File, you can
use the Speed Scroll, type the first few letters of the word *attorney*, and the
Card File will locate the attorney or attorneys whom you have used in the
past (see fig. 1.13).

You can also use the Card File to print mailing labels for all or only a
portion of the people listed in your file. Again, use selection criteria to limit
the printing to only those labels that you need. With the new word processor
in Version 4.0, you can use the "mail merge" function to combine form
letters contained in the Wordprocessor with names and addresses in the Card
File.

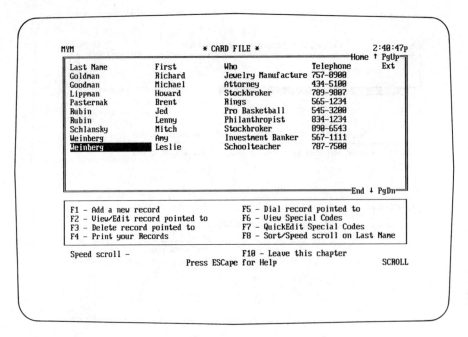

Fig. 1.13. The first Personal Record Keeping screen.

New Main Menu Functions

The five functions on the bottom of the Main Menu screen are relatively new additions to the program (see fig. 1.14). Before the addition of the new functions, these procedures were performed in a roundabout manner by exiting the program and then performing the necessary steps. The new Alt-function keys have greatly simplified the procedures.

```
Alt-F1 Leave Temporarily        Alt-F6 System Setup
Alt-F2 Printer Test             Alt-F7 Portfolio Archives
Alt-F3 Budget Archives

         Always return here before leaving MYM.
Otherwise, you might forget to save data you've entered.

         Press ESCape for Help
```

Fig. 1.14. Version 4.0's functions of the Main Menu.

If you are using a single or two disk system to run the program, you may be prompted to insert one of your working disks into one of the drives.

Alt-F1: Leave Temporarily

When you have to perform a DOS function such as formatting a disk, copying a file, or any of the other DOS functions, you can select Alt-F1 from the Main Menu to do so quickly without having to exit Managing Your Money. After leaving the program by using the Alt-F1 key, return by typing **Exit** and pressing the Enter key and then any other key. You will automatically return to the Main Menu. Remember, when returning to Managing Your Money, don't type **MYM** or you will load the program into working memory again and use up valuable memory space.

If you entered DOS by using the Alt-F1 key, *do not* load any memory resident programs (such as SideKick®, ProKey™, or DOS GRAPHICS.COM) into memory while in DOS. If you do, you may permanently damage your database files. Always load such programs into memory before loading Managing Your Money or after exiting Managing Your Money with the F10 and then F1 keys.

Alt-F2: Printer Test

The Alt-F2 function allows you to test your printer in order to determine whether the proper setup strings have been entered. Press F9 to return to the Main Menu.

Alt-F3: Budget Archives

The Alt-F3 function is a simplified method of accessing your archived Budget and Checkbook data without leaving the program. This function is an improvement over the process that was required in older versions of the program.

Alt-F6: System Setup

Gain quick access to the setup procedures with the Alt-F6 function. If you want to change any of the setup configurations or simply display the current configurations, use this function. Your name will appear on various program reports, and both your name and address will appear on invoices if you print invoices in the program's Budget and Checkbook module.

Alt-F7: Portfolio Archives

Similar to Alt-F3, which allows you to access budget archives, the Alt-F7 function takes you to the portfolio archives, where you can print reports of your archived transactions.

Using the Special Features

Managing Your Money has a number of special features that can be accessed from any point in the program and other features that can be accessed only from within certain modules. Some of these features, which give the program a great deal of flexibility, include the Help screens, the Calculator, and the Notepad. Other valuable features are the report and graph capabilities, the modem capabilities, check printing, and archiving data. Each of these are discussed in the sections that follow.

Help Screens

The program's Help screens truly are helpful (see fig. 1.15). Access a Help screen from anywhere in the program by pressing the ESCape key. While you are in Help mode, no data can be entered into the program and no data can be lost. To return to the active mode, press the ESCape key once again and you will return to the point where you left off.

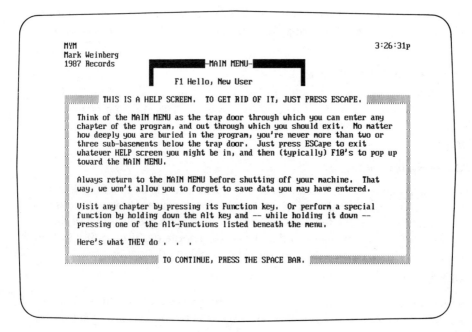

Fig. 1.15. The Main Menu's first Help screen.

The Calculator

Managing Your Money has a built-in calculator. Access the Calculator from anywhere in the program by pressing Ctrl-N. The Calculator display appears at the bottom of the screen (see fig. 1.16). When you press Ctrl-N again, the Calculator disappears, and you return to your place in the program. Note that Ctrl-N is a *toggle*; pressing Ctrl-N once turns on the Calculator feature and pressing Ctrl-N again turns off the feature.

Fig. 1.16. The Calculator.

Try using the Calculator now. Press Ctrl-N, and the Calculator appears. For addition, use the plus key (+); for subtraction, use the minus (-) key; multiplication, the letter X or the asterisk (*); and division, the slash (/). Note that you can use either the plus and minus keys at the top of the keyboard or the ones on the numeric keypad. You do not need to use the equal sign (=). Furthermore, you can put a space between the number and the operation sign, or you can leave spaces out. Unlike some other programs, Managing Your Money is forgiving. Go ahead and try a few calculations.

Type **25 * 10** and your screen should display your entry as shown in figure 1.17. Then press the Enter key, and the answer 250 appears on the far right of the screen—r = 250 (see fig. 1.18).

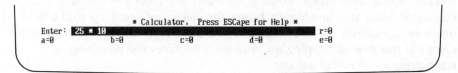

Fig. 1.17. A calculation entered.

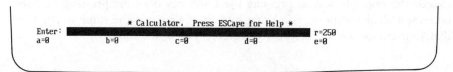

Fig. 1.18. The Calculator with r=250.

Press the F2 function key. The formula then reappears in the Enter line of the Calculator, and the answer is recalculated (see fig. 1.19).

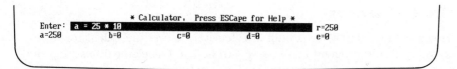

Fig. 1.19. The Calculator with a formula and a result displayed.

To save the answer in one of the program's five memories, type

a = 25 * 10

or

a = 250

and press the Enter key. The result appears in the "a" memory at the left side
of the Calculator. To again retrieve the formula, press F2, and the screen
should look like figure 1.20. The same procedure works for the b, c, d, and e
memories. The results are stored in the memories until you exit the program.

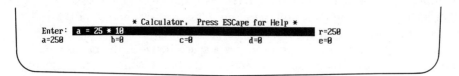

Fig. 1.20. The Calculator with a result stored in memory.

When you complete your calculations, you can exit the Calculator in either
of two ways: press Ctrl-N, or press the Enter key twice. Pressing Ctrl-N takes
you out of Calculator mode. Pressing the Enter key takes you out of
Calculator mode and, in addition, brings the calculated result up to the field
that your cursor was on before you entered Calculator mode. This little trick
saves you the time of retyping the data and eliminates the possibility of
transferring an incorrect amount.

When you are in Calculator mode, pressing the F1 function key works in
exactly the opposite way as pressing the Enter key does. By pressing F1 after
entering Calculator mode, you bring into the Calculator the value in the field
that your cursor was on before you entered Calculator mode.

The Wordprocessor

The Notepad function, which was new to Version 3.0, has evolved into a full-
fledged word processor in Version 4.0.

You can access the Wordprocessor from various locations in the program by pressing Ctrl-E (hold down the Ctrl key while next pressing the E key). The Wordprocessor can be set up to emulate any one of eight popular word-processing programs. The setup is performed either the first time you use the program or by pressing Alt-F6 (System Setup). In the System Setup procedure, you select from the Keystroke Chart screen the specific word-processing program you want to use. (For details, see the section titled "Completing the Setup Procedures" in Chapter 2.)

Reports and Graphs

Managing Your Money has the capability to produce numerous reports and graphs that you can either view on the screen, print to your printer, or print to a disk. Use the reports and graphs in your analysis of your finances. A picture truly is worth a thousand words. (See Chapters 12 and 13 for a list of the reports and graphs and for information on how to access each one.)

You must load a graphics program into the computer's working memory in order to print graphs. Don't worry, you don't have to go out and buy another program. DOS Version 2.0 or later, which already runs your Managing Your Money program, contains a graphics program. To load that program, use the procedures that follow.

Hard disk users:

If you are in Managing Your Money, exit the program by getting back to the Main Menu, and then press F10 and F1. With the C> prompt showing, type **CD\DOS** and press the Enter key. Then type **GRAPHICS** and press the Enter key. Now return to Managing Your Money in the normal fashion (**CD\MYM** and then **MYM**). The graphics program is now in the working memory, and you can print graphs. Caution: Don't use the Alt-F1 method of exiting the program to load the graphics program or you may damage your data files.

One- or two-disk users:

If you are in Managing Your Money, exit the program by getting back to the Main Menu, and then press F10 and F1. With the A> prompt showing and your DOS disk in drive A, type **GRAPHICS** and press the Enter key. Now put your Managing Your Money disk back into drive A and start the program by typing **MYM**. The graphics program is now in the working memory and you can print graphs.

Modem Capabilities

Managing Your Money is equipped to handle telephone communications without using any additional software. To use the modem capabilities, tell Managing Your Money about your modem through the setup program that is described in the "Changing the System Configurations" section of Chapter 2. You can use the modem from within the program's Card File (module 9) to call anyone whose number you have entered into the database. This feature, which can be helpful if you make many phone calls, is discussed more fully in Chapter 11.

You can also use the modem from within the Portfolio Manager (module 7) to update the prices of your stocks and bonds automatically. This capability does require the purchase of additional software, and you will have to pay usage charges in order to tie into the database.

Check Printing

Although the check printing capabilities of the program can be a great timesaver, this option is not for everyone. The details of how to order checks and actually print them are described in Chapter 5 of this book. Basically, this option is helpful if you can sit down and write a number of checks all at one sitting. The option is even more helpful if you have a large number of recurring-item-type checks. If so, then you can program these payments into the computer and write the check with just a few keystrokes.

Archiving Data

Most people have no idea what archiving data means. Because this simple concept has some not-so-simple consequences in the Managing Your Money program, you should take time to understand it fully.

Whether you are running the program on a one- or two-disk computer system or on a hard disk system, your files are divided into program files and data files. A *file* is nothing more than a folder that holds information. The program files make the program do what it is supposed to do. The data files are also contained in folders. When you purchase the Managing Your Money program, the data files contain sample financial data. After you eliminate the sample data and begin to enter your own transactions, the data files then contain your personal financial data. Eventually, the data files become full of data that must be moved to a new file for storage. The new file is called an *archive file*; the process is called *archiving*.

In the Budget and Checkbook (module 3), archiving takes place automatically when you use the program to reconcile your checking account. All the checks and deposits that have cleared the bank will be archived or transferred to an inactive or archive file.

In the Portfolio Manager (module 7), at the end of the year, you must archive all the stocks and bonds that you sold during the year. If you are involved in much trading, you may have to archive before the end of the year, although this is unlikely. You can retrieve and combine archived data with the same year's unarchived data for viewing and printing reports and graphs. However, you should be aware that correcting unarchived data is easier than correcting archived data. Because of this, archiving your data is not recommended unless you run out of space in your working memory. The Managing Your Money program will let you know if this occurs.

Chapters 4 through 11 make up an in-depth Managing Your Money tutorial. You may either go through the tutorial chapter-by-chapter or skip to the chapters about the modules that most interest you. To gain a full understanding of the program, you should work through the entire tutorial.

## Chapter 2

Installing and Starting Managing Your Money

Installing and starting Managing Your Money is really quite simple. The steps vary a little depending on whether you are running the program on a hard disk system or solely with floppy disks. The steps also vary depending on whether you are starting the program for the first time or thereafter.

This chapter provides instructions for installing Managing Your Money on a hard disk system, on a single floppy disk system, and on a two floppy disk system. Just follow the directions for your particular system configuration and you will be up and running in a matter of minutes.

In addition, this chapter gives you the steps for making backup copies of your disks and files, for completing the setup procedures, and for changing your system configurations. You will also find here some advice on caring for your disks and some important information about the copy protection of the Managing Your Money program disks.

Caring for Your Disks

You should handle carefully the four floppy disks that come with Managing Your Money. Do not bend the disks or touch the exposed magnetic surface. Carefully insert and remove the disks from the disk drive. Always keep your disks in their protective envelopes when they are not being used. Do not store a disk in the disk drive. Finally, keep your disks away from heat and magnets.

Note that the disks that came with the program should not be used to run the program. You need to make copies of the program and use the copies as your working disks. Making backup copies is explained later in this chapter.

Understanding Copy Protection

The built-in copy protection scheme in Managing Your Money occasionally requires the insertion of the original Disk 1 that came with the program instead of the working disks. Although this request isn't made very often, you won't be able to proceed until you obey the prompt to insert the original disk. On all other occasions, you should use the working copies that you make of the disks.

Note that the original program disks are "write protected." You can't accidentally copy something else over them.

Getting Up and Running

If you are a seasoned computer user, you probably won't need to work through the following detailed procedures for getting up and running. If you already know the procedure, go ahead and use the DOS command **COPY *.*** to copy the four original disks onto four newly formatted disks (or if you are using high capacity disks, then onto two disks) or onto a subdirectory on your hard disk that you should call \MYM. Don't forget to store the original disks in a safe, accessible place so that you are prepared for those occasional requests by the program for the original Disk 1.

If you are a novice user and are not comfortable with computers, read through the following step-by-step procedures to get you up and running. Three separate and distinct sets of installation instructions are covered here—one if you have a computer with a hard disk, a second if you have two floppy disk drives, and a third if you have a single floppy disk drive on your computer system. Depending on your particular system configuration, you need to read only one set of instructions.

Note that for each type of system, two sets of instructions are provided. The first instructions given are for users who are getting up and running for the first time. The second set of instructions are for those who have already installed Managing Your Money and are merely starting the program.

Installing Managing Your Money on a Hard Disk System

If you are using a hard disk system such as an IBM XT, AT, or compatible, then follow the instructions in this section.

Getting up and running the first time: Assuming that you have already installed DOS on your hard disk, turn on your computer and wait for the C> prompt to appear on the screen. Now you can use the following steps to copy the original program disks onto your hard disk.

1. Type **CD** and press the Enter key to get back to the root directory.

2. Type **MD\MYM** and press the Enter key to create a subdirectory called \MYM.

3. Type **CD\MYM** and press the Enter key to enter your newly created subdirectory \MYM.

4. Put your original Disk 1 into drive A and type

   COPY A:*.* C:

   Press the Enter key to copy all the files from Disk 1 into drive A into the \MYM subdirectory on your hard disk.

5. Remove Disk 1 from drive A and insert Disk 2. Repeat the COPY command in Step 4 to copy the files from Disk 2 to the hard disk.

6. Repeat Step 5 for Disks 3 and 4 in order to copy the files from those disks onto the hard disk.

After all of the copying is complete, type **MYM** and press the Enter key to start up the program. Because this is your first use of the program, you are taken through the setup procedure automatically to inform the program of your hardware configuration.

Getting up and running from then on: After the C> prompt appears, type **CD\MYM**. Press the Enter key and type **MYM**.

Installing Managing Your Money on a Two Floppy Disk System

If you are using a two floppy disk system, follow the instructions in this section.

Getting up and running the first time: Before you begin, you will need four blank, double-sided, double-density disks that will serve as your working copies of Managing Your Money for the current year. Label the disks 1 through 4 and indicate the year and the name of the person using the disks. Then follow these steps:

1. Insert your DOS disk into drive A and turn on your computer. Wait for the A> prompt to appear.

2. Place blank disk 1, which will become your working copy of the original Disk 1, into drive B.

3. Type **FORMAT B:/S** and press the Enter key. This will format the blank disk and will copy the COMMAND.COM file from the DOS disk onto the blank disk. When the formatting of the first disk is complete and you are asked whether you want to format another disk, type **N** for No.

4. Remove the newly formatted working copy of Disk 1 from drive B and insert the blank disk 2 into drive B.

5. Type **FORMAT B:** and press the Enter key. When the formatting is complete and you are asked whether you want to format another disk, type **Y** for Yes.

6. Repeat Steps 4 and 5 for blank disks 3 and 4. When the formatting is complete on disk 4 and you are asked whether you want to format another disk, type **N** for No.

7. Now that the four disks have been formatted, put the original Disk 1 into drive A and the newly formatted disk 1 into drive B. Type

    COPY A:*.* B:

    and press the Enter key to copy all the files from the original Disk 1 to the working copy of disk 1.

8. Remove the original Disk 1 and the working copy of disk 1 from drives A and B, respectively, and insert the original Disk 2 and the working copy of disk 2 into drives A and B, respectively. Repeat the COPY command (as shown in Step 7) for disk 2.

9. Repeat Step 8 for Disks 3 and 4 to copy the contents of those disks onto the working copies of the disks. When you finish, you will have a complete set of working disks to run Managing Your Money.

After all of the copying is complete, remove your original Disk 4 from drive A and your working copy of disk 4 from drive B. Find a safe place to store all four of your original disks. Place the working copy of disk 1 into drive A and the working copy of disk 2 into drive B. Type **MYM** and press the Enter key.

Because this is your first use of the program, you are taken through the setup procedure automatically to inform the program of your hardware configuration.

Getting up and running from then on: Insert working disk 1 into drive A and working disk 2 into drive B and turn on your computer. You do not need to boot up the system first because you have already copied COMMAND.COM onto working disk 1. While you work through the various modules of the program, you will be prompted from time to time to insert the other working disks.

Installing Managing Your Money on a Single Floppy Disk System

If you are using a single floppy disk system, follow the instructions in this section.

Getting up and running the first time: Before you begin, you will need four blank, double-sided, double-density disks that will serve as your working copies of Managing Your Money for the current year. Label the disks 1 through 4 and indicate the year and the name of the person using the disks.

1. Insert your DOS disk into drive A and turn on your computer. Wait for the A> prompt to appear.

2. Type **FORMAT A:\S** and press the Enter key. When you are instructed to insert the *target* disk (the disk to be formatted), insert the blank disk that is labeled disk 1 and press any key to continue. This formats the blank disk that will become your working copy of disk 1 and copies COMMAND.COM onto that disk. When the formatting of this first disk is complete and you are asked whether you want to format another disk, type **N** for No.

3. Remove your newly formatted working copy of disk 1 from drive A and insert the blank disk 2 into drive A.

4. Type **FORMAT A:** and press the Enter key. When the formatting is complete and you are asked whether you want to format another disk, type **Y** for Yes.

5. Repeat Steps 3 and 4 for blank disks 3 and 4. When the formatting is complete on disk 4 and you are asked whether you want to format another disk, type **N** for No.

6. Now that the four disks have been formatted, put your original Disk 1 into drive A, type

   COPY A:*.* B:

   and press the Enter key. Follow the directions on the screen to change the disks between the *source* disk (the original Disk 1, referred to as "the diskette for drive A") and the *target* disk (the newly formatted blank disk, referred to as "the diskette for drive B"). This copies all the files from the original Disk 1 to the working copy of disk 1.

7. Repeat Step 6 for original Disks 2, 3, and 4 to copy the files from each of these disks to the newly formatted disks. When you finish, you will have a complete set of working disks to run Managing Your Money.

After all the copying is complete, find a safe place for all four of your original disks. Place the working copy of disk 1 into drive A, type **MYM**, and press the Enter key. Because this is your first use of the program, you are taken through the setup procedure automatically to inform the program of your hardware configuration.

Getting up and running from then on: Insert working disk 1 into drive A and turn on your computer. You will not need to boot up the system first because you have copied COMMAND.COM onto working disk 1. As you work through the various modules of the program, a prompt tells you from time to time to insert another working disk.

Completing the Setup Procedures

The first time you enter the program, you automatically are taken through a detailed setup procedure. This setup is required in order to alert the program to your particular hardware configuration. For example, you must specify whether you have a hard disk and a modem and the type of printer you are using. This simple procedure should take less than five minutes to accomplish. A step-by-step analysis of the setup procedure follows.

After you have made working copies of your program disks or copied them onto your hard disk, type **MYM** and press the Enter key. If this is your first time using the program, you will be taken automatically to module 1 of the program—Hello New User (see fig. 2.1). You can read through this introductory module later. For now, concentrate on learning how to perform the setup procedures.

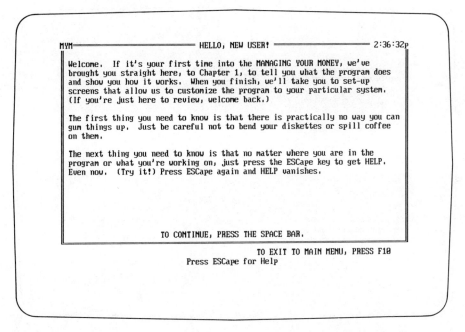

```
MYM═══════════════════ HELLO, NEW USER! ═══════════════ 2:36:32p

 Welcome.  If it's your first time into the MANAGING YOUR MONEY, we've
 brought you straight here, to Chapter 1, to tell you what the program does
 and show you how it works.  When you finish, we'll take you to set-up
 screens that allow us to customize the program to your particular system.
 (If you're just here to review, welcome back.)

 The first thing you need to know is that there is practically no way you can
 gum things up.  Just be careful not to bend your diskettes or spill coffee
 on them.

 The next thing you need to know is that no matter where you are in the
 program or what you're working on, just press the ESCape key to get HELP.
 Even now.  (Try it!) Press ESCape again and HELP vanishes.




              TO CONTINUE, PRESS THE SPACE BAR.

                              TO EXIT TO MAIN MENU, PRESS F10
                 Press ESCape for Help
```

Fig. 2.1. The Hello New User screen.

Press F10 and the setup begins. Your screen should look like figure 2.2. On this screen, you must verify or correct the date. After you type the date, press the F1 key to continue. Your screen should now look like figure 2.3. Assuming that the date is correct, press F1 to continue. Your screen should look like figure 2.4. Now enter your name and address, pressing the Enter key after you type each line in order to continue to the next line.

The date is critical. Among other things, in numerous places in the program, the date automatically is used to calculate holding periods and rates of return. The date also alerts you to important appointments in the Reminder Pad. (For more details, see the "Setting the Date" section of Chapter 1.)

Your name will appear on some of the reports you print. If you use the program to print invoices, your name and address will appear on those.

After you have entered your name and address, press F1 to continue. You are now ready to let the program know what disk configuration you have as part of your computer system. Press F1 again (see fig. 2.5).

On your system, do you have one disk drive, two disk drives, or a hard disk? The program indicates the current configuration. If the current configuration agrees with your disk setup, then press F1 to continue. If it does not agree, then press the appropriate function key to change the configuration: F2 if you

```
   MYM                          Enter Today's Date                    2:05:26p


      Before you actually get into Managing Your Money for the first time, please
      verify or correct today's date:  [11/4/87]




   ┌──────────────────────────────────────────────────────────────────────────┐
   │ Press F1 to continue.                                                      │
   └──────────────────────────────────────────────────────────────────────────┘
```

Fig. 2.2. The Enter Today's Date screen.

```
   MYM                          Enter Today's Date                    2:07:51p




      You've told us it's 1987.  Thus, 1987 will be the year with which we "brand"
      this copy of MYM.  It will be for your 1987 records.  So long as this is
      what you intend, that's fine.  We just wanted to give you a chance to
      correct the year in case it's wrong.

      But wait!  If it's near the end of the year and you don't plan to go back
      and enter all this year's transactions into the program, you can save
      yourself some trouble by lying to us and saying it's January 1 of next
      year.  That will spare your going through the little housekeeping chore we
      do called STARTING A NEW YEAR.

   ┌──────────────────────────────────────────────────────────────────────────┐
   │ F1 - Go ahead!  I'm sure 11/4/87 is the date I want.                       │
   └──────────────────────────────────────────────────────────────────────────┘
      F9 - Go back!  I want to change the date.
```

Fig. 2.3. The Enter Today's Date screen.

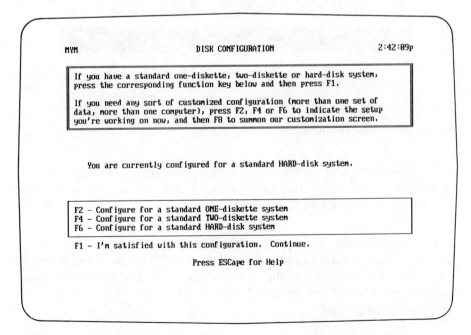

```
   MYM                    Enter Your Name & Address            2:08:38p




              Please enter your name: ████████████████

                      and address:




     ┌──────────────────────────────────────────────────────────────┐
     │ Press F1 to continue.                                          │
     └──────────────────────────────────────────────────────────────┘
```

Fig. 2.4. The Enter Your Name & Address screen.

```
   MYM                      DISK CONFIGURATION                 2:42:09p
     ┌──────────────────────────────────────────────────────────────┐
     │ If you have a standard one-diskette, two-diskette or hard-disk │
     │ system, press the corresponding function key below and then    │
     │ press F1.                                                       │
     │                                                                 │
     │ If you need any sort of customized configuration (more than one │
     │ set of data, more than one computer), press F2, F4 or F6 to     │
     │ indicate the setup you're working on now, and then F8 to summon │
     │ our customization screen.                                       │
     └──────────────────────────────────────────────────────────────┘


             You are currently configured for a standard HARD-disk system.


     ┌──────────────────────────────────────────────────────────────┐
     │ F2 - Configure for a standard ONE-diskette system              │
     │ F4 - Configure for a standard TWO-diskette system              │
     │ F6 - Configure for a standard HARD-disk system                 │
     └──────────────────────────────────────────────────────────────┘
         F1 - I'm satisfied with this configuration. Continue.

                          Press ESCape for Help
```

Fig. 2.5. The Disk Configuration screen.

have one disk drive, F4 if you have two disk drives, and F6 if you have a hard disk system. When you are satisfied, press F1 to continue.

Unfortunately, the Printer Configuration screen (see fig. 2.6) is one of the first screens that appears when you enter the program for the first time. It looks confusing and may overwhelm you a little if you are not a computer whiz. However, informing the program of your printer configuration is quite simple, as is almost everything else in the program.

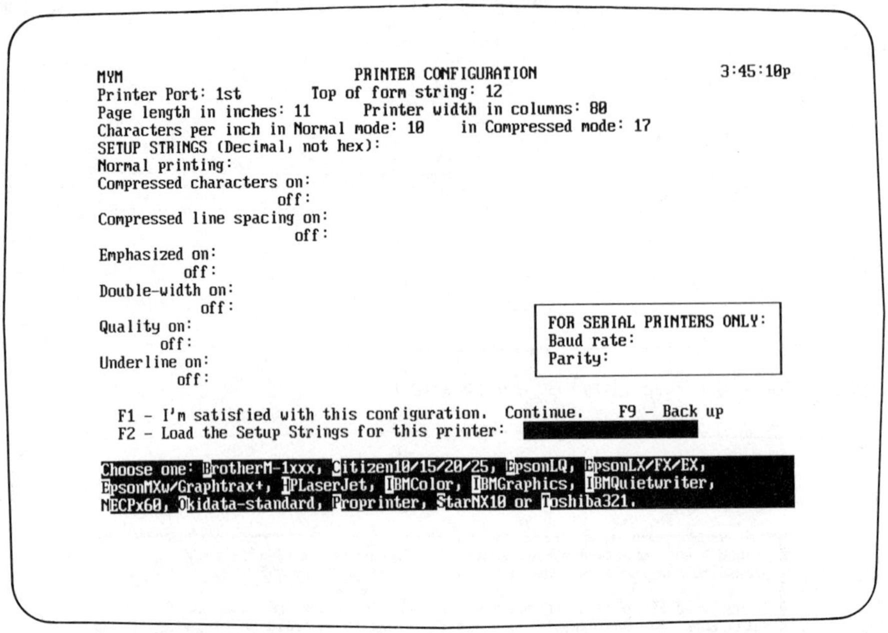

```
MYM                       PRINTER CONFIGURATION                    3:45:18p
Printer Port: 1st         Top of form string: 12
Page length in inches: 11       Printer width in columns: 80
Characters per inch in Normal mode: 10    in Compressed mode: 17
SETUP STRINGS (Decimal, not hex):
Normal printing:
Compressed characters on:
                     off:
Compressed line spacing on:
                        off:
Emphasized on:
          off:
Double-width on:
            off:
Quality on:                         ┌─────────────────────────────┐
        off:                        │ FOR SERIAL PRINTERS ONLY:   │
Underline on:                       │ Baud rate:                  │
          off:                      │ Parity:                     │
                                    └─────────────────────────────┘

    F1 - I'm satisfied with this configuration. Continue.    F9 - Back up
    F2 - Load the Setup Strings for this printer: ▓▓▓▓▓▓▓▓▓▓▓▓▓▓

Choose one: BrotherM-1xxx, Citizen10/15/20/25, EpsonLQ, EpsonLX/FX/EX,
EpsonMXw/Graphtrax+, HPLaserJet, IBMColor, IBMGraphics, IBMQuietwriter,
NECPx60, Okidata-standard, Proprinter, StarNX10 or Toshiba321.
```

Fig. 2.6. The Printer Configuration screen.

Your printer likely will work just fine with the settings as they currently stand. If you are not sure what to do, press F1. If at a later point your printer is not working properly with the program, then you can go back and change some settings.

New to Version 4.0 is the capability of customizing printing for your particular printer. Just move the cursor down to F2-Load the Setup Strings for this printer and select one of the options at the bottom of the screen. Type the first few letters of the printer's name and then press F2 to load the appropriate setup string.

If your printer doesn't work with the program at all and you are sure that your printer is turned on and the cables are all properly connected, try switching the Printer Port entry on the Printer Configuration screen from 1st to 2nd. Then try your printer.

If your printer still doesn't work, then you may have a serial printer instead of a parallel printer. Check your printer manual and enter the baud rate and the parity of your printer. After positioning the cursor in the For Serial Printers Only box, select the baud rate and the parity from the options at the bottom of the screen. If you have a parallel printer, be sure to leave the baud rate and parity boxes blank. Use the space bar to blank them out if something appears in them.

The page length comes preset at 11 inches. If you use legal size paper, change the setting to 14 inches. Also, the printer width is preset at 80 columns. If you have a wide column printer (132 columns), and you are using wide paper, then you should change the printer width to 132.

If you accidentally change some of the numbers and want to get back to the original settings, retype the printer name in the blank at the bottom of the page and then press F2. After you are finished with the printer setup, press F1 to display the Modem Configuration screen (see fig. 2.7).

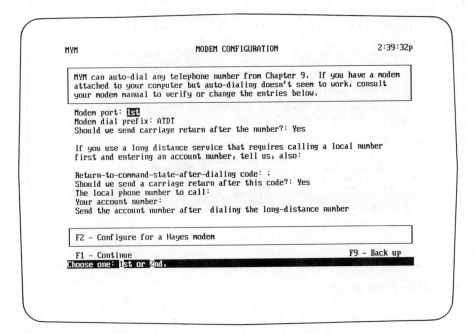

Fig. 2.7. The Modem Configuration screen.

You should be getting good at this by now. You probably do not need to make any changes on this screen if you have a Hayes modem or one that is a Hayes compatible. Press F1 to continue.

A full-fledged word processor is built into Version 4.0 of Managing your Money. The program, which is called WRITE ON THE MONEY, allows you to create complete documents and to keep track of more detail in your financial affairs.

For example, wherever the program provides you with one or two lines for inserting text, you now can enter the word processor and enter as much detail as you like.

The Keystroke Chart screen shown in figure 2.8 allows you to customize the word processor. By using the F2 function key to instruct WRITE ON THE MONEY to resemble one of eight popular word-processing programs, thereby eliminating the need to learn an entirely new set of keystrokes, you can be up and running with your new word processor in a matter of minutes.

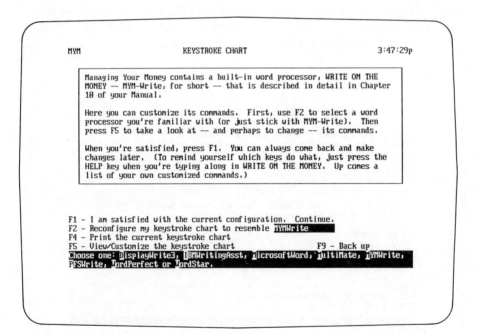

Fig. 2.8. The Keystroke Chart screen.

Press F5 to view the keystroke chart for the specific word processor you selected. This chart gives you the basics for producing and editing a document (see fig. 2.9). Press F9 to back up.

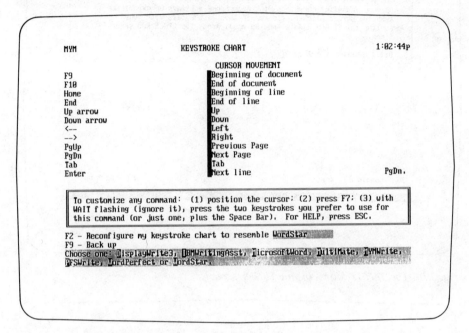

Fig. 2.9. The Keystroke Chart for WordStar.

If you want to print a copy of the keystroke chart, press F4 and then, after you have instructed the program to print to the printer, to the computer screen, or to a disk, press F1.

When you are satisfied with your selection, press F1 to continue.

Do not do anything on the screen that appears unless you have a TANDY® monochrome monitor (see fig. 2.10). Press F1 to continue.

You've made it! You are ready to save the setup information. Your screen should look like figure 2.11.

Press F1 to save the information. Now you should find yourself at the Main Menu of the program (see fig. 2.12).

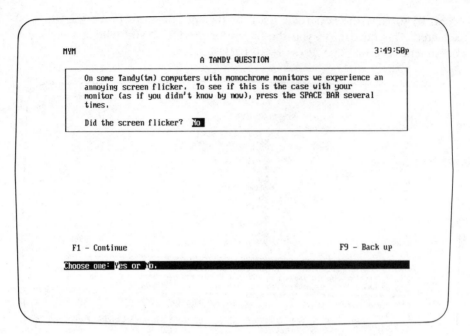

Fig. 2.10. The TANDY Monochrome Flicker screen.

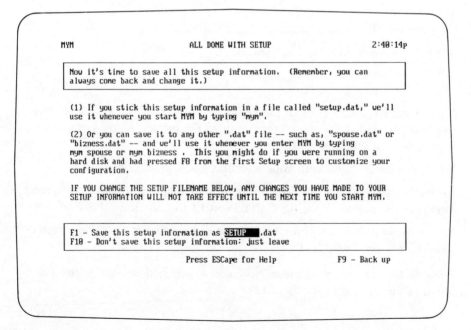

Fig. 2.11. The All Done with Setup screen.

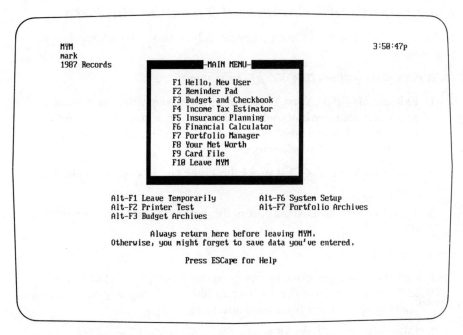

```
 MYM                                                         3:58:47p
 mark
 1987 Records            ┌────────MAIN MENU────────┐
                         │ F1 Hello, New User       │
                         │ F2 Reminder Pad          │
                         │ F3 Budget and Checkbook  │
                         │ F4 Income Tax Estimator  │
                         │ F5 Insurance Planning    │
                         │ F6 Financial Calculator  │
                         │ F7 Portfolio Manager     │
                         │ F8 Your Net Worth        │
                         │ F9 Card File             │
                         │ F10 Leave MYM            │
                         └──────────────────────────┘

       Alt-F1 Leave Temporarily       Alt-F6 System Setup
       Alt-F2 Printer Test            Alt-F7 Portfolio Archives
       Alt-F3 Budget Archives

             Always return here before leaving MYM.
         Otherwise, you might forget to save data you've entered.

                        Press ESCape for Help
```

Fig. 2.12. The Main Menu.

You are now ready to begin exploring the program capabilities. Note that if Managing Your Money isn't working properly on your system, you can change the setup configuration by pressing Alt-F6 from the Main Menu. (See the "Changing the System Configuration" section later in this chapter.)

Making Backup Copies

The importance of having backup copies of your data files cannot be overemphasized. Get into the habit of making backup copies after each working session. That way, the most data you can lose is what you have entered into the program in the most recent working session.

You can back up your files in either of two ways. The first method is to exit the program and use the DOS COPY command. The other method is to use Version 4.0's backup capability. The latter method involves using the function keys prior to exiting the program. Both methods are covered in the sections that follow.

Using the COPY Command To Make Backups

To back up by using the COPY command, follow the steps appropriate for your system.

On a hard disk system (IBM XT, AT, or compatible):

1. Exit the Managing Your Money program through the Main Menu and insert into drive A your backup disk; or, if this is your first time backing up, insert a blank formatted disk. Make sure that you are still in the \MYM subdirectory.

2. Type **COPY *.DB A:** and press the Enter key to copy your database files.

3. Type **COPY *.ARK A:** and press the Enter key to copy your archive files.

On a two floppy disk system:

1. Exit the Managing Your Money program through the Main Menu and insert into drive B your backup disk; or, if this is your first time backing up, insert a blank formatted disk.

2. Insert into drive A the disk that you want to back up.

3. Type **COPY A:*.DB B:** and press the Enter key to copy your database files from your working disk in drive A to your backup disk in drive B.

4. Type **COPY A:*.ARK B:** and press the Enter key to copy your archive files from your working disk in drive A to your backup disk in drive B.

5. Remove your working disk from drive A and repeat Steps 3 and 4 for each of your working disks on which you have made changes since the last time that you backed up your files.

On a single floppy disk system:

1. Exit the Managing Your Money program through the Main Menu and have your backup disk handy, or a newly formatted disk if this is the first time that you are backing up.

2. With the working disk that you want to back up in drive A, type **COPY A:*.DB B:** and press the Enter key. After the prompt, insert your backup disk into drive A. The program will copy your database files from your working disk to the backup disk.

3. Type **COPY A:*.ARK B:** and press the Enter key. After the prompt, insert your backup disk into drive A. The program will copy your archive files from your working disk to the backup disk.

4. Remove your backup disk from drive A and repeat Steps 2 and 3 for each of your working disks on which you have made changes since the last time that you backed up your files.

On single floppy disk systems, note that the disk that you want to copy from is the *source* disk (your working disk) on drive A, and the disk that you are copying to is the *target* disk (your backup disk) on drive B. This is true even though no drive B exists on your system.

Using Managing Your Money To Make Backups

The capability to back up through the program is a relatively new enhancement to Managing Your Money. Backing up using the program itself is a simpler method than using the COPY command.

To back up through the program, you press F10 from the Main Menu in order to leave the program. Go ahead and press F10 from the Main Menu now. If you are running the program on a single disk system or on a hard disk system, your screen should look like figure 2.13. If you are running the program on a two disk system, your screen should look like figure 2.14.

To leave without backing up, press F1 at the Leaving MYM screen, and you will be back in DOS. If you would like to back up, the process is very simple. The cursor will be positioned at the prompt

    My backup disk is in drive: _.

Type the letter of the drive where you have placed your backup disk.

If you have two disk drives, you typically place the backup in drive B, put each working disk in drive A one at a time, and press F3 and/or F4 for each disk. The database files and the archive files from each disk are then copied onto the backup disk. After you have completed this process (which takes no more than a minute or two), press F1 to leave Managing Your Money.

If you have a hard disk system, you typically place the backup in drive A, and you have the additional option of using the F5 and F6 functions to back up your database and archive files instead of copying them. This is just one more possibility, and does not provide any distinct advantages. If the F5 and F6 functions are used, to retrieve such backed up files, you must use the DOS RESTORE command.

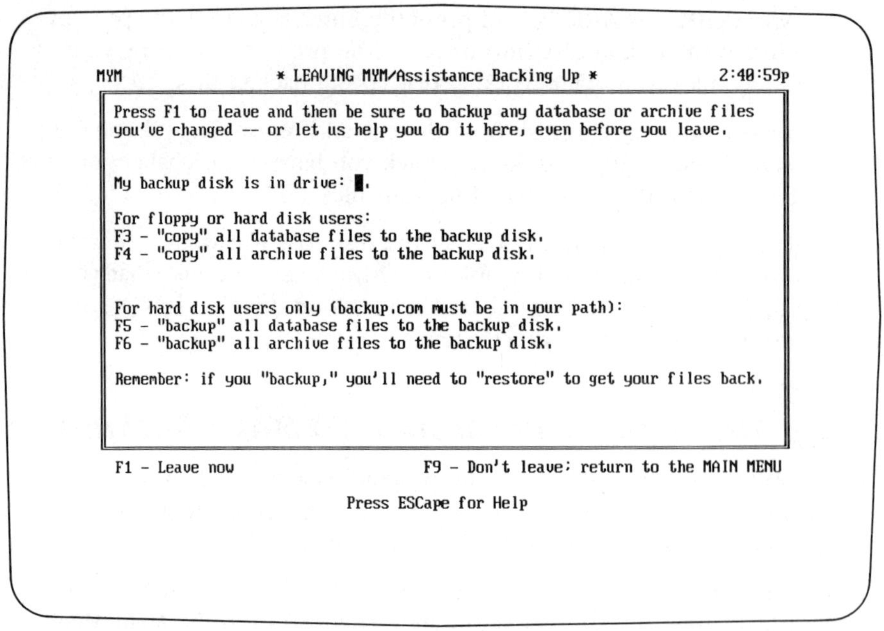

```
MYM              * LEAVING MYM/Assistance Backing Up *              2:40:59p

  Press F1 to leave and then be sure to backup any database or archive files
  you've changed -- or let us help you do it here, even before you leave.


  My backup disk is in drive: █.

  For floppy or hard disk users:
  F3 - "copy" all database files to the backup disk.
  F4 - "copy" all archive files to the backup disk.


  For hard disk users only (backup.com must be in your path):
  F5 - "backup" all database files to the backup disk.
  F6 - "backup" all archive files to the backup disk.

  Remember: if you "backup," you'll need to "restore" to get your files back.



  F1 - Leave now                    F9 - Don't leave; return to the MAIN MENU

                      Press ESCape for Help
```

*Fig. 2.13. The Leaving MYM/Assistance Backing Up screen for single disk
and hard disk systems.*

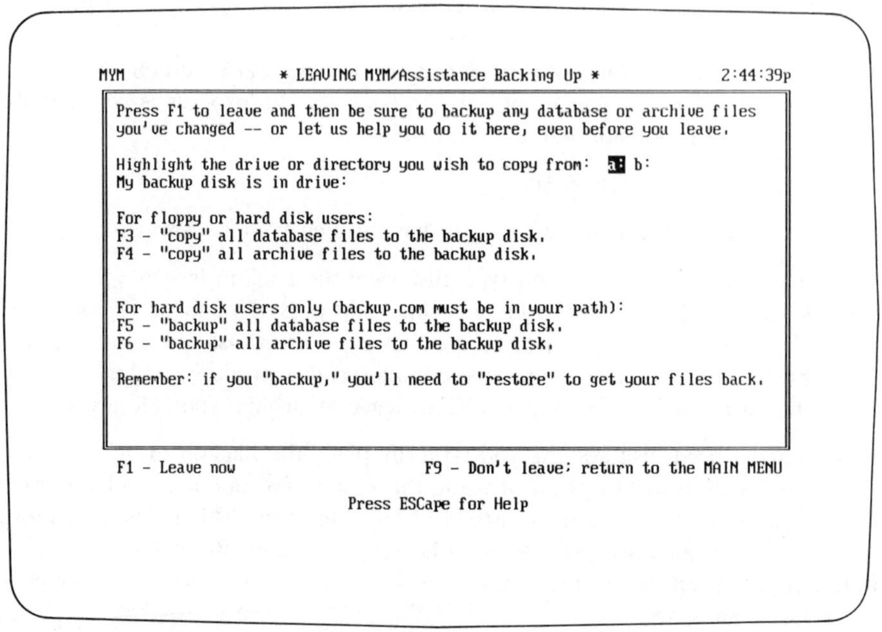

```
MYM              * LEAVING MYM/Assistance Backing Up *              2:44:39p

  Press F1 to leave and then be sure to backup any database or archive files
  you've changed -- or let us help you do it here, even before you leave.

  Highlight the drive or directory you wish to copy from:  a  b
  My backup disk is in drive:

  For floppy or hard disk users:
  F3 - "copy" all database files to the backup disk.
  F4 - "copy" all archive files to the backup disk.


  For hard disk users only (backup.com must be in your path):
  F5 - "backup" all database files to the backup disk.
  F6 - "backup" all archive files to the backup disk.

  Remember: if you "backup," you'll need to "restore" to get your files back.



  F1 - Leave now                    F9 - Don't leave; return to the MAIN MENU

                      Press ESCape for Help
```

*Fig. 2.14. The Leaving MYM/Assistance Backing Up screen for two disk
systems.*

Changing the System Configurations

If you change your system setup, you must alert Managing Your Money to those changes. For example, you might change your setup by acquiring a new printer, changing to a color monitor, installing a modem, or making another equipment change. Version 4.0 makes specifying new system configurations simple. You can either modify the standard disk configurations, or you can create customized configurations.

Modifying the Standard Disk Configurations

To change the standard disk configurations, first enter the program as you normally would and go to the Main Menu. Press Alt-F6 to get to the setup screens. Proceed as you did the first time that you entered the program and inform the program about your disks, modem, and printer. If you have trouble getting the system set up properly, ask the dealer from whom you purchased your computer to help you, or better yet, complete the setup screens and then try running the program to see whether it works. If you guess wrong, just a few minutes are needed for you to go back and set up again.

Creating Customized Configurations

Instead of using the standard configurations, you can create your own customized setup. The program's setup screens discuss how to use the program with several sets of data or with one set of data on more than one computer. From the Main Menu, press Alt-F6. Notice at the top of the Disk Configuration screen the discussion about customized configurations (refer to fig. 2.5).

After specifying your disk configuration, you are instructed to press F8. The Customized Setup screen should be displayed (see fig. 2.15).

Because you may find the directions on this screen a little confusing, step-by-step instructions are provided later in this section. Suppose, for example, that several members of your family want to use the Managing Your Money program to separately keep track of their personal finances, or that you merely want to keep track of your personal and business finances separately. You can proceed in one of several ways.

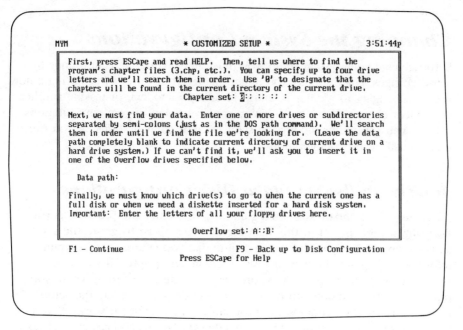

MYM   * CUSTOMIZED SETUP *   3:51:44p

First, press ESCape and read HELP. Then, tell us where to find the
program's chapter files (3.chp, etc.). You can specify up to four drive
letters and we'll search them in order. Use '0' to designate that the
chapters will be found in the current directory of the current drive.
                      Chapter set: █:: :: :: :

Next, we must find your data. Enter one or more drives or subdirectories
separated by semi-colons (just as in the DOS path command). We'll search
them in order until we find the file we're looking for. (Leave the data
path completely blank to indicate current directory of current drive on a
hard drive system.) If we can't find it, we'll ask you to insert it in
one of the Overflow drives specified below.

  Data path:

Finally, we must know which drive(s) to go to when the current one has a
full disk or when we need a diskette inserted for a hard disk system.
Important: Enter the letters of all your floppy drives here.

                      Overflow set: A::B:

F1 - Continue   F9 - Back up to Disk Configuration
                      Press ESCape for Help

Fig. 2.15. The Customized Setup screen.

If you have a single disk or a two disk computer system, then just make
several copies of the four program disks and give a set to each member of
the family. Don't forget to label each set of disks with a felt-tip marker so
that they don't get mixed up.

If you have a hard disk computer system, then you can copy the entire set of
files, both program and data files, into separate working subdirectories on
your hard disk. For example, you could create a subdirectory to store the
Managing Your Money program files and store within a sub-subdirectory your
personal records. In the same way, you could create another subdirectory to
hold another copy of the program files and store in a sub-subdirectory your
business records. This approach, wherein you store multiple copies of the
program files, is not recommended because it takes more than 500K of
storage for each such set of files. A better approach is to make one \MYM
subdirectory that contains the program files on your hard disk and keep each
family member's data files on a separate floppy disk or in a separate
subdirectory on the hard disk. Each of these methods is discussed in the
sections that follow.

Using the Floppy Disk Method

If you elect to use the floppy disk method, the program speed is reduced, but you have greater flexibility and increased privacy. You have the flexibility to transport your data files between your home and your office and to update them at either location. You also maintain private control of the data on the floppy disks.

If this method sounds attractive, follow these steps to copy your data files onto a floppy disk:

1. After copying the four original program disks into the \MYM subdirectory on your hard disk, place a newly formatted disk into drive A.

   If you don't have a formatted disk, then place an unformatted disk into drive A and type **FORMAT A:** and press the Enter key.

2. When the formatting is complete, go back into your \MYM subdirectory (CD\MYM) and with your newly formatted disk in drive A, type

   COPY *.DB A:

   and press the Enter key. This copies your database files onto the floppy disk. When this is completed, type

   COPY *.ARK A:

   and press the Enter key. This copies your archive files onto the floppy disk.

You now have one disk that holds your database and archive files. Each time you use the program, you must insert this disk into drive A. To make additional disks for other family members, merely repeat Steps 2 with a separate formatted disk for each family member or for each set of data that you want to maintain. Don't forget to label the disks properly so that you don't confuse your personal data with your business data or your own data with your daughter's data.

You must now direct the program to look for your database files and archive files on the floppy disks and not on your hard disk. Here are the setup procedures:

1. From the Main Menu, press Alt-F6 to display the Disk Configuration screen (see fig. 2.5).

2. After specifying your disk configuration, press F8 to access the Customized Setup screen (see fig. 2.15).

3. The first question on the Customized Setup screen concerns the chapter set. Enter the number 0 to tell the program to look in the default drive (drive C) for the program files.

4. The next question concerns the data path. Enter the letter of the disk drive where your data will reside. Generally, this will be drive A. This information tells the program to look for the database and archive files in the specified drive.

5. To answer the next question on the Customized Setup screen, indicate the drive where the program should look for data when the data disk is full. This can either be the same drive as specified in Step 4 or another floppy drive if you have both an A and a B drive.

   You are now ready to go back into the program.

6. Press F1 to continue.

   You will have to respond to the remaining questions on the Customized Setup screen in order to complete the setup procedure. If you haven't changed anything else, you can merely press F1 for each screen. Then type **MYM** to start the program. Don't forget to insert your floppy disk in the drive that you specified to handle the data.

Using the Separate Subdirectory Method

Using the separate subdirectory method has some advantages over the floppy disk method. The separate subdirectory method allows you to maintain separate sets of data on the same hard disk. Also, by working only on the hard disk, you don't sacrifice any program speed. Reading and writing to a floppy disk drive requires much more computer time than the same procedures on a hard disk drive.

The separate subdirectory method is also superior to copying all the files, both program and data files, into separate subdirectories on the hard disk. You save disk space by storing only one set of program files rather than several. You can copy one set of program files into a subdirectory on your hard disk and then store numerous sets of database and archive files in separate subdirectories. Each set of data files uses the same set of program files contained in the \MYM subdirectory.

If the separate subdirectory method is for you, follow these steps to set up the program:

1. From the Main Menu, press Alt-F6 to access the setup procedures displayed on the Disk Configuration screen (see fig. 2.5).

2. After pressing F6 to indicate that you have a hard disk, press F8 to access the Customized Setup screen (see fig. 2.15).

3. On the Customized Setup screen, respond to the chapter set question by entering the number 0. This tells the program to look in the default drive (drive C) for the program files.

4. Assuming that you want to maintain one set of files for personal records and one set of files for business records, store the personal data files in a subdirectory called \MYM\PERS and the business data files in a subdirectory called \MYM\BUS. Set up each set of files separately. The second question on the Customized Setup screen asks for the data path or where the program should look for the data files. Type **\MYM\PERS** and press the Enter key. (You will repeat this process for the business records in just a moment.) Your answer to this question will allow you to place your personal data files in a subdirectory under the \MYM subdirectory called \PERS.

5. The answer to the question regarding the overflow set of data instructs the program where to look for data when the data disk is full. You should respond to the question by indicating the same drive that you specified in Step 4. However, in addition, you can indicate a floppy drive to allow for when the hard disk is full.

6. Assuming that you haven't changed anything else, you can merely press F1 for each screen to answer the remaining setup questions and then save the setup under the name PERS.DAT.

7. Press F1 to save the setup data and to return automatically to the Main Menu.

To create the subdirectory for your business files repeat the preceding Steps 1 through 6, making the following changes:

1. In Step 4, instead of typing \MYM\PERS for the data set, type **\MYM\BUS** and press the Enter key.

2. In Step 6, instead of saving the setup under the name PERS.DAT, type **BUS.DAT** and then press the F1 key.

To create additional sets of data, for other members of your family or for others in your office, repeat the separate subdirectory procedure. Each time you use the procedure, substitute a different subdirectory name for the data set and use a different name for storing the setup data.

You are not quite finished yet. You have instructed the program to store the separate sets of data files in separate subdirectories, but you have not yet created the subdirectories nor have you copied those files into the subdirectories. To do that, first go to the Main Menu and press F10 and then F1 to exit the program. Next, follow these steps to create the subdirectories and to copy your data files into those subdirectories:

1. At the C> prompt, type **CD** and press the Enter key. This assures that you are back at the root directory.

2. To create the first subdirectory, type **MD\MYM\PERS** and then press the Enter key.

3. To create the second subdirectory, type **MD\MYM\BUS** and then press the Enter key.

4. Now type **CD\MYM** to go into the \MYM subdirectory.

5. Type **COPY *.DB\MYM\PERS** to copy the database files into the \MYM\PERS subdirectory.

6. Type **COPY *.ARK\MYM\PERS** to copy the archive files into the \MYM\PERS subdirectory.

7. Type **COPY *.DB\MYM\BUS** to copy the database files into the \MYM\BUS subdirectory.

8. Type **COPY *.ARK\MYM\BUS** to copy the archive files into the \MYM\BUS subdirectory.

You now have one set of Managing Your Money database and archive files in a subdirectory for your personal records and another full set of database and archive files in a subdirectory for your business records. There is nothing magical about the names PERS and BUS. You can choose your own names for your subdirectories.

Whenever you start the program and the C> prompt appears, type **CD\MYM** to get into the \MYM subdirectory. Then, instead of typing MYM to start the program, type **MYM PERS** to access your personal data and **MYM BUS** to access your business data.

## Chapter 3

An Introduction to Financial Planning

The topic of financial planning has received more than its share of press during the past couple of years. A person literally cannot open a newspaper or turn on a television without coming in contact with some aspect of the financial planning boom. In January, 1986, a *Consumer Reports* article entitled "Financial Planners: What Are They Really Selling?" chronicled the confusion surrounding today's complex financial markets and the difficulty that the average person has in obtaining competent advice. Eight months later, *The New York Times* devoted an entire Sunday pull-out section to personal finance and cautioned readers to choose financial planners carefully.

Despite these and other articles, more people are asking: What is financial planning and what do financial planners really do? The question has no simple answer because the financial planning industry is currently undergoing tremendous growth and constant change. Financial planning, though not a new industry, was historically used only by wealthy people. Planners now are beginning to serve middle income individuals by offering them strategies for selecting investments, improving cash flow, minimizing taxes, and building wealth.

Should You Hire a Financial Planner?

The number of financial planners and those who call themselves financial planners has grown at a tremendous rate to meet the increasing demand for their services. Among those devoting their energies to capturing a portion of what can be a lucrative market are bankers, insurance agents, accountants, lawyers, and brokers. Stockbrokers who work for major investment houses have changed their titles to "financial consultants." And finding life insurance salespeople today has become difficult because they have become "financial planners," many with little or no additional training.

As in any other business (and financial planning is big business), you find good planners and bad planners. Although stories of the bad ones abound, some extremely well-qualified people can help you save money on your taxes and can steer you in the right direction in plotting your investment strategy.

Despite the recent trend, not everyone needs a financial planner. Depending on your financial sophistication, you may be best able to determine your own investment strategy. After all, you understand better than anyone your tolerance for risk and your financial goals.

In the past, even many of the people who understood the concepts went to professionals because they didn't want to spend their time calculating and recalculating the numbers. Those days are gone. Personal computers and sophisticated money-management computer programs such as Managing Your Money will do most of the necessary calculations for you. What's more, coupling this book and the program should help you understand the concepts underlying every financial plan. If you don't have complete trust in yourself and the program, then work out your own financial plan and take the results to an accountant or a financial planner for review. In time, you should find that your results are not significantly different from those you would obtain from a professional.

If you are determined to hire a professional, then understanding the concepts will help you evaluate planners and make an informed decision about the one best suited to your needs. In addition, because the program will help you organize your financial data, the fee you are charged will be less than that for someone who carries to the planner a shoe box full of data.

How Do You Choose a Financial Planner?

Selecting a financial planner from among the large number available is not an easy task. The majority of financial planners are associated with one of two primary trade organizations: the International Association for Financial Planning (IAFP), which is the larger of the two with approximately 22,000 members (see fig. 3.1), and the Institute of Certified Financial Planners (ICFP), which has about 18,000 members. These figures represent an overall 400 percent increase in membership in the two organizations since 1981, and the numbers keep growing. No accurate figures are available for the number of additional financial planners who are not members of one of these two trade organizations, although estimates range from 50,000 to 150,000.

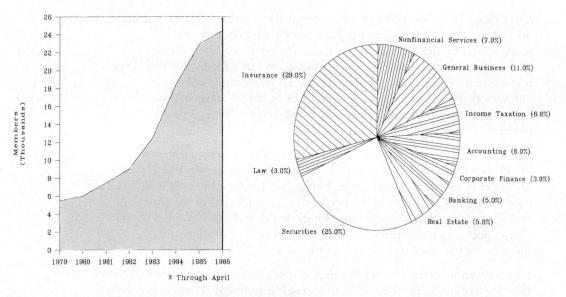

*Fig. 3.1. Membership in the International Association for Financial
Planners and members' backgrounds. Source: IAFP.*

Although the number of available planners is large, virtually no regulation of
their industry exists. Almost anyone can take the title "financial planner" and
hang out a shingle, although several well-documented abuses have created a
move by both planners and legislators for tighter regulation. The ICFP argues
that additional regulation is not needed, but instead, that existing laws should
be more strictly enforced. The IAFP favors the creation of a self-regulatory
organization, similar to the Financial Accounting Standards Board for
accountants, that would set and enforce standards for financial planners. Until
these changes occur, and that may not be any time soon, the best advice is
to be wary.

Membership in either of the trade groups does not guarantee that a selected
planner is competent. Membership in the IAFP means merely that the
planners each have paid a $125 fee and that they have agreed to abide by a
code of ethics that requires them to be honest, to avoid misleading
representations, and to disclose potential conflicts of interest. No tests are
required, and no specific educational requirements must be met. However, to
be listed in the IAFP's Registry of Financial Planning Practitioners, planners
must have three or more years of financial planning experience, meet
specified educational requirements, and pass a written examination
administered by the organization. In addition, planners must submit
references and sample financial plans for review by a committee.

Approximately 12,000 planners have earned the "certified financial planner" title. That title indicates that they have passed a number of tests— administered by the College for Financial Planning—covering taxation, insurance benefits, estate planning, investing, and other similar topics. Other planners have earned the "chartered financial consultant" title, which indicates that they have passed a number of tests that are generally considered more demanding than the tests taken by certified financial planners.

Basically, three types of planners are available. The *fee-only* planner sells only the financial plan and then sends you to other people to purchase investments. Another type of planner charges a fee for plans and then earns a commission, often as high as 70 percent of the total cost of the plan, for selling the investments that are recommended in it. Finally, some planners charge nothing for the plan but earn their entire fee by selling the investments that they recommend in the plan.

Naturally, an inherent conflict of interest arises in relationships with the latter two types of planners. Their incentive to sell investment products may be a larger factor in their financial advice than whether the products are truly good investments and right for you. Although you do not need to avoid entirely the planners who earn commissions, you would be wise to exercise extra caution when dealing with them.

Fee arrangements with financial planners vary as widely as the planners themselves. Most planners charge either an hourly fee, a fixed fee, or a percentage of your wealth or income. Set the fee at the beginning so that neither you nor the planner will be surprised when the plan is completed.

As in choosing any other professionals—accountants and lawyers included—don't rely solely on credentials. Ask any planners that you interview about their educational and professional experience before you commit to anything. Also ask for recommendations. Above all, trust your instincts.

Using Managing Your Money as a Financial Planner

Although many financial planners use fairly sophisticated financial planning computer programs to generate "customized" financial plans, these programs (which usually are expensive) won't give you much more relevant information than you can obtain from Managing Your Money. One such professional program costs $6,000 for all the modules required to fully utilize the applications. The program requires the input of a client's personal financial data, attitude toward risk, financial objectives, and certain other factors. The result—a comprehensive financial report ranging from 40 to 80 pages—includes a cash flow analysis, tax planning, estate planning, a section on wealth growth, and possible risk management. Undeniably, the reports are impressive, but their necessity is questionable.

All financial plans have some basic characteristics in common. The next sections in this chapter cover the basics of sound financial planning and then explain how to use Managing Your Money to implement the plan.

Organizing Your Financial Data

All good financial plans begin with the organization of your financial data. To begin, you should divide your relevant data into qualitative data and quantitative data.

Qualitative data involves such factors as your family situation, your marital status, and the number of children you have. A qualitative analysis also involves your personal attitudes about risk (Do you prefer insured bank deposits or high risk start-up computer ventures?), leverage (Are you willing to make investments with borrowed funds or only with money you have saved?), and the types of investments you are interested in (stocks, bonds, real estate, mutual funds, government securities).

Quantitative data encompasses your current assets and liabilities as well as your current and projected income level. Included in such figures are your investments, pension plans, IRAs, life insurance, disability insurance, loans outstanding, and a myriad of other factors.

Write down the qualitative factors in an organized manner and summarize the quantitative data by preparing a net worth statement. Then you can look at the data in its entirety. You may be surprised to learn that your current investments do not satisfy your needs or your comfort level.

Identifying Your Financial Goals

After the data is assembled, you should identify your financial goals and objectives, and begin to create a plan. Using the data, you also should identify any possible financial problems, considering your current situation and objectives. Be sure to follow the plan, which certainly should suggest how to avoid those problems. After you prepare your plan, using the guidelines that follow, you can begin to draw conclusions.

A comprehensive plan includes the following, all of which can be accomplished with Managing Your Money:

- A cash flow analysis—takes both the inflow and the outflow of cash from all sources and determines whether an excess is available for savings and investment or whether a deficit must be met by reducing your savings or by borrowing.

- A balance sheet or net worth statement—lists your assets and liabilities as of a given point in time and (if you're lucky) discloses that your assets are greater than your liabilities. It also indicates the amount that you currently owe to see whether your debts should be consolidated or paid off (assuming that cash is available).

- An insurance review—covers your life insurance, liability and disability, homeowners', automobile, and other policies that you may have. The review determines whether you are underinsured or overinsured and whether you are getting the most for your money.

- An analysis of your investments—includes an assessment of whether you are too heavily invested in any area. Are you paying too much in commissions on your stock trades, and how well have you actually done on the stocks that your favorite broker recommended to you? Does your current investment portfolio reflect your investment philosophy, or are those high risk stocks inappropriate now that you have three children?

- A tax analysis—covers your anticipated tax liability and makes suggestions about how to reduce your taxes, an especially important area in light of the recent tax overhaul. You must reassess your thinking to reflect the current tax and economic situation now that rates are lower, capital gains provide no tax benefit, and interest on certain types of debt may not be deductible.

- A retirement analysis (which is probably the area that causes the most concern)—determines how much you will need at retirement to maintain the standard of living that you have attained, and whether your current level of savings and investments will provide for these needs.

- Estate planning—may prevent the asset base that you worked so hard to build from being eroded by taxes and legal fees when you die. Several basic estate planning techniques can save you significant amounts of money.

Before you try to develop your personal comprehensive financial plan, get comfortable with the workings of Managing Your Money, either by working through the modules on your own or with the help of the tutorials in the following chapters of this book. Don't try to accomplish everything at once. You might want to make a list in order to give priority to the things that you would like to accomplish. Whatever your objectives—whether you want to provide for your children's college education, assess your current life insurance situation, or analyze the returns that you have received on your investments—try to accomplish them one step at a time. When you are finished, you should have a much better grasp of your current and future financial health.

Analyzing Your Cash Flow

Cash flow analysis is the cornerstone of your financial plan. One objective of financial planning is to make more money accessible to you for your present and future needs. Before you attempt to make changes in the ways that you earn and spend money, get a clear picture of where your cash is coming from and where you are spending it.

You can use the Budget and Checkbook module to obtain a cash flow analysis. Your first step is to go into module 3 (press F3 from the Main Menu). From the Budget and Checkbook's Mini Menu, press F1-Budget Categories.

A budget is merely an estimate of your income and expenses for the coming year. Don't worry if the figures that you select aren't exact—that's what budgets are all about. If your money always seems to run short at the end of the month but you have no idea how much you are spending or on what, then you need a budget.

To get started, pull out last year's check register from your old files. If you spend money or deposit funds in more than one account, then get the registers for all the accounts. By looking through the registers, you should be able to come up with your budget categories. Total the amounts that you spent last year in each of the budget categories and make adjustments, up or down, for the amount that you anticipate spending in each category this year. Try to take into account as many factors that have changed as you can, such as increased prices, additions to the family, a new job, better insurance and the resulting lower medical bills, and so on. Then enter the categories and the numbers into the Managing Your Money program. As the months go by, you will begin to get a feel for how well you estimated your expenses. You also will get a better picture of where your money comes from and where it goes.

After your budget is set up, you can go into the cash forecasting section of the program. From the Budget and Checkbook's Mini Menu, press F3-Cash Forecasting. Here you will see whether your current budget will provide you with excess cash at the end of each month and year, or whether you are spending more than you are taking in.

Although setting up a budget and performing a cash flow analysis is worthwhile, most people have better things to do with their time than to enter data just to find out what they already know—that they just aren't saving enough to provide for their future needs, or worse, to provide for their current obligations. Creating budgets and cash flows makes sense only if you take the output from the program and make some changes in the way that you are spending and investing your money. Without such changes, some of your financial dreams may never become a reality.

You may be surprised to see just how much you are spending in certain budget categories. Sometimes, just viewing the figures motivates you to make changes. People often write check after check without bothering to see how much all those checks add up to. For example, how much does paying the gardener cost, and is the service worth that much? What about those dinners in restaurants that you seem to be enjoying more and more frequently? And what about paying baby-sitters to watch your children while you are out? Maybe you can't cut down on these expenses, or maybe you just don't want to. In any case, look at the figures in black and white (or in color, if you have a color monitor), and evaluate the importance of your expenditures.

Preparing your budget and analyzing your cash flow are only the first steps in developing your financial plan. Certain expenditures that you put into your budget (income taxes, for example) may appear fixed at this point, but they actually can be reduced through proper planning. Other parts of your budget may not need any adjustments; for example, you may look at your cash flow analysis and decide that you are saving an adequate amount of money each month. Further into the planning process, you may find that your current savings will never enable you to save enough for your child's college education or for your retirement years. These facts won't become apparent until you perform some additional calculations.

In short, don't try to do too much too fast. Enter your budget estimates into the computer. Then, for several months, compare your actual expenditures with the budgeted amounts. As you begin to fine-tune your budget, make the required changes, but don't change everything at once.

Don't forget about the graphing capabilities of Managing Your Money. A graph is a very helpful tool for analyzing data. You can prepare graphs to show the distribution of your income sources and your expense categories.

The program's pie graphs list the percentage that each budget category represents to the total income or total expense. You might want to print these graphs so that you can compare your current distribution with the distribution later in the year and in future years.

Creating a Personal Balance Sheet

When most people think of balance sheets and income statements, they think of a business. However, individuals can have balance sheets as well. Generally, a balance sheet for an individual is known as a *net worth statement*, but it provides the same information as a balance sheet.

A net worth statement shows an individual's assets (things that he or she owns or is owed) and the individual's liabilities (amounts that he or she owes). The assets are totaled as are the liabilities, and the difference between the two is an individual's net worth.

You can use module 8 of Managing Your Money to produce your own personal net worth statement. You either can enter the information directly into module 8 of the program; or, if you have been using the other modules of the program, Managing Your Money will automatically extract the relevant information from the other modules and import it into the Your Net Worth module.

While you may be satisfied to generate a net worth statement and marvel at the equity you have built up over the years, the real value is in comparing your net worth from one year to the next. Only then will you be able to determine whether the growth that you require to meet your future needs is taking place.

By delving into the details, you can discover the reasons for a lack of adequate growth. You may find that you are spending too much in a particular area. Possibly the amount you are spending is not a problem, but the way you are spending it is. For example, with the changed tax laws, interest on consumer debt is being phased out as a deduction on your income taxes. By analyzing your net worth statement, you may find that consolidation of numerous consumer loans into one home equity loan would provide significant tax savings and, in addition, would reduce the amount of interest you are paying.

As with all aspects of financial planning, you cannot sit back and be a passive observer. If your net worth is not growing as fast as you would like, then you must make changes. Only you are in a position to make those changes.

Reviewing Your Insurance Needs

Many people ignore insurance planning because they think they are too young to worry about it or because they have gotten by so far without it. Insurance, however, is a key area of financial planning.

Proper insurance planning encompasses a variety of insurance types. These include life insurance, disability, medical, personal property (automobile/homeowners), and liability insurance.

Proper insurance coverage does not mean that you have as much of each type of insurance as you can possibly afford. In fact, more people are probably overinsured than underinsured. You can use module 5 of Managing Your Money to organize your insurance policies and to help you calculate the amount of life insurance you should have based on your current financial situation and your future financial obligations.

When you review your overall insurance needs, you should ask an insurance consultant to help you. The prices of insurance vary so widely and the contracts are so difficult to understand that making an informed decision as a consumer is often impossible. Very often, the savings that the consultant is able to achieve in putting together your overall insurance package will far exceed the fee charged to you by the consultant.

Analyzing Your Investments

Investment analysis is one of the more complicated areas of financial planning, yet it is also the one in which Managing Your Money will be most helpful to you. Modules 6 and 7 (the Financial Calculator and the Portfolio Manager) are loaded with all the necessary tools to help you determine your overall investment performance. In addition, you will be able to assess whether you have properly diversified your investments and whether your current investment portfolio is consistent with your long-term objectives in terms of its level of risk.

For those individuals who are earning more than they currently need to live and who are able to set aside a certain amount each year for investment, deciding on the proper investments can turn into quite a chore. Very often, people will make bad investment decisions because they just don't have the time to perform the necessary research. The best advice for those who can't or won't take the time to properly investigate investments prior to putting their money on the table is to turn their money over to a professional money manager. More and more people who have historically made their own investment decisions are now allowing money managers to make those important decisions for them.

The simplest and often the cheapest way to obtain professional money management is to invest in mutual funds. If you like stocks, you can choose from numerous very successful stock funds. If bonds are your thing, then look into a bond fund. One of the keys to mutual funds is that they allow you to invest in a much more diversified portfolio than you could on your own with limited funds.

When choosing a mutual fund, look at the fund manager's track record. One good year does not make for a good track record. Look for the funds that have performed well in up markets and down markets. While this fund may not be the one that has had the highest return in any given year, the fund will provide you with greater likelihood of success in years to come.

Mutual funds are not for everybody. If, in performing your investment analysis, you determine that you have outperformed the market and the professional money managers, then by all means continue to invest on your own. The key is to analyze your performance so that you can make an informed decision.

Performing a Tax Analysis

While analyzing your taxes does involve the calculation of your tax liability, this is only the beginning of proper tax planning. Managing Your Money allows you to calculate your taxes, but the program also enables you to perform "what if" analysis. This type of analysis can help you rearrange your financial affairs and minimize your taxes.

A very famous United States Court of Appeals judge by the name of Learned Hand once said in one of his opinions:

> Over and over again, courts have said that there is nothing sinister in so arranging one's affairs as to keep taxes as low as possible. Everybody does so, rich or poor; and all do right, for nobody owes any public duty to pay more than the law demands; taxes are enforced exactions, not voluntary contributions.

The real beauty of Managing Your Money's Income Tax Estimator (module 4) is that it allows you to perform timely calculations. Assuming that you use the Budget and Checkbook module to record your income and expenses as they occur throughout the year, you can perform a comprehensive tax analysis in a matter of minutes. By varying your income or your expenses, you will be able to determine the best way to organize your affairs and ultimately achieve savings in taxes.

Planning For Retirement

For many people, retirement seems so far off that planning for it just doesn't seem to make sense. For others, retirement planning becomes almost an obsession that begins to occupy more and more of their productive lives. Financial planning will help to take some of the mystery out of retirement planning, and ideally it will neither be ignored nor dwelled on.

The basic objective of retirement planning is to provide sufficient assets during retirement to allow you to maintain the standard of living you have grown accustomed to during your working life. Without proper planning, inevitably, some people will sacrifice too much during their working lives and will find themselves with assets far in excess of anything that they could reasonably spend during their retirement. Other people will fail to provide adequately for this period in their lives.

Determining the right amount to set aside involves many variables. Some of the factors that go into the calculation are the rate at which your assets will grow before tax, the future tax rates, your future income and future expenditures, the number of working years that you have left, and, finally, the number of years that you will live after you retire.

Many will decide that because of all these variables, planning is impossible. For those of you who feel this way, remember that planning for your financial future is similar in many ways to corporate planning. A good corporate controller is presented with at least as many variables when he or she tries to plot the future financial needs of a corporation. And yet the most successful companies are the ones that were able to plan most accurately. Granted, a lot of variables must be considered. However, you aren't likely to argue with the axiom that to plan in the face of uncertainty is better than not to plan at all.

Managing Your Money's Insurance Planning module will help you plan for your retirement. In a short amount of time, you can quantify the effects of each of these variables. You can use the program to do "what if" analyses. What happens if you alter the number of years that you work, or if you vary the tax rate or the rate of return on your investments? Alter all the above or only some of them. When you are finished, you should have a pretty good idea as to whether your current and future savings will be sufficient to provide for your retirement years. Without question, you will have a better idea of your situation than if you didn't plan at all.

Planning Your Estate

Many people expend a great amount of time and energy maximizing their wealth during their lifetime, and then avoid making any plans for their estates. Contrary to what many might believe, federal estate taxes are still quite high. In fact, federal estate tax rates can be as high as 50 percent of the taxable estate. Many states assess their own estate or transfer taxes. Without proper planning, a large portion of a person's estate can go to paying state and federal taxes. In addition, legal fees for estate administration can take another large bite out of an estate.

With proper planning and the simplest of wills, you can achieve significant savings. A will can be drafted so that up to $1,200,000 can pass tax free to the next generation. Without proper planning, this amount will be reduced to $600,000 with taxes of $192,800 on the other $600,000. Furthermore, assets can be placed in joint names so that they can pass by law to the surviving owner. This saves administration fees and makes the asset immediately available to the survivor. Note that a will can do more than provide for the disposition of assets and the payment of debts. A will also can provide for the care of minors through the appointment of a guardian.

Setting up a gift-giving program also can produce significant estate tax savings. Under current law, a husband and wife can give each of their children (or anyone else, for that matter), up to $20,000 each year. Depending on the ultimate size of the estate, each such $20,000 gift could save up to $10,000 in estate taxes when the donor dies.

Estate planning, which involves more than just a financial analysis, cannot begin too early. If, after analyzing your retirement needs, you determine that you are well provided for, then maybe this is the time to start giving some away.

## Part II

Managing Your Money Tutorial

## Chapter 4

Using the Reminder Pad

The Reminder Pad is one of the nine basic modules that make up the Managing Your Money program. This module consists of four sections: Appointments, Reminders, To-Dos, and Birthdays and Anniversaries.

The Appointments section allows you to prepare a printed schedule of your appointments for any given day, including the specific time of the appointment.

The Reminders section reminds you of upcoming events. For each reminder, you specify the number of days in advance that the program should begin reminding you. For some reminders, you may want to specify a longer period of advance notice so that you can prepare for the event. For other reminders, notice on the particular date in question may be sufficient. As with so much of this program, you set the parameters.

The To-Dos section is for noting long-term projects. This section differs from the Reminders in that items in the To-Do section do not automatically disappear when the date in question passes. This allows you to miss a deadline once in a while and still be reminded that the project exists.

The Birthdays and Anniversaries section allows you to import dates from the Card File (module 9). This saves you the time of reentering this information.

This chapter provides step-by-step instructions on how to use each of the functions of the Reminder Pad.

Unless you already have done so, turn on your computer and get the
Managing Your Money program up and running. After the C> prompt
appears, hard disk users should type **CD\MYM** and then **MYM**. If you are
operating on a one- or two-disk system, then with the A> prompt showing
and Disk 1 in drive A, type **MYM**. After the Welcome screen appears, insert
the appropriate date (MM/DD/YY) and press Enter.

Managing Your Money gives you the option of having the Reminder Pad
appear on your screen automatically the first time you start the program each
day. If the Reminder Pad is currently set to appear automatically the first
time you use the program every day, then your screen should now display
the Reminder Pad module. If the Reminder Pad is not set to appear
automatically, go to the Main Menu and press F2-Reminder Pad. Your screen
should look similar to figure 4.1.

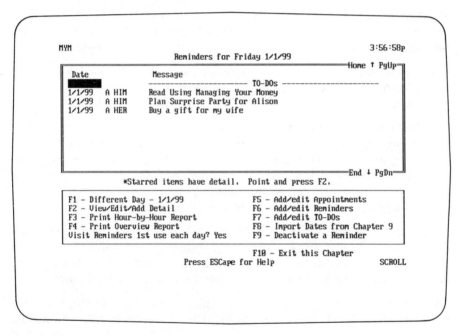

Fig. 4.1. Reminders for Friday, 1/1/99.

To change the default for displaying the Reminder Pad:

1. In the screen's lower left corner, you will see the question:

   Visit Reminder's 1st use each day?

Move the cursor down to the question, decide whether you want the reminder to appear automatically, and then type **Y** (for Yes) or **N** (for No).

Keep in mind that you can see Help screens any time by pressing the ESCape key. If you want, press ESCape now, and you will see one of the Help screens behind the Reminder Pad (see fig. 4.2).

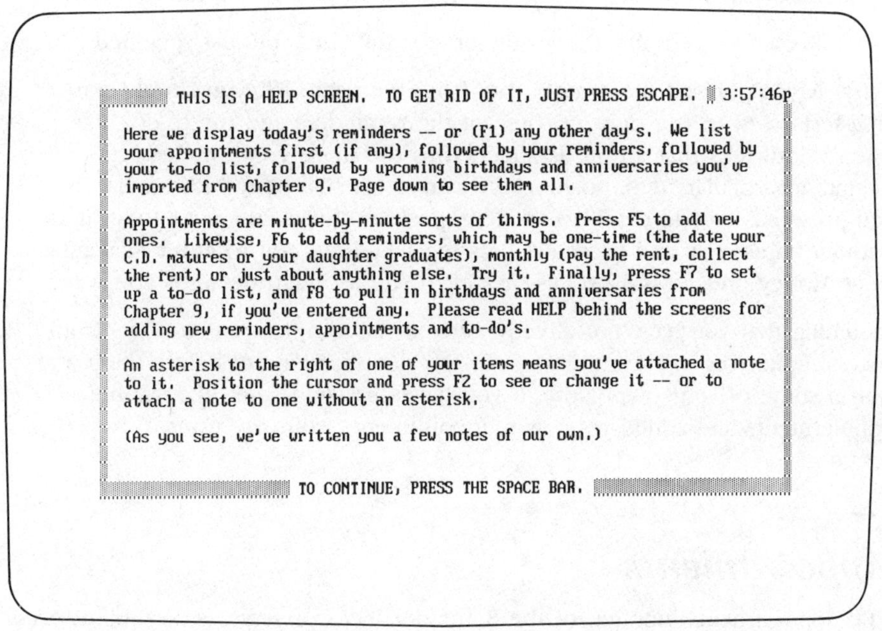

```
      THIS IS A HELP SCREEN.  TO GET RID OF IT, JUST PRESS ESCAPE.    3:57:46p

   Here we display today's reminders -- or (F1) any other day's.  We list
   your appointments first (if any), followed by your reminders, followed by
   your to-do list, followed by upcoming birthdays and anniversaries you've
   imported from Chapter 9.  Page down to see them all.

   Appointments are minute-by-minute sorts of things.  Press F5 to add new
   ones.  Likewise, F6 to add reminders, which may be one-time (the date your
   C.D. matures or your daughter graduates), monthly (pay the rent, collect
   the rent) or just about anything else.  Try it.  Finally, press F7 to set
   up a to-do list, and F8 to pull in birthdays and anniversaries from
   Chapter 9, if you've entered any.  Please read HELP behind the screens for
   adding new reminders, appointments and to-do's.

   An asterisk to the right of one of your items means you've attached a note
   to it.  Position the cursor and press F2 to see or change it -- or to
   attach a note to one without an asterisk.

   (As you see, we've written you a few notes of our own.)

              TO CONTINUE, PRESS THE SPACE BAR.
```

Fig. 4.2. The first Help screen for the Reminder Pad.

Press the ESCape key to reenter the active mode of the Reminder Pad (see fig. 4.1).

The screen displays the reminders for the current day or any other day that you select.

The reminders for the day include your appointments, reminders, to-dos, and upcoming birthdays and anniversaries imported from the Card File (module 9).

Appointments, if any, are listed first. These are the things that you must do hour-by-hour on a certain day. Reminders are upcoming events. Everyone knows what to-dos are because we all have too many of them, but it's a good idea to try to keep track of them.

Remember that this screen contains today's reminders. By pressing certain function keys, you can view and edit your list of appointments, reminders, or to-dos for any day you specify.

To display the reminders for a particular day:

1. On the Reminders screen, move the cursor to the date in the F1-Different Day option so that the date is highlighted.

2. Enter the new date for the reminders that you would like to view.

3. Press F1 to display the reminders for the date you just specified.

If you haven't erased the sample data from the data files, you should notice an asterisk (*) to the right of some of the reminders and the to-dos. The asterisk indicates that a note is attached to the item. To view the detail behind a particular item, position the cursor over an item with an asterisk and press F2. To add detail to an item, position the cursor next to an item without an asterisk and press F2. Pressing F2 allows you to enter Managing Your Money's new word processor and to add as much detail as you want.

Assuming that you have not already deleted the sample appointments from this module, you will use the steps in the next sections to delete them and put in some of your own. Note: If you have already deleted the sample appointments and added your own appointments, you may want to skip this section.

Appointments

The Appointments function of the Reminder Pad can serve as a computerized appointment calendar. Its principal advantage over traditional appointment calendars is that you don't have space constraints; therefore, you can include much more detail about each of your appointments. Some people may decide that this function's advantages are not significant enough to warrant its use. Others will turn on their computers when they first walk into their offices and print out their daily appointments.

To begin, press F5-Add/Edit Appointments, and your screen should look similar to figure 4.3. You may or may not have appointments for the current day, but you may have some for other days.

To delete appointments:

1. From the Reminders screen, press F5-Add/Edit Appointments.

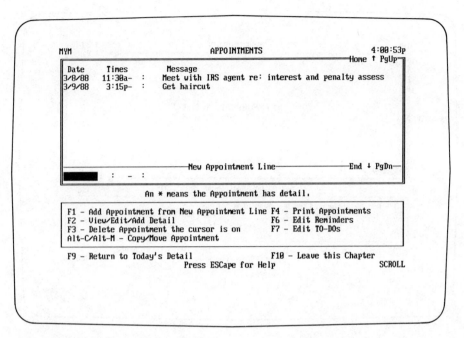

```
 MYM                              APPOINTMENTS                        4:00:53p
                                                                  ╥Home ↑ PgUp╖
  ┌─────────────────────────────────────────────────────────────────────────┐
  │ Date    Times        Message                                              │
  │ 3/8/88  11:30a-  :    Meet with IRS agent re: interest and penalty assess │
  │ 3/9/88   3:15p-  :    Get haircut                                         │
  │                                                                           │
  │                                                                           │
  │                                                                           │
  │                                                                           │
  │                      ─New Appointment Line─              ─End ↓ PgDn─     │
  │ ▆▆▆▆▆▆▆▆    :   -  :                                                       │
  └─────────────────────────────────────────────────────────────────────────┘
                   An * means the Appointment has detail.
  ┌──────────────────────────────────────────────────────────────────────────┐
  │ F1 - Add Appointment from New Appointment Line  F4 - Print Appointments    │
  │ F2 - View/Edit/Add Detail                       F6 - Edit Reminders        │
  │ F3 - Delete Appointment the cursor is on        F7 - Edit TO-DOs           │
  │ Alt-C/Alt-M - Copy/Move Appointment                                        │
  └──────────────────────────────────────────────────────────────────────────┘
     F9 - Return to Today's Detail              F10 - Leave this Chapter
                         Press ESCape for Help                      SCROLL
```

Fig. 4.3. The Appointments screen.

2. Move the cursor to the top item on the screen and press F3-Delete Appointment the Cursor Is On. Then press F1 to proceed with the deletion.

   The appointment is deleted and the cursor should then be positioned at the first remaining appointment.

3. Press F3 and then F1 as many times as necessary to delete all the appointments.

   Afterward, your screen should look like figure 4.4.

   Notice at the bottom of this screen that pressing F3-Delete Appointment the Cursor Is On is no longer an option. That's because no appointments are left to delete. As soon as you add an appointment, the option to delete will reappear.

To add an appointment:

1. With the Appointments screen displayed, use the arrow keys to move the cursor to the New Appointment Line.

   You easily can see where the cursor is positioned by the different color (or contrast) and the flashing underline.

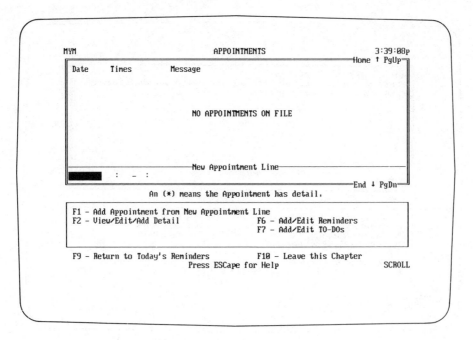

```
MYM                           APPOINTMENTS                    3:39:00p
                                                        ⌐Home ↑ PgUp⌐
  Date      Times       Message



                         NO APPOINTMENTS ON FILE




                     ⌐New Appointment Line⌐
  ████████     :   -   :
                                                        ⌐End ↓ PgDn⌐
                    An (*) means the Appointment has detail.

  ┌───────────────────────────────────────────────────────────────┐
  │ F1 - Add Appointment from New Appointment Line                  │
  │ F2 - View/Edit/Add Detail              F6 - Add/Edit Reminders  │
  │                                        F7 - Add/Edit TO-DOs      │
  │                                                                 │
  │ F9 - Return to Today's Reminders       F10 - Leave this Chapter │
  │             Press ESCape for Help                     SCROLL    │
  └───────────────────────────────────────────────────────────────┘
```

Fig. 4.4. No appointments on file.

2. Position the cursor at the far left blank on the New Appointment Line and type

   5/19/87

   Then press the Enter key.

   The cursor moves over to Times column.

3. First, type **11**. Next, type **15**. Then type **a** for 11:15 a.m. Because you can't tell when your appointment will end, press the Enter key three times.

   Next, you must describe the nature of the 11:15 a.m. appointment on May 19, 1987.

4. Type **Meet with IRS Agent**.

   You are ready to add this appointment.

5. Press F1-Add Appointment from New Appointment Line. The appointment moves to the top of the screen, as shown in figure 4.5.

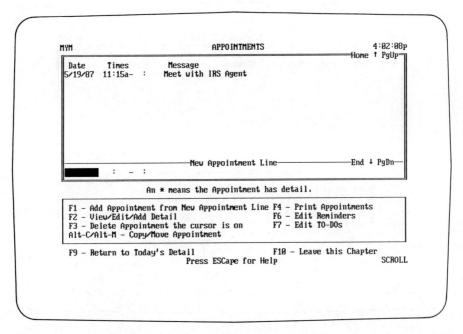

```
MYM                        APPOINTMENTS                      4:02:00p
                                                       Home ↑ PgUp
 Date    Times       Message
 5/19/87 11:15a-  :   Meet with IRS Agent




                    ─New Appointment Line──────────End ↓ PgDn─
 ▄▄▄▄▄▄      :  -  :
           An * means the Appointment has detail.

 F1 - Add Appointment from New Appointment Line F4 - Print Appointments
 F2 - View/Edit/Add Detail                      F6 - Edit Reminders
 F3 - Delete Appointment the cursor is on       F7 - Edit TO-DOs
 Alt-C/Alt-M - Copy/Move Appointment

 F9 - Return to Today's Detail          F10 - Leave this Chapter
                  Press ESCape for Help                  SCROLL
```

Fig. 4.5. An appointment to "Meet with IRS Agent" added.

Look at your options. From among the choices, you can select F2 (which automatically takes you into the word processor) to add some detail to the appointment. You can press F3 to delete the appointment. Or you can press F4 to print appointments.

To print an appointment:

1. Press F4-Print Appointment, and your screen should look like figure 4.6.

   Notice the possibilities here. You can mark certain appointments manually with an "x" and then press F1 to print all the marked items. Or, if you want a list of all appointments for all days, you can press F3 to mark all appointments automatically, and then press F1 to print all marked items.

   Remember, Version 4.0 has the capability to print to the screen, to your printer, or to a file on a disk.

   The F2 function key allows you to mark all appointments in a given period, say for the week beginning May 11, 1987, and ending May 15, 1987.

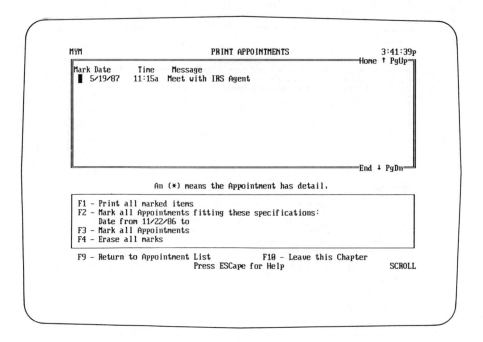

Fig. 4.6. The Print Appointments screen.

2. Experiment with any or all the printing options, as you wish, until
   you are satisfied with your changes. Then, from the Print
   Appointments screen, press F9 twice to return to the Reminders
   screen (see fig. 4.1).

Reminders

Reminders are upcoming events, either personal or business, that you would
be wise not to forget. You have the option to specify how many days in
advance you want to be warned of such events. Also, if you know some
important specifics about an event, you can add a significant amount of detail
to a reminder.

Delete the sample reminders now, if you haven't done so already.

To delete reminders:

1. From the Reminders screen, press F6-Add/Edit Reminders (see
   fig. 4.7).

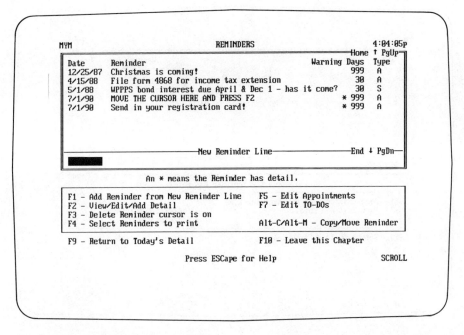

```
MYM                              REMINDERS                            4:04:05p
                                                                ┌Home ↑ PgUp┐
   ┌─────────────────────────────────────────────────────────────────────┐
   │ Date      Reminder                                   Warning Days Type │
   │ 12/25/87  Christmas is coming!                              999   A    │
   │ 4/15/88   File form 4868 for income tax extension           38   A    │
   │ 5/1/88    WPPPS bond interest due April & Dec 1 - has it come? 38 S    │
   │ 7/1/90    MOVE THE CURSOR HERE AND PRESS F2              *  999   A    │
   │ 7/1/90    Send in your registration card!               *  999   A    │
   │                                                                        │
   │                                                                        │
   │─────────────────────New Reminder Line──────────────End ↓ PgDn─────│
   │ ███████████                                                            │
   └─────────────────────────────────────────────────────────────────────┘
           An * means the Reminder has detail.
   ┌─────────────────────────────────────────────────────────────────────┐
   │ F1 - Add Reminder from New Reminder Line    F5 - Edit Appointments    │
   │ F2 - View/Edit/Add Detail                   F7 - Edit TO-DOs          │
   │ F3 - Delete Reminder cursor is on                                     │
   │ F4 - Select Reminders to print           Alt-C/Alt-M - Copy/Move Reminder │
   │                                                                        │
   │ F9 - Return to Today's Detail               F10 - Leave this Chapter  │
   └─────────────────────────────────────────────────────────────────────┘
                      Press ESCape for Help                      SCROLL
```

Fig. 4.7. Sample Reminders.

2. If you haven't deleted the samples yet, use the up-arrow key to move the cursor to the first reminder.

3. Press F3-Delete Reminder Cursor Is On and then press F1 to proceed with the deletion.

   The reminder disappears.

4. Press F3 and then F1 as many times as necessary to delete all the reminders.

   When you are finished, your screen should look like figure 4.8.

To add a reminder:

1. With the cursor positioned at the far left blank on the New Reminder Line, type **1/21/88**. Then press the Enter key.

2. For the text of the reminder, type **My sister Amy's birthday** and press Enter.

3. For Warning Days, type **10** and press the Enter key.

   Warning Days indicates the number of days in advance that the message begins to appear on the Reminders screen. By typing **10**

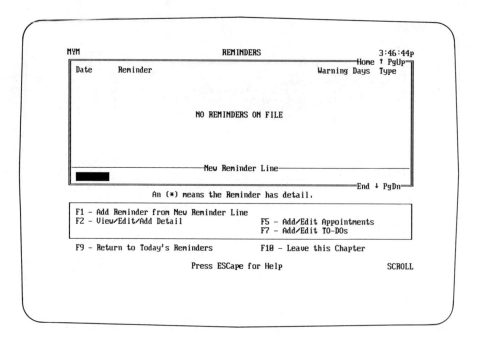

```
MYM                          REMINDERS                        3:46:44p
                                                      ┌Home ↑ PgUp┐
 Date       Reminder                        Warning Days  Type



                     NO REMINDERS ON FILE




                  ┌New Reminder Line┐

 ▐▬▬▬▬▬▬                                              └End ↓ PgDn┘
          An (*) means the Reminder has detail.

  ┌─────────────────────────────────────────────────────────┐
  │ F1 - Add Reminder from New Reminder Line                 │
  │ F2 - View/Edit/Add Detail          F5 - Add/Edit Appointments │
  │                                    F7 - Add/Edit TO-DOs  │
  │                                                          │
  │ F9 - Return to Today's Reminders   F10 - Leave this Chapter │
  └─────────────────────────────────────────────────────────┘

               Press ESCape for Help              SCROLL
```

Fig. 4.8. No Reminders on file.

for a January 21 reminder, you instruct Managing Your Money to
start calling up the reminder on January 11 and each day thereafter
until (and including) January 21.

Note: Obviously, the reminder will not appear if you do not use
Managing Your Money from January 11 through January 21. Also, if
you play around with the date on the Welcome screen, you may
lose your reminders. For example, if you type 1/1/99 just for fun,
all your reminders from now to January 1, 1999, may be eliminated.

The cursor now is positioned at Type (see fig. 4.9). At the bottom
of the screen, Managing Your Money prompts you to select a Type.
The reminder can either be One-time, Weekly, Bi-weekly, Half-
monthly, Monthly, Quarterly, Semi-annual, or Annual.

4. Type **A** for annual because this reminder should appear once a year.

   Note that the reminder will appear on January 11 of each year
   because this is an annual reminder.

5. Press F1-Add Reminder from New Reminder Line, and the reminder
   will move to the top of the screen (see fig. 4.10).

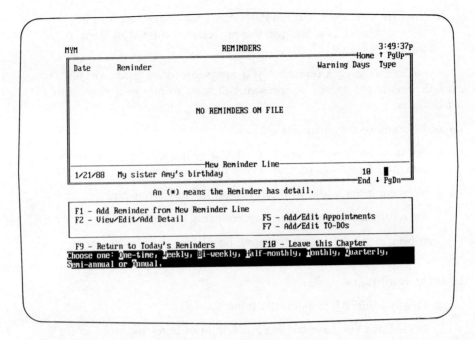

Fig. 4.9. A new Reminder being added.

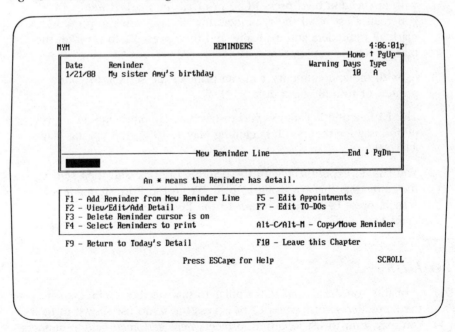

Fig. 4.10. A new Reminder added.

6. Now try to enter a few reminders on your own. Move to the New Reminder Line and use the procedure outlined in Steps 1 through 5.

After you have entered a reminder, you may want to add some details. For example, you might specify the present you want to buy your sister Amy for her birthday.

To add details to a reminder:

1. Position the cursor over the particular reminder and press F2-View/ Edit/Add Detail in order to access the word processor.

2. Now enter any additional information for this reminder.

3. To return to the Reminders screen, press F2 again.

You can print reminders using the same procedure you used to print appointments.

To print reminders:

1. Press F4-Select Reminders To Print.

   Notice that you have the same possibilities here that you had for printing appointments. You can mark certain reminders manually with an "x" and then press F1 to print all the marked items. Or, if you want a list of all the reminders for all days, you can press F3 to mark all reminders automatically, and then press F1 to print all the marked items.

   As with the appointments, you can print to the screen, to your printer, or to a file on a disk.

   The F2 function key allows you to mark all appointments in a given period, say for the month beginning May 1, 1987, and ending May 31, 1987.

2. You should experiment with the printing options, and then select the reminders that you want to print. From the Print Reminders screen, press F9 twice to return to the Reminders screen (see fig. 4.1).

To-Dos

The information on the to-do list is similar to that on the reminders list. From the Reminder screen, press F7 to access the to-do list shown in figure 4.11. You may want to list long-term projects here and keep daily reminders in the reminders list. Or you might not use this list at all. You should have no trouble deleting the sample to-dos. Like everything else in Managing Your Money, the decisions are up to you.

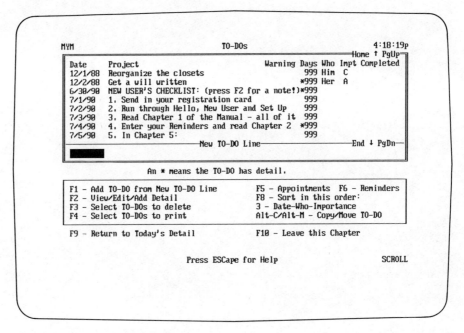

```
MYM                              TO-DOs                              4:18:19p
                                                              ┌Home ↑ PgUp┐
 ┌─────────────────────────────────────────────────────────────────────────┐
 │ Date     Project                        Warning Days Who Impt Completed   │
 │ 12/1/88  Reorganize the closets                999 Him  C                 │
 │ 12/2/88  Get a will written                   *999 Her  A                 │
 │ 6/30/90  NEW USER'S CHECKLIST: (press F2 for a note!)*999                 │
 │ 7/1/90   1. Send in your registration card     999                       │
 │ 7/2/90   2. Run through Hello, New User and Set Up  999                   │
 │ 7/3/90   3. Read Chapter 1 of the Manual - all of it  999                 │
 │ 7/4/90   4. Enter your Reminders and read Chapter 2  *999                 │
 │ 7/5/90   5. In Chapter 5:                      999                        │
 │ ▄▄▄▄▄▄▄▄▄▄▄▄▄▄▄▄▄▄▄▄▄▄New TO-DO Line────────────────End ↓ PgDn┘           │
 └─────────────────────────────────────────────────────────────────────────┘
                    An * means the TO-DO has detail.

 ┌─────────────────────────────────────────────────────────────────────────┐
 │ F1 - Add TO-DO from New TO-DO Line    F5 - Appointments  F6 - Reminders   │
 │ F2 - View/Edit/Add Detail             F8 - Sort in this order:            │
 │ F3 - Select TO-DOs to delete          3 - Date-Who-Importance             │
 │ F4 - Select TO-DOs to print           Alt-C/Alt-M - Copy/Move TO-DO       │
 │                                                                           │
 │ F9 - Return to Today's Detail         F10 - Leave this Chapter            │
 └─────────────────────────────────────────────────────────────────────────┘

                    Press ESCape for Help                      SCROLL
```

Fig. 4.11. The To-Dos screen.

You can specify the person responsible for accomplishing each to-do and determine the importance of each to-do in relation to the others. Using F8-Sort in This Order, you also can sort the items into any one of six different orders.

Use the same procedure for printing to-dos as you use for printing appointments and reminders. Take some time to try printing some to-dos. The more you work with the functions in this module, the more proficient you will become at using the functions.

Birthdays and Anniversaries

One final note about this module. If you press the F8 key from the Reminders screen, you can import dates—such as birthdays and anniversaries —from the Card File (module 9). This saves you the time of reentering dates that have already been entered in the other module.

## Chapter 5

Using the Budget and Checkbook

The Budget and Checkbook module encompasses much more than a computerized checkbook. As you work through the tutorial presented in this chapter, you will learn to use the Budget and Checkbook module to do the following:

- Set up a budget. A budget—the cornerstone of a financial plan—is nothing more than a plan for the inflow and outflow of cash. Therefore, a budget does not need to be complicated.

- Set up your checking account (or accounts, if you have more than one), credit card accounts, and other accounts on the computer. You may elect to print checks on the computer or continue to write your checks manually. Reconciling your bank statements will become a painless process.

- Set up automatic or recurring transactions in your accounts so that they can be processed with just a few keystrokes. A recurring transaction is one that occurs repeatedly. The amount of an automatic transaction payment may be either fixed or varied. The rent for an apartment is an example of a fixed automatic transaction, and an electric bill is an example of a payment that varies from month to month.

- Integrate an accounts payable and an accounts receivable system into your accounts. If you know that you have to pay a certain bill later in the month, or if your brother-in-law owes you money, then you can set up these transactions in advance.

- Perform cash flow analyses to better predict whether you will have enough cash to meet your budgeted obligations as they become due.

- Account for any loans that you have outstanding or that are owed to you. In addition, create an amortization schedule for each loan to determine what portion of the payments is interest and what portion is principal.

- Archive your transactions temporarily. This allows you to combine temporarily your active transactions with those in storage and see how your situation looks. After viewing the combined figures and printing any reports that you request, Managing Your Money automatically separates the transactions as if the temporary archiving had never happened.

- Save your transactions, or if you were experimenting with your accounts, leave the module without saving the changes that were made in the last session. Your accounts then will reflect your account status as of the last time you saved your transactions.

- Perform home banking. If you have a modem and an account at a bank that has a home banking system compatible with Managing Your Money, then you can access your account in order to receive information and to pay bills. (Only Chase Manhattan's Spectrum System currently is accessible in this way.)

Getting Started

Don't be overwhelmed by the length of this chapter. The Budget and Checkbook module is probably the most comprehensive module in the program. By the time you complete this section of the tutorial, you should be comfortable with Managing Your Money (if you aren't already). Although you may need to work slowly through the steps in this chapter, you will be able to pick up the pace in the remaining chapters.

Use as much or as little of the Budget and Checkbook module as you like. Create a budget, enter your checkbook data, or both. The budget figures are fed into the cash flow analysis section of this module and into the Income Tax Estimator (module 4) regardless of whether your actual checkbook figures are entered in Managing Your Money.

From the Main Menu, press F3-Budget and Checkbook to display the
module's Mini Menu, as shown in figure 5.1. If you are running the program
on a one- or two-disk system, you will be prompted to insert Disk 3 into
drive A or drive B depending on your particular setup (see fig. 5.2). Insert
the appropriate disk and press any key, and then you can continue. The Mini
Menu displays your basic options in this module. Sometimes, you must use
one of the options to learn what further action you may take in the module.
You may find the flow chart in the Appendix helpful for finding some of the
most commonly used functions.

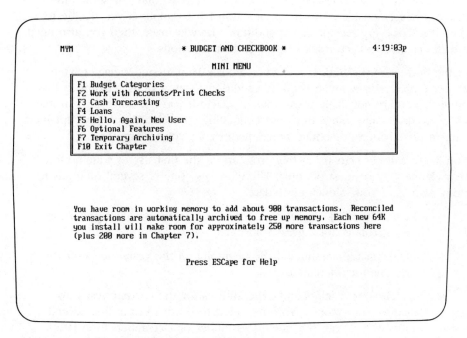

MYM   * BUDGET AND CHECKBOOK *   4:19:03p

                              MINI MENU

    F1 Budget Categories
    F2 Work with Accounts/Print Checks
    F3 Cash Forecasting
    F4 Loans
    F5 Hello, Again, New User
    F6 Optional Features
    F7 Temporary Archiving
    F10 Exit Chapter

    You have room in working memory to add about 900 transactions. Reconciled
    transactions are automatically archived to free up memory. Each new 64K
    you install will make room for approximately 250 more transactions here
    (plus 200 more in Chapter 7).

                        Press ESCape for Help

Fig. 5.1. The Budget and Checkbook's Mini Menu.

    Please put Disk 3 (or disk containing budget.db) in drive A.
    Adjust the disk and press any key to try again.
    Press F10 to return to the previous screen.

Fig. 5.2. The prompt to insert Disk 3.

If you decide to use the program to keep track of your actual checkbook receipts and expenditures, then you must decide whether to continue writing the checks manually and to enter the data into your computer thereafter or to use Managing Your Money and your computer to write your checks for you. You probably should begin by writing your checks manually because you probably will not receive your computerized checks until several weeks after ordering them.

Managing Your Money refers throughout this module to the word *account*, which may be a checking account or a credit card account, or something that you never considered to be an account. For example, if you decide to keep track of every receipt or expenditure that you make, then you also need a *cash account* to keep track of your cash transactions.

At the bottom of the Budget and Checkbook's Mini Menu, Managing Your Money indicates how much room for additional transactions remains in this module. You are not likely to run out of space. If you do, however, you may either archive some transactions by reconciling your checkbook (as explained later in this chapter) or obtain more memory for your computer.

You likely will not start using this program on the first day of your taxable year (January 1, for most people). Therefore, use one of several methods to bring Managing Your Money up-to-date:

1. Wait until the first day of next year to begin to use Managing Your Money. (This is not a great solution.)

2. Enter estimated amounts at the beginning of the year, and enter the actual amounts thereafter.

3. Enter all your receipts and expenditures for the current year into Managing Your Money. You may want to do this in the first several months of the year, but not in November or December. Even late in the year, bringing the program up-to-date should make preparing your tax return simpler.

Setting Up or Reviewing Your Budget Categories

From the Budget and Checkbook's Mini Menu, press F1-Budget Categories. If you have not worked with the program yet, your screen should look like figure 5.3.

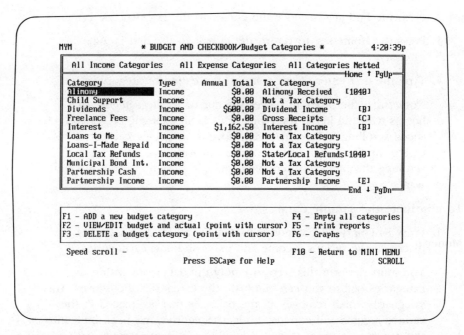

Fig. 5.3. Sample budget categories.

Don't be overwhelmed by the many general categories, types, tax categories, and other figures. They represent the sample data that the manufacturer of Managing Your Money included in the program. You soon will see how easily you can build your own set of data.

Income, as used in this module, may not necessarily be income as it generally is perceived. Although it may represent wages or interest, it also may be a repayment of a loan. Therefore, income may or may not be taxable. It reflects an inflow of cash, regardless of the resulting tax consequences.

Expense, likewise, is not necessarily a tax concept. Although an expense represents an outflow of cash and may be an actual expense, some expenses may be deductible for tax purposes, and others may represent the purchase of an asset, such as a car.

To view the income and expense categories:

1. With the cursor positioned on the All Income Categories blank, press the down-arrow key to scroll through the income and expense categories.

   Notice that the income and expense categories are alphabetized automatically for easy access.

2. Press the End key to move the cursor to the last expense category.

3. Press the Home key to return the cursor to the first income category.

4. Type the first letter of any name in the expense category.

   Notice that the program moves the cursor to the category that begins with the letter you typed. This is an example of Version 4.0's speed scrolling feature. You can move to a specific category by typing the first letter or two of the category name. Instead of scrolling through each item, you can skip directly to the one you want.

To eliminate the sample data:

1. Press F4-Empty All Categories to remove all the balances that are placed in the various income and expense budget categories.

   You must perform this step to empty the data from within the categories before you can eliminate the categories themselves. This safeguard, which removes all the balances that are placed in the various income and expense budget categories, has been built into the program in order to make deleting a budget category with a non-zero balance impossible.

2. Press F1 in response to the program's request that you verify your decision to erase all budget and actual amounts (see fig. 5.4).

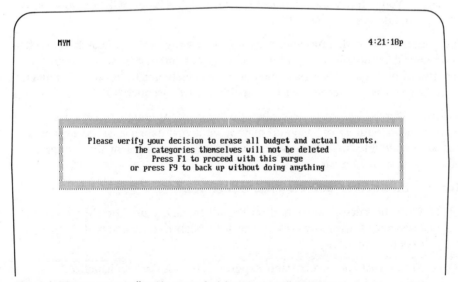

Fig. 5.4. The program's "verify your decision to erase" message.

Whenever you erase data, print a schedule, exit a module of the program without saving your changes, or archive data, the program gives you the opportunity to back up and cancel the request. This safeguard can be a real time-saver if you accidentally press the wrong key.

Now that the balances in all the income and expense budget categories are zero, you can eliminate the budget categories.

3. Scroll down by pressing the down-arrow key and verify that all the balances are zero.

4. Press Home to return to the top budget category.

5. Press F3 as many times as necessary to eliminate all the budget categories. This procedure may take a minute or two, so be patient. When you are finished, the screen should look like figure 5.5.

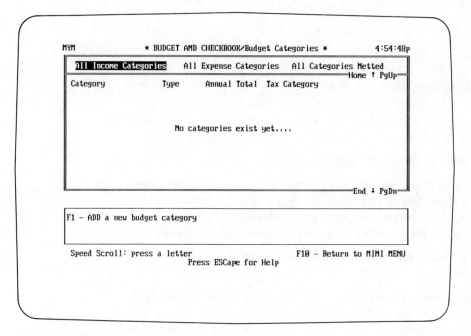

Fig. 5.5. All budget categories eliminated.

Your only option on this screen is F1-Add a New Budget Category.

To add a budget category:

1. Press F1 to display the Add Budget Category screen shown in figure 5.6.

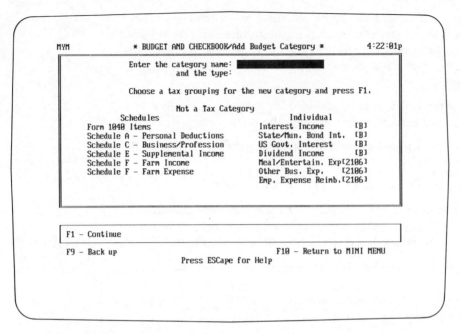

Fig. 5.6. The Add Budget Category screen.

Notice that the cursor and the blinking underline are positioned at the top of the screen to the right of Enter the category name:.

2. Type **Salary - Husband** and press Enter.

The cursor automatically moves down to type:. Here, you must specify the category type from among the choices listed at the bottom of the screen. The prompt says Choose one: Income or Expense. All budget categories are either income or expense.

3. Type **I** for Income, and the cursor automatically moves to Not a Tax Category.

The remaining options on this screen represent the various Tax Category groupings. All income or expense items are included in one of the groupings listed on this screen. Items either will have no income tax effect, will be part of the Internal Revenue Service's Form 1040 (the regular individual tax return), or will go on Schedule A or on one of the other IRS tax forms. If you are not sure how to classify a particular budget category, then you can look at one of your old tax returns, go to your accountant with your proposed budget categories and ask for assistance in assigning tax categories to these budget categories, or classify everything as Not a

Tax Category. Because the last option gives erroneous results when you use the Income Tax Estimator, that approach is not recommended.

Throughout this section of the tutorial, you are told how to code the tax categories. Because Salary is a Form 1040 item, press the down-arrow key or the Enter key once in order to move the cursor to Form 1040 Items (see fig. 5.7).

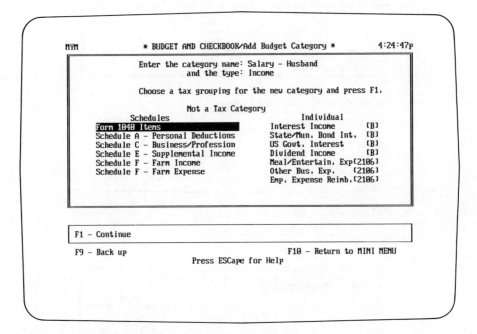

```
MYM              * BUDGET AND CHECKBOOK/Add Budget Category *          4:24:47p

              Enter the category name: Salary - Husband
                        and the type: Income

              Choose a tax grouping for the new category and press F1.

                        Not a Tax Category
              Schedules                          Individual
       Form 1040 Items                     Interest Income       [B]
       Schedule A - Personal Deductions    State/Mun. Bond Int.  [B]
       Schedule C - Business/Profession    US Govt. Interest     [B]
       Schedule E - Supplemental Income    Dividend Income       [B]
       Schedule F - Farm Income            Meal/Entertain. Exp[2106]
       Schedule F - Farm Expense           Other Bus. Exp.   [2106]
                                           Emp. Expense Reimb.[2106]



     F1 - Continue

     F9 - Back up                                F10 - Return to MINI MENU
                        Press ESCape for Help
```

Fig. 5.7. A budget category name and type specified.

4. Press F1 to display the Choose Tax Category screen shown in figure 5.8.

   This screen displays all the possible Form 1040 items. Use the arrow keys or the Enter key to move among the various categories.

5. Position the cursor on the first income category—Salary [1040]— and press F1 to display the screen shown in figure 5.9.

   Now you are ready to enter the budgeted amount for the Husband's Salary.

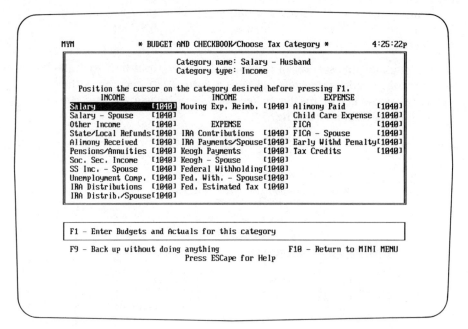

Fig. 5.8. Form 1040 options for husband.

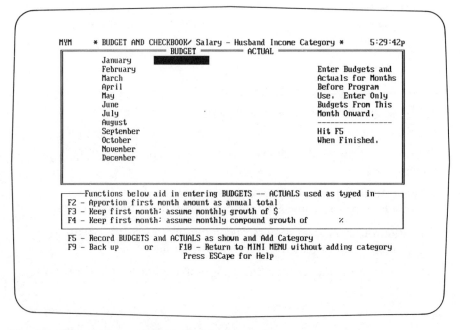

Fig. 5.9. Columns for monthly budget and actual amounts.

6. Type **47000** in the blank for January's budget and press the Enter key.

You do not need to enter the dollar sign or commas. The program enters these for you. Your screen should look like figure 5.10.

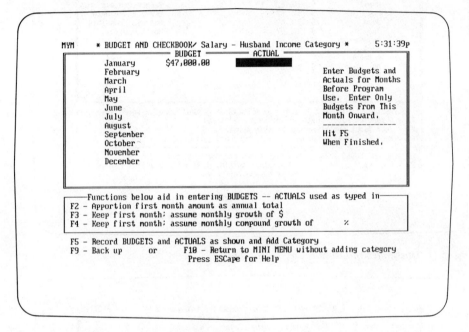

```
MYM    * BUDGET AND CHECKBOOK/ Salary - Husband Income Category *    5:31:39p
                     ══════ BUDGET ══════   ══════ ACTUAL ══════
         January       $47,000.00          ▮▮▮▮▮▮▮▮▮▮▮▮▮▮
         February                                           Enter Budgets and
         March                                              Actuals for Months
         April                                              Before Program
         May                                                Use. Enter Only
         June                                               Budgets From This
         July                                               Month Onward.
         August                                             ──────────────────
         September                                          Hit F5
         October                                            When Finished.
         November
         December



   ┌────Functions below aid in entering BUDGETS -- ACTUALS used as typed in───┐
   │ F2 - Apportion first month amount as annual total                        │
   │ F3 - Keep first month; assume monthly growth of $                        │
   │ F4 - Keep first month; assume monthly compound growth of            %    │
   └──────────────────────────────────────────────────────────────────────────┘
     F5 - Record BUDGETS and ACTUALS as shown and Add Category
     F9 - Back up      or      F10 - Return to MINI MENU without adding category
                           Press ESCape for Help
```

Fig. 5.10. Husband's annual salary entered.

7. Press F2 to apportion the husband's annual salary.

The $47,000 is divided evenly into monthly amounts (see fig. 5.11). You could also enter actual amounts here, but that isn't necessary now.

8. Press F5 to add your first budget category to the program and to return to the Add Budget Category screen (shown in fig. 5.6).

To add a second budget category:

1. On the Add Budget Category screen, type **Salary - Wife** and press the Enter key.

2. Type **I** for Income.

3. Move the cursor to Form 1040 Items and press F1 (see fig. 5.12).

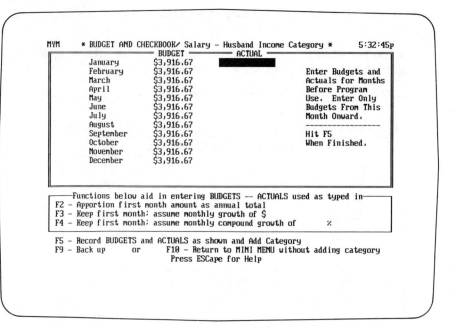

Fig. 5.11. Husband's monthly salary calculated.

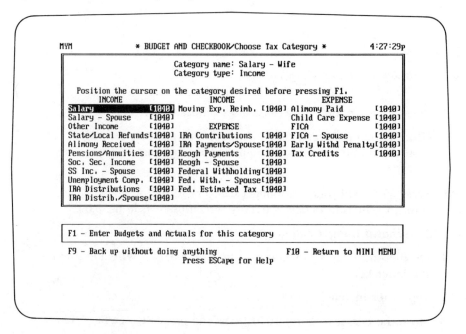

Fig. 5.12. Form 1040 options for wife.

4. Move the cursor down one line to Salary - Spouse [1040] and press F1.

5. Type **52000** in the January budget blank and press Enter.

6. Press F2 to apportion the $52,000 salary over 12 months (see fig. 5.13).

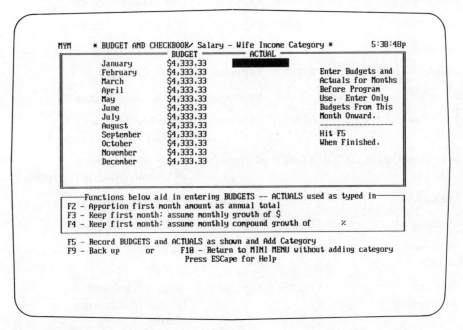

```
MYM       * BUDGET AND CHECKBOOK/ Salary - Wife Income Category *       5:38:48p
                            ═══ BUDGET ═══        ═══ ACTUAL ═══
          January          $4,333.33        ██████████████
          February         $4,333.33                            Enter Budgets and
          March            $4,333.33                            Actuals for Months
          April            $4,333.33                            Before Program
          May              $4,333.33                            Use.  Enter Only
          June             $4,333.33                            Budgets From This
          July             $4,333.33                            Month Onward.
          August           $4,333.33                            ──────────────────
          September        $4,333.33                            Hit F5
          October          $4,333.33                            When Finished.
          November         $4,333.33
          December         $4,333.33

        ┌─Functions below aid in entering BUDGETS ── ACTUALS used as typed in─┐
        │ F2 - Apportion first month amount as annual total                    │
        │ F3 - Keep first month; assume monthly growth of $                    │
        │ F4 - Keep first month; assume monthly compound growth of        %    │
        └──────────────────────────────────────────────────────────────────────┘
          F5 - Record BUDGETS and ACTUALS as shown and Add Category
          F9 - Back up        or        F10 - Return to MINI MENU without adding category
                                   Press ESCape for Help
```

Fig. 5.13. Wife's monthly salary calculated.

7. Press F5 to record the budgeted amount.

   You should now be back at the Add Budget Category screen (see fig. 5.6).

You now have entered your first two budget categories. Perform the same steps for each of the following budgeted income and expense categories. Soon you will fly through these steps with ease. You will be able to use many of these budget categories when you set up your personal budget. After your budget is set up, you will just need to change the amounts (and maybe the tax groupings) because most of the work will be done.

Category Name	Annual Amount	Type	Tax Grouping
Interest Income	$1,200	Income	Interest Income [B]
Loan Repayment	$6,200	Income	Not a Tax Category
Groceries	$2,400	Expense	Not a Tax Category
Telephone	$600	Expense	Not a Tax Category
Student Loan	$3,000	Expense	Not a Tax Category
Gasoline	$360	Expense	Not a Tax Category
Utilities	$3,000	Expense	a Tax Category
Pay T.V.	$420	Expense	Not a Tax Category
Cash Contributions	$2,000	Expense	Schedule A-Pers. Ded. Charity Contributions [A]
IRA Contribution	$2,000	Expense	Form 1040 Items; IRA Contributions [1040]
Laundry	$600	Expense	Not a Tax Category
Clothing	$1,500	Expense	Not a Tax Category
FICA-Social Security	$3,003	Expense	Form 1040 Items; FICA
Federal Withholding	$23,000	Expense	Form 1040 Items; Federal Withholding [1040]
State Withholding	$6,500	Expense	Schedule A-Pers. Ded. State Withholding

Your budget is now complete and you are in position to start entering the sample data. The Add Budget Category screen should be displayed (see fig. 5.6).

Press F9 to back up. Your sample budget should now look similar to figure 5.14. Some of the amounts on the screen may be different depending on what month it is. Figure 5.14 represents two months of the budget for each budget category. If your budget was created in May and no actual amounts were entered for January through April, then the screen would reflect four months of the budget and any actual amounts entered for May.

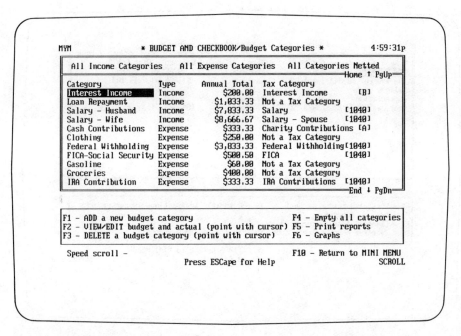

```
MYM                  * BUDGET AND CHECKBOOK/Budget Categories *        4:59:31p

   All Income Categories    All Expense Categories   All Categories Netted
                                                            Home ↑ PgUp
   Category             Type        Annual Total  Tax Category
   Interest Income      Income        $200.00     Interest Income     [B]
   Loan Repayment       Income      $1,033.33     Not a Tax Category
   Salary - Husband     Income      $7,833.33     Salary            [1040]
   Salary - Wife        Income      $8,666.67     Salary - Spouse   [1040]
   Cash Contributions   Expense       $333.33     Charity Contributions [A]
   Clothing             Expense       $250.00     Not a Tax Category
   Federal Withholding  Expense     $3,833.33     Federal Withholding[1040]
   FICA-Social Security Expense       $500.50     FICA              [1040]
   Gasoline             Expense        $60.00     Not a Tax Category
   Groceries            Expense       $400.00     Not a Tax Category
   IRA Contribution     Expense       $333.33     IRA Contributions [1040]
                                                             End ↓ PgDn

   F1 - ADD a new budget category                F4 - Empty all categories
   F2 - VIEW/EDIT budget and actual (point with cursor) F5 - Print reports
   F3 - DELETE a budget category (point with cursor) F6 - Graphs

   Speed scroll -                                F10 - Return to MINI MENU
                          Press ESCape for Help                    SCROLL
```

Fig. 5.14. Budget categories entered.

Try scrolling with the down-arrow key. Position the cursor next to any category and press F2 to view the budget for that category. At this point, you know how to change the budgeted or actual amounts. The Actual column should have nothing in it, but it will be updated as you write checks or receive money in other sections of the program.

Working with Your Accounts

Press F10 to return to the Budget and Checkbook's Mini Menu. To prepare to set up your first checking account, press F2-Work with Your Accounts (see fig. 5.15). From this screen, you can perform numerous functions on your accounts. You can add to, delete from, or make changes in any of your accounts. You can set up automatic transactions, transfer money between your accounts, or rearrange the order of your existing accounts.

If you have not yet erased the sample data that came with the program or entered your own personal data, you will see a sample checking account, a savings account, a charge account, and some cash accounts. Look at the

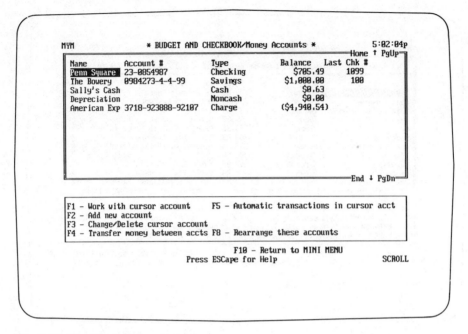

```
MYM                    * BUDGET AND CHECKBOOK/Money Accounts *              5:02:04p
                                                              ┌Home ↑ PgUp┐
 Name          Account #        Type          Balance   Last Chk #
 Penn Square   23-8054987       Checking        $705.49      1099
 The Bowery    8984273-4-4-99   Savings       $1,000.00       100
 Sally's Cash                   Cash             $0.63
 Depreciation                   Noncash          $0.00
 American Exp  3718-923888-92187 Charge       ($4,940.54)


                                                              └End ↓ PgDn┘

 F1 - Work with cursor account     F5 - Automatic transactions in cursor acct
 F2 - Add new account
 F3 - Change/Delete cursor account
 F4 - Transfer money between accts F8 - Rearrange these accounts

                              F10 - Return to MINI MENU
                 Press ESCape for Help                        SCROLL
```

Fig. 5.15. The Money Accounts screen.

information provided for each type of account: the balance in the account and the last check number written for accounts that allow you to write checks on them.

The cursor automatically goes to the first account when you call up this screen. To save time, put first on the list the account that you use most often. You can use the F8 key to rearrange the accounts in any order you like.

To continue in the tutorial, you need to delete the sample accounts. If you have already entered your personal data into Managing Your Money and do not want to delete it, make an additional set of working copies of the four disks for use in the tutorial.

To delete the sample accounts:

1. From the Budget and Checkbook's Money Accounts screen (see fig. 5.15), position the cursor at the top account and press F3.

2. Press F2-Delete This Account.

    The program asks you to verify your decision to delete the account (see fig. 5.16).

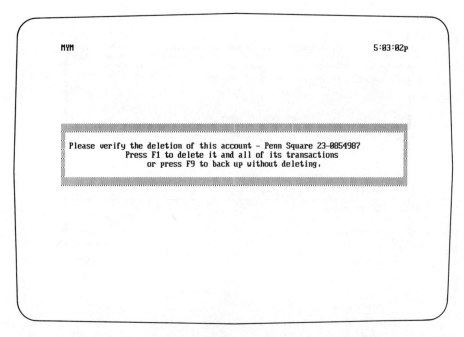

Fig. 5.16. The program's "verify the deletion of this account" message.

3. Press F1, and the account disappears, including all of its transactions.

   The cursor is automatically positioned at the top of the remaining accounts.

4. In succession, press F3, F2, and F1 as many times as necessary to delete all the accounts.

   When you are finished, the screen should look like figure 5.17.

   Notice that the only option is to add a new account.

In this tutorial, you will create one checking account, write checks on that account, and process several deposits. You also will learn how to create and process automatic transactions.

To create a checking account:

1. From the Money Accounts screen, press F2-Add New Account to display the screen shown in figure 5.18.

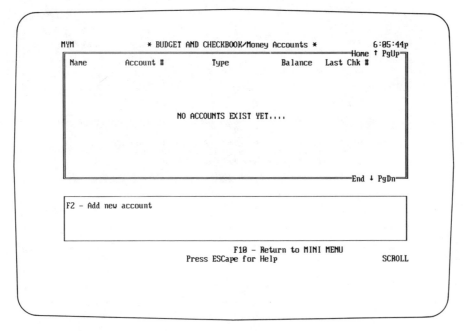

Fig. 5.17. All accounts eliminated.

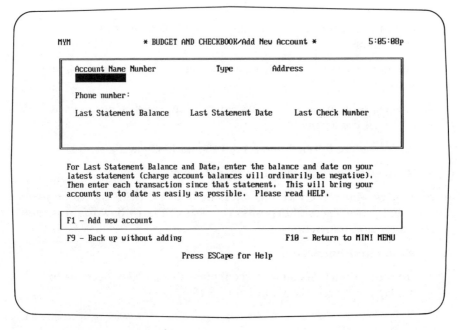

Fig. 5.18. The Add New Account screen.

2. Enter the information that follows in the appropriate blanks. After
   you complete each blank, press Enter.

   Account Name: **Baby Boomer**

   Account #: **1234-000**

   Type of Account: **Che** (for checking)

   Address: **1 Main Street, Anytown, USA**

   Phone Number: **786-1234**

   Last Statement Balance: **1800**

   Date: **1/31/87**

   Last Check Number: **0**

   If you make an error, go back by pressing the Enter key or the up-
   arrow or down-arrow keys. After all the information is entered
   correctly, your screen should look like figure 5.19.

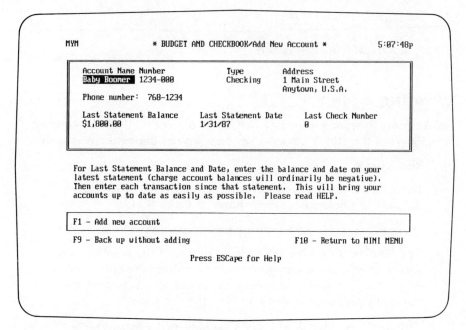

Fig. 5.19. New account information entered.

3. Press F1-Add New Account.

   Your screen should look like figure 5.20.

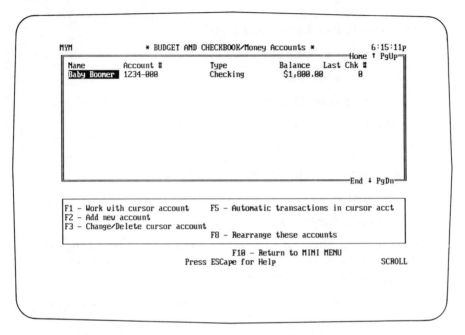

Fig. 5.20. New checking account added.

Spending Money

You are ready to work with your newly created account. Begin by entering
the amounts of the sample checks that were written during the past month.

To write a check:

1. From the Money Accounts screen, press F1-Work with Cursor
    Account to display the screen shown in figure 5.21.

2. Press F1-Spend Money to display the screen shown in figure 5.22.

    The first check number is provided for you. If the number were
    incorrect, you could change it easily by moving the cursor to the
    check number blank and making the correction. You move the
    cursor by pressing the arrow keys or the Enter key.

    The date you entered on the Welcome screen when you first
    entered the program is also provided. If the date were incorrect,
    you could change it here. Keep things simple and assume that all
    checks were written on the date shown so you don't have to enter
    information unnecessarily.

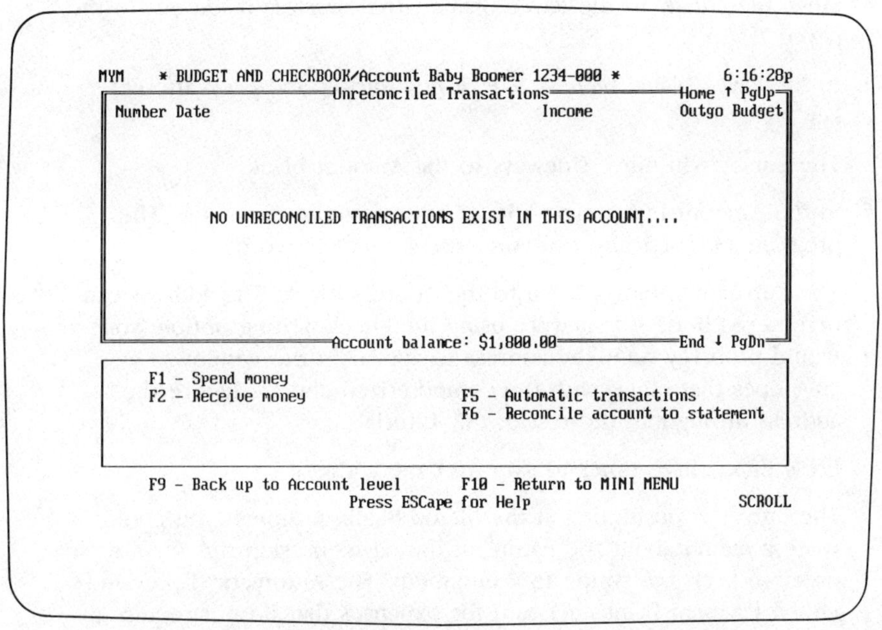

```
MYM    * BUDGET AND CHECKBOOK/Account Baby Boomer 1234-000 *         6:16:28p
                    ═══════Unreconciled Transactions═══════    Home ↑ PgUp
       Number Date                              Income          Outgo Budget




                   NO UNRECONCILED TRANSACTIONS EXIST IN THIS ACCOUNT....




                    ═══════Account balance: $1,000.00═══════  End ↓ PgDn

          F1 - Spend money
          F2 - Receive money             F5 - Automatic transactions
                                         F6 - Reconcile account to statement


          F9 - Back up to Account level     F10 - Return to MINI MENU
                           Press ESCape for Help                  SCROLL
```

Fig. 5.21. The Unreconciled Transactions screen.

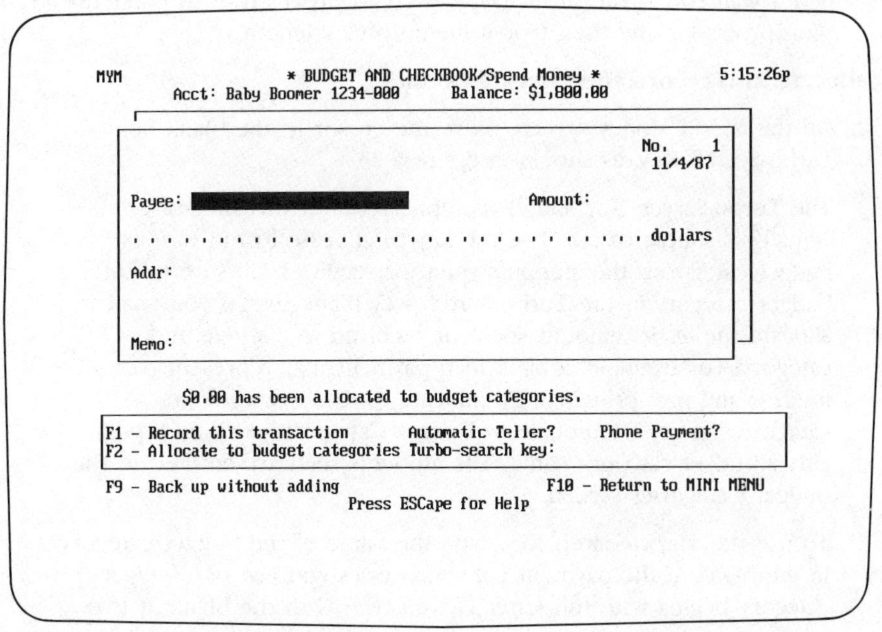

```
MYM                    * BUDGET AND CHECKBOOK/Spend Money *          5:15:26p
            Acct: Baby Boomer 1234-000      Balance: $1,000.00

                                                          No.     1
                                                          11/4/87

          Payee:                              Amount:
          . . . . . . . . . . . . . . . . . . . . . . . . . . . . dollars
          Addr:


          Memo:

              $0.00 has been allocated to budget categories.
       F1 - Record this transaction       Automatic Teller?   Phone Payment?
       F2 - Allocate to budget categories Turbo-search key:

       F9 - Back up without adding                 F10 - Return to MINI MENU
                           Press ESCape for Help
```

Fig. 5.22. The Spend Money screen.

3. Move the cursor to the Payee blank. (The check is made out to the payee.)

4. In the Payee blank, type **M & P Supermarket** and press the Enter key.

   The cursor will move sideways to the Amount blank.

5. In the Amount blank, type **156.22** and press the Enter key. The program automatically will enter the amount in words.

   The cursor will move down to the Address blank. The address can be entered here. If you were using the check-writing option, you would probably want the address to appear in the window envelopes that come with the computerized checks. Ignore the address throughout the rest of this tutorial.

6. Press Enter three times to skip over the address.

   The cursor is positioned at the Memo blank. Although you could write a memo about the nature of the payment, skip this for now in order to keep the typing to a minimum. The Automatic Teller and Phone Payment blanks account for expenses that do not require a check to be written. Skip over those blanks as well.

   If you wanted to enter a memo, you could press Ctrl-E to enter the Wordprocessor and then type a memo of any length.

To allocate and record the check amount:

1. On the Spend Money screen, move the cursor to the blank next to Turbo-Search Key, as shown in figure 5.23.

   The Turbo-Search Key sounds complicated, but this time-saver actually is simple to use. Use the key to allocate to the various budget categories the amounts spent or received. Be sure to enter a budget category in the Turbo-Search Key blank only if you want to allocate the *entire* amount spent or received to a *single* budget category. For example, a bank loan payment may represent part interest and part principal. To allocate to these two budget categories, press F2-Allocate to Budget Categories without typing either budget category name. The amounts then are entered in the Budget Categories screen.

   To use the Turbo-Search Key, type the name of the budget category in the blank. If the payment is for groceries and just one budget category begins with the letter *G*, you type **G** in the blank. If two

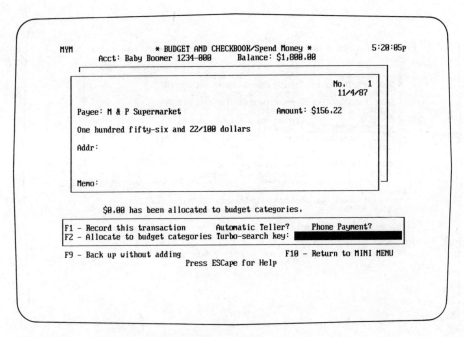

```
MYM                    * BUDGET AND CHECKBOOK/Spend Money *              5:20:05p
               Acct: Baby Boomer 1234-000      Balance: $1,800.00
        ┌─
        │                                                      No.      1
        │                                                      11/4/87
        │
        │    Payee: M & P Supermarket                 Amount: $156.22
        │
        │    One hundred fifty-six and 22/100 dollars
        │
        │    Addr:
        │
        │
        │    Memo:
        └

               $0.00 has been allocated to budget categories.
        ┌─────────────────────────────────────────────────────────────┐
        │ F1 - Record this transaction      Automatic Teller?   Phone Payment? │
        │ F2 - Allocate to budget categories Turbo-search key: ███████████████ │
        └─────────────────────────────────────────────────────────────┘
          F9 - Back up without adding                F10 - Return to MINI MENU
                              Press ESCape for Help
```

Fig. 5.23. Check payment information entered.

budget categories begin with the letter *G*, then the Budget
Categories screen is displayed automatically, and the cursor is
positioned at the first budget category that begins with *G*.

After entering the budget category that you name, you press F1 to
process the transaction. If the cursor ever ends up at the Budget
Categories screen accidentally, or if you press F2 and do not insert
a budget amount in the Turbo-Search Key blank, then enter directly
into the budget category the amount to be allocated and press F1
to process the transaction.

For this example, assume that you cannot remember in which
budget category to enter the payment to M & P.

2. From the Spend Money screen, press F2 and scroll down until the
   cursor is positioned at Groceries (see fig. 5.24).

   Look at the information that is provided for you. Notice that you
   don't have to remember the check amount. If you allocate to
   various budget categories, then the amount remaining to be
   allocated is automatically calculated for you after each such partial
   allocation.

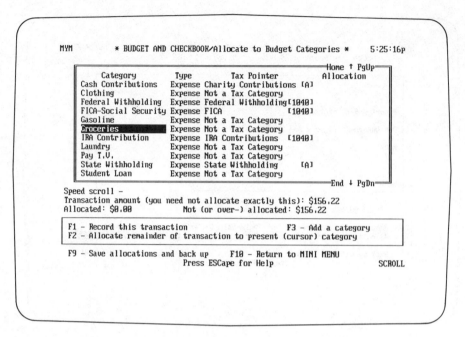

Fig. 5.24. The Allocate to Budget Categories screen.

3. Move the cursor to the right, type **156.22** in the Groceries blank, and press Enter (see fig. 5.25).

   The full amount has been allocated and no over- or under-allocation has occurred. Remember that sometimes you split the payment or the receipt among various budget categories or even decide not to allocate the entire amount.

4. Press F1-Record This Transaction.

   Your screen should display the Spend Money screen, from which you can record another check.

The screen is prepared for the next check entry. Enter the checks that follow in the same manner as the first one. For the remaining checks, use the Turbo-Search Key to allocate to the budget categories, because you are given the budget category name. After you type the budget category in the Turbo-Search Key blank, press F1 to record the transaction.

When you use the Turbo-Search Key, be sure to spell the budget category *exactly* as you did when you set up your budget. If you don't, the program performs as if no such budget category exists, and you will automatically return to the Budget Categories screen. Don't be alarmed if this happens. Just

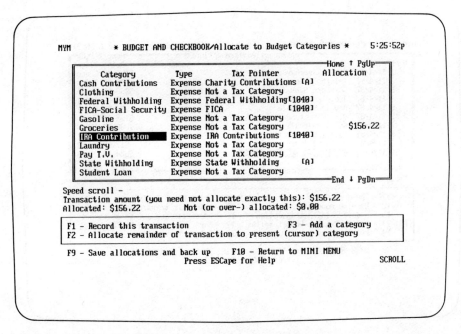

Fig. 5.25. Payment allocated to Groceries budget category.

search through the budget categories and proceed as you did on the first check. Then press F1 when you are ready to record the transaction.

Now enter the information from these nine checks:

Check #	Payee	Amount	Budget Category
002	Telephone Company	$96.12	Telephone
003	Southern Bank	$250.00	Student Loan
004	Jerry's Service Station	$65.60	Gasoline
005	New Jersey Cable	$35.00	Pay T.V.
006	U.S Cancer Society	$150.00	Cash Contributions
007	American Equity	$2,000.00	IRA Contribution
008	Palisade's Electric	$110.90	Utilities
009	Moe's Cleaners	$17.00	Laundry
010	Paul's Department Store	$520.00	Clothing

After you enter the information from the last check, press F9-Back Up to Unreconciled Transactions Level. Compare your screen to figure 5.26.

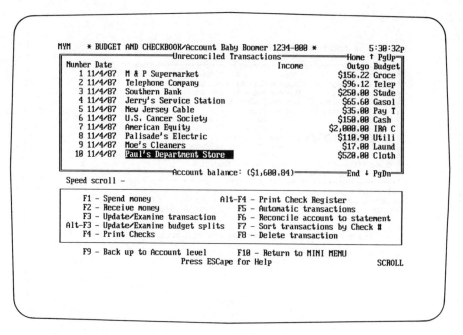

Fig. 5.26. Information on check payments recorded.

Your account balance should be displayed at the lower edge of the upper box. If the balance is not ($1600.84), then you incorrectly entered one of the check amounts. Scroll through the checks until you find the error, and then position the cursor on that check. Press F3 to make the correction. After the correction is made, press F1 to record the modified transaction.

Study the options on the Unreconciled Transactions screen. You can spend more money, receive money, or update or examine a transaction that has already been entered. Version 4.0 can go directly to the Update/Examine Budget Splits screen; move to check printing; print a check register to the screen, the printer, or a disk; work with automatic transactions; reconcile the account with the bank statement; sort the transactions in any of four possible ways (move the cursor to F7 to see the sorting options); or delete a transaction.

The tutorial does not cover every option, so try them on your own. With practice, you will be able to move through the program quickly. Look now at some of these options.

Receiving Money

You are ready to enter the sample deposits for the month into the account. Record each deposit, set up the receipt of a paycheck as an automatic transaction, and execute the automatic transaction.

To enter a deposit:

1. From the Unreconciled Transactions screen, press F2-Receive Money (see fig. 5.27).

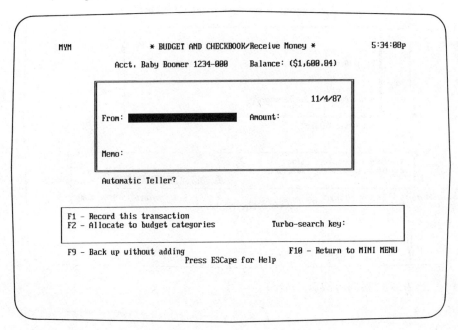

```
  MYM                  * BUDGET AND CHECKBOOK/Receive Money *        5:34:00p

                Acct. Baby Boomer 1234-000     Balance: ($1,600.84)

      ┌──────────────────────────────────────────────────────────┐
      │                                              11/4/87       │
      │                                                            │
      │  From: ███████████████████       Amount:                   │
      │                                                            │
      │                                                            │
      │  Memo:                                                     │
      └──────────────────────────────────────────────────────────┘

         Automatic Teller?

      ┌──────────────────────────────────────────────────────────┐
      │  F1 - Record this transaction                              │
      │  F2 - Allocate to budget categories      Turbo-search key: │
      └──────────────────────────────────────────────────────────┘

         F9 - Back up without adding              F10 - Return to MINI MENU
                         Press ESCape for Help
```

Fig. 5.27. The Receive Money screen.

The date is provided for you again. Later, you can change an incorrect date. For purposes of the tutorial, assume that everything occurred on the same date.

2. The first receipt is the monthly payment on a loan that the sample family made to a relative. Enter the information that follows into the appropriate blanks. After entering information into each blank, press the Enter key.

   From: **Danny Default**

   Amount: **889.78**

Memo: **Partial Loan Repayment** (Press Ctrl-E to enter the Wordprocessor.)

Turbo-Search Key: **Loan Repayment**

When you finish, your screen should look like figure 5.28.

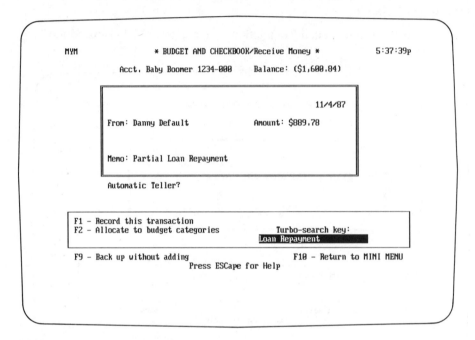

```
MYM                  * BUDGET AND CHECKBOOK/Receive Money *        5:37:39p
              Acct. Baby Boomer 1234-000     Balance: ($1,600.84)

                                              11/4/87

      From: Danny Default            Amount: $889.78


      Memo: Partial Loan Repayment


   Automatic Teller?


   F1 - Record this transaction
   F2 - Allocate to budget categories        Turbo-search key:
                                             Loan Repayment

   F9 - Back up without adding              F10 - Return to MINI MENU
                    Press ESCape for Help
```

Fig. 5.28. Deposit information entered.

3. Press F1 to record the transaction.

4. Press F9-Back Up to Unreconciled Transactions Level.

5. Then press F9 again to back up to the account level.

Figure 5.29 shows the current balance in the Baby Boomer account.

Making Automatic Transactions

An automatic transaction is a receipt or disbursement of cash that you program into Managing Your Money because it occurs regularly. For example, payment of your monthly rent, which doesn't vary in amount, can be set up as a timesaving fixed automatic transaction.

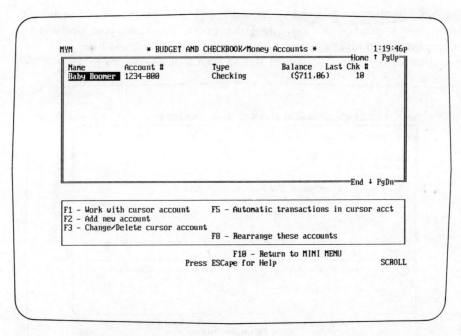

Fig. 5.29. Updated balance displayed on Money Accounts screen.

With the cursor positioned at your only account on the Money Accounts screen, press F5-Automatic Transactions in Cursor Acct. If you have not deleted the sample transactions, then your screen will look like figure 5.30.

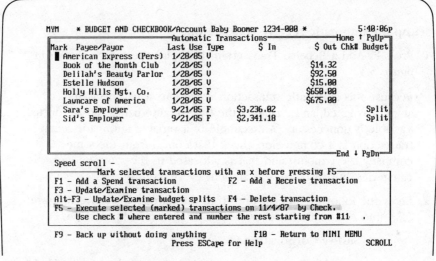

Fig. 5.30. Sample automatic transactions.

To delete all the sample automatic transactions, position the cursor anywhere
on the first transaction and press F4. Then press F1 to verify your decision to
delete. Press F4 and F1 as many times as necessary to delete all the
automatic transactions. The screen should then look like figure 5.31.

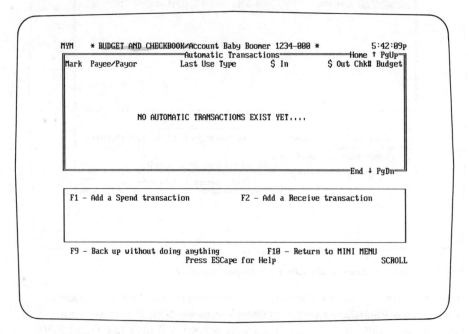

```
MYM     * BUDGET AND CHECKBOOK/Account Baby Boomer 1234-000 *           5:42:09p
                          ═Automatic Transactions═           ═Home ↑ PgUp═
 Mark  Payee/Payor           Last Use Type        $ In        $ Out Chk# Budget




           NO AUTOMATIC TRANSACTIONS EXIST YET....




                                                            ═End ↓ PgDn═

   F1 - Add a Spend transaction          F2 - Add a Receive transaction




   F9 - Back up without doing anything       F10 - Return to MINI MENU
                         Press ESCape for Help                    SCROLL
```

Fig. 5.31. Automatic transactions eliminated.

To set up an automatic receive transaction:

1. Press F2-Add a Receive Transaction to display the screen shown in
   figure 5.32.

   Because this automatic transaction represents a paycheck, its
   amount is Fixed, and changing the type of automatic transaction to
   Variable is unnecessary. An example of a variable automatic-receive
   transaction is a commission check that comes from the same
   company every month and that is allocated to the same budget
   categories, but that varies in amount every month.

2. Enter the following information from the paycheck shown in figure
   5.33 into Automatic Receipts screen, as shown in figure 5.34.

   From: **Sunny Corporation**

   Amount: **1356.42** (the net amount that is deposited in the bank)

```
MYM    * BUDGET AND CHECKBOOK/Acct. Baby Boomer 1234-000 *                    5:43:14p
                        * Automatic Receipts *

            Type of automatic transaction: Fixed

    ┌──────────────────────────────────────────────────────────────┐
    │ From:                                    Amount:               │
    │                                                                │
    │                                                                │
    │ Memo:                                                          │
    │                                                                │
    └──────────────────────────────────────────────────────────────┘



    ┌──────────────────────────────────────────────────────────────┐
    │ F1 - Record this transaction                                   │
    │ F2 - Allocate to budget categories                             │
    │                                                                │
    │ F9 - Back up without adding            F10 - Return to MINI MENU│
    └──────────────────────────────────────────────────────────────┘
    Choose one: Fixed or Variable Amount.
```

Fig. 5.32. The Automatic Receipts screen.

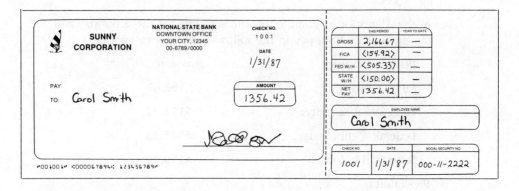

Fig. 5.33. Carol Smith's paycheck.

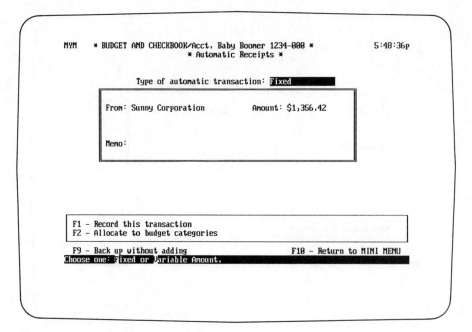

```
MYM    * BUDGET AND CHECKBOOK/Acct. Baby Boomer 1234-000 *          5:48:36p
                        * Automatic Receipts *


             Type of automatic transaction: Fixed

        ┌─────────────────────────────────────────────────────────┐
        │  From: Sunny Corporation          Amount: $1,356.42       │
        │                                                           │
        │                                                           │
        │  Memo:                                                    │
        │                                                           │
        └─────────────────────────────────────────────────────────┘




        ┌─────────────────────────────────────────────────────────┐
        │  F1 - Record this transaction                             │
        │  F2 - Allocate to budget categories                       │
        │                                                           │
        │  F9 - Back up without adding           F10 - Return to MINI MENU │
        └─────────────────────────────────────────────────────────┘
        Choose one: Fixed or Variable Amount.
```

Fig. 5.34. Deposit information entered.

3. Press F2-Allocate to Budget Categories.

   This step displays the budget categories that you set up earlier (see
   fig. 5.35).

4. In the Allocation column, enter the amounts for the gross pay and
   the deductions from pay in the following budget categories:

Budget Category	Amount
Salary - Wife:	$2,166.67
FICA-Social Security:	$154.92
Federal Withholding:	$505.33
State Withholding:	$150.00

5. Press Enter.

   The entire $1356.42 should have been allocated as shown in
   figure 5.36.

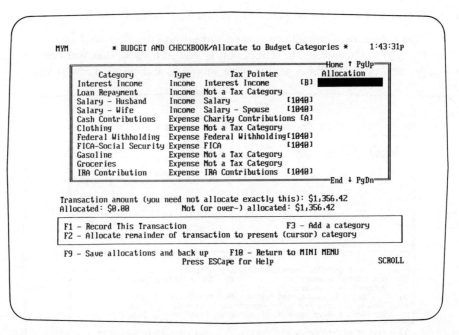

Fig. 5.35. Deposit amount ready to be allocated.

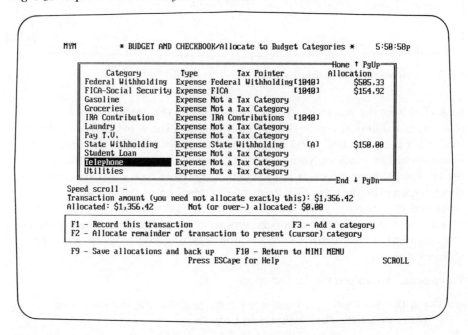

Fig. 5.36. Deposit amount allocated to budget categories.

6. If everything is correct, press F1-Record This Transaction.

The Automatic Transactions screen should now be displayed (see fig. 5.37). The automatic transaction is now set up so that you can process every paycheck you receive simply by executing a few steps.

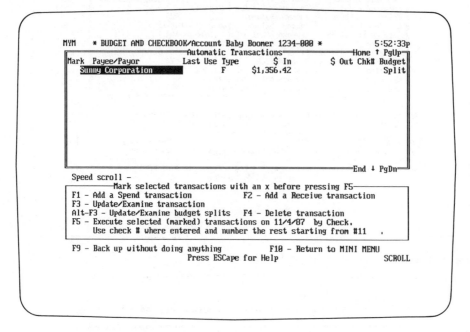

```
MYM    * BUDGET AND CHECKBOOK/Account Baby Boomer 1234-000 *            5:52:33p
                            ┌Automatic Transactions                ┐Home ↑ PgUp┐
┌Mark  Payee/Payor          Last Use Type      $ In          $ Out Chk# Budget│
│ Sunny Corporation                     F    $1,356.42                   Split│
│                                                                             │
│                                                                             │
│                                                                             │
│                                                                             │
│                                                                             │
│                                                                             │
│                                                           └End ↓ PgDn┘
 Speed scroll -
        ┌─────Mark selected transactions with an x before pressing F5─────┐
        │ F1 - Add a Spend transaction          F2 - Add a Receive transaction │
        │ F3 - Update/Examine transaction                                      │
        │ Alt-F3 - Update/Examine budget splits  F4 - Delete transaction       │
        │ F5 - Execute selected (marked) transactions on 11/4/87  by Check.    │
        │      Use check # where entered and number the rest starting from #11 .│
        └──────────────────────────────────────────────────────────────────────┘
  F9 - Back up without doing anything          F10 - Return to MINI MENU
                         Press ESCape for Help                      SCROLL
```

Fig. 5.37. Automatic transaction recorded.

Look closely at the Automatic Transactions screen. The amount of the transaction is listed in the In flow of cash column. The F in the Type column indicates a fixed amount. Versions 3.0 and 4.0 have a Last Use column, which should be blank on your screen. This column indicates the date that the automatic transaction was last executed; therefore, you don't have to check back in the unreconciled items to see whether you've already processed this transaction for the month. The Budget categories column, which is also new, shows the budget allocation of the automatic transaction. The word Split means that the transaction was allocated to more than one budget category.

To execute an automatic transaction:

1. On the Automatic Transactions screen, position the cursor at the blank under the Mark column and type **x**.

The screen is complete except for a check number, which is unnecessary in this case.

2. Press the Enter key.

   The cursor moves down to the F5-Execute option.

3. Press Enter and ignore the date. You are ready to execute the transaction (see fig. 5.38).

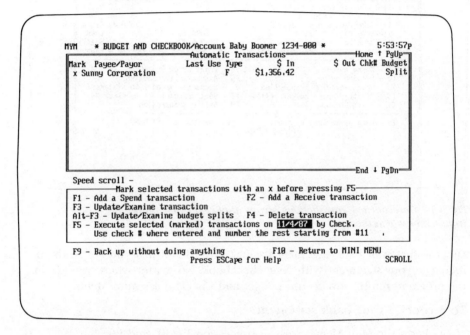

Fig. 5.38. Automatic transaction marked.

4. Press F5 to process the automatic transaction.

   The Unreconciled Transactions screen is automatically displayed (see fig. 5.39). All your transactions for the month have been entered.

Reconciling Your Bank Account

Some people feel that balancing their checkbooks is a monthly chore and a true waste of time. Others are so overwhelmed by the task that they just ignore it. Managing Your Money allows you to have fun balancing your checkbook, and reduces the amount of time you spend doing it (assuming that you *do* reconcile your bank statement with your checkbook register).

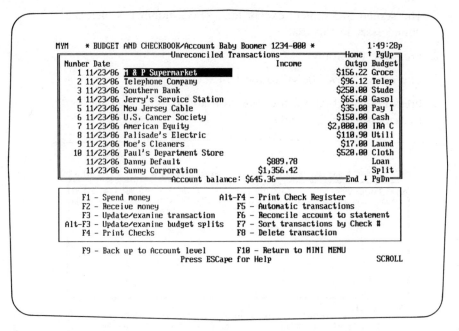

Fig. 5.39. Unreconciled Transactions screen displayed after automatic transaction is executed.

Suppose that your bank statement has just arrived and that you are ready to reconcile your statement with your checkbook. No matter where you are in the program, return now to the Budget and Checkbook's Mini Menu.

To reconcile your bank statement:

1. From the Mini Menu, press in succession F2, F1, and F6.

   Your screen should look like figure 5.40.

2. With the bank statement shown in figure 5.41 by your side, type an **x** in the Mark column on the Transactions to be Reconciled screen beside every check and deposit that cleared the statement.

3. Enter the ending bank balance in the Statement Balance blank at the bottom of the screen.

   Your screen should look like figure 5.42.

4. Press F1 to attempt reconciliation of the account.

   If the account is reconciled, then the screen shown in figure 5.43 appears.

```
MYM    * BUDGET AND CHECKBOOK/Account Baby Boomer 1234-000 *          5:57:31p
            ══════════Transactions to be Reconciled══════════Home ↑ PgUp═
 Mark Number Date       Payee                 $ In           $ Out
   █    1 11/4/87   M & P Supermarket                      $156.22
        2 11/4/87   Telephone Company                       $96.12
        3 11/4/87   Southern Bank                          $250.00
        4 11/4/87   Jerry's Service Sta                     $65.60
        5 11/4/87   New Jersey Cable                        $35.00
        6 11/4/87   U.S. Cancer Society                    $150.00
        7 11/4/87   American Equity                      $2,000.00
        8 11/4/87   Palisade's Electric                    $110.90
        9 11/4/87   Moe's Cleaners                          $17.00
       10 11/4/87   Paul's Department S                    $520.00
            ══════════Account balance: $645.36═══════════End ↓ PgDn═
      Mark (x) all of your canceled checks and credited deposits.

 ┌─────────────────────────────────────────────────────────────────────┐
 │ Statement Balance:                    Interest Earned:                │
 │ Finance Charges:          Check Fees/Service Charges:                 │
 │ Statement Date: 11/4/87                                               │
 │ Check your statement against the items here. Press F1 to attempt      │
 │ reconciliation of this account. Use F9 to back up and add new transactions │
 │ or update existing ones. (Entries on this screen will not be lost.)   │
 └─────────────────────────────────────────────────────────────────────┘

 F9 - Back up to Unreconciled level              F10 - Return to MINI MENU
                        Press ESCape for Help                     SCROLL
```

Fig. 5.40. Transactions to be Reconciled.

BABY BOOMER BANK STATEMENT

Carol Smith   Account #   1234-000
1111 Locust Way
Anytown, USA

Previous Statement Balance $1,800.00

Ending Bank Balance $ 887.38

CLEARED CHECKS		CLEARED DEPOSITS
#	Amount ($)	Amount ($)
001	$ 156.22	$ 889.78
003	250.00	1,356.42
004	65.60	
006	150.00	
007	2,000.00	
009	17.00	
010	520.00	

Fig. 5.41. Bank statement.

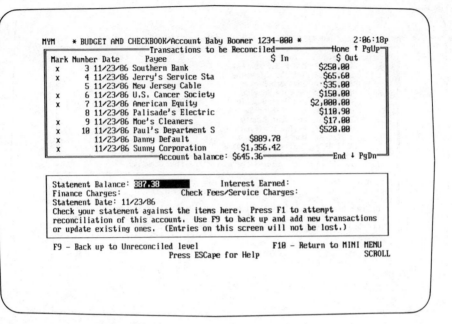

```
MYM    * BUDGET AND CHECKBOOK/Account Baby Boomer 1234-000 *        2:06:18p
              ═════════════Transactions to be Reconciled═════════Home ↑ PgUp═
Mark Number Date        Payee                      $ In          $ Out
 x      3 11/23/86 Southern Bank                               $250.00
 x      4 11/23/86 Jerry's Service Sta                          $65.60
        5 11/23/86 New Jersey Cable                             ·$35.00
 x      6 11/23/86 U.S. Cancer Society                         $150.00
 x      7 11/23/86 American Equity                           $2,000.00
        8 11/23/86 Palisade's Electric                         $110.90
 x      9 11/23/86 Moe's Cleaners                               $17.00
 x     10 11/23/86 Paul's Department S                         $520.00
 x        11/23/86 Danny Default              $889.78
 x        11/23/86 Sunny Corporation        $1,356.42
              ═════════════════Account balance: $645.36═══════════End ↓ PgDn═

    Statement Balance: [387.38]          Interest Earned:
    Finance Charges:            Check Fees/Service Charges:
    Statement Date: 11/23/86
    Check your statement against the items here. Press F1 to attempt
    reconciliation of this account. Use F9 to back up and add new transactions
    or update existing ones. (Entries on this screen will not be lost.)

    F9 - Back up to Unreconciled level          F10 - Return to MINI MENU
                    Press ESCape for Help                      SCROLL
```

Fig. 5.42. Checks that cleared the bank marked and statement balance entered.

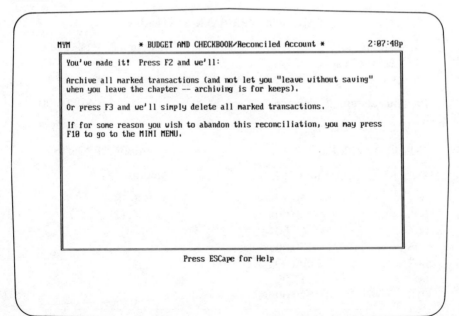

```
MYM            * BUDGET AND CHECKBOOK/Reconciled Account *        2:07:48p

    You've made it! Press F2 and we'll:

    Archive all marked transactions (and not let you "leave without saving"
    when you leave the chapter -- archiving is for keeps).

    Or press F3 and we'll simply delete all marked transactions.

    If for some reason you wish to abandon this reconciliation, you may press
    F10 to go to the MINI MENU.










                    Press ESCape for Help
```

Fig. 5.43. Account reconciled.

If the account does not reconcile, keep trying until it does. A message on the screen tells you whether you need to spend or receive more or less money in order for the account to balance.

5. Most of the time, after your account is reconciled, you should press F2 to archive the transactions that clear the bank. Because this is sample data, however, press F10 to abandon the reconciliation and return to the Budget and Checkbook's Mini Menu.

Keep in mind that entering the correct data properly into the program ensures easy reconciliation of your checkbook. The program performs all addition, subtraction, and other calculations for you, thus reducing errors. Managing Your Money keeps your checkbook balance in its memory so that you do not have to remember it. The program also uses your balance as a component of your net worth in the Your Net Worth module.

Printing Checks

If you write most of your monthly checks in one or two sittings, then Managing Your Money's check-printing capability generally will save you time. If you write one or two checks a day, however, and you cannot change this practice, then the amount of time spent setting up the printer and the checks may be greater than the time saved by having the computer write your checks. Make your decision based on your check-writing habits and the number of checks that you write every month.

If you decide to use this option, you *must* order checks from your bank. The manufacturer of Managing Your Money has made arrangements with the major check-printing companies so that they can print the exact type of checks you need.

To prepare to print checks, first press F2 from the Budget and Checkbook's Mini Menu. Then position the cursor at the desired account and press F1. Press F4 to display the check-printing menu shown in figure 5.44.

The most difficult part of check printing is lining up the checks properly so that everything is printed on the proper line. The F1-Print One Line-up Check function is designed to help you line up the checks properly.

Insert your checks into your printer and press F1 to see if the checks are properly lined up. If not, realign the checks and press F1 again. Repeat this procedure as many times as necessary to line up the checks. Eventually, as you become familiar with your printer, you should be able to line up the checks visually.

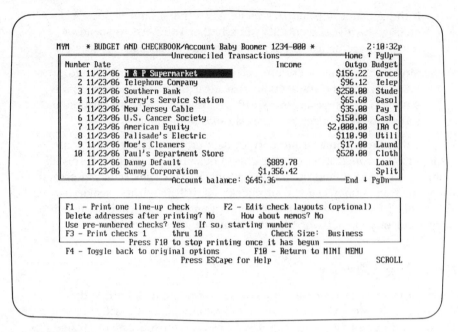

Fig. 5.44. The check-printing menu displayed at the bottom of the screen.

You probably will not have to use the F2-Edit Check Layouts function key. Use it if you use checks other than the two standard types that the program is designed to handle. By editing the check layouts, you can change the print locations of the payee, the date, the amount, and various other details. Using one of the two standard types of checks is recommended.

On the bottom portion of the screen shown in figure 5.44, you are asked several questions. You can move the cursor down to this section of the screen in order to change the answers to the questions.

The first question is whether you want to delete the addresses after printing. If you select Yes, then you will save some space in your archive files because the information will be deleted. The address information will not be deleted from your automatic transactions file if you have set up automatic transactions for any of the checks that you print. The only advantage of deleting the addresses is saving space in your files.

For the next question—concerning deleting memos—saving space is again an issue. You can decide how to answer the question.

Next, you are asked whether you use prenumbered checks. If you answer Yes, your printer will not print check numbers on your checks. If you answer No, your printer prints the check numbers.

Prenumbered checks give you greater control over the account, but they have several disadvantages. First, if you will be writing checks manually from the account *and* printing checks on the computer, you probably will not want to carry the checks with you because they are all attached to each other in one continuous form with perforations. If you tear the checks apart, you will be unable to feed them into your printer. In addition, you will have many voided checks if you make several attempts to line up individual checks properly on your printer.

If you use non-numbered checks, you can keep several with you for writing checks manually. When you line up the checks on your printer, you can use checks that you do not assign a number.

If you use prenumbered checks, then you must indicate the starting number of the checks. Fill in this number after you have lined up the checks, because the number may change.

On the line F3-Print Checks ___ Thru ___, enter the starting and ending check numbers that you will print. Then indicate the size of your checks. The program can accommodate two standard sizes.

To print the checks, press F3. The selected series of checks should be printed.

Creating and Using Loan Records

The Loan Records section of the Budget and Checkbook module is useful if you have a mortgage and need to calculate what portion of each payment is principal and what portion is interest. Even if you do not have this type of loan, you still may want to enter the data for any loans that you have outstanding (either money borrowed or money lent) into Managing Your Money in order to get an accurate picture of your net worth in the Net Worth module of the program.

Setting Up Loan Records

This tutorial sets up two loans—a student loan taken out by the Smith family and a loan made by the Smith family. The student loan is considered a liability (money that the Smiths owe), and the loan made by the Smiths is considered an asset (money owed to them).

From the Mini Menu, begin by pressing F4-Loan Records. The Loan Records screen appears (see fig. 5.45).

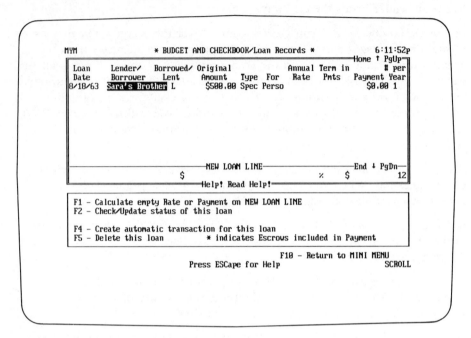

Fig. 5.45. Sample loan records.

If you have not eliminated the sample loans already, then do so before you begin the tutorial. Use the steps for deleting data from the Loan Records screen.

To delete data from the Loan Records screen:

1. On the Loan Records screen, position the cursor at the loan you want to delete.

2. Press F5-Delete This Loan.

3. Press F1 to verify that you want to delete the loan.

4. Repeat Steps 1–3 until all loans are deleted.

    After all loans are deleted, the screen should look like figure 5.46.

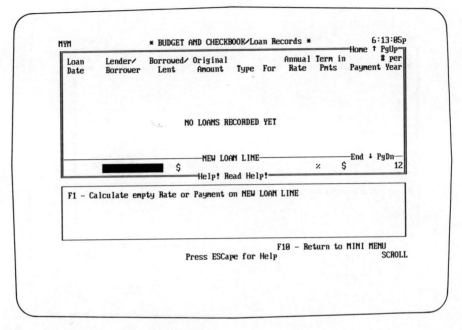

Fig. 5.46. Loans records eliminated.

To set up a loan you've taken out:

1. With the cursor positioned at the New Loan line on the Loan
   Records screen, enter the following information about the student
   loan. Be sure to press the Enter key after each item is entered.

   Loan Date: **1/1/83**

   Lender/Borrower: **Southern Bank**

   Borrowed/Lent: **B** (for borrowed)

   Original Amount: **20605** (the original amount borrowed)

   Type: **M** (for mortgage loan, in which most of the initial payment
   is interest and only a small portion is principal).

   For: **E** (for education)

   Annual Rate: **8** (for 8 percent)

   Term: **120** (12 payments per year for 10 years)

   After you have entered this data, your screen should look like
   figure 5.47.

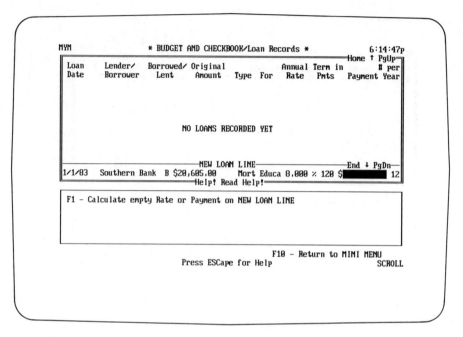

Fig. 5.47. New loan information entered.

2. Press F1 and Managing Your Money will calculate your monthly payment for you.

3. Press F1 to add the loan to your records (see fig. 5.48).

To set up a loan you've made to another:

1. With the cursor positioned at the New Loan line on the Loan Records screen, enter the following information about the loan made by the Smith family to Danny Default. Be sure to press Enter after each item is entered.

   Loan Date: **1/1/86**

   Lender/Borrower: **Danny Default**

   Borrowed/Lent: **L** (for lent)

   Amount: **40000** (for $40,000)

   Type: **M** (for mortgage)

   For: **P** (for personal)

   Annual Rate: **12** (for 12 percent)

   Payments: **60** (12 payments per year for 5 years)

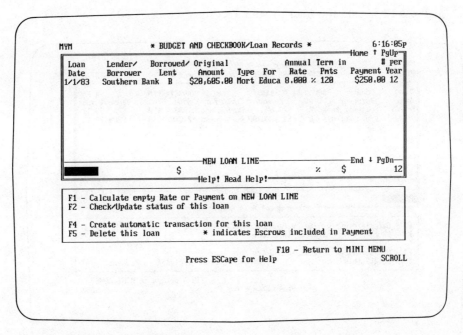

Fig. 5.48. New loan added to records.

2. Press F1 and Managing Your Money calculates the monthly payment
   that Danny Default must make to repay in five years the loan that
   you gave him (see fig. 5.49).

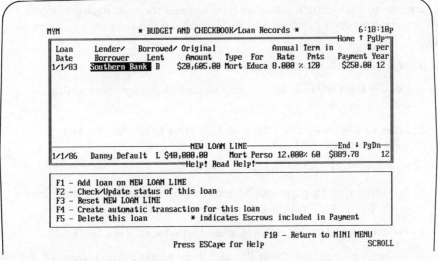

Fig. 5.49. Information entered for a second loan.

3. Press F1 to add the loan to your records (see fig. 5.50).

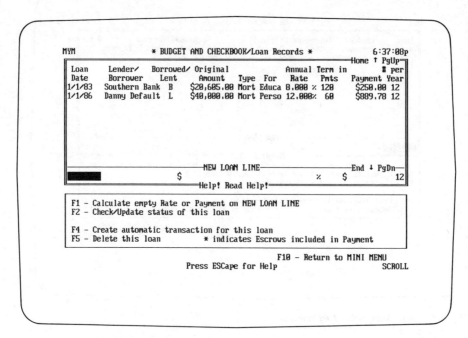

```
MYM                    * BUDGET AND CHECKBOOK/Loan Records *            6:37:00p
                                                              ┌Home ↑ PgUp┐
 Loan    Lender/   Borrowed/ Original              Annual Term in     # per
 Date    Borrower   Lent     Amount     Type For    Rate  Pnts   Payment Year
1/1/83  Southern Bank  B   $20,605.00 Mort Educa  8.000 %  120   $250.00 12
1/1/86  Danny Default  L   $40,000.00 Mort Perso 12.000%   60   $889.78 12




                         ─NEW LOAN LINE─                  ─End ↓ PgDn─
 ▓▓▓▓▓▓▓▓▓▓     $                        %      $             12
                        ═Help! Read Help!═
 ┌─────────────────────────────────────────────────────────────────────┐
 │ F1 - Calculate empty Rate or Payment on NEW LOAN LINE                 │
 │ F2 - Check/Update status of this loan                                 │
 │                                                                       │
 │ F4 - Create automatic transaction for this loan                       │
 │ F5 - Delete this loan          * indicates Escrows included in Payment │
 └─────────────────────────────────────────────────────────────────────┘
                                    F10 - Return to MINI MENU
                   Press ESCape for Help                      SCROLL
```

Fig. 5.50. Two loan records displayed.

Printing an Amortization Schedule

By printing an amortization schedule, you can see the split between interest
and principal for each payment and the balance of the loan on any given
date.

To print an amortization schedule:

1. On the Loan Records screen, use the arrow keys to position the
   cursor over the second loan.

2. Press F2-Check/Update Status of This Loan to display the screen
   shown in figure 5.51.

   First you must update the status of the loan.

3. Assuming that 15 payments have been made so far, move the cursor
   down to the F1 function line and type **15** in the blank.

4. Press F1-Calculate Your Status after 15 Payments (see fig. 5.52).

   Updated information about the loan is provided at the middle of the
   screen.

```
MYM          * BUDGET AND CHECKBOOK/Calculate/Update Loan Status *      6:21:11p
                       You're paid up through 1/1/86
   Date of Loan: 1/1/86            Payments already made: 0
   Borrower: Danny Default         Balance Due: $40,000.00
   Amount of Loan: $40,000.00      Total Principal Paid: $0.00
   Interest Rate: 12.000%          Total Interest Paid: $0.00
   Total Number of Payments: 60    Payments Remaining: 60
   Monthly Payment: $889.78        Expected Pay Off Date: 1/1/91
                   Memo:

   After 0 payments:  There are 60 payments left to go.  So far, you have been
   paid $0.00 of the $40,000.00 principal.  You still are owed $40,000.00.  Of the
   next payment:  $400.00 will be interest; $489.78 will be principal . Over the
   remaining life of this loan, you will be paid $53,386.67 -- the $40,000.00 in
   principal plus $13,386.67 in interest.

   F1 - Calculate your status after 0    payments
   F2 - Print amortization schedule starting as of 1    payments
   F3 - Change the interest rate of this loan to 12.000%
   F4 - Return to Loan Records and UPDATE your status to 0 payments

   F9 - Return to Loan Records              F10 - Return to MINI MENU
 Press Ctrl-E to edit.
```

Fig. 5.51. Loan Status screen.

```
MYM          * BUDGET AND CHECKBOOK/Calculate/Update Loan Status *      6:23:06p
                       You're paid up through 1/1/86
   Date of Loan: 1/1/86            Payments already made: 0
   Borrower: Danny Default         Balance Due: $40,000.00
   Amount of Loan: $40,000.00      Total Principal Paid: $0.00
   Interest Rate: 12.000%          Total Interest Paid: $0.00
   Total Number of Payments: 60    Payments Remaining: 60
   Monthly Payment: $889.78        Expected Pay Off Date: 1/1/91
                   Memo:

   After 15 payments:  There are 45 payments left to go.  So far, you have been
   paid $7,883.90 of the $40,000.00 principal.  You still are owed $32,116.10.  Of
   the next payment:  $321.16 will be interest; $568.62 will be principal . Over
   the remaining life of this loan, you will be paid $40,040.01 -- the $32,116.10
   in principal plus $7,923.91 in interest.

   F1 - Calculate your status after 15  payments
   F2 - Print amortization schedule starting as of 1    payments
   F3 - Change the interest rate of this loan to 12.000%
   F4 - Return to Loan Records and UPDATE your status to 15 payments

   F9 - Return to Loan Records              F10 - Return to MINI MENU
                        Press ESCape for Help
```

Fig. 5.52. Loan status after 15 payments.

5. Move the cursor to the F2 line and type **15** in the blank.

6. Press F2-Print Amortization Schedule Starting as of 15 Payments.

   The program displays the screen shown in figure 5.53. Version 4.0 can print to the screen or to a disk, as well as print to your printer.

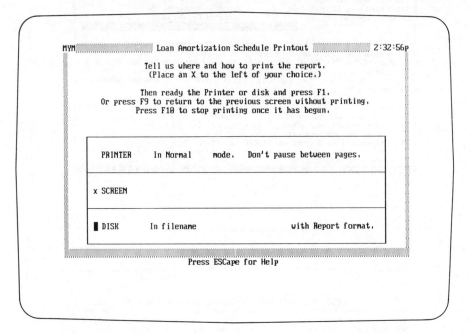

Fig. 5.53. Printout selection.

7. Type an **X** in the desired box.

8. Press F1 to print the amortization schedule (see fig. 5.54).

9. Exit this loan by pressing either F4 to update the status of the loan or F9 to continue the loan amortization schedule until the last payment and leave the loan status the same as it was before you entered the loan records.

Archiving Temporarily

In just a short time, your bulky monthly bank statements, the documents you save for your tax return preparation, and your other personal financial data

```
11/23/86                    Amortization Schedule              Page 1
Mark D. Weinberg

Borrower        Type              Amount       Rate  Periods    Payment
Danny Default   Lent    Mortgage  $40,000.00   12.000%  60      $889.78

Payment  Date             Principal          Interest      Balance Due
 14                                                          $32,679.08
 15     4/1/87            $562.99            $326.79         $32,116.10
 16     5/1/87            $568.62            $321.16         $31,547.48
 17     6/1/87            $574.30            $315.47         $30,973.18
 18     7/1/87            $580.05            $309.73         $30,393.13
 19     8/1/87            $585.85            $303.93         $29,807.28
 20     9/1/87            $591.71            $298.07         $29,215.58
 21     10/1/87           $597.62            $292.16         $28,617.96
 22     11/1/87           $603.60            $286.18         $28,014.36
 23     12/1/87           $609.63            $280.14         $27,404.72
 24     1/1/88            $615.73            $274.05         $26,788.99
 25     2/1/88            $621.89            $267.89         $26,167.10
 26     3/1/88            $628.11            $261.67         $25,539.00
 27     4/1/88            $634.39            $255.39         $24,904.61
 28     5/1/88            $640.73            $249.05         $24,263.88

PRESS ANY KEY TO CONTINUE....
```

Fig. 5.54. A portion of an amortization schedule.

tend to accumulate. In the same manner that your file drawer becomes cluttered with all that data, Managing Your Money's working files also become cluttered.

Although organizing the clutter probably is an all-day affair for people who do not have their personal financial data on a computer, the process is quite simple for those who do. In fact, Managing Your Money archives most data automatically. The archiving process merely takes data that is no longer necessary for current purposes and places it in separate files. The data does not get lost; it just moves to a less cluttered file.

Managing Your Money has the capability to archive data either permanently or temporarily. Any transaction that is entered into the Managing Your Money program is automatically stored in a particular file. For example, the information on a check that you record in the Budget and Checkbook module immediately finds its way into the check file. The information is stored in a file while you continue to work on the program and is erased when you exit that particular module. The information is stored permanently in the file when you direct your computer to save your changes before you exit the module.

Suppose, for example, that you want to do some tax planning in October. Much of your financial data from January through September is automatically permanently archived after you reconcile your checkbook each month. All the checks that have cleared the bank are located in permanent archive files.

Some of your outstanding checks, which have not been archived yet, may have an impact on your tax planning calculations. To complete your calculations, you will need to archive these outstanding checks temporarily. Then you can combine your archived data with your unarchived data and print a report with the combined data. Afterward, the two sets of data automatically separate again.

To temporarily archive data:

1. From the Budget and Checkbook's Mini Menu, press F7-Temporary Archiving (see fig. 5.55).

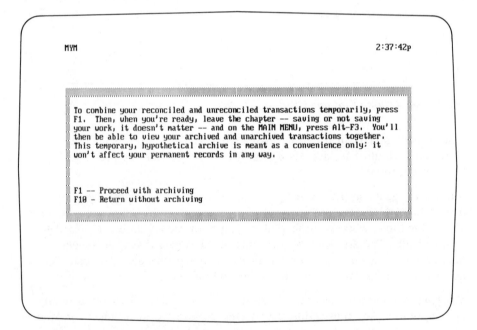

Fig. 5.55. Temporary archiving screen.

2. Press F1-Proceed with Archiving.

   Your screen should now display the Budget and Checkbook's Mini Menu.

This sequence may be confusing at first, because you return to the Budget and Checkbook's Mini Menu, which is where you began. If your screen displays the Mini Menu, then you've made no mistakes. By pressing F7 and then F1, you inform the program that you are going to archive temporarily. These first two steps format the files for the temporary archiving procedure.

3. From the Budget and Checkbook's Mini Menu, press F10 and then F1 and **Y** (or F5, if you want to save the data you entered in the last working session).

You now should be back at the Main Menu.

4. From the Main Menu, press Alt-F3-Budget Archives to display the screen shown in figure 5.56.

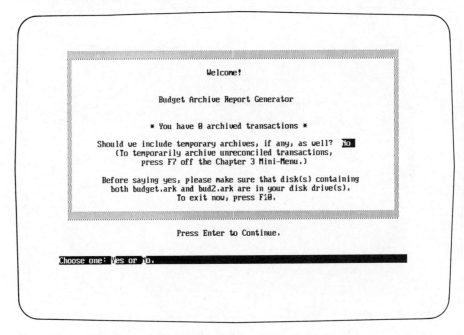

```
                          Welcome!

                 Budget Archive Report Generator

               * You have 0 archived transactions *

    Should we include temporary archives, if any, as well?  No
         (To temporarily archive unreconciled transactions,
                press F7 off the Chapter 3 Mini-Menu.)

       Before saying yes, please make sure that disk(s) containing
         both budget.ark and bud2.ark are in your disk drive(s).
                      To exit now, press F10.


                     Press Enter to Continue.

Choose one: Yes or No.
```

Fig. 5.56. The Welcome screen of the Budget Archive Report Generator.

You no longer have to exit the program in order to archive.

Notice the absence of Help screens here. If you follow the steps in this tutorial, you should have no trouble with temporary archiving. Also, notice that you should have no archived transactions at this point.

The Welcome screen indicates how many archived transactions you have and asks whether you would like to include unarchived transactions in your reports as well. The screen says No. If you leave the No in response to the inquiry, then your unarchived transactions will not be combined with the archived transactions for your reports. You may, for some purposes, want to print reports of only archived transactions. For now, change your answer to Yes.

5. Type **Y** for Yes and press Enter.

   If you have already deleted the sample data that was on the disks when you bought the program and have completed the Budget and Checkbook tutorial in the first part of this chapter, the screen should look like figure 5.57.

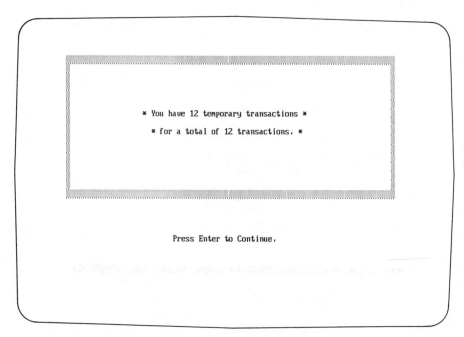

```
                    * You have 12 temporary transactions *
                     * for a total of 12 transactions. *




                           Press Enter to Continue.
```

Fig. 5.57. The number of temporary and archived transactions displayed.

6. Press Enter to display the Budget Archive Report Generator screen shown in figure 5.58.

Creating Reports

The Budget Archive Report Generator screen is the control center for the creation of your reports. Suppose that you want to analyze your medical

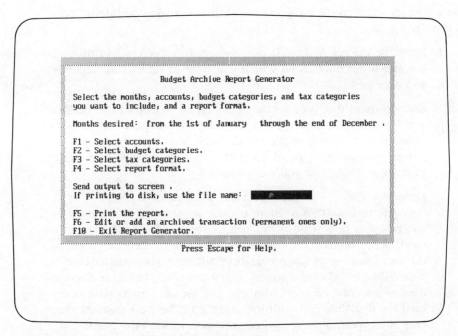

Budget Archive Report Generator

Select the months, accounts, budget categories, and tax categories
you want to include, and a report format.

Months desired: from the 1st of January   through the end of December .

F1 - Select accounts.
F2 - Select budget categories.
F3 - Select tax categories.
F4 - Select report format.

Send output to screen .
If printing to disk, use the file name:

F5 - Print the report.
F6 - Edit or add an archived transaction (permanent ones only).
F10 - Exit Report Generator.

Press Escape for Help.

Fig. 5.58. The Budget Archive Report Generator.

expenses from the two months that you were sick in the hospital. First,
select the months that you want to include in the report. Change the Months
desired on the screen to February and March so that you can focus on that
period. You may want your report to show all your income and expenses for
each month, or maybe you want to see only the expenses that will have an
impact on your tax return. You can do all this with the Budget Archive
Report Generator.

At the end of the year, you surely will want to print by budget category all
your income and expense items with their respective totals. You also might
want at that time a printout of all the budget categories that affect your tax
situation.

In this section of the tutorial, you will create and print two reports from the
sample transactions that you entered earlier. If you did not enter the sample
transactions or if you have already entered some of your personal financial
data, the screens will not be identical to those in this book, but the
explanations should still be helpful.

Before you actually create a report, review the following outline of the general procedure:

1. From the Budget Archive Report Generator screen, select the account or accounts from which you want to select your receipts and expenses.

    Keep in mind that your accounts, which are set up in the Budget and Checkbook module of the program, are composed of groups of transactions that may include both receipts and disbursements of money. Choose any type of account: checking, savings, cash, credit card, or anything else you can imagine.

    From this screen, you can select one account or combine your transactions from two or more of your accounts. For example, if you pay your bills with money from several checking accounts, you most likely combine the transactions from both accounts when you do your planning or tax preparation. Similarly, you may have set up your VISA charge card as one account and your American Express card as a second account. You may pay for car repairs with one card the first time and with the other card the next time. At the end of the year, however, when you want to see how much you spent on car repairs, you would combine the two accounts. The Budget Archive Report Generator allows you to do all of this.

2. Select the budget categories that you want to enter into the report.

    These categories also are set up in the Budget and Checkbook module.

3. Select the tax categories that you want to include in the report.

    You may want to include only the transactions that are classified as employee business expenses, all the transactions that have a tax impact, or only those that have no tax impact.

If you understand just one important concept about the report generator, then you should have no trouble extracting the information that you need for all of your reports:

> *For a transaction (whether it is the receipt of your paycheck or a mortgage payment on your house) to find its way into a report, the transaction must meet one of the selected criteria in each of the three groups: account, budget, and tax.*

That is, the transaction must have occurred in one of the selected accounts, and it must fall into one of the selected budget categories and one of the selected tax categories. Therefore, if you selected your checking account and the Groceries budget category, but failed to select Not a Tax Category, then your expenditure for groceries will not be included in the report.

To create a report:

1. On the Budget Archive Report Generator screen, for simplicity, let the months stand as January through December.

2. Press F1-Select Accounts.

   If you completed the Budget and Checkbook tutorial from the beginning of this chapter and saved your data, then your screen should look like figure 5.59.

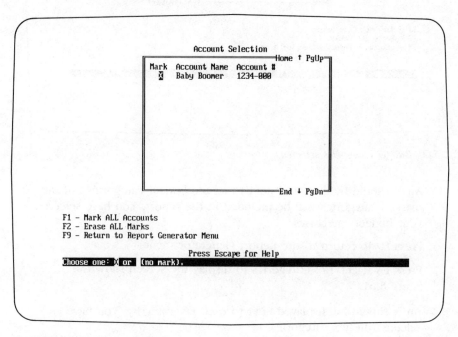

Fig. 5.59. An account selected.

3. An X should be displayed next to this account already. If not, then type an **X** there.

   You have chosen the account from which the transactions will be selected for the report.

4. Press F9 to return to the Report Generator menu.

5. Press F2-Select Budget Categories and the screen shown in figure 5.60 should be displayed.

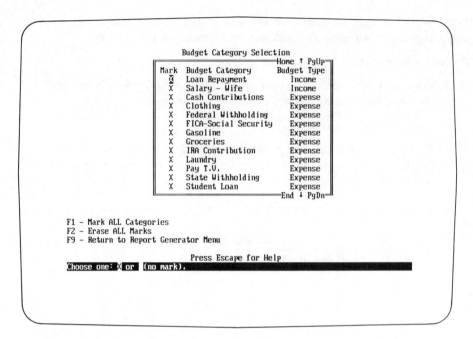

Fig. 5.60. Budget categories selected.

An X should be displayed next to all the budget categories. All the marked categories will be included in the report. You have selected your budget categories.

6. Press F9 to return to the Report Generator menu.

7. Press F3-Select Tax Categories to display the screen shown in figure 5.61.

   An X should be displayed next to each tax category. You have selected the tax categories.

8. Press F9 to return to the Report Generator menu.

   All tax categories are included, and you are ready to select your report format.

9. Press F4-Select Report Format to display the screen shown in figure 5.62.

   The programmed Account Report format, which is adequate for most purposes, is displayed on the screen. You can print reports by Account, Tax Category, or Payee. For example, use Payee to see how much you paid this year to your next-door-neighbor's daughter

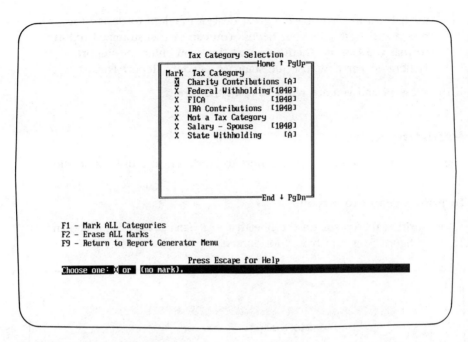

Fig. 5.61. Tax categories selected.

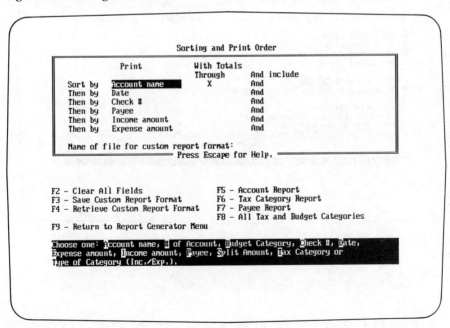

Fig. 5.62. The Sorting and Print Order screen.

for baby-sitting. You have a great deal of freedom to design the
report that best suits your needs. You can save customized reports
so that you can use them the next time you enter the Report
Generator. For now, use the standard Account Report Format.

10. Press F9 and you are ready to print the report.

Printing Reports

You can send the output of your report to a printer, to a disk, or to the
screen.

To print a report to screen:

1. Position the cursor on the line that says Send output to, as shown
   in figure 5.63, and type **S** for Screen.

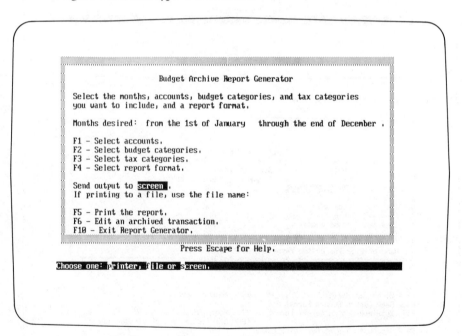

```
                     Budget Archive Report Generator

       Select the months, accounts, budget categories, and tax categories
       you want to include, and a report format.

       Months desired: from the 1st of January   through the end of December .

       F1 - Select accounts.
       F2 - Select budget categories.
       F3 - Select tax categories.
       F4 - Select report format.

       Send output to screen .
       If printing to a file, use the file name:

       F5 - Print the report.
       F6 - Edit an archived transaction.
       F10 - Exit Report Generator.
                          Press Escape for Help.

       Choose one: printer, file or screen.
```

*Fig. 5.63. The Budget Archive Report Generator set to send output to the
screen.*

2. Press F5-Print the Report to display the screen shown in figure
   5.64.

3. Press F5 to print your report and display it on the screen, as shown
   in figure 5.65.

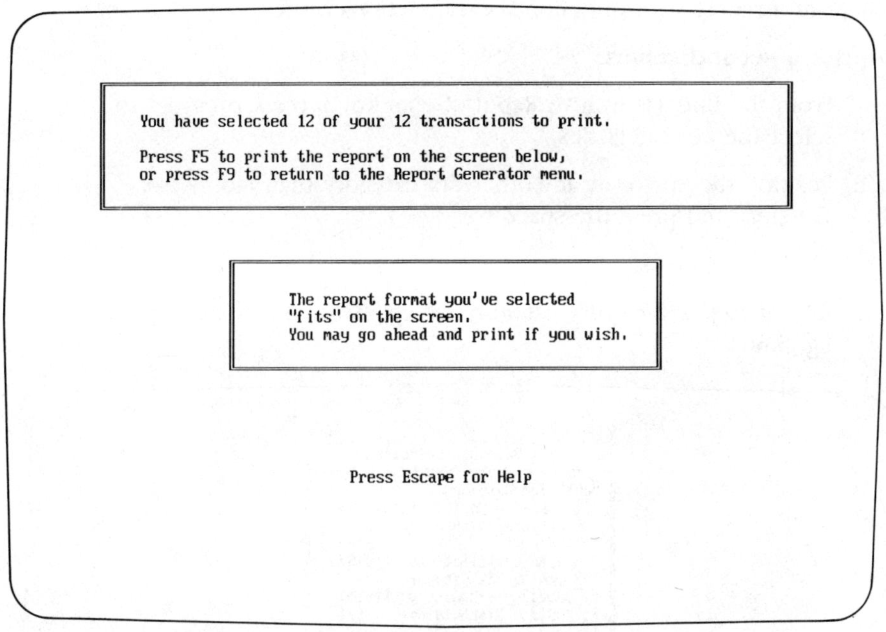

```
┌─────────────────────────────────────────────────────────┐
│  You have selected 12 of your 12 transactions to print.   │
│                                                           │
│  Press F5 to print the report on the screen below,        │
│  or press F9 to return to the Report Generator menu.      │
└─────────────────────────────────────────────────────────┘


        ┌─────────────────────────────────────┐
        │  The report format you've selected   │
        │  "fits" on the screen.               │
        │  You may go ahead and print if you wish. │
        └─────────────────────────────────────┘




                    Press Escape for Help
```

Fig. 5.64. Transactions to be printed selected.

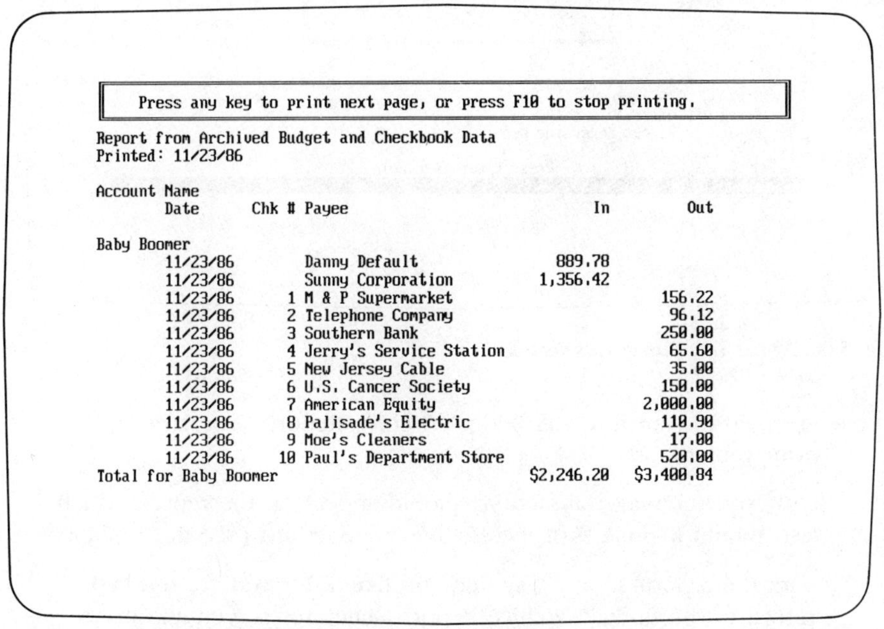

```
┌─────────────────────────────────────────────────────────┐
│  Press any key to print next page, or press F10 to stop printing. │
└─────────────────────────────────────────────────────────┘
Report from Archived Budget and Checkbook Data
Printed: 11/23/86

Account Name
        Date      Chk # Payee                    In         Out

Baby Boomer
        11/23/86        Danny Default           889.78
        11/23/86        Sunny Corporation     1,356.42
        11/23/86      1 M & P Supermarket                  156.22
        11/23/86      2 Telephone Company                   96.12
        11/23/86      3 Southern Bank                      250.00
        11/23/86      4 Jerry's Service Station             65.60
        11/23/86      5 New Jersey Cable                    35.00
        11/23/86      6 U.S. Cancer Society                150.00
        11/23/86      7 American Equity                  2,000.00
        11/23/86      8 Palisade's Electric                110.90
        11/23/86      9 Moe's Cleaners                      17.00
        11/23/86     10 Paul's Department Store            520.00
Total for Baby Boomer                      $2,246.20   $3,400.84
```

Fig. 5.65. A sample report of transactions that have a tax effect,
displayed on the screen.

Now print a report with only non-tax transactions on it.

To print a second report:

1. From the Budget Archive Report Generator screen, press F3 to select the tax categories.

2. Position the cursor at any other tax category than Not a Tax Category and press the space bar.

   The X disappears.

3. Repeat Step 2 for every category except Not a Tax Category (see fig. 5.66).

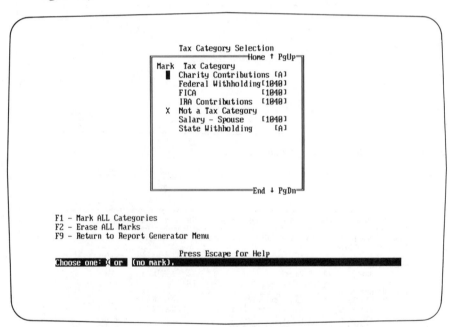

Fig. 5.66. Not a Tax Category selected.

4. Press F9 to return to the Budget Archive Report Generator and print your report.

   Only your non-tax transactions should appear on the report, which also should include 9 of the 12 total transactions (see fig. 5.67).

5. Vary the reports in any way that you like. After you are finished, return to the Budget Archive Report Generator screen and press F10 to return to the Main Menu of Managing Your Money.

```
┌────────────────────────────────────────────────────────────────┐
│    Press any key to print next page, or press F10 to stop printing. │
└────────────────────────────────────────────────────────────────┘
Report from Archived Budget and Checkbook Data
Printed: 11/23/86

Account Name
        Date        Chk # Payee                         In          Out

Baby Boomer
        11/23/86          Danny Default              889.78
        11/23/86        1 M & P Supermarket                        156.22
        11/23/86        2 Telephone Company                         96.12
        11/23/86        3 Southern Bank                            250.00
        11/23/86        4 Jerry's Service Station                   65.60
        11/23/86        5 New Jersey Cable                          35.00
        11/23/86        8 Palisade's Electric                      110.90
        11/23/86        9 Moe's Cleaners                            17.00
        11/23/86       10 Paul's Department Store                  520.00
        Total for Baby Boomer                       $889.78    $1,250.84
```

Fig. 5.67. A sample report of non-tax transactions, displayed on the screen.

Understanding the Budget and Checkbook's Optional Features

The Budget and Checkbook's optional features include Accounts Payable, Accounts Receivable, Graphs, Five Year Planning, and (in Versions 3.0 and 4.0) Home Banking. This tutorial does not discuss the details of how to add and delete accounts payable and receivable or how to graph and plan, because those are fairly simple functions. Furthermore, you probably do not need (or want) any more practice entering data. However, the tutorial does explain how to turn on the optional features and how to access them from the Budget and Checkbook's Mini Menu.

Before you can use any of the optional features, you must turn on the features you want to use. After you turn on the features, you use a different procedure to enter Accounts Payable, Accounts Receivable, Graphs, Five Year Planning, or Home Banking.

To turn on an optional feature:

1. From the Budget and Checkbook's Mini Menu, press F6 to display the screen shown in figure 5.68.

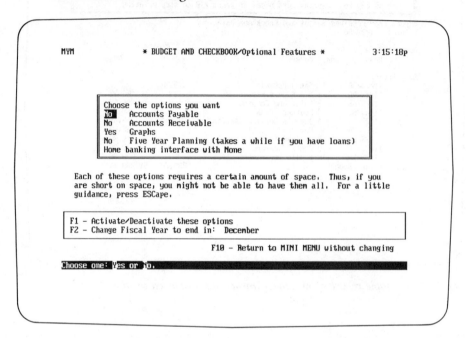

Fig. 5.68. The Budget and Checkbook's optional features.

Whether or not you want to use the optional features (except for Home Banking), you might as well turn them on. Using the options does use up space in the computer's memory. However, unless you have a huge number of transactions, or unless you have less than 256K of memory on your computer, you should have no problem. Besides, Managing Your Money alerts you if it has a memory problem, and you can then turn off any of the features.

2. Press F1 to activate the options.

If you forget to press F1 and you instead press F10 to return to the Mini Menu, the options will remain in the mode that they were in before any changes were made. Pressing F1 will, in effect, store the changes in the computer's memory.

After the optional features are activated, they are accessed by various function keys in the Budget and Checkbook module. Accounts Payable and Accounts

Receivable are accessed by pressing F2-Work with Your Accounts, and Graphs and Five Year Planning are accessed by pressing F3-Cash Forecasting.

Accounts Payable and Accounts Receivable

Exactly what is an account payable or an account receivable? An *account payable* is simply an amount that you owe someone, and an *account receivable* is an amount that someone owes you. For example, the amount that you owe on your American Express bill is an account payable, and the money that your brother-in-law promised to pay back last year but still owes you is an account receivable. (The money owed by your brother-in-law might also be called a bad debt.)

The accounts payable and accounts receivable capabilities of Managing your Money are designed to help you better manage your cash flow—to help you better predict your upcoming cash receipts and cash expenditures. Often, when a bill arrives at your house, payment is not due immediately. You may not want to pay the bill for a week or two, but you may want to note the date that payment is due. Similarly, although you may not have the cash today to pay all the bills that arrive, you would like to make sure that you will have the cash by the time the bills are due to be paid. Recording the amount of money that is owed to you will help you determine whether the cash will be in your account in time.

After you enter your first account payable or account receivable, you can print an aged listing of all your payables or receivables. An aged listing report tells you whether the various amounts owed to you or owed by you are current, whether they are 1 to 30 days past their due dates, whether they are 31 to 60 days past due, and so on. These reports will give you a clear picture of how well you are keeping up with your payments to creditors and how well those that owe you money are keeping up with their payments to you.

Graphs and Five Year Plans

Graphs and Five Year Planning, two more optional features, can help you forecast your future cash requirements. The graphing function displays how your cash position will change according to your budgets and actual expenditures to-date. Five Year Planning allows you to predict your cash position up to five years from now depending on your projected levels of income and expense. With a little experimentation, you should become proficient with these functions.

Home Banking

The Home Banking function, which is currently compatible only with Chase Manhattan Bank's Spectrum System, is new to the Managing Your Money program. The Home Banking option, as its name indicates, allows you to perform banking transactions from your home or office. You can transfer money between Chase Manhattan accounts, pay off your credit card, and perform various other functions. After Home Banking is activated as one of this module's optional features, the function F8-Read Data from Spectrum will appear on the Budget and Checkbook's Mini Menu. This service is available to customers in 48 states by calling the toll-free number 1-800-522-7766. (In New York, call 212/223-7794.)

## Chapter 6

Using the
Financial Calculator

Managing Your Money's powerful, built-in Financial Calculator allows you to answer many of the financial questions that you are likely to encounter in today's complex world. Will you have enough money to pay for your daughter's college education? Should you refinance your home mortgage because interest rates have fallen? With the Financial Calculator, you easily can find the answers.

You probably will not need to use all the Financial Calculator's capabilities, but you surely will want to use some of them. You should at least skim through this chapter to familiarize yourself with the available features.

From the Main Menu, press F6 to display the Financial Calculator's Mini Menu (see fig. 6.1). If you are running the program on a one- or two-disk system, the program prompts you to insert Disk 2 into either drive A or drive B before continuing (see fig. 6.2). After inserting the proper disk, press the Enter key to continue.

Here is an overview of the sections within the module:

Financial Calculator

This part of the module has the same name as the module itself. The module's Financial Calculator is made up of four sections: Compound Interest, Loans and Annuities, Current Yield & Yield to Maturity, and Interest Rate vs. Yield.

The Compound Interest section calculates present and future values. For example, if you invest $500 in a money market fund, and you want to calculate how much it will have grown in 14 years at 7.2 percent, then this section can help you. On the other hand, this section also can help you determine how much you must deposit in your money market fund in order to accumulate $20,000 during the next 10 years.

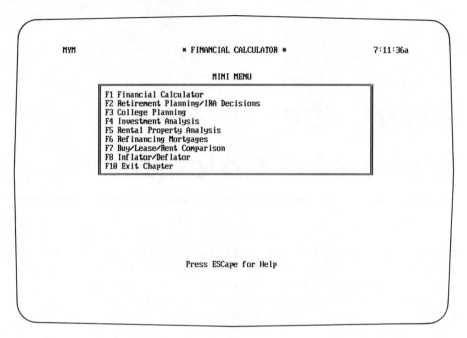

Fig. 6.1. The Financial Calculator's Mini Menu.

Fig. 6.2. The prompt to insert Disk 2.

The Loans and Annuities section calculates the monthly payments for the $7,500 car loan you are considering. Or suppose that you have determined the maximum monthly payment you can afford on a new house. The calculator tells you the maximum loan you can obtain for that payment.

The Current Yield & Yield to Maturity section determines the rate of return you can obtain on a bond investment. A bond is a financial instrument that a corporation, government, or other entity uses to borrow money from you, with a promise to repay the money and the interest that it accumulates. The calculator helps determine the advisability of investing in certain bonds.

The Interest Rate vs. Yield section calculates the real interest rate that you will obtain on an investment. Banks generally quote two interest rates in their ads. An ad might say that the account pays 8% compounded daily for an effective annual yield of 8.45%. This means that the interest earned on the original investment also will earn interest and that when the year is complete, you will have earned 8.45% on your money instead of 8%. Therefore, when you determine the rate of return on an investment, the effective annual yield is much more meaningful than the stated interest rate.

Retirement Planning/IRA Decisions

Retirement planning cannot begin soon enough. Proper planning lets you look forward to maintaining your current standard of living during your retirement years. In contrast, lack of planning can lead to a financial nightmare. Predicting exactly what lies in store for you is impossible. However, by working through several scenarios in the Retirement Planning section, you can determine whether your current and future savings will put you on the right track. The decision whether to invest in an IRA has become more complicated under the new tax law. IRA contributions may no longer be deductible, depending on your level of income.

College Planning

By inserting a series of numbers in the blanks, you can use the College Planning section to estimate the total cost of your children's education as well as the estimated annual amount that you must set aside in order to provide for it. Granted, you must make certain assumptions here. However, by entering information for various cost and inflation scenarios, you can determine your ability to meet these important future expenditures.

General Investment Analysis

Use the General Investment Analysis section to analyze the attractiveness of various investment opportunities. This section helps determine the investment's *internal rate of return*—the after-tax rate of interest you would have to earn in order to equal the results obtained from a specified investment. Some complex financial calculations are involved here, but Managing Your Money's calculator makes the process simple.

After you enter your estimates of the cash inflow and outflow for an investment along with the anticipated tax deductions from the investment, the calculator adds up the cash you invest, the cash you receive, the tax benefits, and the year in which each event occurs. The calculator then provides a single figure, such as 12 percent, that you can compare to the rates of return on your other investment opportunities. With this information, you can make informed decisions about your investments.

Rental Property Analysis

Suppose that you are thinking about buying a single family house near the college campus and renting it out to students. Or maybe you and your partner are considering the purchase of a 52-unit apartment building. Regardless of the size of your investment, the Financial Calculator helps you analyze the investment.

The program's Rental Property Analysis section calculates your projected after-tax cash flow as well as your internal rate of return on investments. In other words, the calculator computes all the cash you expect to invest, the tax benefits you will receive from depreciation, the cash you expect to receive from the investment, and your tax rate, and converts the results into a figure that you can compare to your other investment opportunities.

Refinancing a Mortgage

The powerful Refinancing a Mortgage section of the calculator may be the first function you use. Because of the sharp drop in interest rates over the past several years, many homeowners probably have asked whether this is the best time to refinance their mortgages. After you enter the financial details of both your current mortgage and a mortgage that is now available, the Financial Calculator can answer the question quickly and easily.

You may want to refinance in order to obtain a larger loan amount or to take advantage of the recent changes in the tax laws. Whatever your reasons and however you want to structure the new mortgage, the calculator tells you plainly whether refinancing makes sense and, if so, how much you will save.

Buy/Lease/Rent

Some people have to consider daily whether to buy, lease, or rent assets. Enter the details of a transaction (such as the price of the asset, the portion you will depreciate, how much money you will borrow, and your tax bracket), and the calculator, in simple terms, tells you which form of acquisition makes the most financial sense.

The decision whether to buy, rent, or lease often is governed by factors other than the numbers. Some people enjoy the convenience of leasing, and others would rather buy because, later on, they can give the asset to their children. Whatever your reasons are for making certain decisions, you can be more informed about them by quickly running through the numbers.

Inflator/Deflator

"Plug in" various figures to see the devastating effects that inflation can have on your wealth. At least for the past couple of years, inflation has not been a problem. Let's hope that it doesn't return anytime soon.

The examples for each of the following sections of the tutorial are independent of the other sections. Therefore, if you want to learn how just one function of the Financial Calculator operates without reading through the others, skip the others for now and come back to them later.

Financial Calculator

From the Mini Menu, press F1 to get to the Financial Calculator (see fig. 6.3). Remember that the first section of the Financial Calculator module is also called the Financial Calculator.

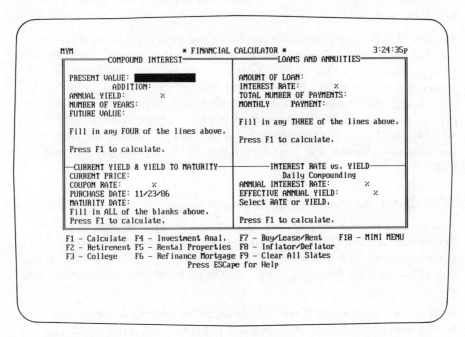

Fig. 6.3. The Financial Calculator screen.

Notice that the screen is divided into quadrants. The upper left corner is used for compound interest calculations (present and future values); the lower left corner for the current yields and the yields to maturity of investments in bonds; the upper right corner for loan amounts and payments; and the lower right corner for the yields on investments with specified interest rates and daily compounding.

Compound Interest

Although the concepts inherent in compound interest problems are quite simple, the calculations often turn out to be overwhelming. The Financial Calculator keeps the process simple by calculating the results for you, without requiring that you understand the concepts completely.

Always ask yourself one question before you perform any of these calculations: "What do I know, and what am I trying to determine?" Either you know the amount of money that you have and that you want to invest, and you need to determine how much that amount will grow in a fixed number of years; or, conversely, you know the amount that you want to obtain, and you want to know how much you have to invest today in order to achieve your goal.

All present value and future value problems are basically that simple, with only minor variations. The calculations all rest on the premise that a dollar today is worth more than a dollar next year, because you can invest the money you receive today and it will earn interest. *Present value* represents any starting dollar amount. *Future value* represents the amount that the present sum will reach after a specified number of years at a specified interest rate. The calculator asks you whether you will add to the amount you originally invested, and if so, how much and how often you will add to it.

Determining the Future Value of an IRA

Suppose that you are 45 years old and want to set up your first Individual Retirement Account (IRA). You also want to make a one-time $2,000 contribution this year to the IRA, which will earn 8 percent per year. You would like to know how much the IRA will be worth in 20 years when you retire.

Look at the Compound Interest calculator in the upper left corner of your screen. You know that the present value is $2,000, and you want to determine the future value—how much that amount will grow in 20 years. Remember that the annual yield you enter into the formula should be an after-tax yield. In the case of your IRA, the before-tax and after-tax yields are the same because the internal buildup in an IRA is not taxed until it is withdrawn.

To determine the future value of an IRA:

    1. In the Compound Interest quadrant of the Financial Calculator screen, enter the following figures into four of the five blanks:

Present Value: **2000** (for $2,000; dollar signs and commas are unnecessary.)

Addition: **0** (the amount that you later can add to the IRA)

Annual Yield: **8** (for 8 percent)

Number of Years: **20**

2. The Future Value blank should be empty. If it isn't, position the cursor over the blank and press the space bar.

   Your screen should look like figure 6.4.

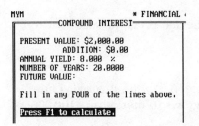

Fig. 6.4. The Compound Interest quadrant.

3. Position the cursor at Press F1 to Calculate and press F1.

   All values in this section of the Financial Calculator are calculated by pressing the F1 key.

   The Future Value should be $9,321.91. After 20 years at 8 percent, $2,000 will grow to $9,321.91 (see fig. 6.5).

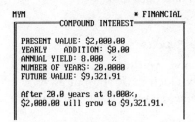

Fig. 6.5. The future value of an IRA calculated.

Making Yearly Additions to an IRA

Leave everything the same as in the preceding example, but instead of contributing $2,000 in the first year only, contribute $2,000 every year. See how the future value in this example differs from that of the preceding example.

To determine the future value of an IRA with yearly additions:

1. In the Compound Interest quadrant of the Financial Calculator screen, position the cursor on the second line, at the blank directly preceding the word Addition.

2. Type **Y** (for yearly).

   The cursor moves automatically to the right.

3. Type **2000** (for $2,000) and press Enter (to indicate that you are adding $2,000 annually to the IRA).

4. Move the cursor to the Future Value line and press the space bar to empty the blank.

5. Press F1 to calculate the future value.

The future value should be $100,845.84 (see fig. 6.6). Isn't it amazing how quickly $2,000 invested annually for 20 years grows to more than $100,000?

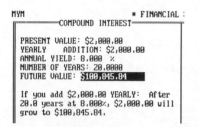

```
MYM                    * FINANCIAL :
        =COMPOUND INTEREST=
 PRESENT VALUE: $2,000.00
 YEARLY    ADDITION: $2,000.00
 ANNUAL YIELD: 8.000 %
 NUMBER OF YEARS: 20.0000
 FUTURE VALUE: $100,845.84

 If you add $2,000.00 YEARLY: After
 20.0 years at 8.000%, $2,000.00 will
 grow to $100,845.84.
```

Fig. 6.6. The future value of an annual IRA contribution calculated.

Determining the Present Value of a Future Expense

Your daughter is 16 years old. Ten years from now, you want to have $30,000 to cover the cost of her wedding. How much must you put away today? In this example, you know the future value, and you want to calculate the present amount that you must invest.

Don't forget to use an after-tax return in your calculations. The earnings will not be sheltered from tax as they were in the IRA examples. Assume that a 4 percent after-tax return is reasonable.

To determine the present value of a future expense:

1. In the Compound Interest section of the Financial Calculator, move the cursor to the Present Value blank and press the space bar to empty the blank, because this is the unknown value.

2. Complete the other blanks as follows:

   Yearly Addition: **0** (because you do not want to add more money after the first year)

   Annual Yield: **4** (for 4 percent)

   Number of Years: **10**

   Future Value: **30000** (for $30,000)

3. Position the cursor at the Present Value blank and press F1 to calculate the present value.

The answer is $20,266.93. After 10 years at 4 percent, $20,266.93 will grow to $30,000 (see fig. 6.7).

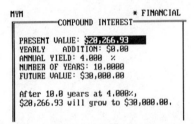

Fig. 6.7. The lump sum needed for a future expense.

Suppose that you do not have $20,000 to invest today in anticipation of your daughter's wedding. With Managing Your Money, you can test different scenarios quickly in order to develop a plan that combines your financial goals with your financial ability. Work through the steps in the next example in order to find a more realistic solution to this problem. Keep in mind that you can use the Financial Calculator to solve your real-life financial problems as well as to test hypothetical ones.

Making Monthly Additions To Fund a Future Expense

Use the same assumptions as in the preceding example, and also assume that you are able to add $125 per month to the amount you originally invest for the wedding.

To make monthly additions to fund a future expense:

1. In the Compound Interest section of the Financial Calculator, position the cursor at the Present Value blank and press the space bar to empty the blank, because this is the unknown value.

2. Press the Enter key to move the cursor down one line.

3. Type **M** (for monthly, because this is how often you plan to add to the investment).

4. Type **125** (because you intend to add $125 every month).

   The remaining figures should stay the same. The annual yield remains constant at 4 percent; 10 years still remain; and the future value is $30,000.

5. Position the cursor at the Present Value blank and press F1.

The present value should be $7,879.11. If you add $125 monthly, $7,879.11 will grow to $30,000 after 10 years at 4 percent (see fig. 6.8). This sum may be more manageable. Although you do not have $20,000 to set aside today, you may be able to find approximately $7,900 now, and then make monthly additions.

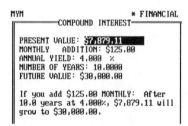

Fig. 6.8. The lump sum and monthly additions needed for a future expense.

Be aware that you eventually may start earning less on your investment than you originally projected. Or perhaps, later on, you may be able to afford to set aside more than $125 per month. In any case, sit down at your computer and recalculate the figures with your new information. Keep in mind that financial planning is not something you do today and then forget about until retirement. Financial planning requires periodic attention in order to adjust for changing conditions in the financial markets and changes in your personal financial situation.

Loans and Annuities

An *annuity* is essentially a stream of payments, which you make or receive, that may last for a period of years or indefinitely. In the Loans and Annuities section of the Financial Calculator, loans generally are considered amounts that you have borrowed and must repay, and annuities are amounts that you have loaned (to an insurance company, for example) and that must be repaid to you.

Determining the Size of Loan Payments

Suppose that you are buying a house, and you would like to borrow $200,000 from your bank. Your property will serve as collateral for the loan. Your banker says that the interest rate will be 9.25 percent on a 30-year fixed rate mortgage. You want to determine whether you can make the payments on this sizable mortgage.

To determine the size of a loan payment:

1. In the Loans and Annuities section of the Financial Calculator, enter the following information:

   Amount of Loan: **200000** (for $200,000)

   Interest Rate: **9.25** (for 9.25 percent)

   Total Number of Payments: **360** (12 payments per year for 30 years)

2. Leave the Monthly Payment blank empty.

3. Position the cursor over the Monthly Payment blank and press F1 to calculate.

The Monthly Payment should be $1,645.35. To pay off a $200,000 loan at 9.25 percent, you must pay $1,645.35 per month for 360 months (see fig. 6.9).

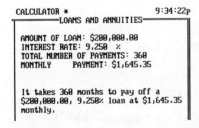

Fig. 6.9. A monthly payment calculated from a mortgage loan amount.

Determining the Amount of a Loan by the Payment Limit

After discussing the matter with your spouse, you decide that you will be unable to make payments of $1,645.35 per month and that $1,200 per month is your limit. So try again, this time to determine the size of a loan that you can obtain with your $1,200 per month payment limit.

To determine the amount of a loan by the payment limit:

1. In the Loans and Annuities section of the Financial Calculator, position the cursor at the Amount of Loan blank and press the space bar to empty the line.

2. Leave the interest rate at 9.25 percent and the number of payments at 360.

3. For Monthly Payment, enter **1200** (for $1,200).

4. Position the cursor at the Amount of Loan blank and press F1 to calculate the amount of the loan.

The loan amount should be $145,865.55 (see fig. 6.10). Unless you can find a lower interest rate, the maximum monthly payment that you can afford will allow you to borrow $145,865. To buy the house you have in mind, you will have to increase your down payment by approximately $54,000 over the amount you would have put down with a $200,000 mortgage.

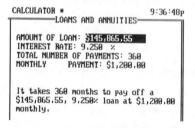

Fig. 6.10. A mortgage loan amount calculated from a fixed monthly payment.

Work through other changes in the variables. Remember to fill in any three of the four variables and leave blank the item that you are seeking.

Current Yield and Yield to Maturity

The Current Yield & Yield to Maturity quadrant of the Financial Calculator is fairly specialized and applies specifically to bond investments. The quadrant calculates the current yield or rate of return on an investment in a bond and the yield to maturity on the bond investment. If you have no interest in such investments, then you probably will not need to use this function. If you do invest in bonds, then you must understand some basic terminology.

A *bond* is basically a financial instrument that represents a loan. The loan is made by a buyer of a bond to the entity that issued the bond. The interest and repayment terms of the bond are set forth in the *bond indenture agreement*. Bonds, which are issued in multiples of $1,000, generally pay a stated interest rate or *coupon rate*. The amount that the borrowing entity is obligated to repay to the bondholder upon maturity of the bond is called the *face amount*.

Bonds do not always trade at their face amount. For example, if the prevailing interest rate for a particular company was 10 percent when the bond was issued and the rates have fallen since then, then the bond probably will trade at a *premium*—at an amount above its face amount. When interest rates rise, the bond probably will trade at a **discount**. Follow this general rule: When interest rates fall, bond prices rise, and vice versa.

The *current yield* on a bond is the coupon interest rate divided by the price you paid for the bond. For example, if the coupon rate is 5 percent and you paid $500 for a $1,000 bond, then the current yield is 5 divided by 500, or 10 percent.

The *yield to maturity* is much more difficult to calculate. It takes into account the coupon rate of interest that you will be paid over the life of the bond as well as the fact that you will receive $1,000 at maturity for a bond that cost $500. The yield to maturity therefore depends on the length of time that remains between the bond purchase date and the maturity date, as well as on several other factors.

Determining Current Yield and Yield to Maturity

Suppose that you are considering purchasing a bond that is trading at 86 (at a discount). The $1,000 bond therefore would cost you $860. Before you decide to buy, you want to calculate the current yield and the yield to maturity on the bond. If you buy the bond on September 15, 1987, the coupon rate would be 5 percent, and the maturity date would be June 30, 2001.

To determine the current yield and yield to maturity:

1. In the Current Yield & Yield to Maturity section of the Financial Calculator, enter the following information:

   Current Price: **86**

Coupon Rate: **5** (for 5 percent)

Purchase Date: **9/15/87**

Maturity Date: **6/30/101** (the year after 1999 is "Nineteen one hundred," so 2001 is 101.)

2. Position the cursor over any blank in this quadrant.

3. Press F1 to calculate the current yield and the yield to maturity.

The current yield should be 5.814 percent, and the yield to maturity should be 6.6 percent (see fig. 6.11). The coupon rate of interest, which you will receive as a return on your investment in the bond, is 5.814 percent. The total yield on the bond, which you will receive if you hold the bond to maturity, is 6.6 percent. The 5.814 percent represents the return you receive based on the interest payments. The 6.6 percent takes into account both the interest payments and the fact that if you hold the bond to maturity, you will receive $1,000 for something for which you originally paid only $860.

```
┌─CURRENT YIELD & YIELD TO MATURITY─┐
│ CURRENT PRICE: 86.00              │
│ COUPON RATE: 5.000 %              │
│ PURCHASE DATE: 9/15/86            │
│ MATURITY DATE: 6/30/101           │
│ CURRENT YIELD: 5.814%             │
│ YIELD TO MATURITY:  6.5%          │
└───────────────────────────────────┘
```

Fig. 6.11. The current yield and yield to maturity calculated.

Interest Rate Versus Yield

The Interest Rate vs. Yield quadrant of the Financial Calculator simply converts a specified interest rate to the equivalent yield, and vice versa, assuming daily compounding of interest.

The difference between the interest rate and the effective annual yield arises from the compounding of interest. When a bank compounds, you earn interest on your interest. Banks generally compound interest daily, which means that the $1,000 you deposit today will be just a little more than $1,000 tomorrow. How much greater? The balance in your account will be $1,000 plus one day's interest on the $1,000 at the stated interest rate. (This balance may not be reflected in your passbook or on your statement because interest is typically posted in your account monthly or quarterly.) The $1,000 plus the one day's interest then will earn interest for the second day. The third day's interest then will be calculated on the $1,000 plus two day's interest, and so on.

Banks typically compound interest daily, although the compounding period may be a week, a month, or any other period. Naturally, the shorter the compounding period, the greater the difference between the stated interest rate and the effective annual yield. An 8 percent stated interest rate that is compounded daily results in an 8.45 percent effective annual yield, and an 8 percent interest rate compounded monthly would be only about 8.299 percent. The difference could be substantial on large sums of money.

Finding the Effective Annual Yield

Suppose that a bank advertises a 7 percent interest rate but does does not state the effect that daily compounding has on the rate.

To find the effective annual yield:

1. In the Interest Rate vs. Yield quadrant of the Financial Calculator, position the cursor at the Annual Interest Rate blank and type **7** (for 7 percent).

2. Make sure that the Effective Annual Yield blank is empty. If it is not empty, position the cursor at the blank and press the space bar.

3. Position the cursor at the Effective Annual Yield blank and press F1.

The Effective Annual Yield should be 7.36 percent (see fig. 6.12).

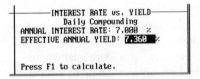

```
┌──────INTEREST RATE vs. YIELD──────┐
│            Daily Compounding      │
│ ANNUAL INTEREST RATE: 7.000 %     │
│ EFFECTIVE ANNUAL YIELD: 7.360 %   │
│                                   │
│ Press F1 to calculate.            │
└───────────────────────────────────┘
```

Fig. 6.12. The effective annual yield calculated.

Remember: When performing all financial calculations, you always should use the effective annual yield and not a stated interest rate as the Annual Yield component.

Retirement Planning

How do you know that your current savings and the amount that you will save during the remainder of your working years will be sufficient to carry you through your retirement years? You probably don't know. Too many unknowns exist, such as your future earnings, your future cash needs, inflation rates, tax rates, yields on your investments, and the number of years you will live after retirement. So why plan? Because planning enables you to predict whether you are on the right track.

After using Managing Your Money to work through several possible scenarios, you may realize that you are spending too much of your earnings now and that you will probably pay for this habit in your retirement. On the other hand, you may be surprised to see how much your nest egg can grow during a 30- to 40-year period (especially if some of your investments are compounding tax free). Maybe you are putting aside too much today, and you will be unlikely to spend it all during your retirement years. You might also consider whether your children could make better use of some of your money today, rather than after you die.

Planning under unknown circumstances certainly is difficult. However, planning is truly impossible if you don't take time to consider the range of possibilities. Clearly, any amount of planning is better than no planning at all, and the Retirement Planning section of the Financial Calculator can help make the planning process less painful.

From the Financial Calculator screen, press F2 to go directly to the Retirement Planning screen without first going to the Financial Calculator's Mini Menu. Or, from the Financial Calculator's Mini Menu, press F2 to achieve the same result. Your Retirement Planning screen should look similar to figure 6.13. To erase the sample data, or any other data that may be on the screen, press F2 to clear the upper slates.

In this section of the Financial Calculator, you will enter data into three basic divisions: the *present balance* that you already have invested in various categories, the *estimated annual contribution* that you anticipate making to each of the investment categories, and the *estimated annual yield* or return that you expect to earn on your investments during a specified period.

The investments are divided between taxables and nontaxables, because the full yield on the nontaxable investments accumulates in your account and only the after-tax yield accumulates on the taxable investments. Your taxable savings include savings accounts, money market funds, certificates of deposit, and any other interest-bearing instruments. Other taxables items might include a variety of investments such as stocks, rental property, and loans to a friend. Nontaxable investments might include such items as municipal bonds, IRA accounts, and Keogh accounts.

The estimated annual yield that you enter should be the full yield of the investment. Ignore taxes here because the calculator automatically adjusts the returns on the taxable portfolios for the proper tax effect.

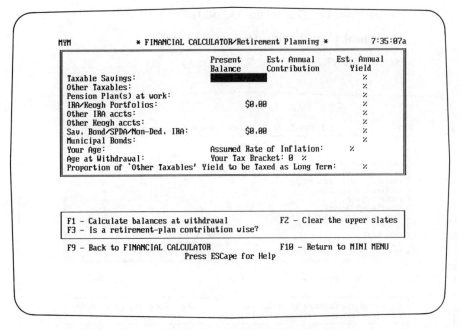

Fig. 6.13. The Retirement Planning screen showing sample data.

Calculating Account Balances at Retirement

Suppose that you have a present balance of $37,500 in savings accounts and that you plan to put an additional $3,500 per year into those accounts. You expect to earn an annual 7.5 percent return on your savings before taxes. In addition, you have a present balance of $23,300 in other taxable investments. You plan to put an additional $500 per year into your other taxable investments, and you expect to earn an annual 8 percent return before taxes on those investments. Suppose that you also have an IRA account with a present balance of $6,000. You do not expect to contribute more to your IRA, but the existing income should earn 8 percent per year. Furthermore, suppose that you have $50,000 earning 5 percent per year; you are 36 years old; you expect to withdraw the balances at age 65; you have assumed an inflation rate of 3 percent; and you are in the 28 percent tax bracket. How much will you have in your accounts at retirement?

To calculate the balances in the accounts at retirement:

1. On the Retirement Planning screen, enter the following information for Taxable Savings, as shown in figure 6.14:

Present Balance: **37500** (for $37,500)

Est. Annual Contribution: **3500** (for $3,500)

Est. Annual Yield: **7.5** (for 7.5 percent)

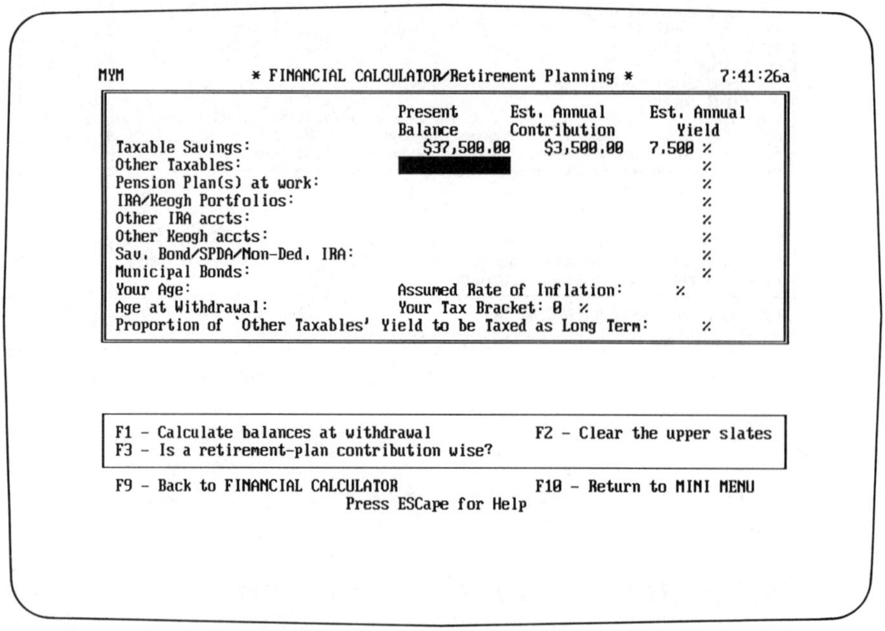

```
MYM              * FINANCIAL CALCULATOR/Retirement Planning *          7:41:26a
                              Present      Est. Annual      Est. Annual
                              Balance      Contribution        Yield
         Taxable Savings:     $37,500.00    $3,500.00       7.500 %
         Other Taxables:      ███████                          %
         Pension Plan(s) at work:                             %
         IRA/Keogh Portfolios:                                %
         Other IRA accts:                                     %
         Other Keogh accts:                                   %
         Sav. Bond/SPDA/Non-Ded. IRA:                         %
         Municipal Bonds:                                     %
         Your Age:                  Assumed Rate of Inflation:   %
         Age at Withdrawal:         Your Tax Bracket: 0 %
         Proportion of `Other Taxables' Yield to be Taxed as Long Term:   %


         F1 - Calculate balances at withdrawal        F2 - Clear the upper slates
         F3 - Is a retirement-plan contribution wise?

         F9 - Back to FINANCIAL CALCULATOR            F10 - Return to MINI MENU
                          Press ESCape for Help
```

Fig. 6.14. Taxable savings entered on the Retirement Planning screen.

2. Enter the following information for Other Taxables:

    Present Balance: **23300** (for $23,300)

    Est. Annual Contribution: **500** (for $500)

    Est. Annual Yield: **8** percent

3. Enter the following information for your IRA:

    Present Balance: **6000** (for $6,000)

    Est. Annual Contribution: **0**

    Est. Annual Yield: **8** (for 8 percent)

4. Enter the following information for your municipal bonds:

    Present Balance: **50000** (for $50,000)

Est. Annual Contribution: **0**

Est. Annual Yield: **5** percent

5. Enter the following additional information:

Your Age: **36**

Age at Withdrawal: **65**

Assumed Rate of Inflation: **3** (for 3 percent)

Your Tax Bracket: **28** (for 28 percent)

Other Taxables To Be Taxed as Long Term: **0**

6. Press F1 to calculate the balances in the accounts at retirement.

The program alerts you that you have been aggressive in your yield assumptions (see fig. 6.15).

7. Stick with the assumptions and press F1 again (see fig. 6.16).

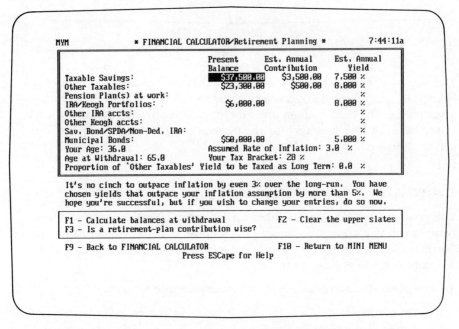

Fig. 6.15. Other taxables entered on the Retirement Planning screen.

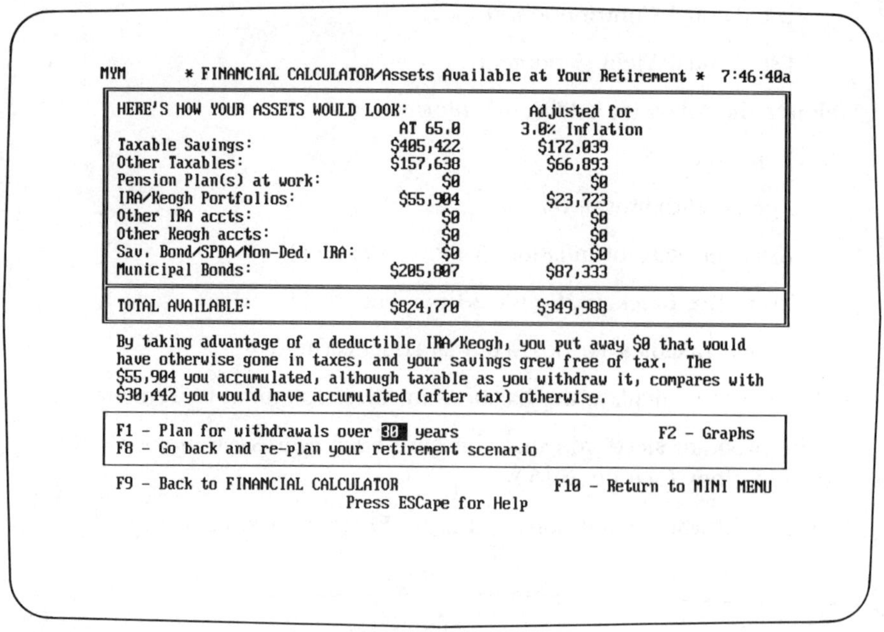

```
MYM      * FINANCIAL CALCULATOR/Assets Available at Your Retirement *  7:46:40a

   HERE'S HOW YOUR ASSETS WOULD LOOK:              Adjusted for
                                      AT 65.0       3.8% Inflation
   Taxable Savings:                   $405,422       $172,039
   Other Taxables:                    $157,638        $66,893
   Pension Plan(s) at work:                $0             $0
   IRA/Keogh Portfolios:               $55,904        $23,723
   Other IRA accts:                        $0             $0
   Other Keogh accts:                      $0             $0
   Sav. Bond/SPDA/Non-Ded. IRA:            $0             $0
   Municipal Bonds:                   $205,807        $87,333

   TOTAL AVAILABLE:                   $824,770       $349,988

   By taking advantage of a deductible IRA/Keogh, you put away $0 that would
   have otherwise gone in taxes, and your savings grew free of tax.  The
   $55,904 you accumulated, although taxable as you withdraw it, compares with
   $30,442 you would have accumulated (after tax) otherwise.

   F1 - Plan for withdrawals over 30  years                F2 - Graphs
   F8 - Go back and re-plan your retirement scenario

   F9 - Back to FINANCIAL CALCULATOR              F10 - Return to MINI MENU
                     Press ESCape for Help
```

Fig. 6.16. The assets available at retirement.

This screen displays two columns. The left column indicates the projected balance in each of the asset categories, taking into consideration all your assumptions. The right column gives the present-day buying power for each of the balances after adjusting for the projected inflation rate over the specified period.

Calculating Assets Available for Retirement

The program also can provide other retirement information, such as the benefits you will accumulate in an IRA. Suppose that you expect to live to be 80 years old. Therefore, you would like to withdraw the money during the 15 years that follow your retirement.

To calculate the assets available during your retirement:

1. On the Assets Available at Your Retirement screen, position the cursor at the blank in the line

   `F1-Plan for withdrawals over ___ years`

2. Type **15** (for 15 years).

3. Press F1 to calculate your assumptions.

Your screen should display a summary of your pre-tax income during retirement (see fig. 6.17).

```
MYM              * Annual Income After Retirement: age 65.0 to 79.0 *        7:48:14a
 ┌───────────────────────────────────────────────────────────────────────────┐
 │ Assuming your money continued to appreciate, if you withdrew it all over 15 │
 │ years, your pre-tax income would be $90,705 a year (plus Social Security -- │
 │ see HELP).  Because of inflation, that would equal about $38,490 in today's │
 │ dollars in the first year, and -- with inflation's continued erosion --     │
 │ $25,447 in the last year.  (To keep your buying power constant, you could   │
 │ withdraw fewer dollars at first, to have more later on.)                    │
 │                                                                             │
 │ It's tough to say what tax brackets will look like in the future.  But if   │
 │ they do not rise (fat chance), and are adjusted to keep pace with inflation │
 │ (fat, fat chance), then yours would be about 15%.  Thus, at age 65.0, your  │
 │ annual income after tax would be $83,273, or $35,336 in today's dollars.  By│
 │ age 79.0, your after-tax income would be $89,040 (you're in the 15% bracket │
 │ now), or $24,980 in today's dollars (inflation rages on).                  │
 │                                                                             │
 └───────────────────────────────────────────────────────────────────────────┘
 ┌───────────────────────────────────────────────────────────────────────────┐
 │ F7 - Alter the number of years for withdrawal                               │
 │ F8 - Re-plan your entire retirement scenario                                │
 └───────────────────────────────────────────────────────────────────────────┘
   F9 - Back to FINANCIAL CALCULATOR                      F10 - Return to MINI MENU
                         Press ESCape for Help
```

Fig. 6.17. *The annual income after retirement.*

To vary the number of years that you expect to live after age 65:

1. Press F7.

2. Make the necessary changes.

3. Press F1 to recalculate.

To view the various graphs:

1. Press F7 to return to the Assets Available at Your Retirement screen.

2. Press F2 to try the graphing capabilities.

3. Press the function keys one at a time to view the various graphic information that is available. One example—a pie graph—is shown in figure 6.18.

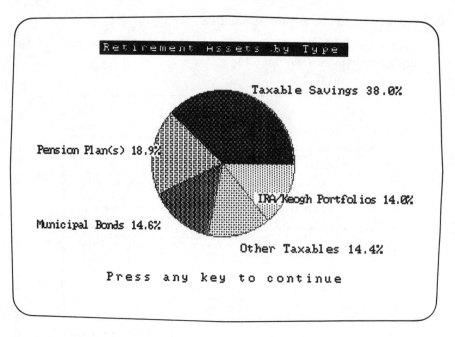

Fig. 6.18. A graph of retirement assets by type.

You can print the graphs to your printer by pressing the Shift key and holding it while you next press the PrtSc key. Remember, however, that you must first have loaded a graphics program into your computer's memory before you can print any graphs. (See Chapter 12 for an explanation about how to load the DOS GRAPHICS program into the working memory of your computer.)

Repeat the steps in this section using your own figures. Then print the screens and graphs.

Is Contributing to a Retirement Plan Wise?

New to Version 4.0 is the F3 function on the Retirement Planning screen. This function helps you decide whether contributing to a retirement plan makes any sense. To try out the function, press F3 (see fig. 6.19). When you are comfortable with this function, return to the Financial Calculator's Mini Menu so that you can explore College Planning.

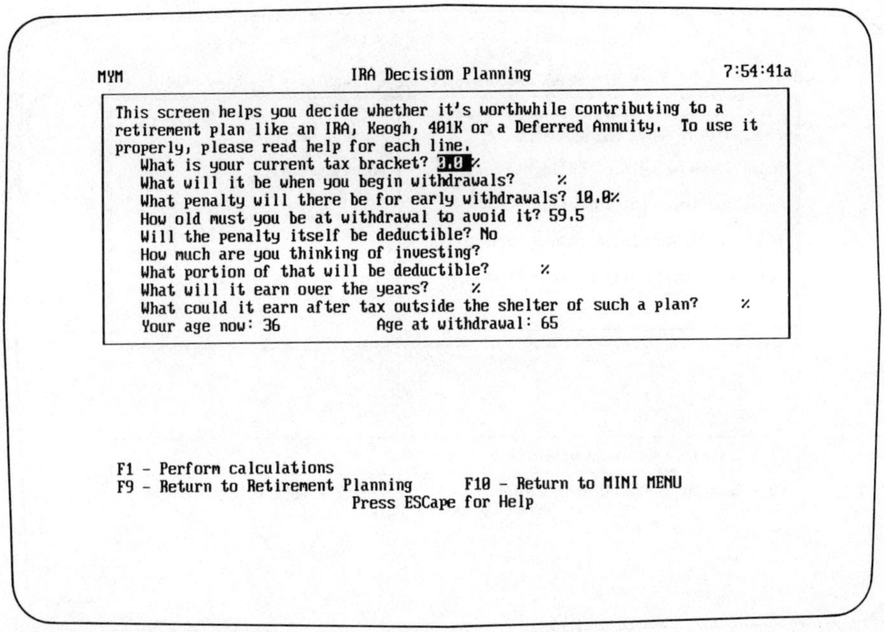

```
MYM                         IRA Decision Planning                    7:54:41a

This screen helps you decide whether it's worthwhile contributing to a
retirement plan like an IRA, Keogh, 401K or a Deferred Annuity. To use it
properly, please read help for each line.
    What is your current tax bracket? 0.0 %
    What will it be when you begin withdrawals?     %
    What penalty will there be for early withdrawals? 10.0%
    How old must you be at withdrawal to avoid it? 59.5
    Will the penalty itself be deductible? No
    How much are you thinking of investing?
    What portion of that will be deductible?     %
    What will it earn over the years?    %
    What could it earn after tax outside the shelter of such a plan?    %
    Your age now: 36            Age at withdrawal: 65




    F1 - Perform calculations
    F9 - Return to Retirement Planning      F10 - Return to MINI MENU
                        Press ESCape for Help
```

Fig. 6.19. The IRA Decision Plan screen.

College Planning

Planning for children's college education is probably one of today's most
essential goals of financial planning. As college costs continue to rise (even
with inflation under control), beginning the planning process while children
are very young becomes increasingly important.

From the Financial Calculator's Mini Menu, press F3-College Planning. Your
screen should look like figure 6.20.

Suppose that you have an 8-year-old daughter named Alison. Ten years from
now, you expect her to attend a 4-year college. Assume that the current cost
of a year in college is $9,000 and that the cost will increase at a rate of 3
percent per year. You already have set aside $2,500 for Alison's college
education, an amount that will grow at an after-tax annual rate of 4 percent.

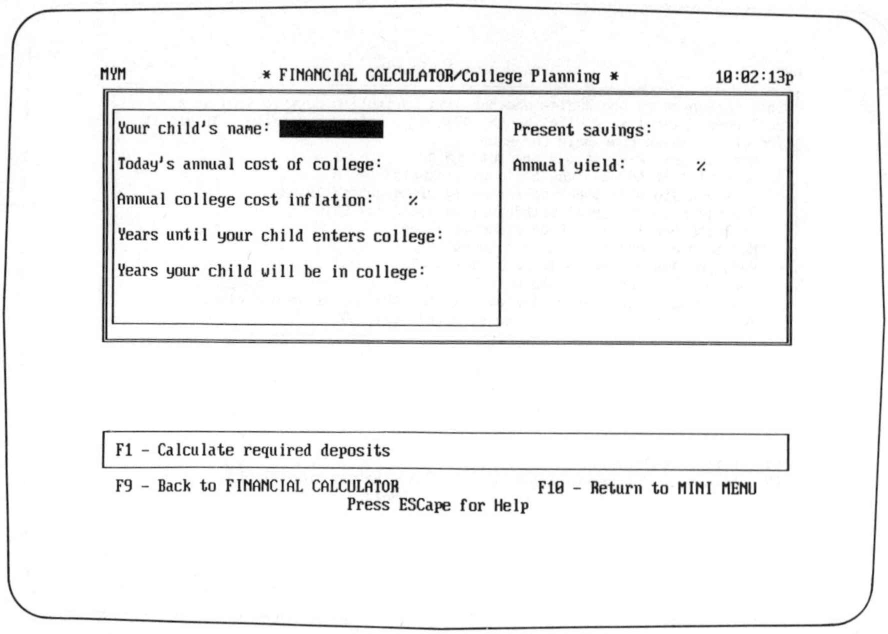

```
MYM              * FINANCIAL CALCULATOR/College Planning *        10:02:13p

    Your child's name: ██████████        Present savings:

    Today's annual cost of college:      Annual yield:        %

    Annual college cost inflation:   %

    Years until your child enters college:

    Years your child will be in college:




    F1 - Calculate required deposits

     F9 - Back to FINANCIAL CALCULATOR              F10 - Return to MINI MENU
                        Press ESCape for Help
```

Fig. 6.20. The College Planning screen.

To complete the College Planning screen and calculate the required deposits:

1. For Your Child's Name, enter **Alison**.

   Although the name information is not necessary, you must enter your child's name if you want it printed in the college planning results. If you are planning for more than one child's education, insert each name so that the results will not be confused.

2. For Today's Annual Cost of College, enter **9000** (for $9,000).

   This is an estimate of the net cost for a year at college. You may have the exact current yearly cost of a particular college in mind. Don't forget to include such expenses as room, board, books, travel to and from school, and miscellaneous expenses. Don't forget to subtract any loans or scholarships that may be available to your children. If you expect your children to pay a portion of the cost themselves from earnings after school or during the summer season, also subtract that amount.

3. For Annual College Cost Inflation, enter **3** (for 3 percent).

   The annual cost of college today will rise at this rate. (Enter a different figure or try several to see the variations in the results.)

4. For Years Until Your Child Enters College, enter **10**.

   Calculate the number of years until your child begins to attend college (the number of years you have left in which to save for this expense). If you have more than one child, then this blank and the child's name blank may be the only blanks you have to change in order to calculate the results for each of your children.

5. For Years Your Child Will Be in College, enter **4**.

   Although the most common answer is 4, you may want to plan for graduate school as well. If the current costs of graduate school are different than they are for college (and they probably will be), then calculate the college and the graduate school costs separately and add the two amounts.

6. For Present Savings, enter **2500** (for $2,500).

   Enter the amount of your savings that you have already set aside for your child's college education. If you have more than one child, don't count your savings more than once. Remember to divide the savings among the children.

7. For Annual Yield, enter **4** (for 4 percent).

   Unlike the Retirement Planning section of the calculator, here you must enter the *after-tax* yield that you expect to earn on your college savings.

   When you finish entering the data, your screen should look like figure 6.21.

8. Press F1 to calculate the required deposits (see fig. 6.22).

The college planning results include a number of figures. First, the results give the projected total cost of a college education. Second, the screen displays the yearly addition that you must make to your current savings in order to achieve your goal. Also supplied is an alternate yearly addition which assumes that you will continue to save while your child is in school, and another alternate which assumes that your yearly addition will increase at the same rate as college costs. The screen also gives the amount that you must set aside today in addition to your current college savings in order to prevent having to set aside any more money later. The last figure is the present value

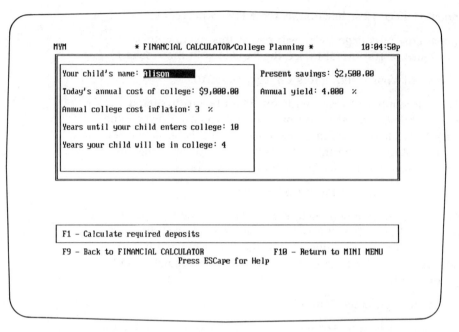

```
MYM              * FINANCIAL CALCULATOR/College Planning *        10:04:50p

  ┌─────────────────────────────────────────┐  ┌──────────────────────────┐
  │ Your child's name: Alison               │  │ Present savings: $2,500.00│
  │                                          │  │                          │
  │ Today's annual cost of college: $9,000.00│  │ Annual yield: 4.000  %   │
  │                                          │  │                          │
  │ Annual college cost inflation: 3  %      │  │                          │
  │                                          │  │                          │
  │ Years until your child enters college: 10│  │                          │
  │                                          │  │                          │
  │ Years your child will be in college: 4   │  │                          │
  │                                          │  │                          │
  └─────────────────────────────────────────┘  └──────────────────────────┘

  ┌─────────────────────────────────────────────────────────────────────┐
  │ F1 - Calculate required deposits                                      │
  └─────────────────────────────────────────────────────────────────────┘
    F9 - Back to FINANCIAL CALCULATOR              F10 - Return to MINI MENU
                        Press ESCape for Help
```

Fig. 6.21. College planning data entered.

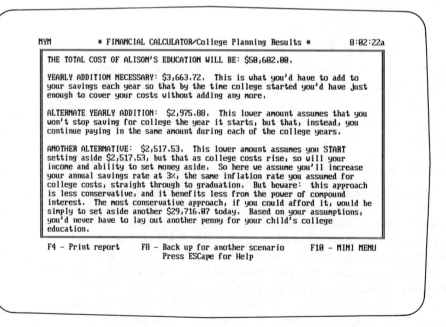

```
MYM         * FINANCIAL CALCULATOR/College Planning Results *      8:02:22a
  ┌─────────────────────────────────────────────────────────────────────┐
  │ THE TOTAL COST OF ALISON'S EDUCATION WILL BE: $50,602.00.             │
  │                                                                       │
  │ YEARLY ADDITION NECESSARY: $3,663.72.  This is what you'd have to add │
  │ to your savings each year so that by the time college started you'd   │
  │ have just enough to cover your costs without adding any more.         │
  │                                                                       │
  │ ALTERNATE YEARLY ADDITION: $2,975.88.  This lower amount assumes that │
  │ you won't stop saving for college the year it starts, but that,       │
  │ instead, you continue paying in the same amount during each of the    │
  │ college years.                                                        │
  │                                                                       │
  │ ANOTHER ALTERNATIVE: $2,517.53.  This lower amount assumes you START  │
  │ setting aside $2,517.53, but that as college costs rise, so will your │
  │ income and ability to set money aside.  So here we assume you'll      │
  │ increase your annual savings rate at 3%, the same inflation rate you  │
  │ assumed for college costs, straight through to graduation.  But       │
  │ beware: this approach is less conservative, and it benefits less from │
  │ the power of compound interest.  The most conservative approach, if   │
  │ you could afford it, would be simply to set aside another $29,716.07  │
  │ today.  Based on your assumptions, you'd never have to lay out        │
  │ another penny for your child's college education.                     │
  └─────────────────────────────────────────────────────────────────────┘
    F4 - Print report    F8 - Back up for another scenario   F10 - MINI MENU
                        Press ESCape for Help
```

Fig. 6.22. The college planning results.

of your child's college education, calculated with the assumptions that you have made about inflation, yield, and college costs.

To print a report to the screen:

1. Press F4.

2. Place an X in the box beside the word Screen. (With Versions 3.0 and 4.0, you can print either to your printer, to the screen, or to a disk.)

3. Press F1 to print.

   Your screen should look like figure 6.23.

```
 11/5/87                 College Planning Report              Page 1
 Mark D. Weinberg

     Assuming ALISON has 10 years to go before entering a 4 year
     school that currently costs $9,000.00 a year; and assuming
     that cost will rise steadily at 3% a year while you'll be
     able to earn 4.00% after tax on the money you set aside (on
     top of the $2,500.00 you've already set aside), here's the scoop:

     THE TOTAL COST OF ALISON'S EDUCATION WILL BE: $50,602.00.

     YEARLY ADDITION NECESSARY: $3,663.72. This is what you'd have
     to add to your savings each year so that by the time college
     started you'd have just enough to cover your costs without
     adding any more.

     ALTERNATE YEARLY ADDITION: $2,975.88. This lower amount assumes
     that you won't stop saving for college the year it starts, but that,
     instead, you continue paying in the same amount during each of
     the college years.

     ANOTHER ALTERNATIVE: $2,517.53. This lower amount assumes

     PRESS ANY KEY TO CONTINUE....
```

Fig. 6.23. Alison's college planning report.

4. To view the remainder of the report, press any key twice as you are prompted.

After you finish with College Planning, press F10 to return to the Financial Calculator's Mini Menu.

Investment Analysis

The yield, or rate of return, that you earn on some investments is fairly easy to calculate. For example, if you loan your sister $1,000 today and she promises to repay you $1,500 in 3 years after she graduates from medical school, calculating the yield on your investment is not difficult. In the Compound Interest quadrant of the Financial Calculator, just enter $1,000 for the present value, $1,500 for the future value, and 3 for the number of years. Then solve for the yield.

What if the return on the investment is more complicated? Suppose that you are considering purchasing a share in a limited partnership that will invest in real estate and that you would be making payments in the partnership for several years. As a partner, you might be entitled to tax deductions from the investment as well as cash distributions. All these factors may be spelled out in the form of projections in a prospectus describing the investment. If you believe that the projections are fairly accurate, you can calculate the projected rate of return that you would realize if you made the investment. If you believe that the prospectus paints too rosy a picture—that the actual results will not be quite as good—then make changes to the projections and calculate the return. The investment may still make sense based on your other investment opportunities.

Suppose that you receive a prospectus from your stockbroker for such an investment. Instead of buying real property, the partnership intends to buy two Boeing 747 jets and lease them to a domestic airline. You are required to invest $10,000 today, and you should receive a cash flow of $500 from the investment the first year, $750 the second year, and $1,000 in each of the following 6 years. You also will receive a $2,000 tax deduction in each year of the 8-year period and a $15,000 cash distribution at the end of the eighth year. Although this equation is pretty complicated, the Financial Calculator can solve it for you in seconds.

From the Financial Calculator's Mini Menu, press F4-Investment Analysis. Your screen should look similar to figure 6.24.

If figures appear on your screen and it doesn't say

    No Cash Flows Have Been Recorded Yet

press F7 to delete all the figures. The cursor should be at the far left blank, in the Year column. The information that must be entered in the General Investment Analysis screen would be found in a prospectus or in an other document that describes the investment.

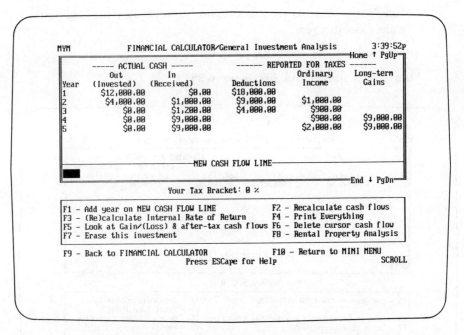

Fig. 6.24. The General Investment Analysis screen with sample data.

To calculate the internal rate of return on an investment one year at a time:

1. In Year 1, you will invest $10,000 and receive $500 from the investment. In addition, you will receive a $2,000 tax deduction. Enter the following information:

    Year: **1**. (Label the years 1 through 8 for now, but remember to use the actual years in your own calculations later.)

The next two entries relate to the actual cash invested and received during the year.

    Actual Cash Out (Invested): **10000** (for $10,000)

    Actual Cash In (Received): **500** (for $500)

The next three entries relate to the tax ramifications of the investment for the year.

    Deductions: **2000** (for $2,000)

    Ordinary Income: **500** (for the $500 cash distribution from the investment, which will be taxable as ordinary income)

Long-Term Gains: Leave this column blank because no long-term gains exist this year.

2. To add the data for this year, press F1.

Your screen should look like figure 6.25.

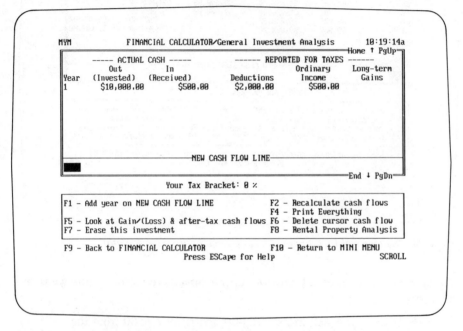

Fig. 6.25. Data entered for the first year of an investment.

3. Enter the data for years 2 through 8. Press F1 to add the New Cash Flow Line after each year is completed.

Enter the following data:

Year 2: **750** received, **2000** tax deduction, **750** ordinary income

Years 3 through 7: **1000** received, **2000** tax deduction, **1000** ordinary income

Year 8: **16000** received ($1,000 plus $15,000), **2000** tax deduction, **16000** ordinary income

4. Type **28** percent for your tax bracket.

After you have entered all the data, your screen should look like figure 6.26.

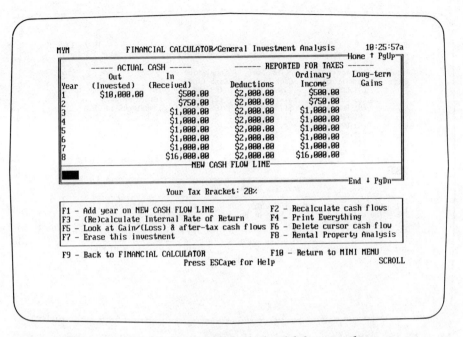

Fig. 6.26. Data entered for the second through the eighth years of an investment.

5. Press F3 to calculate the internal rate of return (see fig. 6.27).

The internal rate of return is 15.4 percent. If the projections for this investment prove to be accurate, then this would be an excellent investment, depending, of course, on the risk factor that is inherent in the endeavor. The rate, you must remember, is the annual after-tax yield on the investment.

Look at the other data on this screen. See how much income or loss you will have to report on your tax return for each year as well as the after-tax cash flow and the cumulative cash flow for the investment at any time. The after-tax cash flow is the amount of extra cash in your pocket or cash that you must pay out from the investment (if the cash flow is negative) after taxes are figured. The cumulative cash flow is the sum of the annual cash flow from the time you made the investment until now.

Look at your options. Press F4 to print all the data, or press F7 to erase the investment and start over.

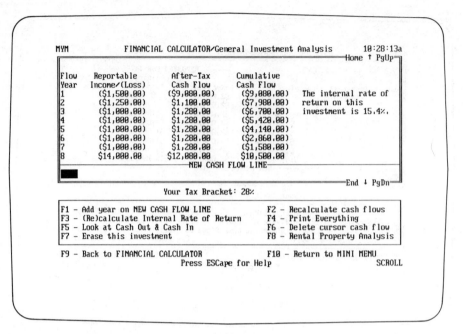

```
MYM              FINANCIAL CALCULATOR/General Investment Analysis      10:28:13a
                                                             Home ↑ PgUp
   Flow    Reportable        After-Tax      Cumulative
   Year    Income/(Loss)     Cash Flow      Cash Flow
   1        ($1,500.00)      ($9,000.00)     ($9,000.00)    The internal rate of
   2        ($1,250.00)      $1,100.00       ($7,900.00)    return on this
   3        ($1,000.00)      $1,200.00       ($6,700.00)    investment is 15.4%.
   4        ($1,000.00)      $1,200.00       ($5,420.00)
   5        ($1,000.00)      $1,200.00       ($4,140.00)
   6        ($1,000.00)      $1,200.00       ($2,860.00)
   7        ($1,000.00)      $1,200.00       ($1,580.00)
   8        $14,000.00       $12,000.00      $10,500.00
                          NEW CASH FLOW LINE
   ████
                                                             End ↓ PgDn
                    Your Tax Bracket: 28%

   F1 - Add year on NEW CASH FLOW LINE        F2 - Recalculate cash flows
   F3 - (Re)calculate Internal Rate of Return F4 - Print Everything
   F5 - Look at Cash Out & Cash In            F6 - Delete cursor cash flow
   F7 - Erase this investment                 F8 - Rental Property Analysis

   F9 - Back to FINANCIAL CALCULATOR          F10 - Return to MINI MENU
                        Press ESCape for Help                    SCROLL
```

Fig. 6.27. *The internal rate of return calculated.*

Rental Property Analysis

If you have just completed work on the General Investment Analysis screen, press F8 to get to the Rental Property Analysis screen. Or, from the Financial Calculator's Mini Menu, press F5. If you have not deleted the sample data, your screen should look like figure 6.28. Press F2 to clear all the numbers from the screen.

The Rental Property Analysis function determines the internal rate of return and the cash flow of a rental property investment. Notice that you are seeking the same figures as in the General Investment Analysis. Only the nature of the investment is different. The General Investment Analysis function should be used to calculate the return on investments that have varying cash flow both into and from the investment. The Rental Property Analysis function generally is used for investments in real rental property; therefore, its screen is set up to consider depreciation, varying financing methods, inflation, and other factors.

The Financial Calculator allows you to enter three estimates for inflation: how fast the maintenance costs of the property will rise, how fast you can

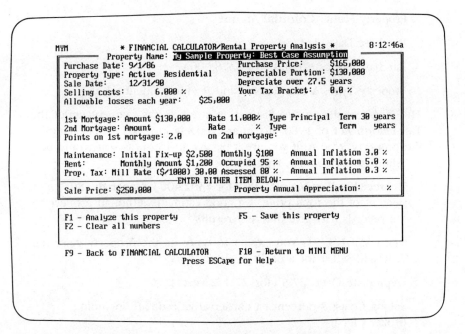

```
MYM              * FINANCIAL CALCULATOR/Rental Property Analysis *      8:12:46a
              Property Name: My Sample Property: Best Case Assumption
 Purchase Date: 9/1/86                 Purchase Price:      $165,000
 Property Type: Active Residential     Depreciable Portion: $130,000
 Sale Date:    12/31/90                Depreciate over 27.5 years
 Selling costs:     6.000 %            Your Tax Bracket:    0.0 %
 Allowable losses each year:    $25,000

 1st Mortgage: Amount $130,000    Rate 11.000% Type Principal Term 30 years
 2nd Mortgage: Amount             Rate      %  Type           Term    years
 Points on 1st mortgage: 2.0      on 2nd mortgage:

 Maintenance: Initial Fix-up $2,500  Monthly $100    Annual Inflation 3.0 %
 Rent:           Monthly Amount $1,200 Occupied 95 %  Annual Inflation 5.0 %
 Prop. Tax: Mill Rate ($/1000) 30.00 Assessed 80 %   Annual Inflation 0.3 %
                        ─────ENTER EITHER ITEM BELOW:─────
 Sale Price: $250,000                  Property Annual Appreciation:      %


  F1 - Analyze this property           F5 - Save this property
  F2 - Clear all numbers


  F9 - Back to FINANCIAL CALCULATOR     F10 - Return to MINI MENU
                     Press ESCape for Help
```

Fig. 6.28. The Rental Property Analysis screen with sample data.

expect to be able to raise the rent on the property, and how fast you can expect property tax rates to rise. The three estimates may all be different or the same. Even if you assume that they will all rise at the same rate, don't ignore them. They still will have an impact on your rate of return on the investment.

Mortgages are classified as either conventional (where the payments consist of both principal and interest) or interest only. Blanks are provided on the screen for both first and second mortgages, if they exist. The primary difference between a first and second mortgage is the priority of the lender's claims. If you default or fail to make payments on your loans and the lenders foreclose, the first mortgage lender has first priority to any proceeds from a sale of the property.

Suppose, for example, that you are thinking about buying a three-family house. The broker has given you the details about the property.

To calculate the projected internal rate of return and the cash flow from the investment:

1. On the Rental Property Analysis screen, enter the following information:

Property Name: **Colonial Manor**

Purchase Date: **1/1/88**

Purchase Price: **378000** (for $378,000)

Property Type: **A** (for active) and **R** (for residential)

The *active* versus *passive* distinction is a new tax concept under the Tax Reform Act of 1986. If you are actively involved in managing the property, type **A**; if you are a passive investor, as you would be in a limited partnership, type **P**.

Depreciable Portion: **302400** (for $302,400). Generally, 80 percent of the total price is a good estimate, although property tax records may give different results.

Sale Date: **1/1/91**. You expect to renovate the property, raise the rent, and sell it for a profit in three years.

Depreciate Over: **27.5** (for 27 1/2 years)

Selling Costs: **8** percent (a conservative estimate including broker's fee)

Your Tax Bracket: **28** (for 28 percent)

Allowable Losses each year: **25000** (for $25,000)

This limitation on losses was imposed by Congress in the Tax Reform Act of 1986. For actively managed properties, a taxpayer is allowed up to $25,000 in aggregate losses for all of his or her properties for the year. If his or her adjusted gross income is above $100,000, then the allowable loss is reduced and ultimately eliminated when adjusted gross income reaches $150,000.

1st Mortgage: **300000** at **9.25** percent; **P** (for principal and interest over 30 years).

Maintenance:

Initial Fix-Up: **5000** (for $5,000)

Monthly: **300** (for $300)

Annual Inflation: **3** (for 3 percent)

Rent:

Monthly Amount: **2800** (for $2,800)

Occupied: **100** (for 100 percent)

Annual Inflation: **5** (for 5 percent)

Prop. Tax:

Mill Rate: **2** (for $2 per $1,000)

Assessed: **100** (for 100 percent assessment)

Annual Inflation: **0** (assuming no reassessment occurs while you hold the property)

Sale Price: **410000** (for $410,000—your best estimate based on recent trends)

When you finish, your screen should look like figure 6.29.

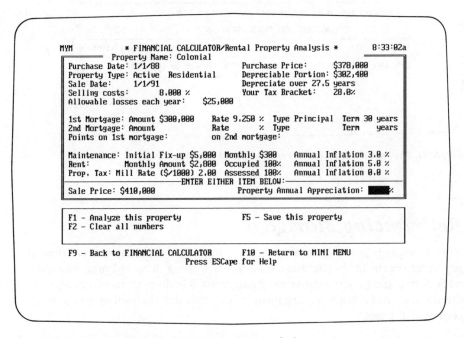

```
MYM              * FINANCIAL CALCULATOR/Rental Property Analysis *        8:33:02a
              Property Name: Colonial
 Purchase Date: 1/1/88                Purchase Price:       $378,000
 Property Type: Active  Residential   Depreciable Portion: $302,400
 Sale Date:     1/1/91                Depreciate over 27.5 years
 Selling costs:        8.000 %        Your Tax Bracket:    28.0%
 Allowable losses each year:    $25,000

 1st Mortgage: Amount $300,000   Rate 9.250 %  Type Principal  Term 30 years
 2nd Mortgage: Amount            Rate       %  Type            Term    years
 Points on 1st mortgage:         on 2nd mortgage:

 Maintenance: Initial Fix-up $5,000  Monthly $300    Annual Inflation 3.0 %
 Rent:         Monthly Amount $2,000 Occupied 100%   Annual Inflation 5.0 %
 Prop. Tax: Mill Rate ($/1000) 2.00  Assessed 100%   Annual Inflation 0.0 %
 ─────────────────────────ENTER EITHER ITEM BELOW:─────────────
 Sale Price: $410,000                  Property Annual Appreciation: ▓▓▓▓ %

 F1 - Analyze this property            F5 - Save this property
 F2 - Clear all numbers

 F9 - Back to FINANCIAL CALCULATOR     F10 - Return to MINI MENU
                Press ESCape for Help
```

Fig. 6.29. Data entered on the Rental Property Analysis screen.

2. Press F1 to analyze the property.

Your screen should look like figure 6.30.

The numbers should lead to one conclusion: This is not a good investment. The internal rate of return is 1.5 percent. You can do many times better than this in a money market fund with much less risk. Look for a new investment, or change the projections to see how high your selling price would have to be in order to make this a good investment.

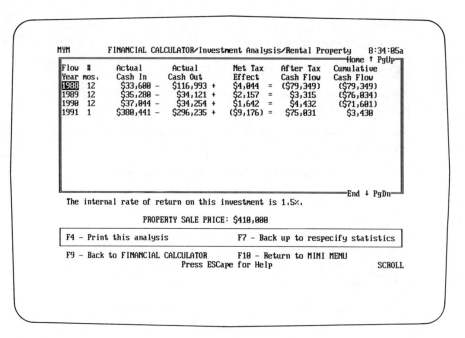

```
MYM         FINANCIAL CALCULATOR/Investment Analysis/Rental Property    8:34:05a
                                                              ┌Home ↑ PgUp┐
 Flow  #     Actual        Actual        Net Tax     After Tax    Cumulative
 Year mos.   Cash In       Cash Out      Effect      Cash Flow    Cash Flow
 1988  12    $33,600 -     $116,993 +    $4,044  =   ($79,349)    ($79,349)
 1989  12    $35,280 -     $34,121 +     $2,157  =   $3,315       ($76,034)
 1990  12    $37,044 -     $34,254 +     $1,642  =   $4,432       ($71,601)
 1991  1     $380,441 -    $296,235 +    ($9,176) =  $75,031      $3,430




                                                              └End ↓ PgDn┘
      The internal rate of return on this investment is 1.5%.

                    PROPERTY SALE PRICE: $410,000

  ┌────────────────────────────────────────────────────────────────────┐
  │ F4 - Print this analysis              F7 - Back up to respecify statistics │
  └────────────────────────────────────────────────────────────────────┘
     F9 - Back to FINANCIAL CALCULATOR       F10 - Return to MINI MENU
                    Press ESCape for Help                         SCROLL
```

Fig. 6.30. The investment analysis of the rental property.

Refinancing Mortgages

More mortgages probably have been refinanced in the past two years than at any other recent time. The main reason is the sharp drop in home mortgage rates during the past several years. Along with this drop in rates, changes in the tax laws make home equity loans more attractive than other types of commercial loans.

The interest on commercial loans—such as car loans, credit card interest, and interest payable to the IRS—is only partially deductible in 1987 and will be phased out entirely by 1991. The interest on debt for a taxpayer's home will be deductible in full, as long as the loan does not exceed the taxpayer's cost for the home plus amounts paid for improvements. A provision allows a taxpayer to borrow extra amounts for certain medical or educational expenses. In light of these changes, many people are using the profits from their home mortgage refinancings to pay off commercial loans.

People often fail to consider all the factors involved in refinancing. Calculating refinancing costs is not as simple as saying that rates have fallen, and therefore it's time to refinance. After all, when you refinance, you also must expect to pay fees to the bank and lawyers, and possibly to pay a prepayment penalty on your old loan.

The Financial Calculator considers all these factors, including your personal tax rate. The Financial Calculator informs you in simple terms whether refinancing makes sense for you.

From the Rental Property Analysis screen, press F10 to return to the Mini Menu. From the Mini Menu, press F6-Refinancing Mortgages. Your screen should look similar to figure 6.31. (Your figures may be different.)

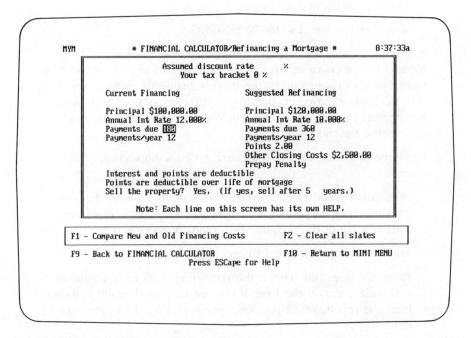

Fig. 6.31. The Refinancing a Mortgage screen.

The Refinancing a Mortgage screen is divided into two sections. On the left side, you enter the details of the current financing you have on your home. On the right side, you enter the figures for the suggested refinancing. When you enter data, you can type over any figures that may be on the screen.

Suppose that you pay an exorbitant 13 percent interest rate on your $150,000 mortgage. Although you have 15 years left on this loan, you want to refinance and borrow $210,000 at a considerably more reasonable 9.25 percent rate for a 30-year term. You will have to pay points of 3 percent, and you estimate that other closing costs will be $1,000.

In this refinancing, you are attempting to borrow more than you currently owe. The extra money you borrow may be used to put an addition on the house, to purchase a new car, or to pay off a credit card debt. Whatever you do, make sure that when you increase the size of your loan, you will be able to make the new payments.

To compare your current financing with a new loan at a lower rate:

1. Move the cursor to the blanks at the top of the screen and enter the following information:

   Assumed Discount Rate: **4** (for 4 percent)

   Your Tax Bracket: **28** (for 28 percent)

   A *discount rate* is the after-tax return that you can earn on your money. The discount rate measures the value of money to you. The higher your discount rate is, the more valuable the refinancing is for you. Remember, however, that if your after-tax cost of borrowing is higher than your discount rate, borrowing extra funds may not make sense for you.

2. Enter the following data in the Current Financing section of the screen:

   Principal: **150000** (for $150,000). This is the amount that you currently owe on your loan. Unless you have an "interest only" loan, this is not the amount you originally borrowed.

   Annual Int Rate: **13** (for 13 percent)

   Payments Due: **180**. This is the remaining number of payments you must make on the loan. If you are halfway through a 30-year loan and you make 12 payments per year, then 180 payments are due.

   Payments/Year: **12** (the most common number because most loans require payments once a month).

3. Enter the following data in the Suggested Refinancing section of the screen:

   Principal: **210000** (for $210,000)

   Annual Int Rate: **9.25** (for 9.25 percent)

   Payments Due: **360** (12 payments per year for 30 years)

   Payments/Year: **12**

   Points: **3** (an up-front cost that banks generally charge when they make loans)

Other Closing Costs: **1000** (for $1,000). Do you have to pay your lawyer or your accountant for assisting in the refinancing? If so, include the amount here.

4. Move the cursor to the bottom of the screen and fill in the answers to the questions as follows:

Interest and Points Are: **deductible**

Points Are Deductible: **when paid**. Check with your accountant to determine whether the points are deductible when paid or whether you must spread the deductions over the life of the loan.

Sell the Property?: **No**. All the transaction costs that are inherent in refinancings typically are paid up front. Whether you should refinance may depend on the period over which you spread the expense. If you expect to sell the property in a short time, the costs of refinancing may be greater than the savings of a lower interest rate.

After you have entered all the data, your screen should look like figure 6.32.

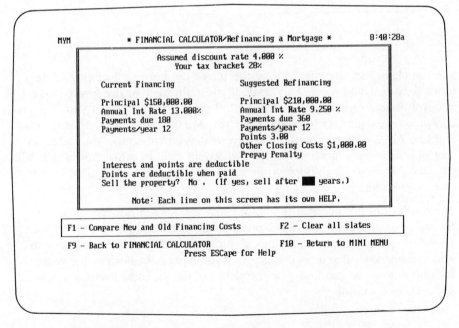

Fig. 6.32. Data entered on the Refinancing a Mortgage screen.

5. Press F1 to compare your new and old financing costs (see
   fig. 6.33).

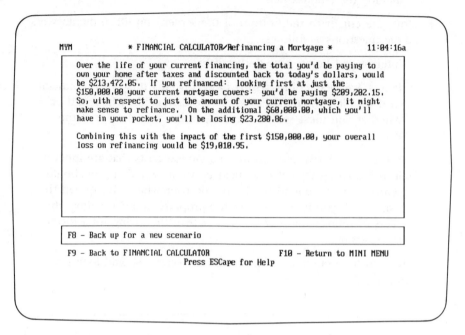

```
MYM              * FINANCIAL CALCULATOR/Refinancing a Mortgage *        11:04:16a

      Over the life of your current financing, the total you'd be paying to
      own your home after taxes and discounted back to today's dollars, would
      be $213,472.05.  If you refinanced:  looking first at just the
      $150,000.00 your current mortgage covers:  you'd be paying $209,202.15.
      So, with respect to just the amount of your current mortgage, it might
      make sense to refinance.  On the additional $60,000.00, which you'll
      have in your pocket, you'll be losing $23,280.86.

      Combining this with the impact of the first $150,000.00, your overall
      loss on refinancing would be $19,010.95.




      F8 - Back up for a new scenario

      F9 - Back to FINANCIAL CALCULATOR                F10 - Return to MINI MENU
                          Press ESCape for Help
```

Fig. 6.33. The results of refinancing a mortgage.

The calculator indicates that during the life of the current financing in the
example, you would pay $213,472.05. If you refinanced at the lower interest
rate, you would save approximately $4,200 on the $150,000 that you
currently owe. However, consider the extra $60,000 you are borrowing. You
will lose $23,280.86 during the life of your new loan because your after-tax
cost of borrowing is greater than your discount rate. In other words, you will
pay more to the bank to borrow the extra $60,000 than you will be able to
earn on the money.

The result does not necessarily indicate that you should not refinance. After
all, the interest rate on the new loan is lower than the rate on the old loan.
Therefore, you can realize a savings if you borrow an amount equivalent to
your current loan. Based on this analysis, you better not borrow the extra
$60,000 unless you can find a better place to use the money and adjust your
discount rate accordingly.

Buy/Lease/Rent Comparison

Access the Buy/Lease/Rent function of the Financial Calculator by pressing F7 from the Financial Calculator's Mini Menu (see fig. 6.34).

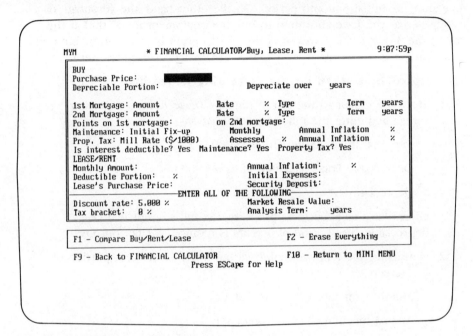

Fig. 6.34. The Buy/Lease/Rent Comparison screen.

The Buy/Lease/Rent comparison is performed in order to determine from a financial standpoint whether you should buy a particular asset, lease it, or rent it. Obviously, finances are not the only consideration in your decision. However, after you know the financial cost of each option, you will be in a better position to make an informed decision.

Suppose that you want to use the least expensive method possible to acquire a new computer system. The entire system should cost about $25,000. Given the speed at which computer equipment becomes obsolete, you are leaning toward rental or lease so that 3 to 5 years down the road you don't get stuck owning a relic.

After your initial investigation, you determine that you could either rent or lease the required hardware for $600 per month. The rental agreement would allow you to cancel any time after the third month. The lease agreement would require you to sign a 3-year contract that could not be canceled. Both the rental and lease agreements would require a $2,000 up-front nonrefundable payment to cover transportation and installation of the equipment.

Consider your options. The advantage of renting is that you can cancel at any time after the initial 3-month period. On the other hand, the advantage of leasing is that you have an option to buy the equipment for $7,000 at the end of the 3-year term, if you so desire. That option is worth something only if the equipment is worth at least $7,000 at the end of the lease term.

To compare the costs of buying vs. renting vs. leasing:

1. Move the cursor to the top of the Buy/Lease/Rent Comparison screen and enter the following information:

   Purchase Price: **25000** (for $25,000)

   Depreciable Portion: **25000** (for $25,000)

   Depreciate Over: **5** (years)

   Given that this is business property, the full amount will be depreciable. The period of 5 years is required for tax purposes.

2. Now enter the following information in the Lease/Rent portion of the screen:

   Monthly Amount: **600** (for $600)

   Annual Inflation: **2** (for 2 percent)

   Deductible Portion: **100** (for 100 percent)

   Initial Expenses: **2000** (for $2,000)

   Lease's Purchase Price: **7000** (for $7,000)

3. Enter the following information in the bottom portion of the screen:

   Discount Rate: **4** (for 4 percent)

   Market Resale Value: **9000** (for $9,000)

   Tax Bracket: **28** (for percent)

   Analysis Term: **3** (for 3 years)

   As explained in a previous section, the discount rate is the after-tax return that you can earn on your money. The discount rate measures the value of the money to you. These figures assume that the computer system can be sold for $9,000 at the end of the lease term.

When you have entered all of the data, your screen should look like figure 6.35.

4. Press F1 to compare the costs of buying, leasing and renting (see fig. 6.36).

Notice the costs for each of the three alternatives are stated both in terms of total net expenses and total net cost in today's dollars. Total net expenses indicates the net outflow of cash over the period, taking depreciation and tax savings into consideration. Total net cost in today's dollars goes one step further by calculating the present value of the payments.

While the cost of purchasing the computer system is cheaper than either leasing or renting the equipment, the present value cost to lease is not significantly greater than it is to buy. Given the advantage of not having to come up with a large amount of cash in order to lease the system, the extra cost may make sense for you.

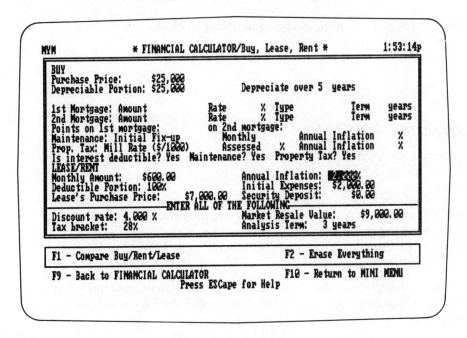

Fig. 6.35. The Buy/Lease/Rent Comparison screen with data entered.

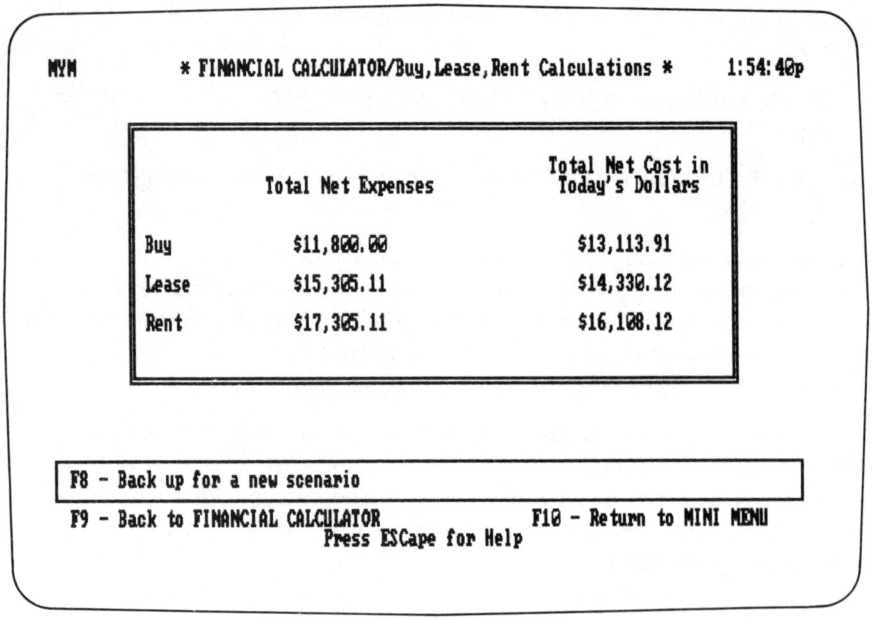

```
MYM          * FINANCIAL CALCULATOR/Buy,Lease,Rent Calculations *      1:54:40p


                                                     Total Net Cost in
                              Total Net Expenses      Today's Dollars

              Buy              $11,800.00              $13,113.91

              Lease            $15,305.11              $14,330.12

              Rent             $17,305.11              $16,108.12



    F8 - Back up for a new scenario

    F9 - Back to FINANCIAL CALCULATOR              F10 - Return to MINI MENU
                          Press ESCape for Help
```

Fig. 6.36. The costs of buying, leasing, and renting compared.

Inflator/Deflator

To access the Inflator/Deflator, press F8 from the Financial Calculator's Mini Menu (see fig. 6.37).

The Inflator/Deflator is designed to show you the effects of inflation. While inflation appears to be under control for the moment, even at a low 3 percent rate, after 10 years, $10,000 would be worth only $7,440.94 (see fig. 6.36). In other words, in 10 years, you would need $13,439.16 in order to buy what $10,000 buys today.

In the bottom portion of the screen, you can enter an amount along with two years of your choice. You'll find that a dollar just isn't worth what it used to be.

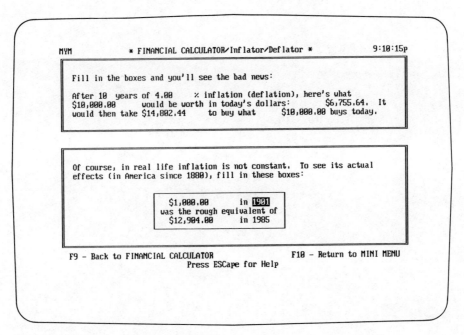

```
MYM                  * FINANCIAL CALCULATOR/Inflator/Deflator *              9:10:15p

    Fill in the boxes and you'll see the bad news:

    After 10  years of 4.00     % inflation (deflation), here's what
    $10,000.00      would be worth in today's dollars:       $6,755.64.  It
    would then take $14,802.44    to buy what      $10,000.00 buys today.


    Of course, in real life inflation is not constant.  To see its actual
    effects (in America since 1880), fill in these boxes:

                        $1,000.00      in 1901
                        was the rough equivalent of
                        $12,904.00      in 1985

    F9 - Back to FINANCIAL CALCULATOR                 F10 - Return to MINI MENU
                            Press ESCape for Help
```

Fig. 6.37. The Inflator/Deflator screen.

## Chapter 7

Using the Insurance Planner

Managing Your Money's Insurance Planning module is fun to work with and can give you some sophisticated answers about life insurance. By using the most current actuarial tables to determine your life expectancy, the module can help you decide how much life insurance will provide adequately for your spouse and your children and can calculate the approximate cost of that insurance.

Less than 30 minutes with this module can give you results equivalent to those that you would obtain from a good financial planner. Review your insurance needs with Managing Your Money, and save the $350 that a planner would charge.

From the Main Menu, press F5-Insurance Planning. Your screen should display the Mini Menu shown in figure 7.1.

If you are running the program on a single- or two-disk system, you will be prompted to insert Disk 4 in either drive A or drive B, depending on your system configuration (see fig. 7.2).

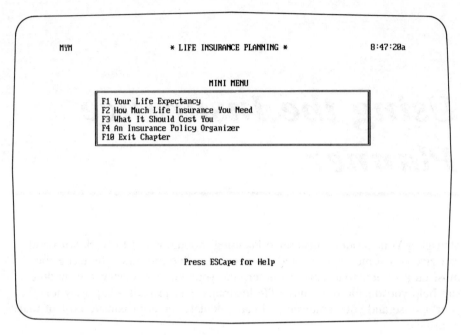

```
    MYM                      * LIFE INSURANCE PLANNING *              8:47:28a


                                    MINI MENU

                  F1 Your Life Expectancy
                  F2 How Much Life Insurance You Need
                  F3 What It Should Cost You
                  F4 An Insurance Policy Organizer
                  F10 Exit Chapter




                              Press ESCape for Help
```

Fig. 7.1. Life Insurance Planning's Mini Menu.

```
        Please put Disk 4 (or disk containing insure.db) in drive A.
        Adjust the disk and press any key to try again.
        Press F10 to return to the previous screen.
```

Fig. 7.2. A prompt to adjust the disk and press any key to try again.

Determining Your Life Expectancy

Insurance companies can predict with a fair degree of accuracy the age at which individuals will die, based on such factors as their overall health, their marital status, whether they smoke, and the age that their parents and grandparents died, as well as other factors. The companies apply these factors to large groups of people in order to compile *actuarial tables* that predict longevity. Because Managing Your Money has incorporated these actuarial tables into the program, you can use the program to make similar predictions and to estimate the cost of insurance.

From the Life Insurance Planning's Mini Menu, press F1 to display the Your Life Expectancy screen (see fig. 7.3). In the steps that follow, and in those throughout this chapter, use your own data to complete the screens. Don't be too concerned about your answers to most of the questions. You can always go back and change the variables later.

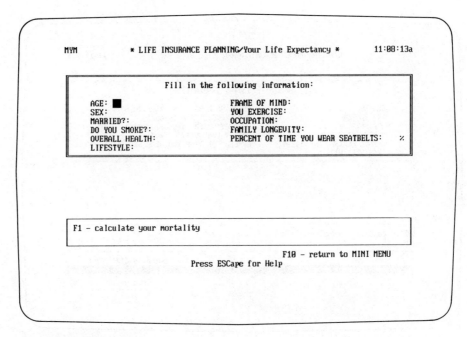

Fig. 7.3. The Your Life Expectancy screen.

The key factors regarding life expectancy are your age, your sex, your marital status, and whether you smoke. You can experiment with the other factors and then recalculate your mortality each time you make a change, but these factors will not do much to alter your life expectancy.

To determine your life expectancy:

1. On the Your Life Expectancy screen, enter your age, your sex, whether you are married, whether you smoke, and descriptions of your overall health and lifestyle.

For some of the blanks, you need to choose an answer from those listed at the bottom of the screen.

2. Fill in a description of your frame of mind, whether you exercise, and the nature of your occupation. Then enter a description of your family's longevity and the percentage of time that you wear your seat belt.

After you have completed all the blanks, your screen should look similar to figure 7.4.

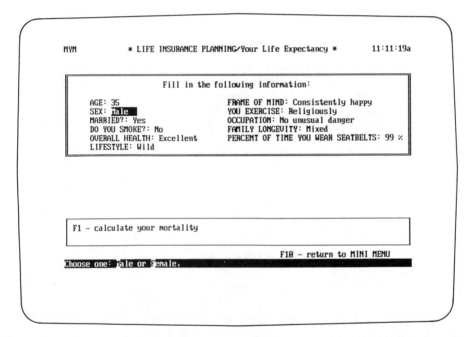

Fig. 7.4. Data entered in the Your Life Expectancy screen.

3. Press F1 to calculate your odds of dying this year and how many more years you have left, according to the actuarial tables (see fig. 7.5).

Determining Your Life Insurance Needs

To see how much life insurance you need, you must enter some more information. Press F2 to display the screen shown in figure 7.6.

```
MYM            * LIFE INSURANCE PLANNING/Your Life Expectancy *         11:12:16a

        ┌─────────────────────────────────────────────────────────────────┐
        │              Fill in the following information:                   │
        │                                                                   │
        │   AGE: 35                    FRAME OF MIND: Consistently happy     │
        │   SEX: Male                  YOU EXERCISE: Religiously             │
        │   MARRIED?: Yes              OCCUPATION: No unusual danger         │
        │   DO YOU SMOKE?: No          FAMILY LONGEVITY: Mixed               │
        │   OVERALL HEALTH: Excellent  PERCENT OF TIME YOU WEAR SEATBELTS: 99 %│
        │   LIFESTYLE: Wild                                                 │
        └─────────────────────────────────────────────────────────────────┘

        Your odds of dying this year are less than 2 in 1,000.  Your life expectancy
        is about 43 more years for a total of 78 years.  Even so, you may need life
        insurance.  To see how much, press F2.

        ┌─────────────────────────────────────────────────────────────────┐
        │  F1 - re-calculate your mortality                                 │
        │  F2 - See how much life insurance you need                        │
        │                                                                   │
        │                                    F10 - return to MINI MENU       │
        └─────────────────────────────────────────────────────────────────┘
        Choose one: Male or Female.
```

Fig. 7.5. Your odds of dying.

```
MYM            * LIFE INSURANCE PLANNING/Calculate How Much You Need    11:12:49a
        ┌─────────────────────────────────────────────────────────────────┐
        │                         Until the kids      After the kids        │
        │                         finish college      finish college        │
        │   Number of years to provide:    12              20               │
        │      Estimated annual need:  $58,000.00      $20,000.00            │
        │   Estimated Social Security:  $9,000.00       $5,000.00            │
        │                                                                   │
        │  The rate of interest your heirs will earn                        │
        │  on the money you leave them (after taxes and inflation).    3%    │
        │                                                                   │
        │  A provision for "final expenses."                   $15,000.00    │
        │                                                                   │
        │  Assets (such as group life insurance, savings                    │
        │  or investments) your heirs may use as a base.      $120,000.00    │
        │                                                                   │
        │  A downward adjustment to reflect other assets                    │
        │  your heirs may have access to.                                   │
        └─────────────────────────────────────────────────────────────────┘


        F1 - Calculate your insurance needs          F2 - Look at costs
                     F10 - Return to MINI MENU
                     Press ESCape for Help
```

Fig. 7.6. Data entered for calculating how much life insurance you need.

Determining your life insurance needs, like many other financial planning calculations, requires that you make some assumptions. Although the results clearly will depend in part on the accuracy of the assumptions you make, making a plan is better than neglecting to plan at all.

To calculate how much life insurance you need:

1. On the Calculate How Much You Need screen, enter in the top left blank the number of years that remain until your youngest child finishes college.

   If you have no children or if you are no longer supporting them, then enter **0**.

2. In the top right blank, enter the number of years for which you want to make provisions for your spouse, your children, or anyone else after your children are grown. If they already are grown, then calculate the number of years from today.

   If you need to provide for no one after your death, then the correct answer for this blank, as well as for the last one, is **0**, because you don't need any life insurance.

   On the other hand, if you are relatively young and need to provide for your dependents for many years, don't be surprised at the amount of life insurance you need. Be thankful, if you are young, that the annual premiums on the insurance probably are lower than you thought they were.

3. Enter your Estimated Annual Need both Until the Kids Finish College and After the Kids Finish College.

   These blanks are asking for the amount needed to support your dependents in your absence. Some experts estimate that this figure is approximately 75 percent of your current after-tax pay before the kids finish college and 60 percent after they finish. You don't have to consider inflation when you calculate this figure. (The program will consider inflation for you in Step 5.)

4. Estimate the Social Security benefits that your family would receive after your death, and fill in the two blanks for Until and After the Kids Finish College.

   These are the current Social Security benefits: if you are a widow or widower with one child, you receive between $8,000 and $14,500 annually; if you have more than one child, you receive between $9,000 and $17,000 annually; and if you have no dependents, you receive no benefits until you reach age 60, and then you receive approximately $5,500 to $9,000 per year.

These amounts are estimates that depend on many factors, including how much and how long you have contributed to the Social Security system. Your local Social Security office can give you more accurate figures.

5. Enter your best estimate of the rate of interest your heirs will earn on the money you leave them (after taxes and inflation).

   A good return after taxes and inflation during a long period is 2 to 4 percent, but you may have a more accurate estimate for your own situation. Try several percentage figures to determine their impact on your insurance needs.

6. Enter a provision for final expenses.

   This amount includes funeral costs, legal and accounting fees for administration of the estate, and taxes that may be owed. Experts estimate this amount as 50 percent of your gross salary. However, you can enter any amount you feel is reasonable.

7. To fill in the amount of assets your heirs may use as a base, enter an approximation of your net worth.

   This amount includes cash, investments, other life insurance policies you may already have, and any other assets your heirs could easily convert into cash.

8. If your heirs are likely to receive assets from another source (from your parents, for example), make a downward dollar adjustment of your life insurance needs in the last blank.

9. Press F1 to calculate your insurance needs.

   At the bottom of the screen, the calculated amount should be displayed after the message Your Insurance Needs Come to (see fig. 7.7).

To change any of the assumptions, move the cursor to the top section of the screen and insert the changes. After you are satisfied, press F1 again to recalculate your insurance needs.

Estimating the Cost of Life Insurance

Press F2 to calculate how much insurance you need. The life insurance planner asks you to confirm the information about yourself: your age, your

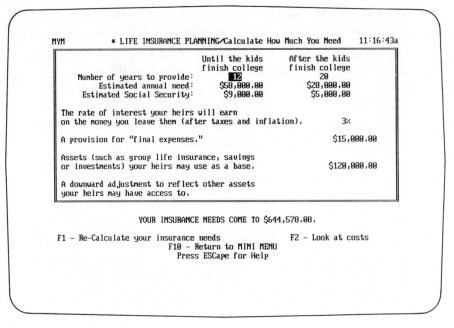

MYM   * LIFE INSURANCE PLANNING/Calculate How Much You Need   11:16:43a

	Until the kids finish college	After the kids finish college
Number of years to provide:	12	20
Estimated annual need:	$58,000.00	$28,000.00
Estimated Social Security:	$9,000.00	$5,000.00

The rate of interest your heirs will earn
on the money you leave them (after taxes and inflation).   3%

A provision for "final expenses." $15,000.00

Assets (such as group life insurance, savings
or investments) your heirs may use as a base. $120,000.00

A downward adjustment to reflect other assets
your heirs may have access to.

YOUR INSURANCE NEEDS COME TO $644,570.00.

F1 - Re-Calculate your insurance needs   F2 - Look at costs
            F10 - Return to MINI MENU
            Press ESCape for Help

Fig. 7.7. *Your total insurance needs calculated.*

sex, whether you smoke, your health, and your required amount of life insurance. Press F1 to display a comment on your needs.

Press F2 to calculate how much the insurance you need will cost. Your screen should look like figure 7.8. Although several types of life insurance are available, the rates listed here are for term life insurance. If you know how much insurance you want, you can press F3 from the Mini Menu to go directly to this screen and to calculate the cost.

Term life insurance covers you against death during the stated term of the policy. The premiums for term insurance are inexpensive while you are young and are very expensive after you reach age 60 or 65. Note that the premiums for a *whole life* policy, which covers you until you die, remain constant throughout your lifetime, but they are higher than the premiums on an equivalent amount of term insurance.

The rates displayed on your screen are for a *reversionary term* policy. The rates are lower than comparable term insurance because this policy requires you to requalify for the insurance every 10 years. If your health deteriorates during that period, then renewing this policy may be difficult or even impossible.

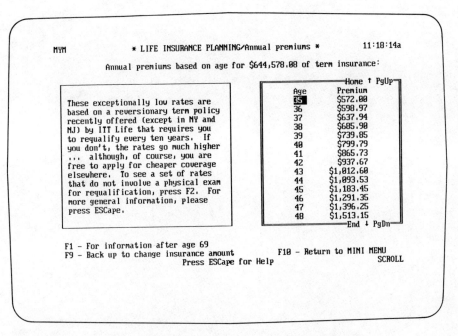

```
MYM              * LIFE INSURANCE PLANNING/Annual premiums *          11:18:14a

          Annual premiums based on age for $644,578.08 of term insurance:

                                                        ┌Home ↑ PgUp┐
  ┌─────────────────────────────────┐        │ Age    Premium          │
  │ These exceptionally low rates are │      │ 35     $572.00          │
  │ based on a reversionary term policy│     │ 36     $598.97          │
  │ recently offered (except in NY and │     │ 37     $637.94          │
  │ NJ) by ITT Life that requires you  │     │ 38     $685.90          │
  │ to requalify every ten years.  If  │     │ 39     $739.85          │
  │ you don't, the rates go much higher│     │ 40     $799.79          │
  │ ... although, of course, you are   │     │ 41     $865.73          │
  │ free to apply for cheaper coverage │     │ 42     $937.67          │
  │ elsewhere.  To see a set of rates  │     │ 43     $1,012.60        │
  │ that do not involve a physical exam│     │ 44     $1,093.53        │
  │ for requalification, press F2.  For│     │ 45     $1,183.45        │
  │ more general information, please   │     │ 46     $1,291.35        │
  │ press ESCape.                      │     │ 47     $1,396.25        │
  └─────────────────────────────────┘      │ 48     $1,513.15        │
                                              └End ↓ PgDn┘

  F1 - For information after age 69
  F9 - Back up to change insurance amount      F10 - Return to MINI MENU
                       Press ESCape for Help                      SCROLL
```

Fig. 7.8. The annual premiums for the amount of life insurance you need.

Press F2 again to display the rates on an equivalent amount of term insurance that does not require requalification every 10 years. After you qualify for this policy, it cannot be canceled as long as you make the premium payments as they become due.

Note: The author and the publisher of this book make no recommendations nor have they made any independent analysis of the insurance companies listed in this module of the program. Before purchasing any life insurance, you should make your own investigation in order to find the best rates and the best insurance company for your needs.

## Chapter 8

Using the Portfolio Manager

What is a portfolio? Quite simply, any collection of assets you decide to group together can be called a portfolio. Your coin collection, your baseball cards, and even your old Superman comic books are examples of portfolios. The stocks and bonds in your Charles Schwab brokerage account also are part of a portfolio. Typically, similar types of assets are grouped together into portfolios. For example, you probably wouldn't include your baseball cards in the same portfolio as your stocks and bonds.

By grouping your assets into portfolios, you can achieve many objectives. Managing Your Money was designed to help you achieve your objectives simply and efficiently. Managing Your Money's Portfolio Manager (module 7):

- Allows you to organize your assets into portfolios so that you can keep track of them and manage them efficiently.

- Assigns values to each one of the assets in your portfolios so that you can determine your net worth and easily track changes as they occur.

- Calculates the simple and annual appreciation or depreciation from your assets so that you can evaluate the investment decisions you have made and make better future decisions.

- Allows you to analyze the various assets or types of assets you own, whether they are located in one or several of your portfolios, and to determine the performance of those assets in relation to your other assets, the Dow Jones Industrial Average, or any other index you specify.

- Calculates for informational and tax purposes your gains and losses on the sale of assets in your portfolios. Several reports that Managing Your Money produces for you in this module are adequate, without further modification, as supporting schedules for your tax returns.

- Provides a graph of the assets in your portfolio or portfolios. In addition to being nice to look at, the graphs often point out problem areas in your overall investment strategy.

A basic rule of successful money management is *Manage your investments, but do not allow your investments to manage you.* This rule is much more than a cute phrase used by your financial planner during your first meeting together. Instead of making investments and then reviewing the results after it is too late to make changes, make investments and then monitor the results as they develop.

Often, if you can work with accurate and up-to-date information, problems or opportunities concerning your investments can be identified while you still can do something about them. A lack of information probably is the most common cause of the lack of attention investors give their investments. Usually, the most in-depth analysis people perform is calculating the gain or loss on certain investments. Real sophisticates determine their after-tax gain or loss by subtracting the taxes they must pay.

The Portfolio Manager automatically calculates the gain or loss on each of your investments (assuming that you have entered their current market values). In addition, the program provides you with the percentage gain or loss on an asset and the annualized appreciation or depreciation.

Annualized appreciation or depreciation is the percentage rate of return that your gain or loss represents on an annual basis. The key phrase is *on an annual basis.* For example, if you purchase 100 shares of a stock that sells for $10 per share today (for an overall investment of $1,000) and sell that stock for $1,350 exactly one year from today, then the annual appreciation is 35 percent. These numbers make a simple calculation: a $1,350 selling price minus a $1,000 cost equals a $350 gain, and a $350 gain divided by the $1,000 original investment equals 35 percent. If the same investment is made and sold at the same price, but the selling date is six months (instead of one year) from the date of purchase, then the same $350 gain on the same $1,000 investment becomes 70 percent annualized appreciation. This second investment took half as long as the first investment did to earn the same amount of money. If an unlimited amount of these investments were available to you (and if they are, I'd love to hear about them so that I can invest too!), then in the second example, you could make the investment twice in one year and earn $700 instead of the $350 earned in the first example.

Even if you are not yet able to calculate the annualized appreciation on an investment, you should understand the basic concept. Knowing the gain on an investment without knowing the length of time in which the gain was earned may be close to a meaningless number. By providing you with annualized appreciation figures, Managing Your Money enables you to determine how well your investments are performing and whether you might be better off with different types of investments.

This description only scratches the surface of the information you can obtain from the program. Some of the Portfolio Manager's features will not interest you, but many of them, if properly used, will help you to invest better and to get the most from your investment dollars. You should take the time to get comfortable with the Portfolio Manager and its operation so that you can take full advantage of its capabilities.

From the Main Menu, press F7-Portfolio Manager to display the module's Mini Menu (see fig. 8.1). If you are running the program on a one or two disk system, you will have to insert Disk 4 into your disk drive.

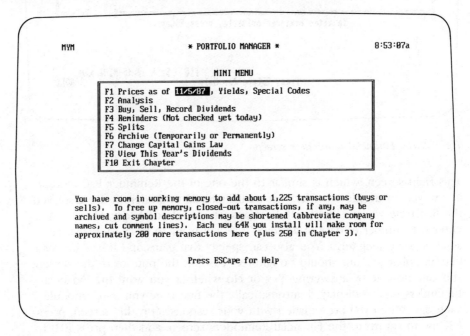

```
MYM                      * PORTFOLIO MANAGER *                    8:53:07a

                              MINI MENU

     ┌──────────────────────────────────────────────────────────┐
     │ F1 Prices as of  11/5/87 , Yields, Special Codes            │
     │ F2 Analysis                                                │
     │ F3 Buy, Sell, Record Dividends                             │
     │ F4 Reminders (Not checked yet today)                       │
     │ F5 Splits                                                  │
     │ F6 Archive (Temporarily or Permanently)                    │
     │ F7 Change Capital Gains Law                                │
     │ F8 View This Year's Dividends                              │
     │ F10 Exit Chapter                                           │
     └──────────────────────────────────────────────────────────┘

     You have room in working memory to add about 1,225 transactions (buys or
     sells).  To free up memory, closed-out transactions, if any, may be
     archived and symbol descriptions may be shortened (abbreviate company
     names, cut comment lines).  Each new 64K you install will make room for
     approximately 200 more transactions here (plus 250 in Chapter 3).


                          Press ESCape for Help
```

Fig. 8.1. The Portfolio Manager's Mini Menu.

Note: If this is the first time you have used the module today, the program
may automatically display the Financial Reminders screen (see fig. 8.2)
instead of the Mini Menu. If you don't want your financial reminders to come
up automatically the first time you use module 7 each day, then press ESCape
to access the Help screen (see fig. 8.3). If the program did not display the
Financial Reminders screen automatically, but you would like to get there
now, press F4 from the Portfolio Manager's Mini Menu and then press
ESCape to access the Help screen.

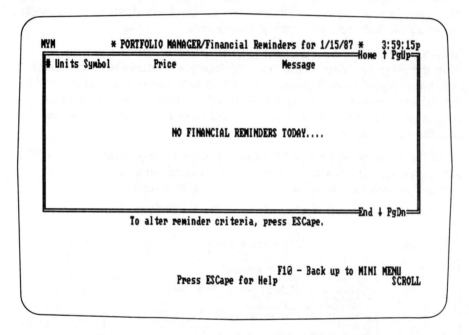

Fig. 8.2. The Financial Reminders screen.

This Help screen, which is similar to the one in the Reminder Pad module,
allows you to decide whether you want financial reminders to be displayed
the first time you use the Portfolio Manager module each day. Here, you can
enter the number of days in advance that you want to be alerted that an
asset is going long-term. You also can specify that gains and losses below a
certain dollar amount should be ignored. Also, at the bottom of the screen,
you can indicate by answering **Yes** or **No** whether you want the Financial
Reminders screen displayed automatically the first time you enter module 7
each day. When you are satisfied with your responses on this screen, press
ESCape to return to the Financial Reminders screen, and then press F10 to
return to the Portfolio Manager's Mini Menu.

```
▓▓▓▓▓ THIS IS A HELP SCREEN.  TO GET RID OF IT, JUST PRESS ESCAPE. ▓ 4:33:29p

  If you've listed securities in this chapter, we'll automatically remind
  you when a position is within 45 days of going long-term. We won't
  bother reminding you if the gain or loss is less than $150.00  . Also, we
  will Omit   assets in your hypothetical portfolios and Omit   assets in
  your IRA/Keogh portfolios.  (Change any of these parameters simply by
  typing over them.)

  If you've specified price objectives for any of your stocks, we'll remind
  you when they've been met.  (Will you sell? Or raise your objective, only
  to see the stock fall back to where you bought it?) If you've entered
  mental stop losses, we'll remind you when they've been reached.  (Will you
  sell? Or lower the stop loss, only to see . . . )

  If you've used the proper symbols for your options (see page 132 in your
  manual), we can deduce the expiration month of the option. We assume
  options expire the 3rd Friday of each month (as all currently do), and
  begin reminding you 20  days in advance thereof.

  Finally, do you want these reminders displayed automatically the first
  time you use Chapter 7 each day? No .
```

Fig. 8.3. The Help screen for Financial Reminders.

If you haven't deleted the sample data that was on your disks when you purchased the program, the module will contain several sample portfolios. You should delete all the sample portfolios before working through the tutorial in this chapter. If you already have deleted the sample portfolios and have entered your own data, you still can complete the tutorial presented in this chapter. If the amount of personal data is significant, you should make a backup copy of all your database and archive files so that you won't lose your data.

If you are using floppy disks to run Managing Your Money, insert program Disk 4 into drive A and a blank formatted disk into drive B. Type **COPY A:*.DB B:** and press Enter. Then type **COPY A:*.ARK B:** and press Enter. You should have a backup copy of your portfolio data, both archived and unarchived, on the disk in drive B.

If you are using a hard disk to run Managing Your Money, type **CD\MYM** to go to the Managing Your Money directory. Place a blank formatted disk into drive A. After the C> prompt appears, type **COPY C:*.DB A:** and press Enter. Then type **COPY C:*.ARK A:** and press Enter. You should have a backup copy of your portfolio data, both archived and unarchived, on the disk in drive A.

You should have a backup of all your portfolio data now. Although you most
likely will not have to use the backup disks to retrieve your data, "better safe
than sorry."

Now, so that your screen will match the figures shown throughout the
chapter, you should delete all of the sample portfolios before working
through the tutorial. Then, at your option, you can save or not save the
changes you make. If you don't save the changes when you exit the Portfolio
Manager module, then the information that was in the data files before the
session began returns and the tutorial portfolio is deleted. If you decide at
any time in this section of the tutorial to exit the Portfolio Manager module
of the program and you want your personal data or the sample data that
comes with the program to return, then exit the Portfolio Manager's Mini
Menu by first pressing F10-Exit Chapter and then **Y**. Then press F1-Exit
Without Saving to confirm that you want to exit without saving.

From the Portfolio Manager's Mini Menu, press F3-Buy, Sell, Record
Dividends. Your screen should look like figure 8.4 if you have not yet deleted
the sample data. (Your screen will reflect any changes that you have made to
the portfolios.)

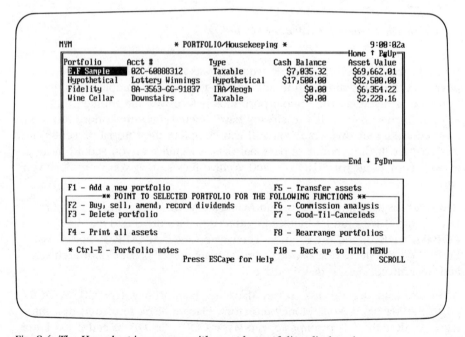

Fig. 8.4. The Housekeeping screen with sample portfolios displayed.

To delete the sample data:

1. At the Housekeeping screen of the Portfolio Manager, position the cursor at the top portfolio and press F3-Delete Portfolio.

2. Press F1 to verify your decision to delete the portfolio.

   The cursor automatically moves to the next portfolio.

3. Press F3 and F1 in succession until you have deleted all the portfolios.

   After you finish, your screen should look like figure 8.5.

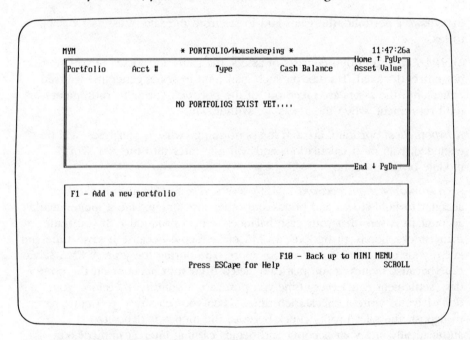

Fig. 8.5. The Housekeeping screen: No portfolios exist yet.

4. Press F10-Back Up to Mini Menu.

Because no portfolios exist yet, fewer options are available to you at the Mini Menu at this point. You aren't given the option to delete a portfolio if no portfolios exist. After you have created a portfolio, though, the option to delete will be provided.

If you have entered your own data into the portfolios and have temporarily deleted that data, DO NOT press F10 and then F5 from the Mini Menu when you leave the Portfolio Manager module because your data will be deleted from the portfolios. If you have entered any data, the preceding steps will have deleted it from the screen, but it still is in memory and can be restored by pressing F10 and F1-Exit Without Saving. Then press **Y** to confirm your decision.

Setting Up Portfolios

A portfolio is a collection of assets that you choose to group together. You can decide to set up a portfolio that is taxable, IRA/Keogh, hypothetical, or CMA.

In a *taxable* portfolio, the gains and losses from the sale of assets are subject to tax.

An *IRA/Keogh* portfolio consists of assets, the gains and losses of which are not currently taxed. The tax on such gains and losses is generally deferred either until the assets are taken out of the portfolio (prior to retirement) or until retirement, when the assets are withdrawn.

A *hypothetical* portfolio, created for performing "what if" analyses, will be excluded from most calculations and will not enter into the Net Worth module of the program.

A *cash management account (CMA)* serves as a combination brokerage account to hold stocks and bonds and other investments and a money market account to ensure that your cash balances remain productive. If you trade many stocks, bonds, or options, a CMA makes sense because it saves time and keeps your cash earning interest for more days during the year. A CMA saves time because money is automatically taken from your account on the proper day (settlement date) every time you purchase a security; therefore, you don't have to write a check each time. When you sell stock, you don't have to deposit the sales profits check because the money is deposited automatically into your account and begins earning interest immediately. Similarly, if you allow your broker to hold your securities for you, dividend checks are deposited automatically into your account.

Many large brokerage houses, such as Merrill Lynch, Shearson Lehman, and American Express, have cash management accounts. These houses charge a reasonable annual fee for the service.

Adding a New Portfolio

Begin by creating a hypothetical portfolio. First, you will set up the portfolio with $75,000 in cash, and then you will purchase some stocks with this money. After the portfolio is set up, you will explore some of the Portfolio Manager's capabilities to analyze the stocks.

To create a hypothetical portfolio:

1. From the Mini Menu, press F3-Buy, Sell, Record Dividends.

2. Press F1-Add New Portfolio to display the screen shown in figure 8.6.

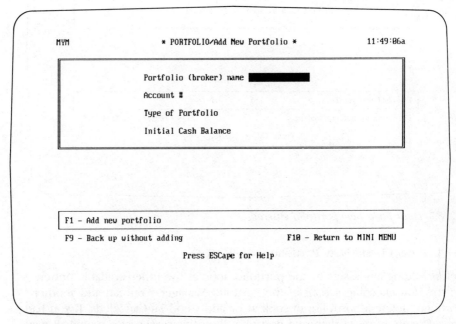

```
   MYM                * PORTFOLIO/Add New Portfolio *           11:49:06a

                  Portfolio (broker) name  ████████████

                  Account #

                  Type of Portfolio

                  Initial Cash Balance


   F1 - Add new portfolio

   F9 - Back up without adding              F10 - Return to MINI MENU

                      Press ESCape for Help
```

Fig. 8.6. The Add New Portfolio screen.

3. Enter the information that follows. After each line, press the Enter key to continue.

   Portfolio (broker) name: **Charles Squat**

   Account #: **9876-000**

   Type of Portfolio: **T** (for taxable)

   Look at the options at the bottom of the screen for the type of portfolios: Taxable, IRA/Keogh, Hypothetical, or CMA. (Version 4.0 allows you to maintain as many as nine CMA accounts, whereas earlier versions could handle only one.)

   Initial Cash Balance: **75000** (for $75,000)

   After the data is entered, your screen should look like figure 8.7.

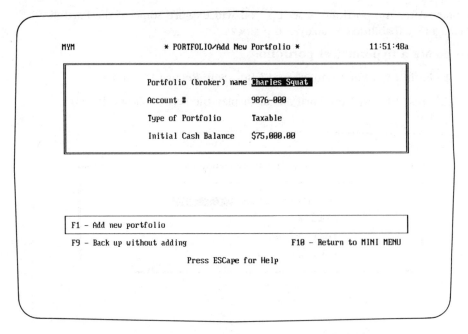

```
MYM                    * PORTFOLIO/Add New Portfolio *              11:51:48a

                 Portfolio (broker) name  Charles Squat
                 Account #                9876-000
                 Type of Portfolio        Taxable
                 Initial Cash Balance     $75,000.00



        F1 - Add new portfolio

        F9 - Back up without adding               F10 - Return to MINI MENU

                           Press ESCape for Help
```

Fig. 8.7. Data for a new portfolio entered.

4. Press F1-Add New Portfolio (see fig. 8.8).

Before adding any assets to the portfolio, look at the other available options on the Housekeeping screen of the Portfolio Manager. You can add another portfolio, delete a portfolio, or look at or add Good-Til-Canceleds. If you had placed assets in more than one portfolio, then this screen also would display the options for rearranging the order of your portfolios (generally, to place first the one in which you transact the most business), for transferring assets between portfolios (which would be a real accounting nightmare without this function), for performing a commission analysis, or for printing all your assets in all your portfolios.

Although most of the functions are self-explanatory, take a look at a few of them that may require descriptions.

Performing a Commission Analysis

If you had already purchased an asset in the Charles Squat portfolio, then your screen would display the F6-Commission Analysis option. A commission analysis can be performed for each one of your portfolios. The program tells you the amount you have spent on commissions on the transactions in each

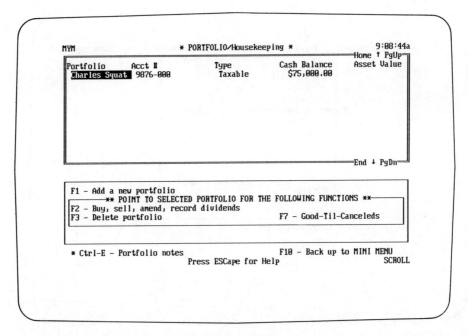

Fig. 8.8. Details of new portfolio account displayed.

portfolio and the approximate amount that a discount broker would have charged for performing the same transactions. Depending on the services you receive from your full service broker (if you are using one), you might want to consider switching brokers. By performing the analysis, you can compare brokers and make an informed decision.

Using Good-Til-Canceleds

Another option on the Portfolio Manager's Housekeeping screen is F7-Good-Til-Canceleds. Press F7 to display the screen shown in figure 8.9.

When you place an order to purchase a security (a stock or a bond, for example), the broker asks you whether you want to buy at the current offering price or at a lower price. If you believe that the market price of the security will fall a little below the current offering price, then you might place the order to purchase at a price below the current offering price. By taking this approach, you don't acquire the security unless the price drops. On the other hand, if the price does drop a little, then you will have made a good decision.

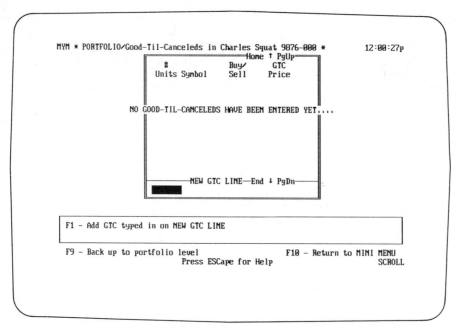

Fig. 8.9. The Good-Til-Canceled screen for a sample portfolio.

If your broker cannot immediately acquire the securities that you want to purchase, then he or she will ask you how long the order should remain in effect. A *day order* remains in effect only for the day that it is placed. If the broker is unable to acquire the security under the terms that you specified, then the order expires. You must place the order again if you still want to acquire the security.

A *good-til-canceled order*, on the other hand, remains intact until the security is acquired under the terms that you have specified. If you place a good-til-canceled order and specify to your broker that you want to acquire 100 shares of the Shop Right Insurance Company's stock at $79 dollars per share and the current offering price is $81, then you won't be able to buy any stock. If the stock rises to $88 per share and 4 months later, after the announcement of poor earnings, it drops to $76, then you probably would acquire the stock on its way down past $79. The danger of this type of order is that you might forget about making it and your broker will remember. By the time you finally acquire the stock, you may no longer be interested in it.

The best advice is to place day orders and to stay away from good-til-canceleds. If you do place good-til-canceleds, however, then enter them into the program. Using the program will prevent you from getting a surprise call from your broker telling you that you own 1,000 shares of a company that is on the verge of bankruptcy.

Adding Assets to Portfolios

Now you will add some stocks and real estate to the Charles Squat portfolio.

To add some common stocks and other assets to the portfolio that you created:

1. Press F9 to return to the Housekeeping screen. If more than one portfolio is displayed, move the cursor to the appropriate portfolio before attempting to buy or sell.

2. Press F2-Buy, Sell, Amend, Record Dividend to display the Unsold Assets screen shown in figure 8.10.

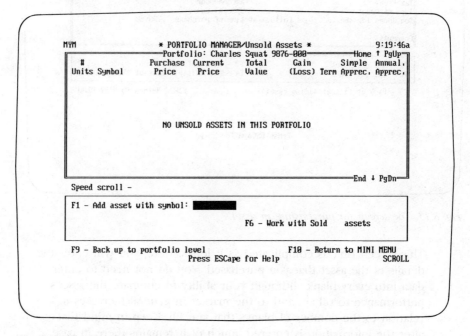

```
MYM                  * PORTFOLIO MANAGER/Unsold Assets *              9:19:46a
                    ─Portfolio: Charles Squat 9876-000──────Home ↑ PgUp─
      #             Purchase  Current    Total      Gain      Simple  Annual.
   Units Symbol      Price     Price     Value     (Loss) Term Apprec. Apprec.




                  NO UNSOLD ASSETS IN THIS PORTFOLIO



                                                        ─End ↓ PgDn─
   Speed scroll -

   F1 - Add asset with symbol: ██████████

                              F6 - Work with Sold    assets

   F9 - Back up to portfolio level          F10 - Return to MINI MENU
                      Press ESCape for Help                     SCROLL
```

Fig. 8.10. The Unsold Assets screen.

3. Be sure that the cursor is positioned at the blank after F1-Add Asset with Symbol:.

4. Type **IBM** (the symbol for the stock of International Business Machines Corporation).

When adding a publicly traded security, use the symbol that the security uses on the exchange where the security is traded. If the assets are of a different nature (such as the various coins in your coin collection), then make up any abbreviation that is easy to remember.

5. Press F1-Add Asset with Symbol to display the Enter New Purchase screen (see fig. 8.11).

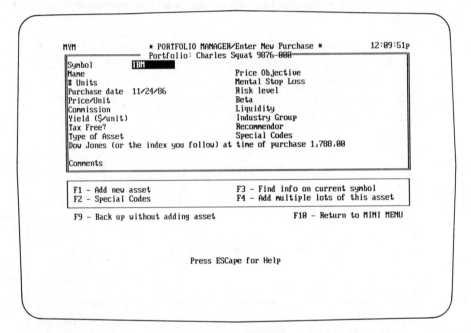

Fig. 8.11. The screen for purchasing an asset.

This screen isn't as complicated as it looks. Here, you will enter the details of the asset that you purchased. You do not need to enter data into every blank, although your ability to compare the asset's performance to others and to the market in general increases in relation to the number of blanks that you fill. Keep in mind that after the information is entered, much of it remains there in case you ever purchase more of the same asset.

6. With the cursor positioned at the Name blank, type **Inter Bus Mach** and press Enter.

The name you enter here will appear on Managing Your Money's Schedule D (for capital gains and losses). The program can print a completed form that you can attach to a blank Schedule D with your tax return.

7. Enter the following information about the IBM stock:

Units: **100**

For stocks, this number indicates shares. If you are buying bonds, then the number represents the number of bonds, which generally have a $1,000 face amount. If you are buying a house, then you would enter 1 as the number of units. Be consistent both in this blank and in the Price/Unit blank.

Purchase date: **2/17/80**

Here, always use the *trade date*, the date you made the transaction. Don't use the *settlement date*, the date you must pay for your purchase. Sometimes these two dates are different.

Price/Unit: **87** (for $87.00)

Remember to be consistent with the number of units you purchase. If you enter 1 after the # Units blank for your asset purchase, then the entire purchase price must be entered after Price/Unit. If you enter 100 in the # Units blank, then you must enter 1/100 of the purchase price in Price/Unit. Either method is acceptable, but the entries must be consistent.

Commission: **50** (for $50.00)

This is the amount you paid the broker to execute the trade or any other expense related to the purchase of the asset.

Yield ($/unit): **4.40**

This number is the dividend that a stock pays per year in dollars per unit or the amount of cash that any other type of asset pays you during the year. If no dividend exists for the asset you have purchased, then leave the space blank or enter 0. Remember that this is the amount paid on each share or bond and not the total you would receive on all the shares or bonds that you hold.

Tax Free?: **N** (for No)

Enter Yes only for municipal bonds or utility dividends in a reinvestment plan. For all others, even if they are in a tax-free portfolio such as an IRA, enter No.

Type of Asset: **C** (for common stock)

Look at the options at the bottom of the screen. If you can't find your type of asset in the list, enter Sp (for Special coded) and insert your own code in another blank. Special codes are discussed later in this chapter.

Price Objective: **120** (the price at which you would like to sell the asset)

An amount is not necessary on this line. However, if you enter one and the price of the asset reaches your objective, then Managing Your Money tells you in the Financial Reminders.

Mental Stop Loss: Leave this line blank for now.

You might think of a mental stop loss as the "down side" of a price objective. You saw that a price objective is the price at which you want to sell your stock because it has performed as you had hoped, and you don't want to get too greedy. A mental stop loss, on the other hand, is the price at which you want to bail out of the investment because you have reached your limit for losing money on it. If an investment decreases to the amount that you have entered on this line, then Managing Your Money informs you in the Financial Reminders. A real stop loss is an order that you give to your broker to sell a particular asset if the price drops to a specified level. Similar to good-til-canceled orders, stop losses are dangerous because your stock may take a quick dip and then recover after your broker sells you out.

Risk: **L** (for Low)

All investments involve some degree of risk, except for United States Treasury bills, which are generally considered to be without risk. (The common belief is that people probably won't have to worry about money if the government of the United States defaults on an obligation.) Stocks are generally considered more risky than bonds, but naturally there are exceptions. An investment in IBM stock carries less risk than an investment in the bonds of a company on the verge of bankruptcy. Although the assessment of risk is as much art as science, try to define the relative risk that is inherent in your investments.

Beta: Leave this line blank for now.

Beta measures the volatility or price movement of a particular stock or other investment relative to the overall market. If the percentage change in the market price of your stock moves in harmony with the market, then your stock has a beta of 1. If your stock price moves up and down twice as fast as the market, then your stock has a beta of 2, and so on. Investors are divided on the issue of the worth of betas. (Betas are published in Standard and Poor's *Stock Guide.*)

Liquidity: **F** (for Full)

Liquidity measures the ease with which you can convert an asset to cash. A fully liquid asset can be converted to cash immediately, such as your 100 shares of IBM stock. An investment in a limited partnership, where you are at the mercy of the general partner, probably has no liquidity. A semi-liquid investment (your house, for example) might need several months to be converted into cash. Liquidity measure tells you how well you will be able to meet unexpected expenditures.

Industry Group: Look at the choices, but don't use this line yet.

No matter how bullish you are on certain industries, diversification is the key to minimizing your investment risk.

Recommendor: Leave this line blank. For your personal portfolios, however, try to find a pattern in your investments. For example, perhaps your broker actually isn't making much money for you.

Special Codes: **P** (for Personal)

By coding your investments, you can use Managing Your Money to perform analyses and to spot opportunities or problem areas. Use any method you like to code your investments. Later, you can extract specific assets based on the codes you have assigned (for example, only those that you read about in the *Wall Street Journal* or in a certain issue of *Money* magazine). When you analyze, look for developing patterns.

Index: Leave this line blank, but use it for your personal portfolios to compare your overall investment performance with the market in general or with any index that you choose.

Here you would enter the Dow Jones Industrial Average or another index on the date of your purchase. The Dow Jones index follows the percentage change in 30 selected stocks. Other indexes follow percentage change trends in the financial markets.

Comments: Use this line to enter information that you want to remember about the investment. To enter a comment, you would press Ctrl-E and enter Version 4.0's new word processor.

After you enter the information, your screen should look like figure 8.12.

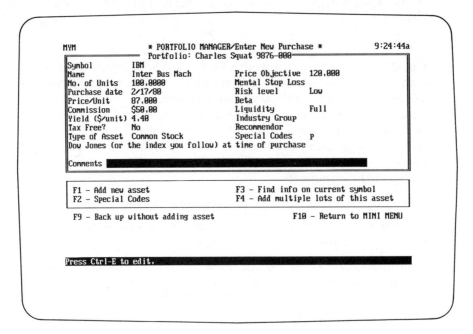

```
MYM                    * PORTFOLIO MANAGER/Enter New Purchase *        9:24:44a
                      Portfolio: Charles Squat 9876-000
Symbol          IBM
Name            Inter Bus Mach      Price Objective  120.000
No. of Units    100.0000            Mental Stop Loss
Purchase date   2/17/80             Risk level       Low
Price/Unit      87.000              Beta
Commission      $50.00              Liquidity        Full
Yield ($/unit)  4.40                Industry Group
Tax Free?       No                  Recommendor
Type of Asset   Common Stock        Special Codes    P
Dow Jones (or the index you follow) at time of purchase

Comments

   F1 - Add new asset              F3 - Find info on current symbol
   F2 - Special Codes              F4 - Add multiple lots of this asset

   F9 - Back up without adding asset            F10 - Return to MINI MENU


Press Ctrl-E to edit.
```

Fig. 8.12. New purchase information entered.

Versions 3.0 and 4.0 have the capability of adding multiple lots of the same asset much more quickly than earlier versions of the program. If you had bought 270 shares of IBM stock at varying prices during the past 10 years, for example, then you would have had to add each purchase separately in previous versions of Managing Your Money. With Versions 3.0 and 4.0, you can quickly add several separate purchases of the same asset.

To add multiple lots of the same asset:

1. From the Enter New Purchase screen, press F4 to add several separate purchases of the same asset (see fig. 8.13).

2. Press F9 to back up without adding anything.

3. Press F1 to add the 100 shares of IBM stock.

   The data on the screen disappears as the asset is added.

4. Repeat Steps 1 through 3 to add the following assets to portfolios:

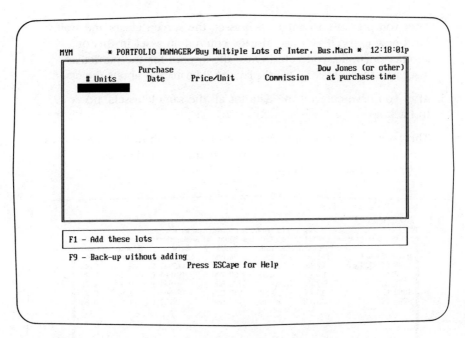

```
MYM        * PORTFOLIO MANAGER/Buy Multiple Lots of Inter. Bus.Mach *  12:18:01p

                Purchase                              Dow Jones (or other)
        # Units   Date     Price/Unit    Commission    at purchase time
       ▉▉▉▉▉▉▉▉




    F1 - Add these lots

    F9 - Back-up without adding
                            Press ESCape for Help
```

Fig. 8.13. The screen for buying multiple lots of the same asset.

Symbol	AFF	HSE	LBI	LLC
Name	Amy's Fast Food	House	Leslie's Bakery	Lou's Landscape
# Units	300	1	1000	200
Purchase Date	3/10/84	5/6/83	2/2/84	8/5/85
Price/Unit	29	175000	18	38
Commission	100	0	250	75
Yield	0	0	0	0
Tax Free?	N	N	N	N
Type of Asset	C	R	C	C
Price Objective	34	–	20	50
Risk Level	H	L	S	M
Liquidity	F	S	F	F
Special Codes	A	–	G	P

After you press F1 to enter each asset, the screen clears and waits for a new entry. If you had already entered an asset in this or another portfolio, you could enter the symbol for the particular asset and then press F3 to display the information about the asset.

5. After you have entered the data for all the sample assets, press F9 to back up.

The assets in your newly created portfolio are shown in figure 8.14. Look at the information on this screen and the additional capabilities that are available.

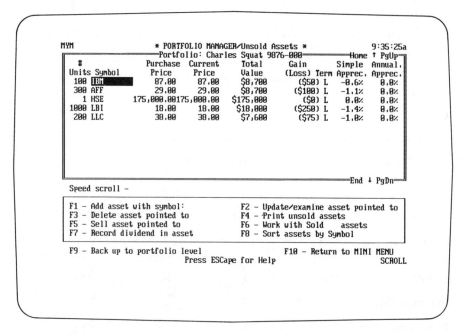

Fig. 8.14. The Unsold Assets screen with sample data displayed.

Printing Lists of Assets

From the Unsold Assets screen, press F9 to back up to the Portfolio Housekeeping screen. The F4-Print All Assets function allows you to print all the assets from all of your portfolios into one report. This capability is especially helpful if you have several portfolios. The program allows you to print the report to your printer, to the computer screen, or to a disk so that you can modify it with a word processor or a spreadsheet program.

Updating Prices

Press F2 to return to the Unsold Assets screen. This screen displays the assets that you currently hold in your portfolio. Notice that the current price equals the purchase price of each asset you have entered because the current price automatically is updated to the newest purchase price of each asset. Before you do anything else, you need to update the prices of the five assets to their current prices.

To update prices:

1. From the Unsold Assets screen, press F10-Return to Mini Menu.

2. Press F1-Prices as of _____, Yields, Special Codes to display the screen shown in figure 8.15.

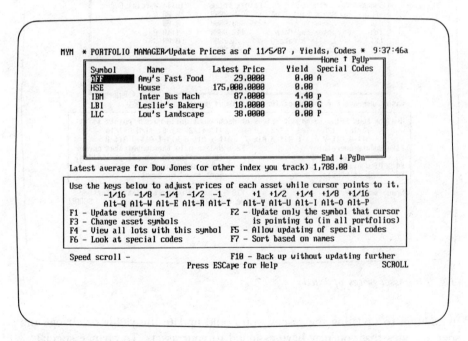

```
MYM  * PORTFOLIO MANAGER/Update Prices as of 11/5/87 , Yields, Codes *  9:37:46a
                                                      ═══Home ↑ PgUp═══
      ┌─────────────────────────────────────────────────────────────┐
      │ Symbol      Name          Latest Price   Yield Special Codes  │
      │ AFF         Amy's Fast Food    29,0000     0.00 A             │
      │ HSE         House         175,000.0000     0.00               │
      │ IBM         Inter Bus Mach     87.0000     4.40 p             │
      │ LBI         Leslie's Bakery    18.0000     0.00 G             │
      │ LLC         Lou's Landscape    38.0000     0.00 P             │
      │                                                               │
      │                                                               │
      │                                                  ══End ↓ PgDn══│
      └─────────────────────────────────────────────────────────────┘
      Latest average for Dow Jones (or other index you track) 1,788.00
      ┌─────────────────────────────────────────────────────────────┐
      │ Use the keys below to adjust prices of each asset while cursor points to it.│
      │     -1/16  -1/8  -1/4  -1/2  -1     +1  +1/2  +1/4  +1/8  +1/16│
      │      Alt-Q Alt-W Alt-E Alt-R Alt-T  Alt-Y Alt-U Alt-I Alt-O Alt-P│
      │ F1 - Update everything         F2 - Update only the symbol that cursor│
      │ F3 - Change asset symbols           is pointing to (in all portfolios)│
      │ F4 - View all lots with this symbol  F5 - Allow updating of special codes│
      │ F6 - Look at special codes     F7 - Sort based on names       │
      └─────────────────────────────────────────────────────────────┘
      Speed scroll -              F10 - Back up without updating further
                          Press ESCape for Help                 SCROLL
```

Fig. 8.15. The Updating Asset Prices screen with sample data displayed.

3. Insert the following prices in the Latest Price blank for each of
these assets:

AFF   35

HSE   245000

IBM   142

LBI   5.75

LLC   44.5

After you finish, your screen should look like figure 8.16.

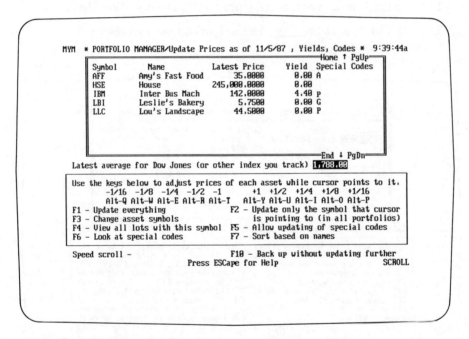

Fig. 8.16. Asset prices updated.

In addition to updating the prices, you could update the yields or change the
special codes that you may have assigned to your assets. To change special
codes, you would first press F5. You can adjust the prices of your assets
either by typing the current price over the existing price or holding down
the Alt key while pressing any of the letters in QWERT YUIOP. Each of those
letters is assigned a value, as shown in figure 8.16. Each key moves the price
up or down a specified amount.

To increase the price of an asset:

1. On the Update Asset Prices screen, position the cursor at the latest price of IBM.

2. Press **Alt-Y** to increase the price by $1.

3. Press **Alt-T** to return the price to its proper level.

   At this point, you have the following options:

   F1   Applies the updated prices to all your portfolios. You may have shares of the same stock in several different portfolios (although that is not the case in this example). This function requires you to enter the price just one time. The updated price then enters every lot in each portfolio automatically.

   F2   Allows you to update only the symbol that the cursor points to in all the portfolios that hold the asset.

   F3   Allows you to change the symbol of a specified asset, in all portfolios that hold the asset, without entering each portfolio separately.

   F4   Lets you view all lots of a specified asset from all portfolios that hold the asset.

   F5   Allows you to update the special codes that you have assigned to your assets.

   F6   Displays the special codes that you have set up.

4. Press F1 to apply the updated prices to your portfolio.

   The prices are updated and you return automatically to the Mini Menu.

5. To return to where you were before you updated the prices, press F3-Buy, Sell, Record Dividends.

6. Press F2-Buy, Sell, Amend, Record Dividends.

   Your screen should reflect your updated prices and the unrealized gains and losses for each asset (see fig. 8.17).

Note: The annual appreciation calculated on your computer will differ from the amounts shown in the figures throughout this chapter. The appreciation differs because of the differences in the date on which the calculations are made.

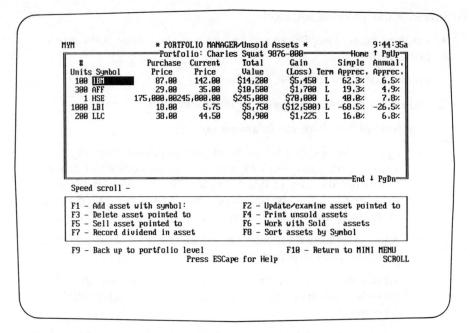

```
MYM                    * PORTFOLIO MANAGER/Unsold Assets *              9:44:35a
                   ┌─Portfolio: Charles Squat 9876-000──────────Home ↑ PgUp┐
      #             Purchase  Current    Total      Gain      Simple  Annual.
   Units Symbol      Price     Price     Value    (Loss) Term Apprec. Apprec.
    100 IBM           87.00    142.00   $14,200    $5,450  L   62.3%   6.5%
    300 AFF           29.00     35.00   $10,500    $1,700  L   19.3%   4.9%
      1 HSE      175,000.00 245,000.00 $245,000   $70,000  L   40.0%   7.8%
   1000 LBI           18.00      5.75    $5,750  ($12,500) L  -68.5% -26.5%
    200 LLC           38.00     44.50    $8,900    $1,225  L   16.0%   6.8%




                                                         └End ↓ PgDn┘
   Speed scroll -
   ┌──────────────────────────────────────────────────────────────────────┐
   │ F1 - Add asset with symbol:        F2 - Update/examine asset pointed to│
   │ F3 - Delete asset pointed to       F4 - Print unsold assets            │
   │ F5 - Sell asset pointed to         F6 - Work with Sold    assets       │
   │ F7 - Record dividend in asset      F8 - Sort assets by Symbol          │
   └──────────────────────────────────────────────────────────────────────┘
   F9 - Back up to portfolio level                F10 - Return to MINI MENU
                        Press ESCape for Help                        SCROLL
```

Fig. 8.17. Updated unsold asset prices and unrealized gains and losses for each asset displayed.

Handling Unsold Assets

The Unsold Assets screen—one of the most powerful tools in this module—shows the current value of each asset in this portfolio, the amount of gain or loss that has yet to be realized, whether the investment is long-term or short-term, and the simple and annualized appreciation of the asset. You can quickly see the current price and the purchase price of each of your assets to see which investments are performing well and which investments you would rather not have made. The total value of each investment shows you where your money is invested and which assets can be sold in order to pay for your new car.

What about the gain or loss on each asset? Maybe you didn't realize exactly how much you are losing on that investment in Leslie's Bakery. Naturally, you should consider several other factors, but maybe this is a good year to take the tax loss in LBI in order to offset your short-term gains from another investment that you sold. As long as you are considering taxes—a good thing to consider in your financial planning—you also can distinguish between your short-term and long-term gains. Look at the Term column; L stands for long and S for short. (Note that this distinction has less importance for gains beginning in 1988.)

The last two columns on the Unsold Assets screen provide the most important information for assessing the performance of each investment as well as your overall investment strategy. These columns give percentages for the simple appreciation and the annual appreciation.

The Simple Appreciation column indicates the percentage increase or decrease in the value of your investment. If you bought a stock for $10 per share and it now sells for $15 per share, then its simple appreciation is 50 percent (a $5 increase divided by a $10 original cost).

While the simple appreciation figure does have some relevance, and is generally the one that people speak of when they tell you how they did on a particular investment, you should focus your attention on the annual appreciation. Managing Your Money calculates the annual appreciation automatically for each of your investments.

The Annual Appreciation column begins with simple appreciation and incorporates the time factor. The more time that earning your simple return took, the lower your annual appreciation will be. For example, if your stock appreciated in price from $10 per share to $15 per share in 1 year, then the annual appreciation would equal the 50 percent simple appreciation. Suppose, however, that the stock shot from $10 per share to $15 per share in just 6 months. In that case, the annual appreciation would be approximately 100 percent, or twice as much as before. You could have made the same amount of money in the first 6 months and then invested the money elsewhere for the second 6 months. Just remember that your investment return is higher if your investment earns money in a shorter period of time.

Printing a List of Unsold Assets

From the Unsold Assets screen, you can print the unsold assets in this portfolio. You can print to your printer, to the screen (if you don't need hard copy), or to a disk (if you later want to modify the report on a word processor or a spreadsheet program).

To print to the screen:

1. From the Unsold Assets screen, press F4-Print Unsold Assets to display the screen shown in figure 8.18.

2. At the Print Full Detail? blank, type **Y** to print a detailed printout or **N** to print a summary.

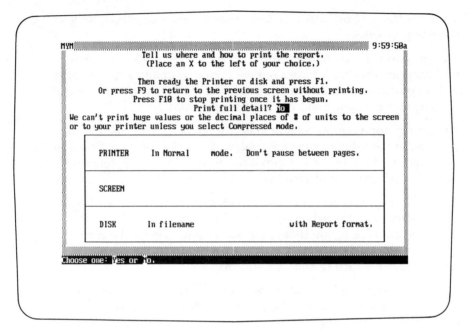

```
MYM▓▓▓▓▓▓▓▓▓▓▓▓▓▓▓▓▓▓▓▓▓▓▓▓▓▓▓▓▓▓▓▓▓▓▓▓▓ 9:59:50a
                Tell us where and how to print the report.
                (Place an X to the left of your choice.)

              Then ready the Printer or disk and press F1.
        Or press F9 to return to the previous screen without printing.
              Press F10 to stop printing once it has begun.
                    Print full detail? No
      We can't print huge values or the decimal places of # of units to the screen
      or to your printer unless you select Compressed mode.

      ┌──────────────────────────────────────────────────────────┐
      │ PRINTER    In Normal    mode.   Don't pause between pages. │
      │                                                            │
      │ SCREEN                                                     │
      │                                                            │
      │ DISK       In filename                  with Report format.│
      └──────────────────────────────────────────────────────────┘

      Choose one: Yes or No.
```

Fig. 8.18. The options for printing unsold assets.

3. Move the cursor to the blank preceding the word Screen.

4. Place an **X** in the box.

5. Press F1 to display the screen shown in figure 8.19.

6. Press any key to return to the Unsold Assets screen.

Selling Stocks

From the Unsold Assets screen, the F6 function key lets you work with any of the unsold assets, assets sold from the portfolio during the current year, or assets that you have sold short (assets that you don't own). When you sell an asset short, you essentially are borrowing the stock (generally from a brokerage house) and repaying the loan by returning the same number of shares of stock that you borrowed. Investors use this risky strategy when they believe that a stock is going to decline in value. After it does, they buy it back at a lower price and repay the loan with their newly purchased stock. If the stock price goes up, then they have to buy it back at a higher price, possibly many times higher than the price at which they sold short. Unlike typical stock investments, your potential loss when selling short is not limited by the amount that you originally invested.

```
  11/5/87                        Unsold Assets                      Page 1
  Mark D. Weinberg

       #                 Initial  Latest    Total     Gain       Simple  Annual
     Units    Symbol      Price    Price     Value    (Loss) Term Apprec  Apprec
  =============================================================================

                  Portfolio: Charles Squat              9876-000
                  ----------------------------------------------------------
      300 AFF             29.00    35.00   $10,500     $1,700 L    19.3     4.9
        1 HSE        175,000.00 245,000.00 $245,000   $70,000 L    40.0     7.8
      100 IBM             87.00   142.00   $14,200     $5,450 L    62.3     6.5
     1000 LBI             18.00     5.75    $5,750   ($12,500)L   -68.5   -26.5
      200 LLC             30.00    44.50    $8,900     $1,225 L    16.0     6.8
                  ----------------------------------------------------------
  TOTALS:                                  $284,350   $65,875



  PRESS ANY KEY TO CONTINUE....
```

Fig. 8.19. A report on unsold assets.

No sold assets are in your portfolio yet. Suppose that you want to sell 100 of the 300 shares of the AFF stock that you previously added to your portfolio.

To sell a portion of the shares held of a stock:

1. From the Unsold Assets screen, position the cursor at the AFF stock.

2. Press F5-Sell Asset Pointed To to display the screen shown in figure 8.20.

    Information about the stock is provided here: the date you bought it, the price, its current value, the length of time you held it, and your current gain. The displayed length of time that the stock was held will differ from figure 8.20 because of the difference in the date on which the calculations were performed.

    To sell, you must supply the sale date (if the one displayed is wrong, just type over it), the sale price, and the commissions you paid (if any).

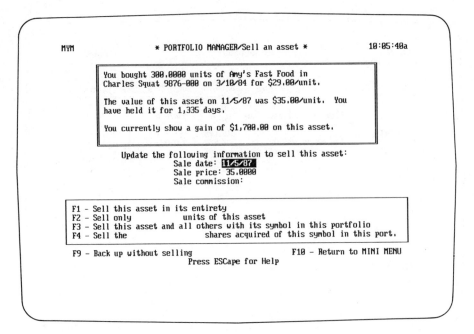

Fig. 8.20. The Sell an Asset screen.

3. Enter the following information:

> Sale Date: the current date
>
> Sale Price: **35**
>
> Sale Commission: **75**

Your screen should look like figure 8.21.

Notice the available options, listed in the menu at the bottom of the screen, for selling the AFF stock:

F1   Use this function to sell the asset that you had pointed to in its entirety.

F2   Insert a number that represents a portion of the shares of the asset and press this function to sell only that number of shares.

F3   Use this function to sell the asset and all others with the same symbol in the portfolio.

F4   This function could help you save significant dollars in taxes. Use this function if you have acquired your current position in a particular investment at different times and at different prices.

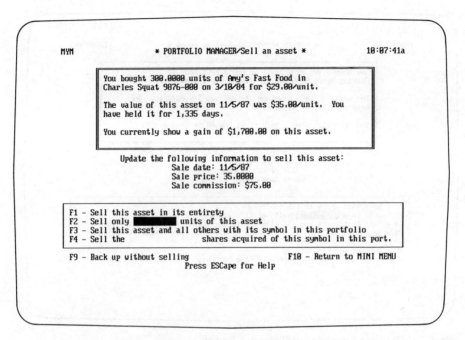

MYM   * PORTFOLIO MANAGER/Sell an asset *   10:07:41a

```
You bought 300.0000 units of Amy's Fast Food in
Charles Squat 9876-000 on 3/10/84 for $29.00/unit.

The value of this asset on 11/5/87 was $35.00/unit.  You
have held it for 1,335 days.

You currently show a gain of $1,700.00 on this asset.
```

Update the following information to sell this asset:
       Sale date: 11/5/87
       Sale price: 35.0000
       Sale commission: $75.00

```
F1 - Sell this asset in its entirety
F2 - Sell only [        ] units of this asset
F3 - Sell this asset and all others with its symbol in this portfolio
F4 - Sell the            shares acquired of this symbol in this port.
```

F9 - Back up without selling   F10 - Return to MINI MENU
                    Press ESCape for Help

Fig. 8.21. The sale information for AFF stock updated.

4. Move the cursor to the blank in the following line:

   F2-Sell only ____ units of this asset

5. Enter **100**, as shown in figure 8.22.

6. Press F2 to effect the sale.

   You should be back at the Unsold Assets screen (see fig. 8.23) with just 200 shares of the AFF stock remaining in the portfolio.

At this point, the menu on the Unsold Assets screen offers you a number of options. This tutorial does not discuss in detail all the options available to you here, but here is a brief description:

F2   Displays the details of any asset in the portfolio and makes the changes that you request.

F3   Deletes an asset that was improperly added.

F4   Prints assets held in your portfolio.

F7   Records stock dividends.

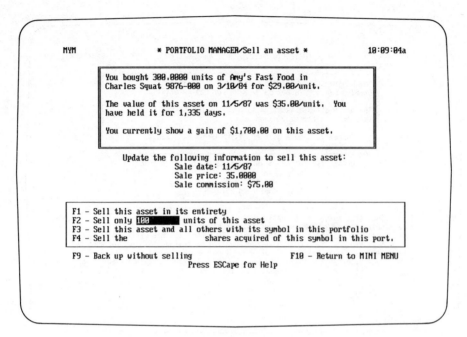

Fig. 8.22. The data for selling 100 shares of stock.

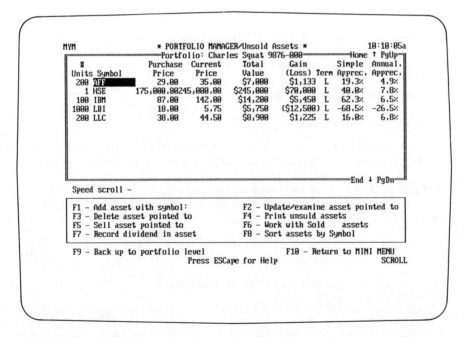

Fig. 8.23. The Unsold Assets screen after the sale.

Versions 3.0 and 4.0 of the program can handle *liquidating dividends*, or dividends that are nontaxable because they represent a return of your original investment. When you receive these dividends, the company or your broker should tell you about their special nature. (The F8 option on the Portfolio Manager's Mini Menu allows you to display all dividends recorded for the year.)

F8   Allows you to sort your assets six different ways, which is important from a financial planning perspective. The presentation of a schedule in a format directed at a particular type of analysis often sheds light on an otherwise cloudy situation.

Selecting Shares To Sell

Contrary to popular belief, one share of IBM stock in your portfolio may not be identical to another share of IBM stock. You could realize a gain on the sale of one block of shares and a loss on the sale of another block, depending on the prices you paid. Or, the gain on the sale of a block may be either long-term or short-term, depending on when you bought the particular stock. Therefore, you can affect legitimately the amount of gain or loss that you must report for tax purposes and the nature of the gain or loss (long-term or short-term) by specifically identifying the shares you are selling.

Suppose that you had purchased 10 shares of IBM stock at $80 per share 10 years ago, 10 shares at $105 per share 3 years ago, and 10 shares at $155 per share last month. You might want to sell 15 of the 30 shares you own because you are not convinced that IBM is going to perform well for the next couple of years. You already have realized short-term capital gains this year, you are in the top tax bracket, and the stock currently sells for $135 per share. You might want to sell the shares that would generate a loss or those that would produce the smallest gain. Therefore, you would sell all the shares most recently acquired at $155 per share and 5 of the shares acquired at $105 per share.

No matter what shares you sell, you would sell 15 shares and retain 15 shares. Depending on the specific shares that you would sell, however, you could affect the gain or loss and the nature of the gain or loss that you must recognize for tax purposes.

If you wanted to sell the most recently acquired shares of IBM, you would start at the Sell an Asset screen, and you would fill in the two blanks on the following line:

```
F4-Sell the ____ ____ shares acquired of this symbol in this port.
```

You would type **L** (for Last) on the first blank, and you would type **15** on the second blank. Your screen would look like figure 8.24. To effect the sale of the last 15 shares you have acquired and to calculate the gains, losses, and proper holding periods, you would press F4.

```
F1 - Sell this asset in its entirety
F2 - Sell only          units of this asset
F3 - Sell this asset and all others with its symbol in this portfolio
F4 - Sell the Last  15          shares acquired of this symbol in this port.
```

Fig. 8.24. The data for selling the most recently acquired shares.

Remember to tell your broker whether you want to sell specific shares or the most recently acquired shares, and to specify the number of shares you would like to sell from each of your purchase dates.

When you get the trade ticket from your broker, it should have the following notation on it: "VSP and a date." VSP stands for versus purchase, which indicates that the shares sold were matched with specific shares you had purchased. Without this notation, you could have problems justifying your tax treatment with the Internal Revenue Service. The IRS assumes that without an intention to the contrary, the shares sold are the first ones you had purchased.

Sorting Assets

When you select F8 on the Unsold Assets screen, you have the option of sorting your assets. The capability to sort assets is invaluable for determining the worth of your current investments. Often, just looking at the portfolio from a new perspective helps you realize the mistakes you have been making so that you can make some improvements in your strategy.

You can sort assets in a number of ways. Sorting the assets in order of their total value may help you determine that you have invested too much in certain areas. Sorting by purchase date might show that you've been holding on to that "dog" of an investment too long and that the time has come to take your loss and move forward. If you sort in order of the total gain that you have in each investment, you may quickly discover the best asset to use for your favorite charitable contribution. By contributing to charity an asset that you have held for at least six months, you are entitled to a deduction equal to the fair market value of the property, and you avoid having to pay any capital gain. You benefit most by choosing the asset with the greatest amount of unrealized gain. If you sort in order of annual appreciation, then you can easily see which of your assets have performed well.

Press F10-Return to Mini Menu to explore additional capabilities of the Portfolio Manager.

Analyzing Assets

This tutorial already has examined the F1 and F3 functions, so now look at F2-Analysis. This function enables you to perform some sophisticated financial planning analyses that are sure to help you improve your investment returns. No program can tell you what to invest in. However, by analyzing the results that you have achieved in the past, you should be able to spot problem areas in your investment approach and eliminate any needless risks.

From the Mini Menu, press F2-Analysis to display the screen shown in figure 8.25.

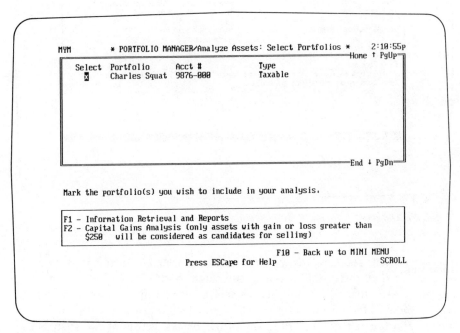

Fig. 8.25. The Analyze Assets: Select Portfolios screen.

Retrieving Information

If you have followed the Portfolio Manager tutorial from the beginning, then only one portfolio is recorded at this point. If you had more than one portfolio, then they would all appear on this screen. From here, you could select one, several, or all of your portfolios on which to perform analyses.

To select one or more portfolios for analysis:

1. Make sure that an X is next to the Charles Squat portfolio.

2. Press F1-Information Retrieval and Reports to display the screen shown in figure 8.26.

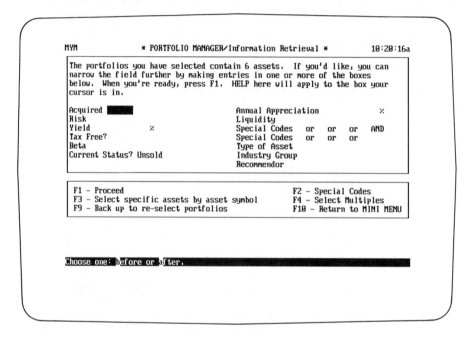

Fig. 8.26. The asset Information Retrieval screen.

The screen tells you how many assets you have selected. In this case, you have selected all the unsold assets in the single portfolio. You can further limit the assets that you would like to analyze. If you insert nothing in the blanks, then all the unsold assets in all your selected portfolios will be included in the analysis. By filling any of the blanks, you limit the analysis to certain assets based on the criteria you select.

Here is a brief explanation of each blank on the screen and how it can be used to analyze your assets:

Acquired: Use these blanks if you want to analyze only the assets acquired before or after a certain date. Type either **B** or **A** (for Before or After) in the first blank. Type the date in the second blank.

Risk: If you coded your assets based on their risk level when you added them to the portfolios, then you can select particular assets based on their level of risk. In the first blank, enter **L**, **E**, or **G** (for Less than, Equal to, or Greater than). In the second blank, enter one of the risk categories. For example, if you entered **Equal to** and **Speculative**, then your analysis would be performed only for the speculative asset codes that also meet all the other selection criteria.

Yield: Select only those assets that pay dividends of a certain percentage or that provide a yield of less than or more than a specified percentage.

Tax Free?: Select only your tax-free municipal bonds for analysis by entering **Y** (for Yes). Enter **N** (for No) to exclude them from the analysis.

Beta: Similar to risk, you can only select assets based on the beta that you have assigned to them if you have assigned a beta when you added the asset to the portfolio.

Current Status?: Include only your unsold or sold assets, or both, in the analysis. Leave the box blank to analyze only your unsold assets.

Annual Appreciation: Select only the assets that have appreciated above or below a specified rate.

Liquidity: Select assets based on the liquidity level that you assigned to them when you added them to the portfolio.

Special Codes: If you have assigned special codes to your assets, then select here the assets based on their codes. Enter from one to four codes on the top line, and only the assets that possess at least one of those codes can be selected. Enter as many as four codes on the bottom line as well, and then the only assets that can be selected are those that possess at least one of the codes from each of both the top and bottom lines.

Type of Asset: Select assets based on their type (for example, common stocks only or bonds only). If you want to select various asset types, enter **Multiple** and press F4. Then select from the list of asset types displayed on your screen (see fig. 8.27).

Industry Group: Select assets based on their industry group (for example, only high-tech stocks). If you want to look at assets from more than one industry group, then enter **Multiple** and press F4. Your screen will display a list of industry groups from which you can make a selection (see fig. 8.28).

Recommendor: Select assets based on who recommended the investment. To select from more than one recommendor, enter **Multiple** and press F4.

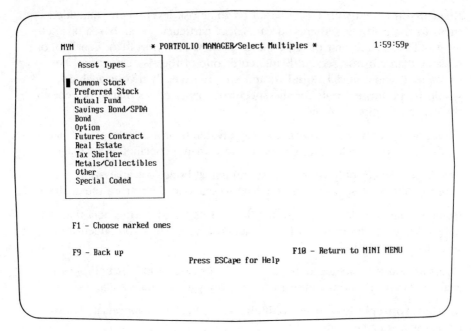

Fig. 8.27. A list of Asset Types.

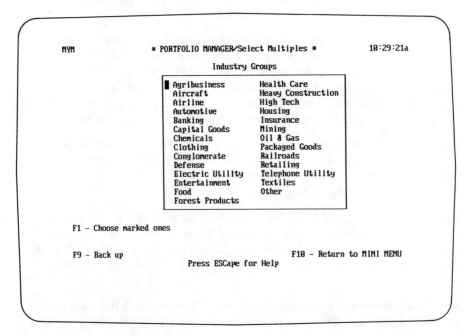

Fig. 8.28. A list of industry groups.

Your screen will display a list of recommendors from which you can make a selection (see fig. 8.29).

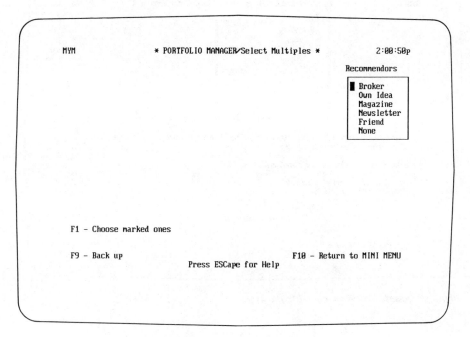

Fig. 8.29. A list of recommendors.

Selecting Specific Assets by Symbol

You can select assets from the selected portfolios (a single portfolio, in this case) either by selecting specific assets or by inserting certain selection criteria. From the Information Retrieval screen, press F3-Select Specific Assets By Asset Symbol to display the screen shown in figure 8.30.

All assets in the portfolio that you created are listed. From this screen, you have an option to place an X beside each asset you want to select for analysis and then to press F1. You also have the option to keep all assets available for analysis by pressing F2.

Press F2 to back up to the Information Retrieval screen and to keep all assets available for analysis. From that screen, you could decide to select only the assets acquired before or after a certain date, only those that are tax-free or taxable, only common stocks, only bonds, only taxable stocks and bonds, or only those recommended by your brother-in-law. The choices are yours and the options are plentiful. After you have created your own portfolios, you will be the one to decide how to analyze your assets.

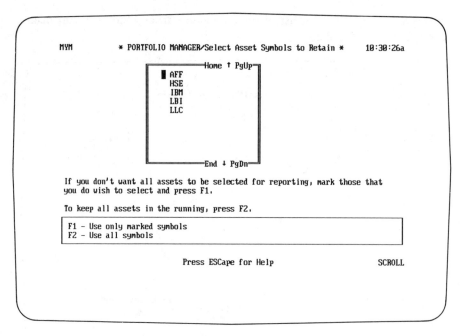

Fig. 8.30. Assets being selected for analysis.

To include all your assets in the analysis, leave all the blanks empty and press
F1 to display the screen shown in figure 8.31. The screen tells you how
many assets meet the criteria you have selected. In this case, you selected all
unsold assets. The screen indicates the percentage of assets that was chosen
from all portfolios, the value of the chosen assets, the total gain or loss on
the chosen assets, and the weighted average beta.

Calculating the Weighted Average Beta

As explained earlier in the chapter, beta measures a stock's volatility. On the
Analyze Chosen Assets screen, the Weighted Average Beta figure should be 0
because you didn't insert any betas.

Analyzing the Risk Distribution

A great deal of subjectivity is involved in determining the difference between
low, moderate, and high risk. After all, you select the classification for your
investments. The final piece of information on the Analyze Chosen Assets
screen measures the percentage of your selected assets that you have
classified as having from no risk to speculative risk.

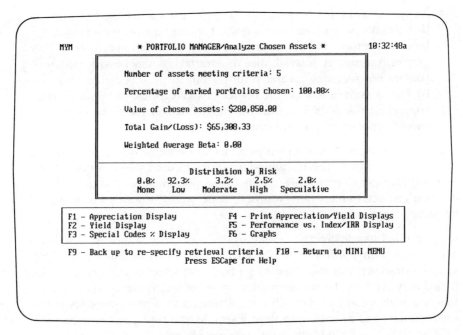

```
    MYM                  * PORTFOLIO MANAGER/Analyze Chosen Assets *        10:32:40a

            ┌──────────────────────────────────────────────────────────────┐
            │  Number of assets meeting criteria: 5                          │
            │                                                                │
            │  Percentage of marked portfolios chosen: 100.00%              │
            │                                                                │
            │  Value of chosen assets: $200,850.00                           │
            │                                                                │
            │  Total Gain/(Loss): $65,300.33                                 │
            │                                                                │
            │  Weighted Average Beta: 0.00                                   │
            │                                                                │
            │────────────────────────────────────────────────────────────  │
            │                    Distribution by Risk                        │
            │          0.0%    92.3%    3.2%    2.5%     2.0%                │
            │          None     Low   Moderate  High  Speculative            │
            └──────────────────────────────────────────────────────────────┘

      ┌───────────────────────────────────────────────────────────────────┐
      │  F1 - Appreciation Display       F4 - Print Appreciation/Yield Displays │
      │  F2 - Yield Display              F5 - Performance vs. Index/IRR Display │
      │  F3 - Special Codes % Display    F6 - Graphs                        │
      └───────────────────────────────────────────────────────────────────┘
          F9 - Back up to re-specify retrieval criteria   F10 - Return to MINI MENU
                               Press ESCape for Help
```

Fig. 8.31. The Analyze Chosen Assets screen.

Don't think that the classification is worthless just because it is subjective. Being able to judge the overall risk is important. These figures allow you to rise above the emotional aspect of investing and to make a somewhat objective assessment of your current investment strategy. Investors often acquire small positions in risky stocks and then acquire more of the same stocks. Soon, their portfolios are unbalanced in relation to their earning capacity, their stage of life, and their future cash requirements. A simple schedule of risk distribution is often sufficient to alert investors that they are not investing according to their overall plans and that they probably will not achieve their desired financial objectives.

Follow some general rules for assessing the risk involved in your investment strategy:

- The basic precept of portfolio risk assessment says that taking greater risks should yield greater returns on your investment, and that taking lesser risks should yield lesser returns. Often, this precept is misinterpreted to mean that if you take greater risks, then you get higher returns. Generally, nothing could be further from the truth. Those who take risks often end up with no return or, worse, they lose their original investment as well.

- Analyze Distribution by Risk in relation to the annual appreciation that you obtain on your investments. The concept of "increased risk, increased return" doesn't mean that taking risks will guarantee greater returns but, instead, that you are taking unnecessary risks if you are not receiving greater returns from them. If your Distribution by Risk is skewed toward the higher risk categories, and your annual appreciation is no higher than the money market rates, then you should reconsider your investment strategy.

The Analyze Chosen Assets screen presents an overview of the performance of the selected assets. The remaining functions in the analysis section of the Portfolio Manager display more details of the performance of your assets so that you can determine where you have done well (or poorly) with your investment approach.

Keep in mind the flexibility available in this section. You have selected all the assets in the only portfolio that you set up, which may be fine for the first analysis. However, you may want to go back and select assets again, possibly by industry category, by recommendor, or by including the assets you sold this year with those that you still own. A tendency of most investors is to sell their winners and to hold onto their losers. Maybe your performance will look better if you include the assets you already sold.

Displaying Appreciation

From the menu at the bottom of the Analyze Chosen Assets screen, select F1-Appreciation Display to display the screen shown in figure 8.32. This screen shows the details of the specified assets in your selected portfolios. Information about your assets is provided: the purchase price, the current price since the last time you updated, the total value of each investment (the current price multiplied by the number of units), the unrealized gain or loss on each asset, and the status (long-term or short-term) of the gain. The simple appreciation and the annual appreciation of each asset are also displayed.

Perhaps only one loss is throwing off your overall return, or perhaps only one winner is masking a bad overall investment history. Use the displays to analyze and identify problems. If you are unsure of how to interpret the results, talk to your accountant or to a friend, and be sure to use the available information.

Displaying and Analyzing Yield

From the Appreciation Display screen, press F1-Yield Display to display the screen shown in figure 8.33. If your stocks pay dividends, if you hold bonds

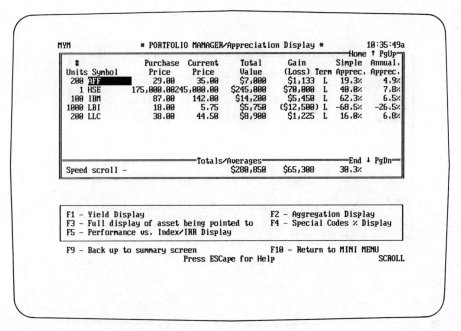

Fig. 8.32. The Appreciation Display screen.

that pay interest, or if you have any investment where cash is distributed, then this screen indicates the return you are receiving from the distribution by showing the percentage of the current value of the asset. The "%" column displays this figure.

The Total Return column displays a very important figure. The return achieved on many stocks is a combination of the dividends paid and the appreciation of the stock price. This last column is the sum of the assets' annualized appreciation plus the yield on the investment as a percentage of the original purchase price. For example, if you paid $100 a year ago for a stock that now sells for $120, and at the end of the year the stock paid a dividend of $4 per share, then your Total Return is 24 percent (20 percent annualized appreciation plus a 4 percent dividend yield). You often might accept lower stock appreciation or be willing to wait longer for the appreciation if the stock pays a dividend. In fact, many stocks are attractive investments simply because they pay good dividends even though their prices are fairly stable.

If any of the results are confusing or seem to be incorrect, press F3 from the Yield Display screen to examine the details of any of the assets displayed.

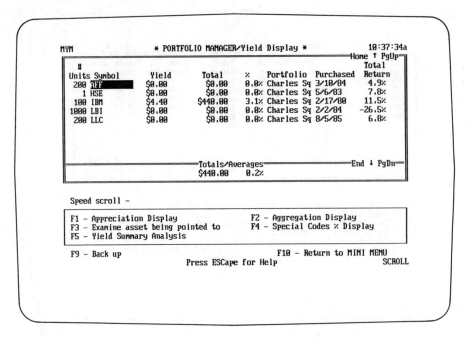

Fig. 8.33. The Yield Display screen.

When you have finished examining those details, press F9 to back up and
then press F5-Yield Summary Analysis to display the screen shown in figure
8.34. This screen summarizes the income you are receiving from your
selected portfolios, broken down by the tax status of the investments, the
risk, and the types of assets. If you are in a high tax bracket and all or most
of your income is taxable, then perhaps you should revise your strategy to
see whether you can benefit from the purchase of tax-free municipal bonds.

Similar conclusions may be drawn from the other categories. If your
moderate risk investments have not been appreciating but they provide a
good portion of your investment income, then maybe they serve their
purpose and you should keep them. The key is not to arrive at quick
conclusions about your investment assets. Several different analyses usually are
necessary before you get a clear picture of your performance.

Aggregating Assets from Various Portfolios

From the Yield Summary Analysis screen, press F9 to back up to the Yield
Display screen. Then press F2 to display the Aggregation Display screen
shown in figure 8.35.

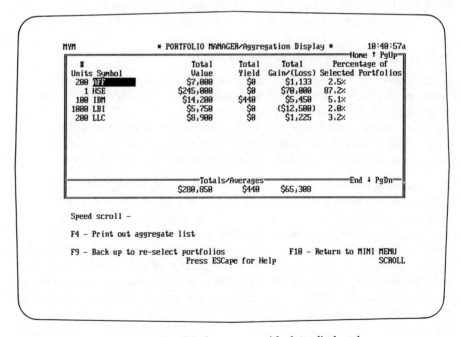

```
MYM              * PORTFOLIO MANAGER/Yield Summary Analysis *        3:51:43p

      The total annual income in the portfolios you selected is $440.00, or
      0.2% of the total current value of those portfolios.  After tax (we
      have 0% as your bracket) it comes to $440.00.

      The total breaks down as follows:
                                          By Asset Type:
      By Tax Status:                      Common Stock         $440 100.0%
      Taxable              $440 100.0%    Preferred Stock             0.0%
      Tax-Free                   0.0%     Mutual Fund                 0.0%
      Unspecified                0.0%     Savings Bonds/SPDAs         0.0%
                                          Bond                        0.0%
      By Risk:                            Option                      0.0%
      None                       0.0%     Futures Contract            0.0%
      Low                  $440 100.0%    Real Estate            $0   0.0%
      Moderate              $0   0.0%     Tax Shelter                 0.0%
      High                  $0   0.0%     Metals/Collectibles         0.0%
      Speculative           $0   0.0%     Other                       0.0%
      Unspecified                0.0%     Special Coded               0.0%


    F9 - Back up                          F10 - Return to MINI MENU
```

Fig. 8.34. The Yield Summary Analysis screen.

```
MYM              * PORTFOLIO MANAGER/Aggregation Display *         10:40:57a
                                                        Home ↑ PgUp
       #          Total      Total     Total      Percentage of
  Units Symbol    Value      Yield   Gain/(Loss) Selected Portfolios
    200 AFF       $7,000       $0      $1,133         2.5%
      1 HSE     $245,000       $0     $70,000        87.2%
    100 IBM      $14,200     $440      $5,450         5.1%
   1000 LBI       $5,750       $0    ($12,500)        2.0%
    200 LLC       $8,900       $0      $1,225         3.2%




                   Totals/Averages                    End ↓ PgDn
                   $280,850      $440    $65,300


   Speed scroll -

   F4 - Print out aggregate list

   F9 - Back up to re-select portfolios        F10 - Return to MINI MENU
                     Press ESCape for Help                        SCROLL
```

Fig. 8.35. The asset Aggregation Display screen with data displayed.

The Aggregation Display is helpful if you have numerous lots or groups of the same stock, either in one or many of your portfolios. For instance, you may have bought 100 shares of stock at $10 per share, another 100 shares at $8 per share, and 300 shares at $13 per share, and the stock now sells for $11 per share. Although you may have both gains and losses on your shares, you should keep in mind the overall performance of your stocks. The Aggregation Display adds all the shares of stock or other investments that have the same symbol and shows their total current value, their yield, their total gain or loss, and the percentage (based on value) of the total selected portfolios that they represent.

A basic rule for reducing your portfolio investment risk is to diversify your holdings. Because you may have shares of the same stock in several different portfolios, you may be surprised to learn that you have too much money tied up in one investment. This fact may not be evident if you look at each portfolio separately. The Percentage of Selected Portfolios figures on the Aggregation Display screen can help you assess your risk. Those figures provide insight into how diversified your investments are and may cause you to readjust your holdings.

Notice that from the Aggregation Display screen, you can print an aggregate list to your printer, to the screen, or to a disk.

When you have finished studying the Aggregation Display screen, you can return to the Analyze Chosen Assets screen by pressing F9, F1, and F1 again.

Comparing Your Performance to an Index

At the Analyze Chosen Assets screen, press F5-Performance vs. Index/IRR Display to display the screen shown in figure 8.36. This screen shows the details of each of your selected assets. You are provided with the number of units of each investment held, the symbol, the purchase price, and the level of the chosen index at the time of the asset's purchase. All this information comes from the data you provided when you added each of the assets.

The remaining four columns are calculated for you by Managing Your Money and serve as the basis for the analysis. The simple appreciation columns indicate how each of your particular assets has performed, in terms of percentage appreciation, in relation to the index. The last two columns display a similar comparison, but these columns are more meaningful in that they incorporate the time element in a comparison of the annual percentage appreciation of the assets and the index. Finally, at the bottom of the screen, is a comparison of the total simple appreciation and annual appreciation of the portfolio vs. the index.

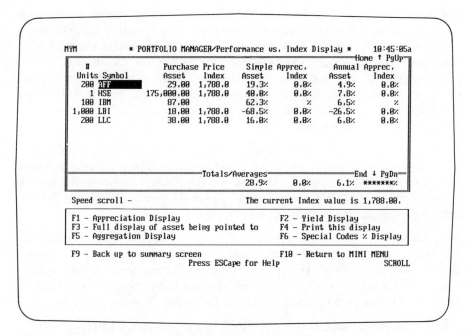

Fig. 8.36. The Performance vs. Index Display screen.

Your ability to analyze your investment results is limited unless you have some standard against which you can compare your results. The Performance vs. Index function is capable of comparing your investment results with a general stock market index such as the Dow Jones Industrial Average or any other average you select.

The Dow Jones Industrial Average (or simply the Dow Jones) is a collection of 30 stocks that are traded on the New York Stock Exchange. These stocks were chosen to represent the overall movement of the stock market. Their performance, however, may actually have no relation to the performance of your investments.

To use this function, you must enter the current value of the chosen index at the time that you add each of your assets to a portfolio. Use the Dow Jones or any other index.

Another informative analysis might be to compare your results to the performance of a mutual fund. Pick a mutual fund that you are thinking of investing in. Use the Performance vs. Index Display to compare your results with the results of the mutual fund to see whether you should continue to invest on your own or whether you should let a professional invest for you.

The index, in this case, is based on the share price of the mutual fund on the day that you begin the comparison. Look up the share price of the mutual fund that you select. Suppose that the price is $30 per share at the time you make your first investment. On the screen that is used to add an asset to a portfolio (see fig. 8.11 earlier in the chapter), a blank is provided for you to fill in the index value at the time you purchased the asset. You would enter **30**. When you buy additional assets, look up the mutual fund price and enter that price as the current index value.

For accuracy, you must keep track of any dividends paid and any stock splits of the mutual fund. If a $1 per share dividend had been paid, then you would add $1 to the current mutual fund price to arrive at the proper index level. If a 2-for-1 stock split had occurred, then you would double the mutual fund price to arrive at the proper level for the current index.

Keep track of the mutual fund price at the time of each of your purchases so that you can use the Performance vs. Index Display screen to compare your performance to the fund's performance. The results may surprise you. If the fund beats you, then perhaps you should transfer some money to the fund. If you beat the fund, then perhaps you're in the wrong business.

When you have finished studying the Performance vs. Index Display screen, press F9-Back Up to Summary Screen to return to the Analyze Chosen Assets screen.

Graphing Portfolio Holdings

From the Analyze Chosen Assets screen, press F6-Graphs to display the screen shown in figure 8.37. From this screen, you can see the breakdown of your selected portfolios by each of the various categories. Try selecting a few of the options.

Press F1 to display the distribution-by-risk graph shown in figure 8.38. Notice that 92.3 percent of the investments are in low risk category, while only 2 percent of the investments are in the speculative category. Perhaps you should consider accepting a little more risk and possibly achieving some of those large gains that other people are achieving in the market. The distribution in a pie graph format often points out that your concentration of investments in a certain industry or type of asset is too heavy. Remember that diversification is the key to proper asset management. You may have to wait longer to achieve your goal, but you have a much better chance of achieving it.

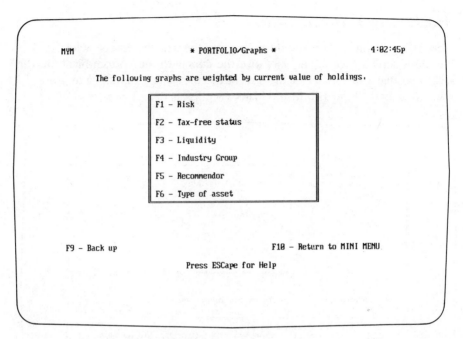

Fig. 8.37. The Portfolio Manager's Graphs screen.

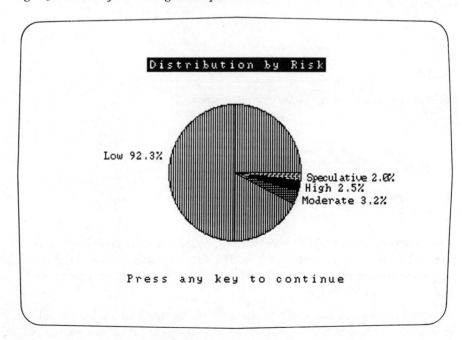

Fig. 8.38. A pie graph of investment risk distribution.

Analyzing Capital Gains

Press F9 three times. You should be back at the Analyze Assets: Select
Portfolios screen (see fig. 8.39). Move the cursor to the bottom blank on the
screen so that you can select the size of the unrealized capital gains you
want to analyze. Type **150** in the blank (see fig. 8.40).

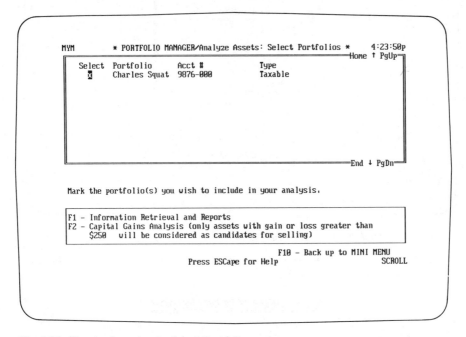

```
  MYM            * PORTFOLIO MANAGER/Analyze Assets: Select Portfolios *      4:23:50p
                                                                    ⌐Home ↑ PgUp⌐
        Select  Portfolio      Acct #            Type
          X      Charles Squat  9876-000          Taxable



                                                                    └End ↓ PgDn┘


        Mark the portfolio(s) you wish to include in your analysis.

      ┌─────────────────────────────────────────────────────────────────────┐
      │ F1 - Information Retrieval and Reports                                │
      │ F2 - Capital Gains Analysis (only assets with gain or loss greater than │
      │      $250  will be considered as candidates for selling)              │
      └─────────────────────────────────────────────────────────────────────┘
                                              F10 - Back up to MINI MENU
                              Press ESCape for Help              SCROLL
```

Fig. 8.39. The Analyze Assets: Select Portfolios screen.

```
┌─────────────────────────────────────────────────────────────────────┐
│ F1 - Information Retrieval and Reports                                │
│ F2 - Capital Gains Analysis (only assets with gain or loss greater than │
│      $150  will be considered as candidates for selling)              │
└─────────────────────────────────────────────────────────────────────┘
```

Fig. 8.40. The Capital Gains Analysis option with amount of assets
specified.

Despite the recent changes in the tax law, taxes still (and probably always
will) affect your investment decisions. The Capital Gains Analysis function
helps you decide whether to take your gains in the current tax year or to
wait.

Investors often place too much importance on the tax considerations and
ignore other relevant factors. Both tax and nontax considerations should play
a role in your decision to sell a particular asset in order to recognize a

capital gain. The decision you make about selling an asset should be primarily influenced by your analysis of its future value. If you believe that the asset is performing at or above your expectations and that it will continue to do so, then don't make a decision to sell based solely on the tax ramifications. Similarly, if the prospects for the investment look bleak but selling would be a bad tax decision, maybe you should sell it anyway.

Keep in mind some basic tax concepts when you make the decision to hold or to sell. First, consider the concept of deferral. You may accomplish more if you recognize a gain sometime *after* the current year ends. If you recognize the gain this year, then you must pay taxes on the gain for this year, and only the net or after-tax amount will be yours to reinvest elsewhere. If you wait until later to recognize the gain, then the taxes will be due later, and the entire invested amount will earn income longer. (Deferral is discussed further in Chapter 10, "Using the Income Tax Estimator.")

Before you decide whether to sell an asset, consider the relative tax rate in the current tax year versus the expected rate in a future tax year. If you expect the rates to decrease (they will be lower in 1988 than in 1987), then you may have an additional tax-related reason to hold onto the investment. If rates are increasing, then the scale tips in favor of selling this year.

Buy-hold decisions must not be made without considering your overall tax situation. Capital gains are treated differently than ordinary income, so be sure to consider the other capital transactions that you have made this year or that you expect to make before the year ends. If you already have taken more than $3,000 in capital losses during the current year, then you probably should take some capital gains.

Press F2 to display the Capital Gains Analyzer, shown in figure 8.41. The top of the screen displays Realized Gains and Losses—ones that have been taken during the current year. For example, if you own 10 shares of stock that have appreciated from $15 per share to $25 per share, then you have $100 ($10 per share multiplied by 10 shares) of unrealized gain (sometimes called paper gain) in the stock. When you sell the stock, the $100 gain becomes a realized gain.

In the Loss Carryforward blanks, you should include the capital losses, both short-term and long-term, that you were unable to recognize for tax purposes in previous years. Capital loss carryforwards occur because the current tax law allows you to recognize only $3,000 in capital losses per year over and above the capital gains that you recognized for that year. If you have more than $3,000 in capital losses, then the excess must be carried ahead to future tax years or back to previous years.

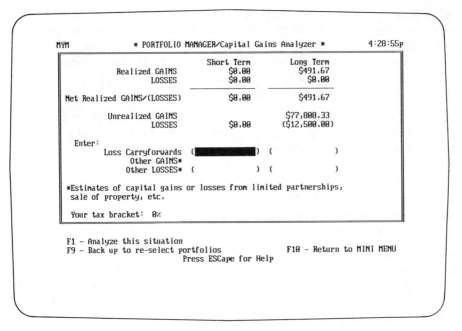

MYM   * PORTFOLIO MANAGER/Capital Gains Analyzer *   4:28:55p

                                  Short Term   Long Term
                  Realized GAINS $0.00 $491.67
                          LOSSES $0.00 $0.00

        Net Realized GAINS/(LOSSES) $0.00 $491.67

                Unrealized GAINS $77,000.33
                          LOSSES $0.00   ($12,500.00)

          Enter:
                Loss Carryforwards (   ) (   )
                      Other GAINS*
                      Other LOSSES* (   ) (   )

        *Estimates of capital gains or losses from limited partnerships,
         sale of property, etc.

         Your tax bracket: 0%

        F1 - Analyze this situation
        F9 - Back up to re-select portfolios   F10 - Return to MINI MENU
                            Press ESCape for Help

Fig. 8.41. The Capital Gains Analyzer screen.

The Other Gains and Other Losses blanks should be filled with any other capital gains and losses from other sources besides the selected portfolios. At the bottom of the screen, you need to enter your expected tax bracket.

To analyze your capital gains situation, press F1. Managing Your Money will give you suggestions as you work through the remaining screens. Some of the advice may not be relevant. Significant changes in the tax laws for 1987 werc enacted; these changes are discussed in detail in Chapter 10.

After you have reviewed the advice, press F10 to return to the Portfolio Manager's Mini Menu.

Using Financial Reminders

Notice that the Mini Menu indicates when the Financial Reminders have not been checked today. From the Mini Menu, select F4-Financial Reminders to display the screen shown in figure 8.42.

You can set the program so that this screen appears either the first time you use the Portfolio Manager module each day or only at your request. To alter the reminder criteria and decide whether you want the screen to appear

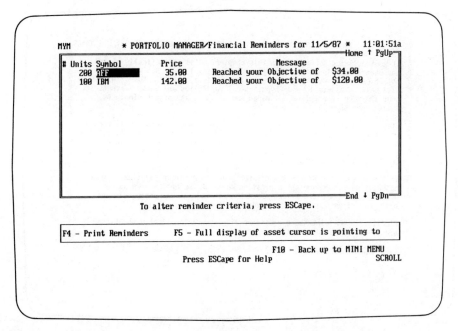

```
MYM              * PORTFOLIO MANAGER/Financial Reminders for 11/5/87 *   11:01:51a
                                                              ┌─────Home ↑ PgUp┐
# Units Symbol         Price                    Message
    200 AFF            35.00       Reached your Objective of  $34.00
    100 IBM           142.00       Reached your Objective of  $120.00




                                                              └────End ↓ PgDn─┘
              To alter reminder criteria, press ESCape.

┌─────────────────────────────────────────────────────────────────────┐
│ F4 - Print Reminders      F5 - Full display of asset cursor is pointing to │
└─────────────────────────────────────────────────────────────────────┘
                                         F10 - Back up to MINI MENU
                        Press ESCape for Help                  SCROLL
```

Fig. 8.42. The Financial Reminders screen.

automatically, press the ESCape key to display the Help screen shown in figure 8.43.

Set your reminder criteria on this screen. Decide how many days in advance you want to be reminded that the holding period on an investment is about to go long-term. If you select 10, then the reminder appears automatically in the financial reminders every day during the 10 days before the investment goes long-term.

The next blank allows you to ignore all gains that are less than the dollar amount you specify. In this way, you can block out any unnecessary reminders.

You can instruct the program not to call up any financial reminders or assets in your hypothetical portfolios or in your IRA/Keogh portfolios. Assets in retirement portfolios generally are meant to be long-term investments that don't have to be watched as closely as the assets in other portfolios.

If you own options, then you can tell the program how many days in advance to alert you that your options are going to expire.

Finally, you can select whether you want the financial reminders to appear automatically the first time you use the Portfolio Manager module.

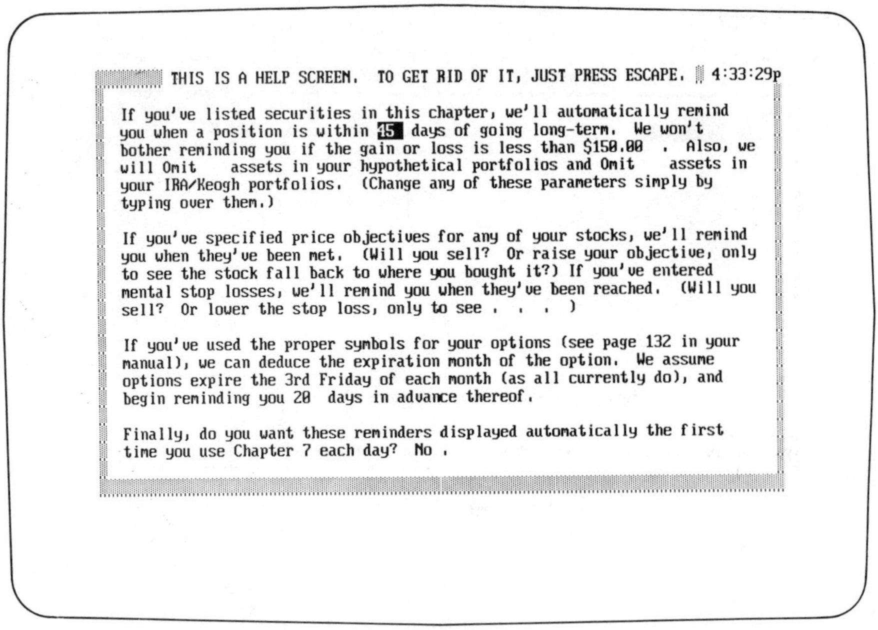

```
▓▓▓▓▓▓ THIS IS A HELP SCREEN.  TO GET RID OF IT, JUST PRESS ESCAPE. ▓ 4:33:29p

  If you've listed securities in this chapter, we'll automatically remind
  you when a position is within ▓45▓ days of going long-term.  We won't
  bother reminding you if the gain or loss is less than $150.00 .  Also, we
  will Omit   assets in your hypothetical portfolios and Omit   assets in
  your IRA/Keogh portfolios.  (Change any of these parameters simply by
  typing over them.)

  If you've specified price objectives for any of your stocks, we'll remind
  you when they've been met.  (Will you sell?  Or raise your objective, only
  to see the stock fall back to where you bought it?) If you've entered
  mental stop losses, we'll remind you when they've been reached.  (Will you
  sell?  Or lower the stop loss, only to see . . . )

  If you've used the proper symbols for your options (see page 132 in your
  manual), we can deduce the expiration month of the option.  We assume
  options expire the 3rd Friday of each month (as all currently do), and
  begin reminding you 20  days in advance thereof.

  Finally, do you want these reminders displayed automatically the first
  time you use Chapter 7 each day?  No .
```

Fig. 8.43. The Help screen for altering reminder criteria.

Press ESCape again to return to the Financial Reminders screen.

You can use the program to display several kinds of reminders on the Financial Reminders screen. When you add assets to a portfolio, you can enter a stop loss or a price objective for the investment. (These concepts were discussed earlier in this chapter.) The Financial Reminder screen alerts you when your investment has reached your specified price objective or when it has dropped to your mental stop loss.

An important money management concept is to stick with the limits that you set when you made your investment. If you decided when you began that you did not want to lose more than a certain amount on the investment and it has lost that amount, then drop the investment and take the loss. Don't let the investment drag you down with it. The same concept applies for your stated price objective: Don't get greedy. If the price of the investment hits your target, then get out and take your gain, or you may watch the price fall below your original purchase price.

None of this advice means that you should ignore new information. For example, if you have invested in a company whose earnings have been growing, then maybe you should raise your price objective as well. Or if the company was hit by a strike in the last quarter but the stock price has leveled off after plummeting to your stop loss level, then maybe you should hold on a while longer. In general, stick to your original decision if you have no new information. After all, what goes up *does* come down.

Notice that from the Financial Reminders screen, you can print reminders to your printer, to the computer screen, or to a disk. From the Financial Reminders screen, press F10-Back Up to Mini Menu.

Accounting for Stock Splits

From the Mini Menu, select F5-Splits to display the screen shown in figure 8.44. This screen lists the symbols for each of your assets in your portfolios. From this list, you select the asset to be split.

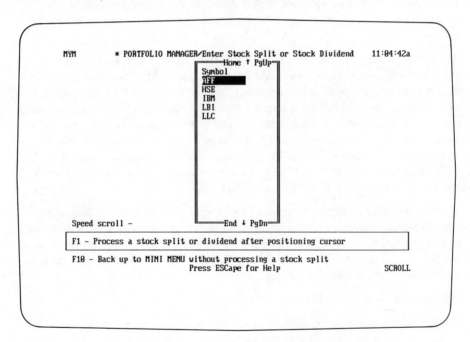

Fig. 8.44. Stocks listed for splits or stock dividends.

Many investors are confused about the meaning of stock splits and stock dividends, although the concept is actually quite simple. Suppose that a company you have invested in has 1 million shares of its stock outstanding in the marketplace. If the stock currently trades for $80 per share, then the market values the company at $80 million, and your 100 shares are worth $8,000. The board of directors of the company may decide that the price of the stock is too high for an average investor to buy 100 shares (the usual minimum number of shares purchased). Therefore, the board splits each outstanding share.

After a board resolution, all the shareholders are asked to turn in their shares and to receive 2 shares of the new stock for every share turned in. Two million shares of the stock would then be outstanding and you would hold 200 shares instead of the 100 shares you originally bought.

Have you made any money on the transaction? No. The price of the stock on that 2-for-1 stock split should drop to half the original price or $40 per share. Your 200 shares would still be worth $8,000 and the company would still be worth $80 million.

A stock split can be compared to dividing a pizza into more slices. If you cut a pizza into 10 slices instead of 6, you don't have a larger pizza. You have more slices, but each slice represents a smaller percentage of the entire pizza.

Then what is the purpose of a stock split? The answer has something to do with investor psychology. You could have bought half the number of shares at the higher stock price just mentioned. A lower stock price, however, enables more people to buy a larger number of shares. For some reason, after a 2-for-1 (or any other) stock split, the stock price often does not go down quite as far as it should mathematically. Basically, investors believe that managements split stock when the prospects for the future are favorable. This belief can become a self-fulfilling prophecy, at least in relation to the stock price, because stock prices often rise after a split.

A stock dividend is similar to a small stock split. For example, a board of directors may announce that a stock dividend of 10 percent will be paid on a certain date. This means that for every 10 shares of stock that you hold, you are given an extra share. If you had bought 100 shares, then you would have 110 shares. The stock price should drop accordingly.

To perform a stock split:

1. On the Enter Stock Split or Stock Dividend screen, position the cursor at any one of the stocks in your portfolio.

2. Press F1 to process the stock split.

   Your screen should look similar to figure 8.45. The screen asks you how many shares you are receiving for each share you own and whether you are receiving fractional shares. If you end up with a fractional number of shares (for example, a 10 percent stock dividend for your 25 shares), then the company usually pays cash for the fractional share. If the company intends to issue a fractional share instead, then enter No. Otherwise, enter Yes.

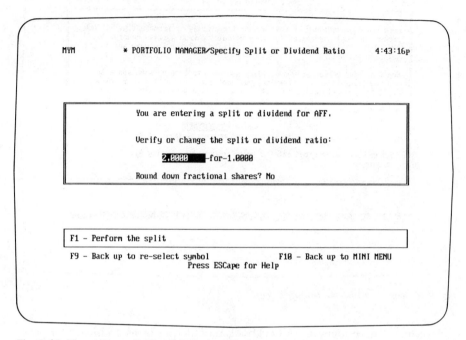

Fig. 8.45. The split or dividend ratio specified.

3. Press F1 to perform a 2-for-1 stock split on the asset that you selected.

    Although you have twice as many shares of the stock as you had before the split, the current price probably will have fallen to about half the pre-split price.

    Your screen should now display the Portfolio Manager's Mini Menu.

Portfolio Archiving

From the Mini Menu, select F6-Archive (Temporarily or Permanently) to display the screen shown in figure 8.46.

Archiving was described in detail in Chapter 5, "Using the Budget and Checkbook." Permanent archiving frees some of the computer's memory by removing closed-out transactions from the current files and storing them in

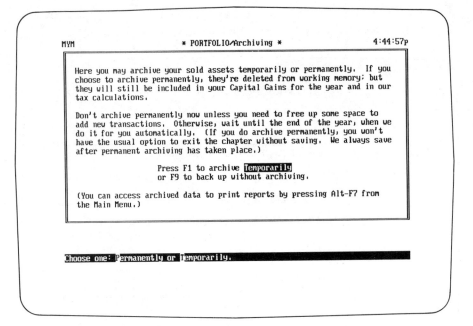

```
MYM                    * PORTFOLIO/Archiving *              4:44:57p

    ┌──────────────────────────────────────────────────────────────┐
    │ Here you may archive your sold assets temporarily or permanently.  If you │
    │ choose to archive permanently, they're deleted from working memory; but   │
    │ they will still be included in your Capital Gains for the year and in our │
    │ tax calculations.                                              │
    │                                                                │
    │ Don't archive permanently now unless you need to free up some space to    │
    │ add new transactions.  Otherwise, wait until the end of the year, when we │
    │ do it for you automatically.  (If you do archive permanently, you won't   │
    │ have the usual option to exit the chapter without saving.  We always save │
    │ after permanent archiving has taken place.)                    │
    │                                                                │
    │               Press F1 to archive Temporarily                  │
    │               or F9 to back up without archiving.              │
    │                                                                │
    │ (You can access archived data to print reports by pressing Alt-F7 from    │
    │ the Main Menu.)                                                │
    └──────────────────────────────────────────────────────────────┘


    Choose one: Permanently or Temporarily.
```

Fig. 8.46. The Portfolio Archiving screen.

archive files. The Budget and Checkbook module performs archiving for you automatically every time you reconcile your checkbook.

In the Portfolio Manager module, the program tells you when you are running out of working memory. In that case, you can permanently archive the asset you have sold in the current year. Do not archive permanently until you start to run out of memory, because changing data or making corrections is more difficult after permanent archiving is performed.

Archiving Temporarily

Temporary archiving in the Portfolio Manager module combines archived and unarchived transactions and then prints reports containing the data. If no permanent archiving has been performed during the year, you still can perform temporary archiving and then print reports for the unarchived data. Versions 3.0 and 4.0 of Managing Your Money can temporarily archive from the Portfolio Manager module without exiting the program to DOS.

To archive temporarily:

1. On the Portfolio Manager's Archiving screen, make sure that the blank says Temporarily.

2. Press F1.

You will return automatically to the Portfolio Manager's Mini Menu.

3. You can exit the module either by saving the changes you have made in the last session or by deleting the changes.

If you don't want to lose your own data that you entered and later deleted when you first began the Portfolio Manager tutorial, press F10-Exit Chapter and then press F1-Exit Without Saving. Press **Y** to verify your decision to exit without saving. The figures entered in the tutorial will be lost, of course, but your own data will reappear.

If you did not enter your own data, then exit either with or without saving. Press F10 and then press F1 and **Y** or F10 and F5.

You should return automatically to the Main Menu.

4. From the Main Menu, press Alt-F7 to display the screen shown in figure 8.47.

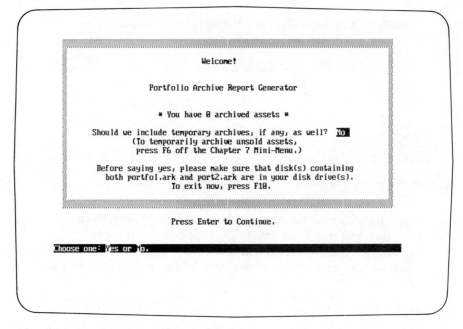

Fig. 8.47. The Portfolio Archive Report Generator.

You probably have **0** archived transactions. The screen asks whether you want your temporary archives included in the report as well. If

you answer Yes, then all assets that were sold but left unarchived
will be included; otherwise, only the archived transactions (if any)
will be included in the report.

5. Type **Y** (for Yes) to include unarchived transactions.

6. Press Enter to continue.

   Your screen should look similar to figure 8.48.

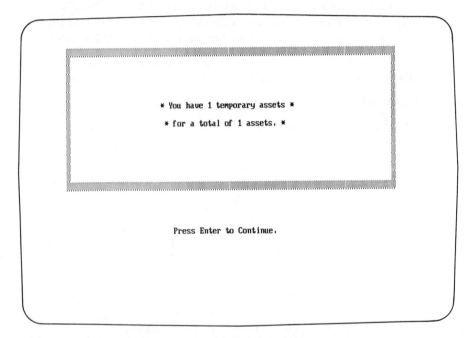

* You have 1 temporary assets *
* for a total of 1 assets. *

Press Enter to Continue.

Fig. 8.48. The number of temporary and total assets displayed.

If you have entered no assets (either archived or unarchived) as
sold, then you will be unable to proceed because no data is
available for printing reports. In that case, return to this screen after
you have sold some assets. If you have sold some assets, then you
may continue.

7. Press Enter to continue.

   Your screen should look similar to figure 8.49.

8. Select the portfolios you want to include in the report, the asset
   names in those portfolios, and the asset types.

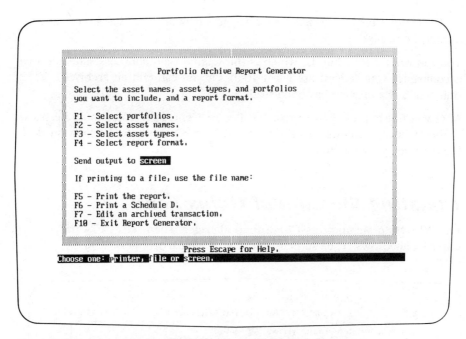

Fig. 8.49. The asset and report format selection screen.

An asset must meet all three of the selection criteria in order to make its way into the report. If you select, for example, the Charles Squat portfolio and include the names of all the assets sold from this portfolio but don't check the common stocks under the asset type, then none of the common stocks sold are included in the report. Remember that the only assets printed are those from the chosen portfolio that have a selected name and a selected type.

Your next task is to design your report. That procedure is described in the next section.

Designing Reports

On the Portfolio Archive Report Generator screen, function F4 allows you to choose the report format. Try a few to see their differences. You can save customized reports so that you can return and use them later. After you design a report, insert a file name into the blank that says

```
Name of file for custom report format:
```

Begin the file name with the letter of the drive where you are sending the file, and then add a colon and the name that you select (for example,

C:CUSTOM). After you design a report, you can send it to the screen, to a printer, or to disk.

You can print a Schedule D, which is the Capital Gain and Loss schedule that accompanies your federal tax Form 1040. Or you can edit an archived transaction if a mistake has been made.

After you finish, press F10 to exit the Report Generator. You should be back at the Main Menu. Return to the Portfolio Manager module to take a quick look at two other functions.

Updating the Capital Gains Laws

From the Main Menu, press F7-Portfolio Manager. Then select F7-Change Capital Gains Laws. Your screen should look similar to figure 8.50.

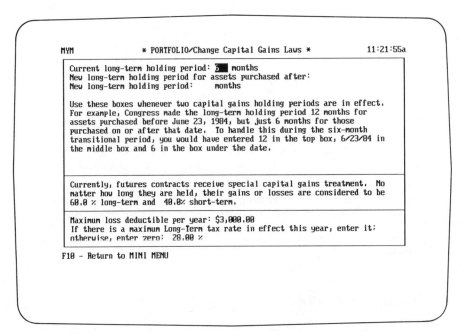

Fig. 8.50. The Change Capital Gains Laws screen.

This function is designed to help you keep the program current with changes in the tax law. For 1986 and 1987, the long-term capital gain holding period remains at 6 months. Beginning in 1988, no difference will exist between the short-term and the long-term capital gains in the tax rates; therefore, for

1988 calculations, you should enter **0** percent in the bottom blank for Long Term tax rate in effect. For 1987, the maximum long-term rate will be 28 percent.

Press F10 to return to the Portfolio Manager's Mini Menu.

Viewing This Year's Dividends

From the Mini Menu, press F8-View This Year's Dividends to display the screen shown in figure 8.51.

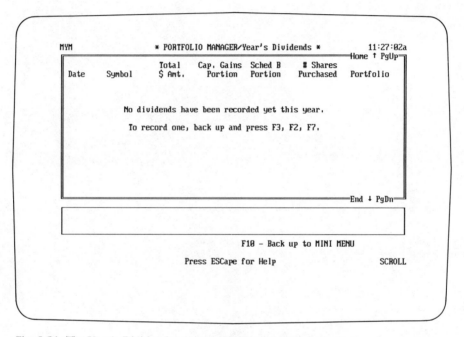

Fig. 8.51. The Year's Dividends screen with no dividends recorded.

You can sort your dividends by date, symbol, or other criteria and print a listing of the dividends received. That capability is helpful at the end of the year when you want to verify that you received all the dividends that you are entitled to. If your broker holds your shares of stock, then the dividends are sent to the brokerage. If your broker accidentally deposits your dividends in the wrong account, then using this function will help you identify the problem.

If you have finished using the Portfolio Manager's features, you now can exit the module. Remember, if you had some personal data in the program before you started the tutorial, then exit the Portfolio Manager without saving your work. Otherwise, you may elect to save or not save as you wish.

You now have had at least a glimpse of all the features in the Portfolio Manager Module. Use the reports you have worked on in the tutorial. Although you may be uncomfortable at first, eventually you will be able to move quickly through the module. Improvements in your investment results should soon be obvious. With Managing Your Money, you can bring your investment strategy in line with your goals and, hopefully, avoid any potentially disastrous results.

## Chapter 9

Analyzing Your Net Worth

Net worth is an amalgamation of everything a person owns (assets) and everything a person owes (liabilities). *Assets* include such things as cash, investments, houses, furnishings, cars, and many other items. *Liabilities* include the mortgage on a house, amounts owed on credit cards, student loans, car loans, and anything owed to anyone else. To calculate your net worth, first you add the dollar amount of all your assets, and then you add the dollar amount of all your liabilities. Next, you subtract the total liabilities from the total assets. The remaining figure is your net worth. A positive number indicates that you own more than you owe.

The Your Net Worth module of Managing Your Money calculates and helps you track your net worth. Much of the necessary data for the net worth calculation does not need to be reentered into this module because it is extracted automatically from data you enter in the other modules. For example, the cash balances that you own and the loans that you owe are entered from the Budget and Checkbook (module 3); your stocks, bonds, and IRA/Keogh portfolios are entered from the Portfolio Manager (module 7); and the cash surrender value of your life insurance is entered from Insurance Planning (module 5).

After your net worth is calculated, the program can print the details in a format known as a *personal balance sheet*. A personal balance sheet displays your assets, liabilities, and net worth. Bankers often require you to have a personal balance sheet when you apply for a business or personal loan. Versions 3.0 and 4.0 have two balance sheet formats: bank style and corporate style. The program also includes the original format provided in the previous versions of the program. The original format allows you to select the level of detail that you want included in the balance sheet. In this module, you also can graph your assets and liabilities, provided that your computer has graphing capabilities.

271

The Net Worth module is organized into a series of levels. You enter the module at the top level, which is your net worth. You move down one level to see the two components—assets and liabilities. You move down further to see the components of your assets and your liabilities. You keep moving down to see the components, if any, of a particular asset or liability.

For example, after moving down to the level where your summer home is listed at an aggregate value of $176,500, you could then move down one level to see the components of that figure (assuming that you had previously entered them). The total may be composed of the house itself, the furnishings in the house, and the swimming pool. You may have entered specific furnishings, or a total may have been sufficient. In this module, you can decide the level of detail that you require for your personal record keeping.

Now that you have an idea of how the module is organized, you are ready to track your net worth. From the Main Menu, press F8-Your Net Worth to display the screen shown in figure 9.1. If you have deleted any of the sample data, then the aggregate net worth displayed on your screen will differ from the amount shown in the figure. If you are running the program on a one- or two-disk system, the program will prompt you to insert Disk 3. You need to insert that disk before you can proceed.

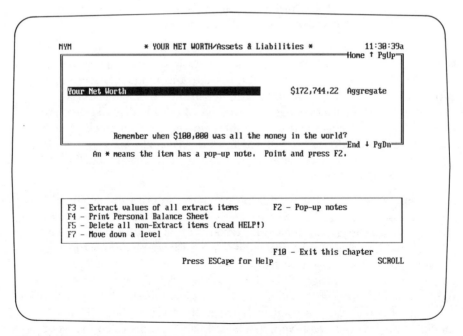

Fig. 9.1. The top level of the Your Net Worth module.

The aggregate net worth value is composed of all the assets and liabilities that are currently in memory. The value can't be changed at this level because it is an aggregate number—a number that can be changed only by changing the value of an underlying asset or liability. As you move down the levels, notice that you cannot change the value of any asset or liability that is composed of items at a lower level. The word Aggregate, which appears in the right-hand column after these assets and liabilities, indicates that they have components at a lower level. You must always reach the lowest level for a particular aggregate asset or liability and change the value before the values at each higher level will change accordingly. Move the cursor to the net worth value and notice that the program will not let you change the amount.

Notice that at this or any of the other levels, you can enter the Wordprocessor by pressing F2. Once in the Wordprocessor, you can add a narrative description of the assets or liabilities.

Press F7 to move down a level. Your screen should look similar to figure 9.2. Two numbers are displayed here. Subtract the aggregate liabilities from the aggregate assets to obtain the net worth figure that was displayed at the top level.

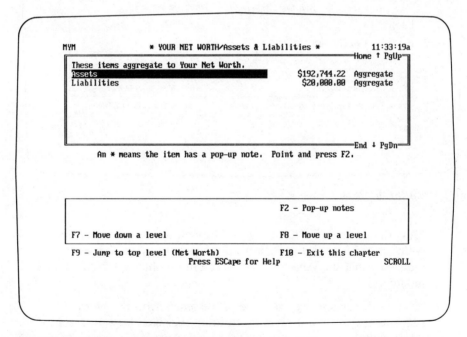

Fig. 9.2. The assets and liabilities that make up net worth.

Reviewing Your Assets and Liabilities

To review your assets and liabilities, you have to move down another level.

To view your assets:

1. On the Assets & Liabilities screen, position the cursor at Assets.

2. Press F7-Move Down a Level.

    The screen should look similar to figure 9.3.

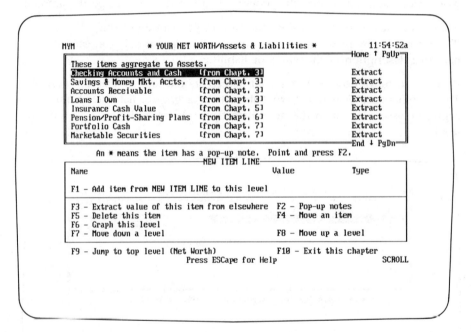

Fig. 9.3. A list of assets.

3. Press the down-arrow key to scroll through the list of assets. See which assets have in the right-hand column the word Extract, indicating that the value for that asset can be obtained from another module.

4. Position the cursor over any one of the assets with the word Extract next to it and press F3 to bring the value forward from the other module.

The assets that have the word Aggregate next to them are composed of assets listed at a lower level or levels. If the sample data is still in the program, notice that Household Inventory is an aggregate asset.

Press the F6 key to graph the various assets at this level as shown in figure 9.4. Your graph may differ if you have deleted any of the sample data or if you didn't extract all the asset values from the other modules. The pie graph in the figure indicates a total asset value of $503,103. In addition, the graph illustrates the breakdown of the other assets and the percentage, in terms of value, that each represents of the total assets.

Note: You will not be able to print graphs to your printer unless a graphing program was loaded into memory before entering the Managing Your Money program. See Chapter 12 for instructions on loading a graphing program.

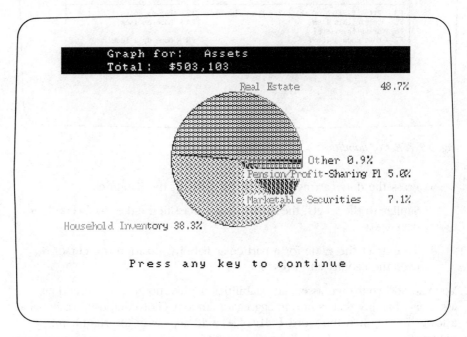

Fig. 9.4. A graph of assets.

Press any key to return to the list of assets. Then press F8 to back up to the Assets and Liabilities level.

To view your liabilities:

1. On the Assets & Liabilities screen, position the cursor at Liabilities.

2. Press F7-Move Down a Level to display the various liabilities that make up the aggregate liability (see fig. 9.5).

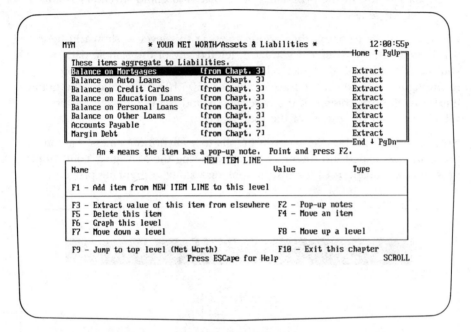

```
MYM                  * YOUR NET WORTH/Assets & Liabilities *          12:00:55p
                                                                ─Home ↑ PgUp─
 ┌──These items aggregate to Liabilities.─────────────────────────────────
 │Balance on Mortgages          [from Chapt. 3]             Extract
 │Balance on Auto Loans         [from Chapt. 3]             Extract
 │Balance on Credit Cards       [from Chapt. 3]             Extract
 │Balance on Education Loans    [from Chapt. 3]             Extract
 │Balance on Personal Loans     [from Chapt. 3]             Extract
 │Balance on Other Loans        [from Chapt. 3]             Extract
 │Accounts Payable              [from Chapt. 3]             Extract
 │Margin Debt                   [from Chapt. 7]             Extract
 │                                                              ─End ↓ PgDn─
      An * means the item has a pop-up note.  Point and press F2.
 ┌───────────────────────────NEW ITEM LINE───────────────────────────
 │Name                                   Value            Type
 │
 │F1 - Add item from NEW ITEM LINE to this level
 ├────────────────────────────────────────────────────────────────────
 │F3 - Extract value of this item from elsewhere  F2 - Pop-up notes
 │F5 - Delete this item                           F4 - Move an item
 │F6 - Graph this level
 │F7 - Move down a level                          F8 - Move up a level
 └────────────────────────────────────────────────────────────────────
     F9 - Jump to top level (Net Worth)          F10 - Exit this chapter
                    Press ESCape for Help                        SCROLL
```

Fig. 9.5. A list of liabilities.

3. Press the down-arrow key to scroll through the liabilities.

   Similar to the assets, the liabilities are classified either as Extract or Aggregate.

4. To extract the value for a particular liability, position the cursor over the liability and press F3.

You can add your own assets and liabilities in this module. If you add an asset or a liability that is not an aggregate amount (not composed of items at a lower level), then the word Individual will appear in the right-hand column.

You can override an amount that has been extracted from another module by typing a new value over the amount and pressing Enter. Keep in mind, however, that the amount in the other module does not change.

Now that you have an idea of how the Your Net Worth module is organized, you can delete the sample data and then enter some data of your own.

To delete the sample data:

1. Press F8 as many times as necessary to return to the top level of the module (see fig. 9.1).

2. Press F5 to delete all non-extract items below assets and liabilities.

3. Press F1 to verify that you want to delete those amounts.

   This step deletes the sample data that was entered directly into the Your Net Worth module, but does not delete the sample data extracted from the other modules.

4. To delete data extracted from the other modules, position the cursor at each of the assets and liabilities individually and use the space bar to blank out the amount or to enter your own amount.

To add an asset (or liability) to your net worth:

1. From the top level of the Your Net Worth Module, press F7 to move down a level.

2. Position the cursor at Assets (or Liabilities) and press F7 again.

3. Press the Enter key to move the cursor down to the New Item Line.

4. Enter the name of the item: **Garage Contents** and press Enter.

5. Enter the value: **775** (for $775) and press Enter.

6. Type **A** (for Aggregate) to list the contents of the garage.

   Your screen should look like figure 9.6.

7. Press F1-Add Item from New Item Line to This Level.

   The item will be added, and the cursor will move to the top of the screen.

8. Hold the Enter key down or use the down-arrow key to position the cursor at the new item—Garage Contents (see fig. 9.7).

9. Press F7 to move down a level (see fig. 9.8).

   The cursor should be on the New Item Line.

10. Add the various contents of the garage, as follows:

    Name: **Lawnmower** and press Enter.

    Value: **400** and press Enter.

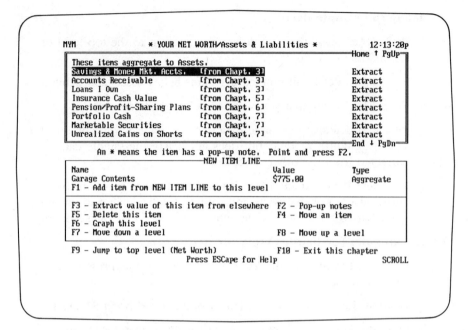

Fig. 9.6. "Garage Contents" entered as an asset.

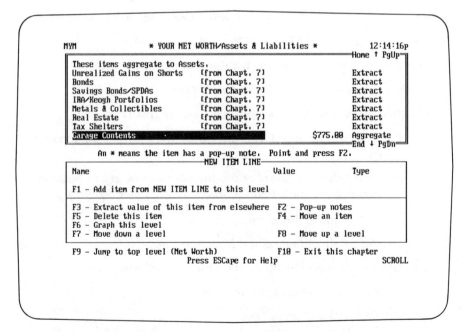

Fig. 9.7. "Garage Contents" added to the list of assets.

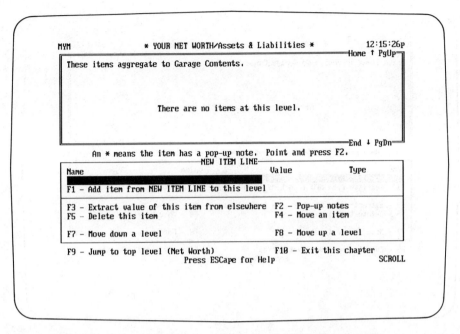

Fig. 9.8. The New Items Line ready to receive items within the contents of the garage.

Type: **I** (for Individual, because you are not going to go to any lower levels).

Compare your screen to figure 9.9.

11. Press F1 to add the lawnmower (see fig. 9.10).

12. Press the Enter key to move the cursor to the New Item Line.

13. Add a $15 rake, and then press F1 (see fig. 9.11).

14. Add spare tires that are worth $100 and miscellaneous items worth $260.

    After you have recorded all the contents of your garage and the value of the items, your screen should look like figure 9.12.

By now, you should be comfortable entering your own financial data. To calculate your net worth, you can either work with each of the other modules and then extract all possible items, or (if you are in a hurry) you can enter your data directly into this module.

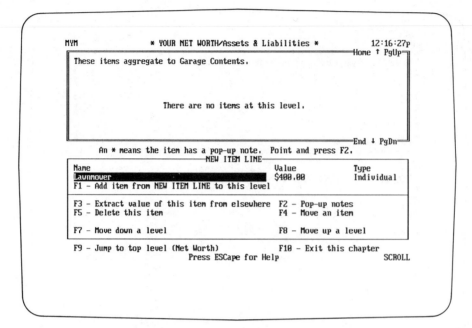

Fig. 9.9. A lawnmower being added as part of the garage contents.

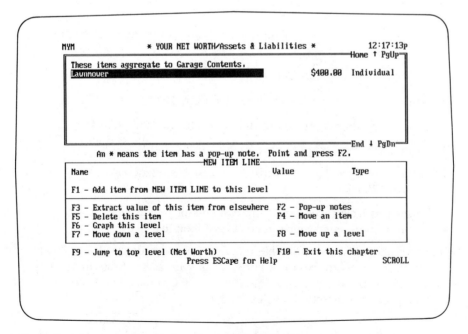

Fig. 9.10. A lawnmower added to the garage contents.

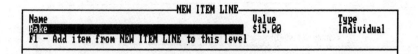

Fig. 9.11. A rake added to the garage contents.

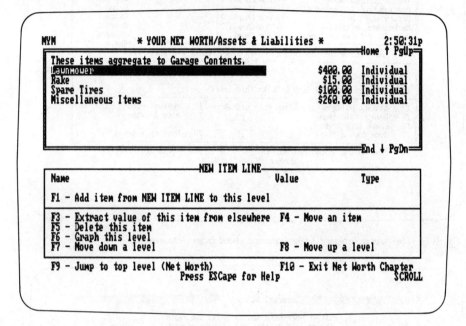

Fig. 9.12. The total contents of the garage.

Printing Balance Sheets

After you have entered all your personal data, you can print a copy of your personal balance sheet. Before you move back to the top level of the module, however, you may want to do a little housekeeping.

To remove the phrase [from Chapt.] from the screens so that it doesn't appear on your printed balance sheet, position the cursor at each of the assets and then the liabilities in succession. Use the right-arrow key to move the blinking underline to the position where the notation begins. Press the space bar to blank out the unwanted language (see fig. 9.13).

After you complete this step, back up to the top level of the Net Worth module and press F4-Print Personal Balance Sheet (see fig. 9.14).

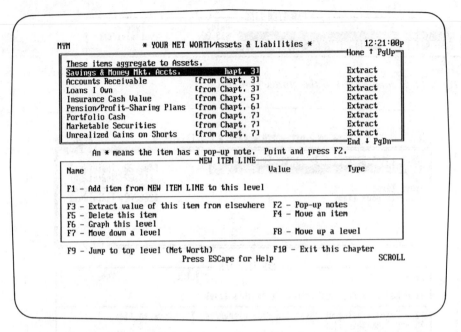

Fig. 9.13. The presentation of the balance sheet being cleaned up.

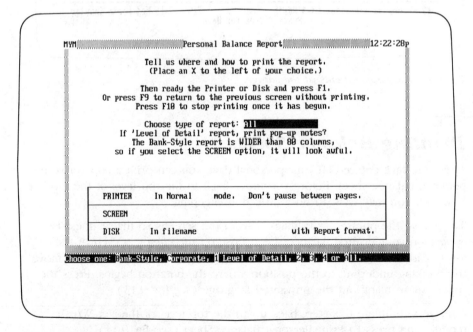

Fig. 9.14. The screen for selecting printing options for the personal balance sheet.

Some new printing options are available in the program. In addition to printing to your printer, you can now print also to the screen or to a file on a disk. Printing to a printer can be in either the normal or compressed printing mode. For balance sheets wider than 80 columns, you might want to use compressed printing unless you have wide paper in your printer. (Note that not all printers will print in the compressed mode.)

In addition to the original style, there are two other styles of balance sheets: a *corporate style*, which lists the assets on top and the liabilities and the net worth below, and a *bank style*, which lists the assets on the left side and the liabilities and net worth on the right side.

You can modify the original balance sheet based on the level of detail you want to include.

Try all the printing options to see which you like best. To begin, type **X** in the box beside `Printer`, `Screen`, or `Disk`. Then press F1 to print your balance sheet in the selected format.

If you don't want to enter your personal financial data now, press the F10 key to exit the Net Worth module and save your most recent changes.

## Chapter 10

Using the Income Tax Estimator

If you have picked up a newspaper, turned on a television, or attended a party during the past couple of years, you probably have heard some discussion about the new tax law. The changes made in the Internal Revenue Code by the Tax Reform Act of 1986 represent the most comprehensive overhaul of the tax system in more than 30 years.

If you were confused about how to save money on your taxes before the Tax Reform Act of 1986, then you certainly need help now. Contrary to the publicized reports about the recent simplification of the tax code, the new tax law is anything but simple. Although rates were slashed from a top personal rate of 50 percent to a top personal rate of 28 percent (or 33 percent for some taxpayers) and the corporate tax rate was reduced from a top rate of 46 percent to 34 percent, the changes are just the tip of a huge iceberg. These changes will affect you in ways that you barely can begin to realize.

The new tax system naturally will produce both winners and losers as well as taxpayers who will not be affected by the changes. In addition, potential winners who are unaware of beneficial changes probably will be sorry. You can't become a tax expert overnight, but you would be wise to gain a basic understanding of some of the changes in the law that are most likely to affect your future financial planning. Read this chapter carefully and use the Tax

Planning module of Managing Your Money to learn about the changes and make more informed investment decisions.

An Overview of the Tax Changes

This discussion about the changes in the tax law covers only a small portion of the changes made by the Tax Reform Act of 1986. Depending on your financial situation, other changes can affect your tax planning significantly. Although this book does not provide a complete explanation of the tax law, the book provides the basic information necessary for planning your finances.

Individual Rate Reductions

The cornerstone of the entire tax reform effort is the reduction of individual tax rates. The reform movement began with a flat-tax proposal by Bill Bradley, a senator from New Jersey, and slowly evolved into the complicated piece of tax legislation that ultimately was passed by Congress. An across-the-board reduction in tax rates gave tax reform the initial push and broad support necessary for it to become law. Although rates actually were cut, the law is more complicated than taxpayers generally were led to believe.

The lower tax rates promised by Congress do not take full effect until 1988. As a result, some of your 1987 income may be taxed at rates that are not much lower than the rates paid on your 1986 income. The 1987 tax rates will range from 11 percent to 38.5 percent, and will include 15 percent, 28 percent, and 35 percent rates along the way. Those rates compare with 15 taxable income brackets in 1986, which ranged from a low of 11 percent to a high of 50 percent.

In 1988, a maximum 28 percent tax rate will go into effect with a 15 percent tax rate for lower taxable incomes. However, the 28 percent "top" rate is deceiving. The new law actually includes 4 tax brackets—15 percent, 28 percent, 33 percent, and 28 percent again—instead of only the 2 tax brackets that many people believed were included.

How did the confusion arise? Congress says that it promised a 28 percent *average effective rate*. The 33 percent rate on a portion of some taxpayers' incomes offsets the benefits of the 15 percent rate for those who have incomes above a certain level. Therefore, a taxpayer may pay tax at the 15 percent rate on a portion of income, at the 28 percent rate on another portion of income, and finally at the 33 percent rate on the remaining income. In total, however, the amount of tax paid will never exceed 28 percent of a taxpayer's total income.

As a logical consequence of the rate reductions, all tax deductions are worth less now than they were before tax reform. Some wise investments that incorporated a tax savings from depreciation or other deductions at the 50 percent tax rate may be real losers under the new tax structure. The new tax law means that investments made and strategies pursued before the 1986 tax law changes may be unwise investments today.

The new rate reductions would have been impossible without other changes in the tax law. To lower the rates and avoid increased budget deficits, both the corporate and the individual income tax bases were broadened. Various tax benefits and other preferences that existed under the old law were eliminated.

Increased Capital Gains Taxes

In terms of personal financial planning, the single most sweeping change in the tax law revision is the elimination of preferential treatment of capital gains for individual taxpayers. The old law required individuals to include in their income only 40 percent of their long-term capital gains, which resulted in a maximum 20 percent tax on such gains. For some taxpayers, depending on their other sources of income, the rate was much lower than 20 percent. Beginning in 1988, the maximum rate on both long-term and short-term capital gains will be 28 percent.

Before the most recent tax reform, financial planners and other tax advisers spent the major portion of their income tax planning time arranging financial affairs in order to take advantage of the preferential capital gains rates. The new law has taken much of the emphasis away from capital gains. Under the new law, an investment that generates ordinary income may be more attractive than one that yields an equal amount of capital gain, because of lower risk involved in the first investment.

Elimination of IRA Deduction

The $2,000 deduction for an IRA investment (or $4,000 if both spouses worked) is significantly curtailed by the new tax law. Beginning in 1987, if neither you nor your spouse is covered by a corporate pension or a profit-sharing plan, then you qualify for an IRA deduction regardless of your income level. If either of you is covered by such a corporate plan, then (depending on your income) only part and maybe none of your IRA investment is deductible.

An estimated 25 percent of all taxpayers no longer can deduct IRA contributions from their taxes. Economically, however, making a nondeductible contribution to an IRA may still be wise, because the earnings on the money invested will continue to accumulate tax free under the new law. New to Version 4.0 is the capability, in the Financial Calculator module, to determine whether making a nondeductible IRA contribution makes sense.

Curtailment of 401(k) Salary Deduction Plans

Beginning in 1987, employees who have taken advantage of company sponsored 401(k) salary deduction plans are limited to an annual deduction of $7,000 instead of $30,000 under the old tax law.

Elimination or Reduction of Certain Individual Itemized Deductions

The elimination of many individual and business deductions by the Tax Reform Act of 1986 is the principal method used to fund the lower overall tax rates. If the deductions were not eliminated, then the lowering of rates would cause federal deficits far worse than the current ones. The enacted law preserves the deduction of state and local income taxes but eliminates the deduction for state and local sales taxes.

Most types of interest expense deductions will be phased out during a five-year period. Certain types of interest, however, remain fully deductible. Here is a description of the changes:

State and Local Sales Tax: Beginning in 1987, the amount of state and local sales taxes you have paid is no longer deductible. No amount of tax planning can lessen the effects of this change. If you live in a state that has a high income tax, you are fortunate that Congress did not change the deduction for state and local income and property taxes. Both deductions were in danger of being eliminated during the early congressional negotiating process, but both were ultimately retained as valid deductions.

Interest Expense: Prior to 1987, individual taxpayers could deduct all interest paid as an itemized deduction regardless of the source of the debt. Some types of interest remain deductible, but others will be completely phased out by 1991. Taxpayers simply should identify the interest that remains deductible and assume that all other types of interest will be phased out.

The deductible interest on the debt taken out to purchase a taxpayer's principal residence or second residence will be limited to the purchase price of the home plus the cost of improvements. A complicated exception to this rule provides that the home mortgage interest on debt in excess of the purchase price of the home and the cost of improvements, but not greater than the fair market value of the home, is deductible if the proceeds of the loan are used to pay for educational or medical expenses of the taxpayer or the taxpayer's dependents. The Internal Revenue Service may have trouble monitoring this exception because of the difficulty of tracing loan proceeds to medical or educational expenses.

By 1991, the deduction for interest on consumer debt (such as interest on credit cards, student loans, car loans, and other loans not secured by principal or second residence) will not be deductible. In 1987, 65 percent of such interest will be allowed as a deduction; in 1988, 40 percent; in 1989, 20 percent; and in 1990, 10 percent.

One type of interest that will remain deductible is interest on debt from the purchase of investments. For example, if you borrow money to buy stocks, then the interest on that loan still is deductible, but only in an amount up to the investment income that you report for the year. Investment income includes interest, dividends, and gains from sales of investments. As in the past, interest on debt from the purchase of tax-exempt securities is not deductible.

Charitable Contributions: Beginning in 1987, you cannot deduct your charitable contributions if you do not itemize deductions on your tax return. If you itemize, then your contributions are deductible. Because of the lower tax rates, however, your after-tax cost of giving will be higher. Also, if you give appreciated property to a charity, then the difference between the asset's current value and its original cost to you is included as a preference item in the new alternative minimum tax. *Preference items* are certain valid deductions, specified under the tax code, that are added back to your tax base in order to calculate the alternative minimum tax. If you take advantage of too many of these specified deductions, then you may find yourself paying additional tax under the alternative minimum tax.

Medical Expenses: Unless you have substantial medical expenses and no insurance to cover the costs, you probably will get no tax relief from medical expenses. Beginning in 1987, you can deduct only the unreimbursed medical costs that exceed 7.5 percent of your adjusted gross income.

Cutback in Employee Business Expenses and Other Miscellaneous Deductions

Beginning in 1987, only a portion of employee business expenses and other miscellaneous deductions are deductible. You can deduct only the amount that exceeds 2 percent of your adjusted gross income. This category includes fees for tax and investment advice, educational expenses, subscriptions to professional journals, and union and professional dues.

Business Meals and Entertainment

You may be in for a shock if you have become accustomed to having the government subsidize many of your restaurant meals and other entertainment related to your trade or business. Under the old law, if you were in the top tax bracket, Uncle Sam paid 50 percent of these valid business expenses, leaving you with the remaining 50 percent of the cost. Under the new law, only 80 percent of such expenses are deductible. Furthermore, this reduced deduction will save you less in taxes as a result of the lower rates. Therefore, by 1988, you will pay almost 78 percent of the cost of such meals instead of 50 percent.

Tax Shelters

Because of the new law, most tax shelters are not as attractive as they once were. Most investors have used tax shelters to deduct losses from their investments (generally created by depreciation or other non-cash expenditures) against income from other sources. For example, a doctor could deduct losses from his investment in a real estate limited partnership against earnings from his medical practice.

The Tax Reform Act ends the use of the *passive loss* deduction against ordinary income. This deduction has been greatly abused during the past decade. Passive losses occur when investors are not *material participants* in the operation of the rental properties or other ventures in which they have invested. For example, a doctor who invests in a real estate limited partnership as a limited partner who has no involvement in the operation of the real estate cannot deduct losses from the investment against medical practice earnings. The doctor can offset losses from the real estate investment or from any other passive investments against income from passive investments. An exception is made for taxpayers who actively participate in the operation of rental real estate. They can offset income from other sources against losses of up to $25,000 from the rental activity, depending on the level of their income from other sources.

Shifting Income

For many years, taxpayers have been able to save on taxes by transferring income-producing assets to taxpayers in a lower tax bracket (either by gift or by sale). For example, parents frequently transferred assets to their children. The assets then grew at a faster rate because a smaller tax bite was taken from the earnings each year.

Beginning in 1987, if a child less than 14 years old has unearned annual income that exceeds $1,000, then the amount is taxed to the child at the parent's top marginal tax rate instead of at the child's tax rate. The provision virtually eliminates the benefit of such income shifting. Parents still may shift assets to their children for other reasons, but the situation must be more carefully analyzed now.

An Overview of the Income Tax Estimator Module

The relatively sophisticated Income Tax Estimator module of the Managing Your Money program allows you to calculate the taxes you would owe in various scenarios. In other words, you can perform "what if" analyses. What if I take the bonus this year instead of next year? What if I sell the stock next year instead of today? What if I get married before the end of the year, or divorced? Minimizing your taxes should be a financial planning priority. Experiment with the countless combinations in order to determine the amount of tax you will ultimately owe.

The program does not print an actual tax return, although it provides the necessary information for filing Form 1040 and all its supporting schedules. The information is printed for each of the various tax return schedules, but not in a manner that is acceptable for filing purposes. When you file your return, either you or your accountant must transfer the final income and expense figures to the appropriate IRS forms.

If your accountant uses the Fast-Tax® program for preparing your return, then Managing Your Money formats your data in a compatible manner. Therefore, at the end of the year, you can give your accountant a floppy disk that contains the information about your return instead of a shoe box full of data. Save time and possibly money by eliminating the need for your accountant to enter the information into a computer manually.

With the Income Tax Estimator, you can print the following information and schedules:

1. The information required for the Form 1040 tax return (including the calculation of your tax liability under the regular tax and the alternative minimum tax)

2. Schedule A for calculating itemized deductions

3. Schedule B for calculating interest and dividend income

4. Schedule C for calculating the profit or loss from a business or profession

5. Schedule D for calculating gains and losses from the sale of capital assets

6. Schedule E for accounting for supplemental income (income or loss from partnerships, trusts, subchapter-S corporations, and other such entities)

7. Schedule F if you have farm income or expense

Version 4.0 of Managing Your Money was designed to help you prepare not
only your 1987 tax return but also (because of its capability to update the
program easily) to incorporate the tax changes in the law for 1988 and
beyond. Updating the program to accommodate future tax changes is covered
in this chapter's tutorial.

Getting Started

Use the Income Tax Estimator tutorial to start planning for this year's taxes
and to find ways to save on your tax bill. From the Main Menu, press
F4-Income Tax Estimator (see fig. 10.1). Notice that this module does not
have a Mini Menu. All of the module's operations center around the Form
1040 screen, which essentially summarizes all the schedules that comprise a
Form 1040 tax return.

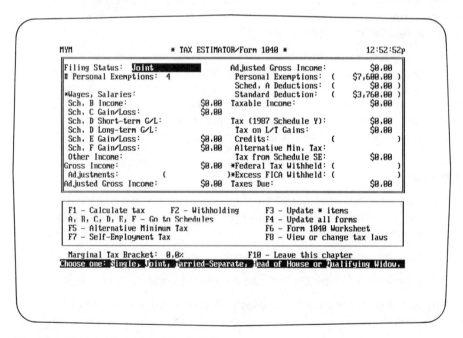

Fig. 10.1. The Tax Estimator/Form 1040 screen.

If you have not worked with the Income Tax Estimator module yet, then all
the blanks on the screen except the Personal Exemptions blank should
contain zeros. If you have already entered your own data into the program

and don't want to lose the information, then you can choose either of the following options:

1. Print each of the schedules to your printer before placing zeros in the blanks. When you complete the tutorial, you can reenter the data from the printouts into the Income Tax Estimator.

2. You can change any of the figures in the schedules as you proceed with the tutorial, but remember to exit the Income Tax Estimator module *without* saving your changes. Although your data is erased from the screen, the information remains in the computer's memory and is restored when you exit the tax module. If you choose this option, you still might want to make printouts of your schedules so that you can be assured that you won't lose your data.

You do not have to be a tax expert to estimate your income taxes in this module, but you must have a basic understanding of the components of your income and the deductions to which you are entitled. In addition to reading this chapter, review an old copy of a tax return that you have filed with the Internal Revenue Service. You also may want to discuss some of the concepts with your tax adviser, if you have one. Once you understand the basics, you should have no trouble using the Income Tax Estimator to help you with your tax planning.

Understanding the Form 1040 Screen

Look at the Tax Estimator/Form 1040 screen. This screen is designed to follow the format of the actual Form 1040 that you file every year with the Internal Revenue Service.

The top of the left column is where you enter your filing status: single taxpayer, joint, or married-filing separate, for example. Next are the number of personal exemptions to be taken. You are entitled to one for yourself, one for your spouse, and one for each of your dependents. You cannot enter a dollar figure in the Personal Exemption blank. The amount of the exemption is calculated automatically based on the number of personal exemptions you enter. Further down are the income items that are part of total gross income. Next are the adjustments to gross income: the adjustment for employee business expenses, IRA deductions, and moving expenses. The Adjusted Gross Income, at the bottom of the column, is a key figure. Many limitations on deductions are calculated as a percentage of the adjusted gross income.

The right column begins with adjusted gross income, from which the personal exemption amount is deducted. The total of Schedule A deductions is listed next, including deductions for medical expenses and drugs, state and local income taxes, home mortgage interest, consumer interest, charitable contributions, and others. The Tax Reform Act of 1986 made significant changes in some of the allowable itemized deductions.

Any tax credits to which you are entitled are entered in the Credits blank, which follows. Alternative minimum tax is included in the next blank. That item is followed by self-employment tax, the amount of federal tax withheld from your paycheck plus estimated tax payments you have made, and credits from overpayment of FICA (Social Security) tax.

The program automatically calculates the amount of tax you would owe based on the figures you have entered and indicates in the bottom left corner of the screen your marginal tax bracket, which is the rate of tax that you pay on your last dollar of income or your highest tax bracket for the year. In 1987, the rates range from 11 percent to 38.5 percent; in 1988 and beyond, the range is from 15 percent to 33 percent and then back to 28 percent.

Keep in mind that the Form 1040 screen is a summary screen. Many other screens display the details for the summary amounts on Form 1040. For example, the Schedule B Income item shows the sum of total interest income and total dividend income. The Schedule A Deductions item shows the sum of all itemized deductions. Although you can enter the totals directly in the blanks on the Form 1040 screen without including the components of each total on the supporting screens, you generally should enter the detailed figures on the supporting screens and allow the program to bring the totals forward automatically.

Loading the Tax Rate Schedules

Even before you enter figures into Form 1040 or the other schedules, you need to set the program for your filing status and load the proper tax rate schedules into memory. The program was designed to accommodate the new tax law. You can load the tax rates for the appropriate year into the program and make other changes that are necessary to account for differences in the law from 1987 on.

This tutorial uses a hypothetical tax situation to help familiarize you with the terminology and the specific workings of this module. Begin by assuming that the hypothetical taxpayer is married and files a joint tax return. Also assume that the hypothetical taxpayer is going to plan for 1987.

To load the 1987 tax rate schedules:

1. On the Form 1040 screen, position the cursor at the Filing Status blank.

2. Type **J** (for joint).

3. Press F8-View or change tax laws to display the screen shown in figure 10.2.

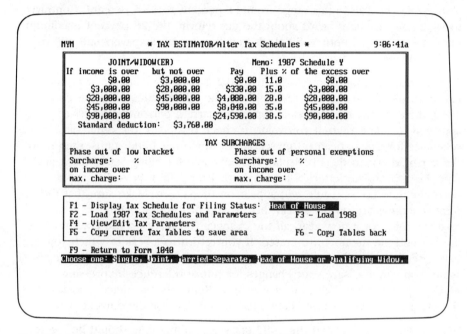

Fig. 10.2. *The screen for loading various years' tax laws.*

Before you do anything, notice the available options. You can display the Tax Schedules for another filing status, view or edit certain of the tax parameters that may change from year to year, copy the Tax Tables to a save area so that if you change them you can retrieve the originals, and you can load the 1988 tax laws into memory.

4. Now press F2-Load 1987 Tax Schedules and Parameters.

The developers of Managing Your Money have entered into the program the tax rate schedules and various other parameters for 1987 and 1988. After you load the proper year into the working memory of your computer, Managing Your Money uses the proper year's schedule to calculate the tax based on the income and deductions that you provide.

When you calculate your own taxes, verify that the rates in the program agree with the rates for that particular year. Compare the rates on the screen with those included with the forms you receive from the Internal Revenue Service. Check with your tax adviser if you have questions about the forms. Although the proper tax schedules are loaded into memory, you must verify that they are correct.

Notice that the 1987 rates range from 11 percent to 38.5 percent. Contrary to what you may have heard about the tax reform, the 28 percent maximum rate does not begin until 1988. And even then, some taxpayers still will pay tax at a 33 percent marginal rate.

The tax rate schedule shown in figure 10.2 is used by taxpayers who file joint returns. If you had entered Single in the Filing Status blank on Form 1040, then the tax rate schedule for an unmarried person would have appeared on the screen. If you want to check or update the other rate schedules for single, head of household, or any other filing status, then move the cursor down to the F1-Display Tax Schedule for Filing Status blank and type the appropriate letter (**S** for Single or **J** for Joint). Press F1, and the corresponding tax schedule will appear on the screen. Make sure that the Joint schedules are on the screen before you proceed. Remember, as you load the rules for a new year, all the changes you made to the tax laws that are currently in memory are erased. If you return to a year in which you have already made changes, then remember to make the necessary changes again. You can also save your changes for future reference by pressing F5-Copy Current Tax Tables to a save area. Remember to make changes in the program to keep it up-to-date with the tax law for the current year.

Because you have selected the 1987 tax year, no amounts should be listed in any of the Surcharge blanks. Surcharges do not go into effect until 1988. If you enter the 1988 tax rate schedules and then look at the tax surcharges, you can see a 5 percent surcharge for each filing status. The surcharge either reduces or eliminates the 15 percent tax rate for some taxpayers depending on their incomes. The surcharge also reduces the amount deductible for each personal exemption.

No changes to this schedule should be necessary for 1987 or 1988.

Changing Items Congress Likes To Change

Press F4-View/Edit Tax Parameters to display the screen shown in figure 10.3. This screen lists some of the tax law items that Congress has had a habit of changing over the years. The screen was designed so that you can use the latest tax law rules to quickly update the program. The figures for 1987 and 1988 are loaded into the program already, so you probably do not have to make changes for those years. Brief explanations of each of the displayed tax law items follow.

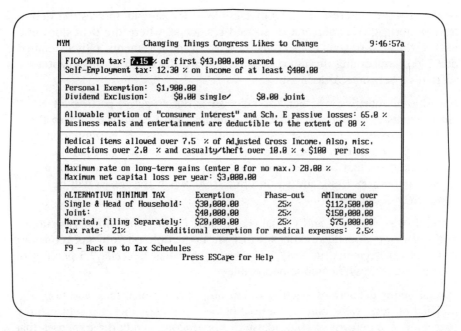

Fig. 10.3. A list of tax law items that Congress has changed over the years.

FICA/RRTA (Social Security) Tax: For 1987, an employee pays 7.15 percent of the first $43,800 earned, and the employer pays a matching amount. No Social Security is paid on amounts exceeding $43,800. A self-employed person pays 12.3 percent Social Security tax on any net income that is more than $400 but not greater than $43,800.

Personal Exemption Amount: The $1,900 that you are allowed to deduct from your gross income for each of your dependents in 1987 rises to $1,950 in 1988. Beginning in 1990, the amount will be adjusted upward for inflation.

Dividend Exclusion: Before 1987, married taxpayers had a $200 exclusion of qualifying dividends, and single taxpayers had a $100 exclusion. Beginning in 1987, the exclusion is eliminated.

Allowable Portion of Consumer Interest and Schedule E Passive Losses: Although most types of interest that you paid before 1987 were deductible as itemized deductions on your tax return, the Tax Reform Act has limited the itemized deduction to home mortgage and investment interest. Consumer interest is being phased out as a deductible item. Also, losses from passive investments, which had been fully deductible from your other earnings in previous years, will be phased out in the next few years.

Certain types of interest are fully deductible—for example, interest on debt from a mortgage on your first or second residence, where the debt does not exceed the cost of your house plus the cost of improvements. Other detailed provisions concerning the interest deduction are discussed in this chapter's section on Schedule A deductions.

Losses from activities in which the taxpayer is not an active participant (investments as a limited partner, for example) will be allowed only to the extent of passive income from such activities. The passive loss limitation rule is being phased in over a period of years. The 65 percent figure on the screen indicates that 65 percent of the losses will be allowed in 1987, a smaller amount in 1988, and so on until 1990, when the losses will be completely disallowed.

Medical, Miscellaneous, and Casualty and Theft Deductions: More reductions in the amount of medical expenses that are deductible on your tax return are taking place. Beginning in 1987, only the amount that exceeds 7.5 percent of your adjusted gross income is deductible.

Miscellaneous deductions, such as union dues, professional fees, and tax preparation fees, were fully deductible before 1987, but they are subject now to a floor of 2 percent of your adjusted gross income. Only the expenses that exceed the 2 percent floor are deductible.

The new law has not changed the deduction of losses from a casualty (generally a sudden, unforeseen event such as an earthquake, a lightning strike) or a theft. Only the amount of the loss that exceeds 10 percent of your adjusted gross income plus $100 per loss is deductible.

The Alternative Minimum Tax will now impact more taxpayers. This tax is designed to ensure that all taxpayers, even those with large deductions, pay their fair share of tax. There is an exemption amount that is phased out for higher income taxpayers. These rates and amounts should not require any adjustment for 1987 and 1988.

If no additional changes need to be made to the tax laws for 1987 or 1988, and if you have loaded the proper year into the computer's memory, then the program should be properly set.

Press F9-Back Up to Tax Schedules. Then press F9 again to return to Form 1040.

Entering Data into the Income Tax Estimator

Look at the following information about the hypothetical taxpayers. Then enter the information into the program by completing the steps in this section of the tutorial.

The taxpayers, Paul and Amy Smith, have the following tax data:

- Two children

- Paul has a $39,000 salary.

- Amy has a $46,000 salary.

- The Smiths expect to earn interest income of $1,400 from their money market account.

- They will receive $220 in dividends from their IBM stock.

- Paul operates from his home a small printing business in which he prepares flyers for local businesses. The business has not been very profitable, but Paul enjoys the work and he can deduct some of the restaurant meals he eats with customers. His relevant financial data for the business follows:

    Gross Receipts: $4,500

    Materials and Supplies: $1,750

    Entertainment: $375

    Depreciation: $175

    Insurance: $472

- The Smiths own 50 shares of IBM stock, purchased in 1976 at $52 per share. They also own 200 shares of Apple Computer purchased at $22 per share on January 23, 1986.

- Their itemized deductions:

    Real property taxes: $3,700

    Medical bills not reimbursed: $640

    Interest expense on credit cards: $1,650

    Interest expense on their house mortgage: $6,600

- The total federal withholding tax taken from their paychecks was $15,000.

To make sure that you have the proper tax schedules loaded into the computer's memory, quickly reload the 1987 tax rate schedules. Make sure that you are at the Tax Estimator/Form 1040 screen.

1. Press F8-View or change tax laws.

2. Press F2-Load 1987 Tax Schedules and Parameters.

3. Press F9-Return to Form 1040.

You should be ready to enter the data into the Form 1040 screen (see fig. 10.4). Except for Personal Exemptions and Standard Deduction, the screen should display zeros in all the blanks.

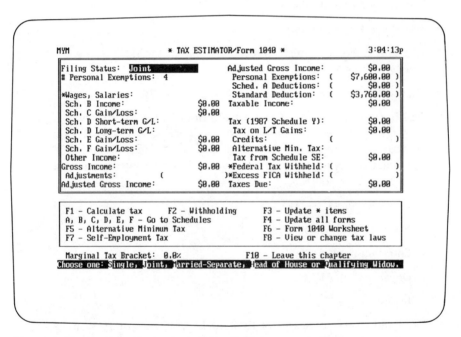

Fig. 10.4. The Form 1040 screen with 1987 tax laws loaded.

To complete the basic information on the Form 1040 screen:

1. Filing Status: The hypothetical taxpayers are married and intend to file a joint tax return, so make sure that the Filing Status item at the top left says Joint. If it doesn't, then position the cursor at the blank and type **J**. (As in the other modules of the program, you move the cursor by pressing either the arrow keys or the Enter key.)

2. # Personal Exemptions: The Smiths have two children and are entitled to four personal exemptions—one for each spouse and one for each of their children. If the number in the Personal Exemptions blank is not 4, position the cursor at the blank, type 4, and then press Enter.

3. Salary: Because both Paul and Amy work, enter the total of their two salaries in the blank. Together, the Smiths earn $85,000 in salary ($39,000 + $46,000). Position the cursor at the appropriate blank, type **85000** (for $85,000), and press Enter. (Remember to omit dollar signs and commas.)

4. Schedule B Income: You must file this schedule with your tax return if you have dividend or interest income that exceeds $400. The Smiths expect interest income of $1,400 and dividend income of $220. You can enter either the $1,620 total amount in the Schedule B Income blank on the Tax Estimator/Form 1040 screen or the detailed amounts in the Schedule B screen (see the detailed steps in the next section).

Completing Schedule B

From the Tax Estimator/Form 1040 screen, type **B** to go to the Schedule B screen shown in figure 10.5. Look at the options. You can either enter actual or estimated amounts directly into the blanks or retrieve budgeted amounts that were entered into the Budget and Checkbook module. If you use the F3 key to retrieve the budgeted amounts from module 3, then the amounts entered in the blanks are the sum of your actual receipts up to this month, the greater of this month's actual or budgeted amounts, and budgeted amounts for the remainder of the year. For this example, instead of retrieving the amounts from module 3, you will enter the actual amounts for the Smiths. Notice that you can move directly to any of the other tax schedules by pressing the letter of that schedule. Note also any tax exempt interest that you may have.

To complete Schedule B:

1. On the Schedule B screen, position the cursor at the Interest Income blank, type **1400** (for $1,400), and press Enter.

2. At the Dividend Income blank, type **220** (for $220), and press Enter.

   The total is calculated automatically, as shown in figure 10.6.

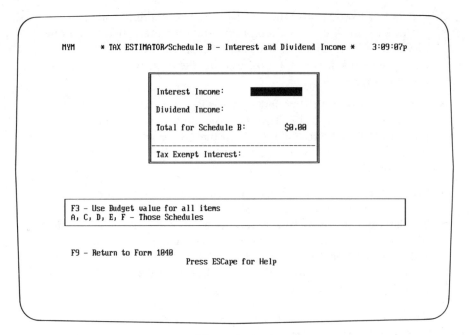

```
   MYM      * TAX ESTIMATOR/Schedule B - Interest and Dividend Income *    3:09:07p


                    ┌──────────────────────────────────────────┐
                    │ Interest Income:        ████████          │
                    │                                           │
                    │ Dividend Income:                          │
                    │                                           │
                    │ Total for Schedule B:      $0.00          │
                    │                                           │
                    │ ----------------------------------------- │
                    │ Tax Exempt Interest:                      │
                    └──────────────────────────────────────────┘


        ┌────────────────────────────────────────────────────────────────┐
        │ F3 - Use Budget value for all items                              │
        │ A, C, D, E, F - Those Schedules                                  │
        └────────────────────────────────────────────────────────────────┘


          F9 - Return to Form 1040
                              Press ESCape for Help
```

Fig. 10.5. The Schedule B – Interest and Dividend Income screen.

3. Press F9 to return to the Form 1040 screen.

    The Schedule B Income blank is updated to reflect the total of the
    dividend and interest income (see fig. 10.7).

Completing Schedule C

Paul's printing business is operated as a sole proprietorship and is included in
Schedule C (Profit or Loss from a Business or Profession). To enter the data
for his business, type **C** for Schedule C to display the screen shown in figure
10.8. If the screen does not look like this one but instead shows Part II-
Deductions for Schedule C, then press F1 to flip to the other side of the
form.

As in all the supporting schedules, complete only those blanks that apply to
you and leave the remaining blanks empty. Also, if you use the function keys
that retrieve your budget values, then the blanks are filled with the sum of
the actual expenses up to the preceding month, the greater of the budgeted
or actual amounts for the current month, and the budgeted amounts through
the end of the year.

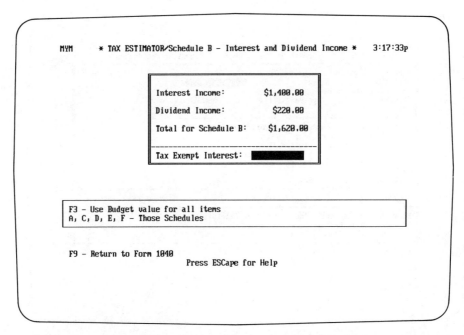

```
MYM          * TAX ESTIMATOR/Schedule B - Interest and Dividend Income *    3:17:33p


               Interest Income:        $1,400.00

               Dividend Income:          $220.00

               Total for Schedule B:   $1,620.00
               ─────────────────────────────────────
               Tax Exempt Interest: ████████████



          F3 - Use Budget value for all items
          A, C, D, E, F - Those Schedules



          F9 - Return to Form 1040
                        Press ESCape for Help
```

Fig. 10.6. The Smiths' interest and dividend income total calculated.

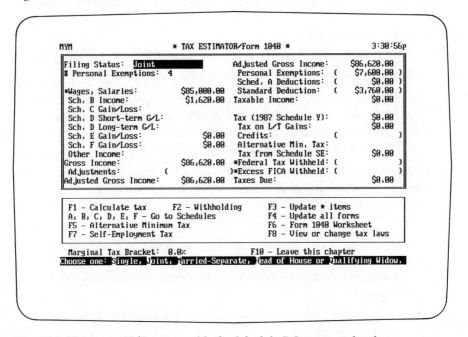

```
MYM                      * TAX ESTIMATOR/Form 1040 *              3:30:56p

Filing Status: Joint            Adjusted Gross Income:     $86,620.00
# Personal Exemptions:  4           Personal Exemptions: (   $7,600.00 )
                                    Sched. A Deductions: (       $0.00 )
*Wages, Salaries:       $85,000.00  Standard Deduction:  (   $3,760.00 )
Sch. B Income:           $1,620.00  Taxable Income:              $0.00
Sch. C Gain/Loss:
Sch. D Short-term G/L:              Tax (1987 Schedule Y):       $0.00
Sch. D Long-term G/L:               Tax on L/T Gains:            $0.00
Sch. E Gain/Loss:           $0.00   Credits:             (              )
Sch. F Gain/Loss:           $0.00   Alternative Min. Tax:
Other Income:                       Tax from Schedule SE:        $0.00
Gross Income:          $86,620.00  *Federal Tax Withheld: (              )
Adjustments:        (          )*Excess FICA Withheld: (              )
Adjusted Gross Income: $86,620.00   Taxes Due:                   $0.00

 F1 - Calculate tax      F2 - Withholding    F3 - Update * items
 A, B, C, D, E, F - Go to Schedules          F4 - Update all forms
 F5 - Alternative Minimum Tax                F6 - Form 1040 Worksheet
 F7 - Self-Employment Tax                    F8 - View or change tax laws

 Marginal Tax Bracket: 0.0%                  F10 - Leave this chapter
Choose one: Single, Joint, Married-Separate, Head of House or Qualifying Widow.
```

Fig. 10.7. The Form 1040 screen with the Schedule B Income updated.

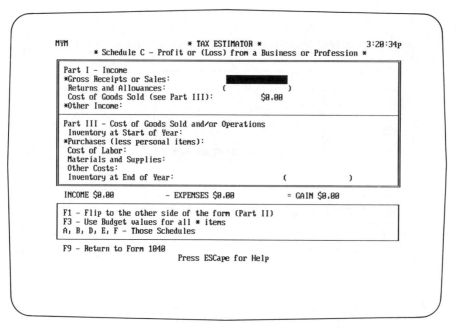

```
MYM                        * TAX ESTIMATOR *                    3:20:34p
          * Schedule C - Profit or (Loss) from a Business or Profession *
 ┌─────────────────────────────────────────────────────────────────────┐
 │ Part I - Income                                                       │
 │ *Gross Receipts or Sales:              ███████████████                │
 │  Returns and Allowances:             (                )               │
 │  Cost of Goods Sold (see Part III):        $0.00                      │
 │ *Other Income:                                                        │
 │                                                                       │
 │ Part III - Cost of Goods Sold and/or Operations                       │
 │  Inventory at Start of Year:                                          │
 │ *Purchases (less personal items):                                     │
 │  Cost of Labor:                                                       │
 │  Materials and Supplies:                                              │
 │  Other Costs:                                                         │
 │  Inventory at End of Year:                   (              )          │
 ├─────────────────────────────────────────────────────────────────────┤
 │ INCOME $0.00          - EXPENSES $0.00            = GAIN $0.00         │
 ├─────────────────────────────────────────────────────────────────────┤
 │ F1 - Flip to the other side of the form (Part II)                     │
 │ F3 - Use Budget values for all * items                                │
 │ A, B, D, E, F - Those Schedules                                       │
 └─────────────────────────────────────────────────────────────────────┘
    F9 - Return to Form 1040
                        Press ESCape for Help
```

Fig. 10.8. Parts I and III of Schedule C - Profit or Loss.

To complete Schedule C:

1. On the Schedule C screen, position the cursor at the Gross Receipts or Sales blank, type **4500** (for $4,500), and press Enter.

2. To enter the Cost of Goods Sold, move the cursor down to Part III-Cost of Goods Sold and/or Operations. Position the cursor at the Materials and Supplies blank. The taxpayer had $1,750 in expenses for this category. Type **1750** and press the Enter key.

   The Cost of Goods Sold (as a reduction of the gross receipts) is entered automatically in Part I. Total Income is entered automatically as INCOME at the bottom of the screen (see fig. 10.9).

   The remaining blanks on this screen do not apply to Paul Smith's situation. He had no returns or allowances and does not maintain any inventories. Next, you will enter the operating expenses for Paul's business.

3. Press F1 to flip to the deductions section of Schedule C (see fig. 10.10).

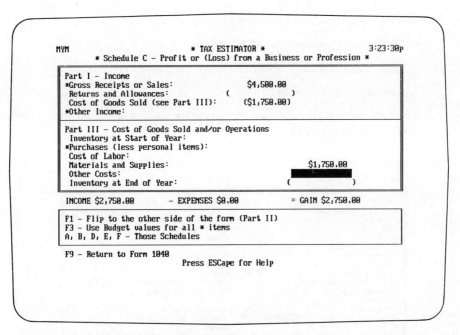

Fig. 10.9. The Cost of Goods Sold entered.

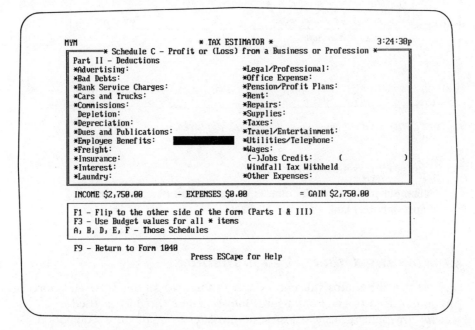

Fig. 10.10. Part II of Schedule C.

4. Enter the expense amounts as follows:

Travel/Entertainment: **375** (for $375)

Depreciation: **175** (for $175)

Insurance: **472** (for $472)

The taxpayer's total expenses are automatically displayed on the screen (see fig. 10.11).

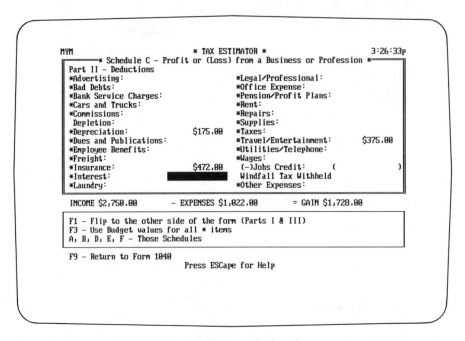

```
MYM                              * TAX ESTIMATOR *                        3:26:33p
      ┌─* Schedule C - Profit or (Loss) from a Business or Profession *─┐
      │ Part II - Deductions                                            │
      │ *Advertising:                     *Legal/Professional:          │
      │ *Bad Debts:                       *Office Expense:              │
      │ *Bank Service Charges:            *Pension/Profit Plans:        │
      │ *Cars and Trucks:                 *Rent:                        │
      │ *Commissions:                     *Repairs:                     │
      │  Depletion:                       *Supplies:                    │
      │ *Depreciation:         $175.00    *Taxes:                       │
      │ *Dues and Publications:           *Travel/Entertainment:  $375.00│
      │ *Employee Benefits:               *Utilities/Telephone:         │
      │ *Freight:                         *Wages:                       │
      │ *Insurance:            $472.00    (-)Jobs Credit:      (        )│
      │ *Interest:            ██████████    Windfall Tax Withheld        │
      │ *Laundry:                         *Other Expenses:              │
      │                                                                 │
      │  INCOME $2,750.00     - EXPENSES $1,022.00     = GAIN $1,728.00  │
      ├─────────────────────────────────────────────────────────────────┤
      │  F1 - Flip to the other side of the form (Parts I & III)        │
      │  F3 - Use Budget values for all * items                         │
      │  A, B, D, E, F - Those Schedules                                │
      └─────────────────────────────────────────────────────────────────┘
          F9 - Return to Form 1040
                            Press ESCape for Help
```

Fig. 10.11. The total of Schedule C deductions displayed.

5. Press F9 to return to Form 1040.

The Schedule C net income is retrieved and placed in the appropriate blank (see fig. 10.12).

Completing Other 1040 Schedules

Suppose that the Smiths will not sell any of their stocks this year. Therefore, you do not need to enter any figures into Schedule D, which is used to account for capital gains and losses. Return later to modify this assumption after you calculate the tax without any sales of stock.

```
MYM                    * TAX ESTIMATOR/Form 1040 *              3:31:40p
┌─────────────────────────────────────────────────────────────────────┐
│Filing Status: Joint           Adjusted Gross Income:      $88,348.00  │
│# Personal Exemptions:  4        Personal Exemptions: (    $7,600.00 ) │
│                                 Sched. A Deductions: (        $0.00 ) │
│*Wages, Salaries:      $85,000.00 Standard Deduction: (    $3,760.00 ) │
│ Sch. B Income:         $1,620.00 Taxable Income:         $76,988.00   │
│ Sch. C Gain/Loss:      $1,728.00                                      │
│ Sch. D Short-term G/L:           Tax (1987 Schedule Y):   $20,035.00  │
│ Sch. D Long-term G/L:            Tax on L/T Gains:            $0.00    │
│ Sch. E Gain/Loss:         $0.00  Credits:             (            )  │
│ Sch. F Gain/Loss:         $0.00  Alternative Min. Tax:              │
│ Other Income:                    Tax from Schedule SE:       $0.00    │
│Gross Income:          $88,348.00 *Federal Tax Withheld: (          )  │
│Adjustments:          (         ) )*Excess FICA Withheld: (         )  │
│Adjusted Gross Income: $88,348.00 Taxes Due:              $20,035.00  │
└─────────────────────────────────────────────────────────────────────┘
┌─────────────────────────────────────────────────────────────────────┐
│ F1 - Calculate tax       F2 - Withholding     F3 - Update * items     │
│ A, B, C, D, E, F - Go to Schedules            F4 - Update all forms   │
│ F5 - Alternative Minimum Tax                  F6 - Form 1040 Worksheet│
│ F7 - Self-Employment Tax                      F8 - View or change tax laws│
└─────────────────────────────────────────────────────────────────────┘
  Marginal Tax Bracket: 35.0%            F10 - Leave this chapter
 Choose one: Single, Joint, Married-Separate, Head of House or Qualifying Widow.
```

Fig. 10.12. The Form 1040 screen with the Schedule C Income updated.

None of the remaining income schedules applies to the Smiths. Schedule E shows income or loss from rental properties, Subchapter-S corporations, partnerships, and trusts. Usually, you can determine whether any of your income must be reported on Schedule E by looking at your tax return from the preceding year. If you acquired a new investment in the current year, then you may need to use the schedule this year, of course, even if you didn't need it last year.

Schedule F is necessary only if you have an investment in a farm or in livestock.

On the Form 1040 screen, look at the Gross Income for the Smiths. Move the cursor to the column on the right of the Form 1040 screen. The Personal Exemption amount is filled in automatically based on the number of personal exemptions you entered earlier. Taxpayers are allowed $1,900 per exemption for 1987 with a reduction for high-income taxpayers. The Smiths have 4 personal exemptions; therefore, the amount displayed for Personal Exemptions should be $7,600.

Entering Schedule A Deductions

In this section of the tutorial, you will enter the Smith's Schedule A deductions. Type **A** for Schedule A to display the screen shown in figure 10.13. Schedule A is used to record a taxpayer's itemized deductions, which include state and local income taxes, medical expenses, interest expenses, real property taxes, and several others.

```
MYM             * TAX ESTIMATOR/Schedule A - Itemized Deductions *       3:36:09p

  *Medicine and drugs:          $0.00  *Misc. deductions:
  *Medical/Dental expenses:             Employee Bus. Expenses:
   Total Medical:            $0.00       Total Misc.:             $0.00
   Less Floor Amount:    $6,626.10       Less Floor Amount:   $1,766.96
   Allowable medical:        $0.00       Allowable misc.:         $0.00

  *Consumer interest:                   Casualty/Theft losses:
   Times Limitation Percentage:  x .65   Less Floor Amount:   $8,934.00
   Allowable interest:       $0.00       Allowable casualty:      $0.00

  *State and local taxes:               Investment interest:
  *Home mortgage interest:              Moving expenses:
  *Charitable contributions:            Other miscellaneous:

       Total Deductions LESS Standard Deduction = Itemized Deductions
            $0.00              $3,760.00              $0.00

  F1 - Employee expenses worksheet     F2 - Investment interest worksheet
  F3 - Use Budget values for * items   F4 - Moving expenses worksheet
  B, C, D, E, F - Those Schedules

  F9 - Return to Form 1040
                          Press ESCape for Help
```

Fig. 10.13. The Schedule A/Itemized Deductions screen.

The F3 function key of Schedule A allows you to retrieve the budget values that you may have entered into the Budget and Checkbook module of the program. In this tutorial, however, you will insert the data manually into the schedules.

To enter the Smiths' itemized deductions:

1. On the Schedule A screen, position the cursor at the Other Medical & Dental Expenses blank.

2. Enter the itemized deductions as follows:

   Medical/Dental Expenses: **640** (for $640)

   Consumer Interest (Credit Cards): **1650** (for $1,650)

   State and Local (Property) Taxes: **3700** (for $3,700)

Home Mortgage Interest: **6600** (for $6,600)

Compare your screen to figure 10.14.

```
MYM              * TAX ESTIMATOR/Schedule A - Itemized Deductions *       3:40:18p
  ┌──────────────────────────────────────────────────────────────────────────┐
  │ *Medicine and drugs:        $0.00    *Misc. deductions:                    │
  │ *Medical/Dental expenses:   $640.00   Employee Bus. Expenses:              │
  │  Total Medical:             $640.00   Total Misc.:              $0.00       │
  │  Less Floor Amount:      $6,626.10    Less Floor Amount:    $1,766.96       │
  │  Allowable medical:         $0.00     Allowable misc.:          $0.00       │
  │                                                                            │
  │ *Consumer interest:       $1,650.00   Casualty/Theft losses:               │
  │  Times Limitation Percentage: x .65   Less Floor Amount:    $8,934.00       │
  │  Allowable interest:      $1,072.50   Allowable casualty:       $0.00       │
  │                                                                            │
  │ *State and local taxes:   $3,700.00   Investment interest:      $0.00       │
  │ *Home mortgage interest:  $6,600.00   Moving expenses:          $0.00       │
  │ *Charitable contributions:            Other miscellaneous:                 │
  │                                                                            │
  │     Total Deductions LESS Standard Deduction = Itemized Deductions         │
  │        $11,372.50              $3,760.00              $7,612.50             │
  │                                                                            │
  │ F1 - Employee expenses worksheet      F2 - Investment interest worksheet   │
  │ F3 - Use Budget values for * items    F4 - Moving expenses worksheet       │
  │ B, C, D, E, F - Those Schedules                                            │
  └──────────────────────────────────────────────────────────────────────────┘
  F9 - Return to Form 1040
                          Press ESCape for Help
```

Fig. 10.14. The Smiths' Schedule A deductions entered.

Tax Law Changes That the Program Calculates

The Income Tax Estimator automatically incorporates most of the relevant provisions of the tax law into the calculation of the total itemized deductions, although you must have some additional knowledge of the law. When you first entered this module of the program, you loaded the tax law for 1987 and verified that the areas of the tax law that Congress has traditionally changed were up-to-date.

Notice that the total of the itemized deductions that you have entered into Schedule A does not equal the Total Deductions on the screen. What accounts for the difference?

First of all, medical and dental expenses for 1987 are deductible only after they exceed 7.5 percent of a taxpayer's adjusted gross income. Form 1040 shows that the Smiths' adjusted gross income is approximately $88,000; therefore, only medical and dental expenses that exceed 7.5 percent of $88,000 (or $6,600) are deductible. The Smiths' medical expenses were $640 and therefore are not deductible. Obviously, if you have any form of medical insurance to cover medical bills, the new tax law probably permits you no tax benefit from your medical expenses.

Another reason for the difference between the sum of the itemized deductions and the total deductions shown on Schedule A is the new tax law's phaseout of interest deductions for interest on debt that is not from a taxpayer's first or second residence. Before 1987, taxpayers could deduct all interest that they paid on credit cards, automobile loans, and a variety of other debts. In 1987, only 65 percent of the interest on consumer-type loans is deductible. The percentage drops to 40 percent in 1988, to 20 percent in 1989, and to 10 percent in 1990. After that, such interest is not deductible. The program considers this information and disallows 35 percent of the $1,650 Other Interest Paid that you entered for the Smiths. The amount accounts for the remainder of the difference between the itemized deductions that you entered and the total of such deductions.

Tax Law Changes That You Enter Manually

You have read about the changes in the tax law that the program calculates automatically. This section covers the information that you must enter into the program manually.

The Tax Reform Act distinguishes between consumer interest and interest on the debt from the purchase of a first or second residence. Although the consumer interest deduction is being phased out between 1987 and 1990, home mortgage interest remains deductible within certain limits. The program does consider this distinction by automatically calculating the limits for Consumer Interest and calculating the full deduction for Home Mortgage Interest. The problem is that for some taxpayers, their home mortgage interest may not be deductible in full.

Interest on the debt from either a taxpayer's principal or second residence is fully deductible if the debt does not exceed the amount of the purchase price of the residence plus the cost of home improvements. If the debt is greater than this cost, then the interest on the debt that exceeds that amount is not deductible unless the extra borrowed amount is used to pay for medical or educational expenses of the taxpayer or the taxpayer's dependents.

The complicated new law will be difficult for the government to administer. The law states that you can deduct interest on home mortgage loans where the loan amount does not exceed your cost plus the cost of improvements to the residence and the cost of any qualifying medical or educational expenses that you incur. If questioned, you will have the burden of establishing that the loan proceeds were used for the permitted purposes.

When you fill the Home Mortgage Interest blank on the Schedule A screen, you must first determine whether the interest is fully deductible, because the program cannot determine that for you. The program treats as deductible the full amount of home mortgage interest that you enter on this line.

The program does provide you with two worksheets designed to assist you with the complexities of the new tax law. F2-Investment Interest worksheet helps you to calculate the permissible deduction for investment interest. Under the new tax law, investment interest is deductible up to the amount of investment income that you earn for the year. Any excess can be carried over and deducted in a future year that you have investment income.

F4-Moving Expenses worksheet assists you in calculating the amount of moving expenses that you can deduct.

You now are finished with Schedule A. Press F9 to return to Form 1040. As you progress through the Form 1040 screen, the taxes due are calculated automatically based on the data entered up to that point (see fig. 10.15).

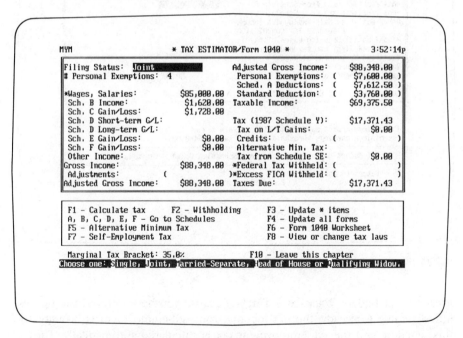

Fig. 10.15. The Smiths' Form 1040 with taxes due calculated.

Entering the Federal Tax Withholding

On the Form 1040 screen, enter the federal tax withholding amount that has been withheld from the hypothetical taxpayers' paychecks. Move the cursor to the Federal Tax Withheld blank, type **15000** (for $15,000), and press Enter.

Calculating Self-Employment Tax

Just as you must pay Social Security taxes on your earnings as an employee, you also must pay self-employment taxes on your net earnings if you are self-employed. Calculate the taxes that Paul Smith owes on his earnings from the printing business.

From the Form 1040, press F7-Self-Employment Tax to display the screen shown in figure 10.16.

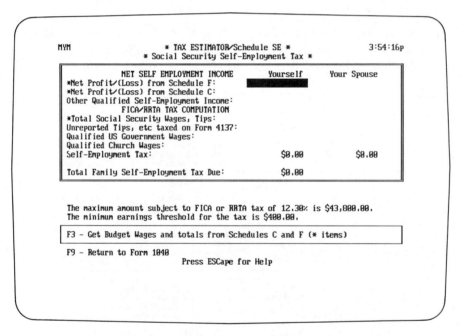

Fig. 10.16. The Schedule SE—Social Security Self-Employment Tax screen.

Press F3-Get Budget Wages and Totals. Because you have entered the figures into Schedule C already, the net income from self-employment is brought to this schedule and the self-employment tax is calculated automatically. The results are displayed on the screen shown in figure 10.17.

If a note begins to flash on the screen, indicating that your budgeted wages and FICA payments do not match the budgeted amounts from module 3, ignore it. The message is designed to alert you that the budget amounts that

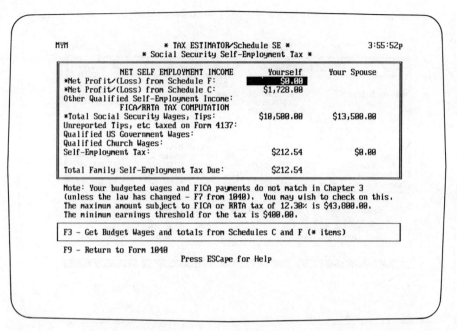

```
MYM                      * TAX ESTIMATOR/Schedule SE *              3:55:52p
                       * Social Security Self-Employment Tax *

            NET SELF EMPLOYMENT INCOME        Yourself      Your Spouse
*Net Profit/(Loss) from Schedule F:             $0.00
*Net Profit/(Loss) from Schedule C:          $1,728.00
Other Qualified Self-Employment Income:
          FICA/RRTA TAX COMPUTATION
*Total Social Security Wages, Tips:         $18,500.00      $13,500.00
Unreported Tips, etc taxed on Form 4137:
Qualified US Government Wages:
Qualified Church Wages:
Self-Employment Tax:                          $212.54          $0.00

Total Family Self-Employment Tax Due:         $212.54

Note: Your budgeted wages and FICA payments do not match in Chapter 3
(unless the law has changed - F7 from 1040).  You may wish to check on this.
The maximum amount subject to FICA or RRTA tax of 12.30% is $43,800.00.
The minimum earnings threshold for the tax is $400.00.

F3 - Get Budget Wages and totals from Schedules C and F (* items)

F9 - Return to Form 1040
                        Press ESCape for Help
```

Fig. 10.17. Paul Smith's self-employment tax displayed.

you may have set up in module 3 of the program are different from the ones in Schedule C that was prepared. For the hypothetical taxpayers, you simply did not conform your budgets to the amounts entered in Schedule C.

Press F9 to return to Form 1040 (see fig. 10.18). The only item still unchecked is whether the Alternative Minimum Tax applies to the Smiths.

Calculating the Alternative Minimum Tax

Although the Alternative Minimum Tax has been part of the tax system for a while, changes made by the Tax Reform Act of 1986 mean that the tax now will apply to more taxpayers. The minimum tax, as it is called, historically has affected high-income taxpayers who have taken advantage of large deductions or who have realized large long-term capital gains. The tax was designed to ensure that all taxpayers pay some amount of tax. Taxpayers with certain large deductions (such as accelerated depreciation or long-term capital gains—both classified as preference items) are required to add them back to their regular income. Special exemptions and deductions are then allowed, and the alternative minimum tax rate is applied to the modified income amount. If the alternative minimum tax is greater than the taxpayer's regular tax, then the alternative minimum tax must be paid.

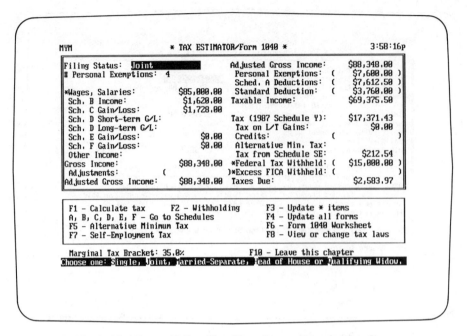

```
MYM                    * TAX ESTIMATOR/Form 1040 *                 3:58:16p

Filing Status:  Joint                Adjusted Gross Income:      $88,348.00
# Personal Exemptions:  4             Personal Exemptions:  (     $7,600.00 )
                                      Sch. A Deductions:    (     $7,612.50 )
*Wages, Salaries:         $85,000.00  Standard Deduction:   (     $3,760.00 )
  Sch. B Income:           $1,620.00  Taxable Income:            $69,375.50
  Sch. C Gain/Loss:        $1,728.00
  Sch. D Short-term G/L:              Tax (1987 Schedule Y):     $17,371.43
  Sch. D Long-term G/L:               Tax on L/T Gains:              $0.00
  Sch. E Gain/Loss:            $0.00  Credits:              (                )
  Sch. F Gain/Loss:            $0.00  Alternative Min. Tax:
  Other Income:                       Tax from Schedule SE:        $212.54
Gross Income:            $88,348.00  *Federal Tax Withheld: (   $15,000.00 )
  Adjustments:        (            )*Excess FICA Withheld: (                )
Adjusted Gross Income:   $88,348.00   Taxes Due:                  $2,583.97


  F1 - Calculate tax      F2 - Withholding      F3 - Update * items
  A, B, C, D, E, F - Go to Schedules            F4 - Update all forms
  F5 - Alternative Minimum Tax                  F6 - Form 1040 Worksheet
  F7 - Self-Employment Tax                      F8 - View or change tax laws

  Marginal Tax Bracket: 35.0%               F10 - Leave this chapter
  Choose one: Single, Joint, Married-Separate, Head of House or Qualifying Widow.
```

Fig. 10.18. The Smiths' Form 1040 with self-employment tax updated.

The basic structure of the alternative minimum tax remains unchanged in the Tax Reform Act. Beginning in 1987, however, the alternative minimum tax rate increases from 20 percent to 21 percent. In addition, the special exemptions that apply to the tax ($40,000 for joint filers, $30,000 for singles, $20,000 for married people filing separately) are phased out for taxpayers with alternative minimum taxable income that exceeds certain amounts. As a result, more taxpayers are subject to the tax.

Beginning in 1987, two items no longer are subject to the minimum tax. The dividend exclusion and the long-term capital gain exclusion both have been eliminated from the tax code. This change occurs not because of a benefit for taxpayers but because these items no longer are preferred items in calculating the regular tax. Therefore, the items no longer are included in the calculation of the minimum tax.

On the other hand, some new preferences must be included in the calculation. If appreciated (non-cash) assets are held longer than six months and are contributed to charity, then the difference between the fair market value of the asset and the cost of the asset must be included as a preference item in the minimum tax calculation.

From the Form 1040 screen, press F5-Alternative Minimum Tax to display the screen shown in figure 10.19. After reading about the background of the Alternative Minimum Tax, you should have some understanding of this screen. If you enter the items that qualify as a tax preference, the program calculates the minimum tax while it considers all the nuances of the new law. Remember that the minimum tax is calculated by re-adding to your income certain tax preferences that were allowed in calculating the regular income tax, and then by subtracting an exemption amount.

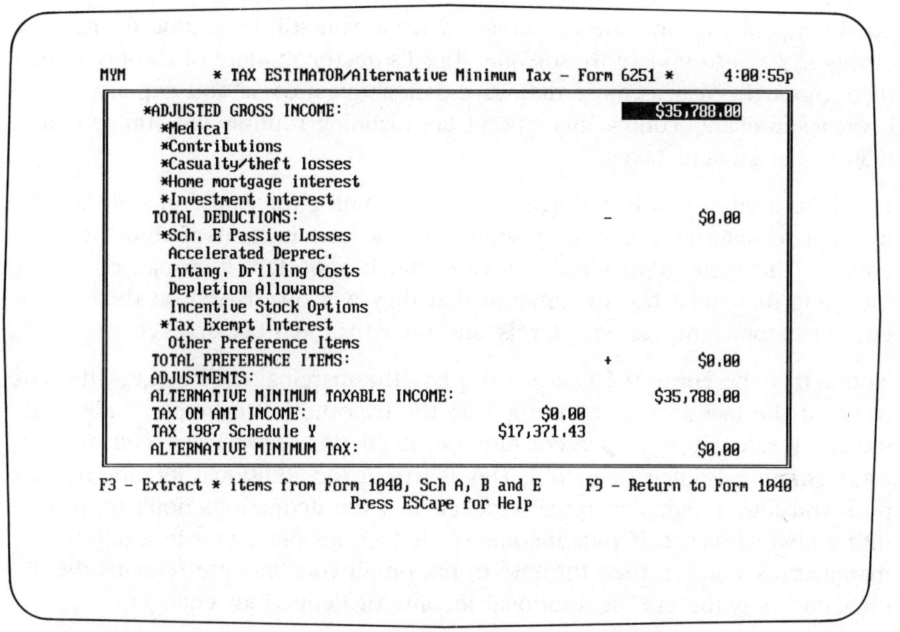

```
MYM              * TAX ESTIMATOR/Alternative Minimum Tax - Form 6251 *       4:00:55p

        *ADJUSTED GROSS INCOME:                               $35,788.00
         *Medical
         *Contributions
         *Casualty/theft losses
         *Home mortgage interest
         *Investment interest
         TOTAL DEDUCTIONS:                           -          $0.00
         *Sch. E Passive Losses
          Accelerated Deprec.
          Intang. Drilling Costs
          Depletion Allowance
          Incentive Stock Options
         *Tax Exempt Interest
          Other Preference Items
         TOTAL PREFERENCE ITEMS:                     +          $0.00
         ADJUSTMENTS:
         ALTERNATIVE MINIMUM TAXABLE INCOME:                 $35,788.00
         TAX ON AMT INCOME:                  $0.00
         TAX 1987 Schedule Y            $17,371.43
         ALTERNATIVE MINIMUM TAX:                              $0.00

        F3 - Extract * items from Form 1040, Sch A, B and E    F9 - Return to Form 1040
                          Press ESCape for Help
```

Fig. 10.19. The Alternative Minimum Tax screen.

New to Version 4.0 is the F3 function key, which extracts any preference items from Schedules A, B, and E. Press F3 now.

Although the Smiths have no preference items to include on the top portion of the screen, you may have some amounts to enter when you calculate your personal taxes. The program automatically calculates the alternative minimum tax and compares it with the regular tax. If the alternative minimum tax is greater, then the amount of the tax that exceeds the regular tax is brought to Form 1040 automatically and is displayed in the Alternative Min. Tax blank.

Press F9 to return to Form 1040. Then press F1-Calculate Tax. The screen, which should look like figure 10.18, did not change because the program already had automatically calculated the tax.

Using the Program To Do Tax Planning

Most taxpayers calculate their tax liabilities after the end of the tax year. Because the tax year is closed, they have no opportunity to make any changes that could lead to a lower tax liability. Determining tax liability after the end of the year often is referred to incorrectly as "tax planning" by many tax professionals.

With Managing Your Money, you can do real tax planning—the kind that's done before the end of the year. With that kind of planning, you can get a good grasp of your income tax situation while you still have time to make changes. You can update the Income Tax Estimator module of the program throughout the year as more definitive data about income and expenses becomes available. Follow this type of tax planning routine and you cannot help saving on your taxes.

In this tutorial, you will perform some tax planning for Paul and Amy Smith in order to determine how they should handle certain items within their control. The Form 1040 screen provides much important information including their total tax, the amount that they will owe based on their current income and expense levels, and their marginal tax bracket.

Notice that the Form 1040 screen displays the marginal tax bracket—the rate of tax at the margin (or at the top). In the hypothetical example, additional income is taxed at a 35 percent rate and deductions save 35 percent on every additional dollar deducted. This is true if the additional income doesn't push you into a higher marginal bracket or if the deductions don't move you into a lower bracket. If your income or deductions place you in a different marginal tax bracket, then the rate of tax on all your income remains the same and only the tax on additional income or deductions changes.

When you do your personal tax planning, you may find that you have a number of income and expense items that could be included in either of two tax years. For now, however, assume that the Smiths have these five items to consider in minimizing their taxes:

1. Individual Retirement Account (IRA): Neither Paul nor Amy qualifies for a company funded retirement plan. Therefore, each is eligible for a $2,000 deduction in an Individual Retirement Account.

2. Sale of Stock: The Smiths believe that the stock market will rise significantly in 1988. They do not plan to sell any stock in 1987, but they may sell in 1988.

3. State Income Taxes: The couple will owe about $1,500 on their state income tax liability and can pay this amount in either 1987 or 1988.

4. Bonus: Paul expects a bonus of approximately $5,500, and Amy expects a $7,000 bonus. Paul and Amy each have the option to take the money in December, 1987, or to wait until the first week of January, 1988, to take the money.

5. Refinancing House Mortgage: The Smiths owe approximately $9,000 on their credit cards. They paid $1,650 in interest in 1987, an amount that is only partially deductible. An even smaller percentage of this interest is deductible in 1988. They could borrow $25,000 against their house, and the interest would be fully deductible.

To perform a crucial "what if" analysis in your tax planning, you must vary one or several variables in the tax calculation formula so that the program can determine their effect on your overall tax liability. If you do not use Managing Your Money or a similar computer program, then the exercise may take hours to perform. In addition, without using a computer, you would have a greater chance of making mistakes because of the numerous calculations required to make a simple income or deduction change. The process is further complicated because of the current transition period created by the Tax Reform Act. The rules and rates are different for 1987 and 1988.

As you work through the following example, you will begin to appreciate the power of this module as a tax planning tool. While considering some of the factors in their financial analysis, the Smiths will ask themselves: Should we make this change? For other factors, they will ask: Should this be done in 1987 or in 1988?

When you perform "what if" tax analysis, get in the habit of making a printout of each Form 1040 screen before making any further changes. The printout should be labeled with the assumptions you made so that you will remember how you obtained the results.

From the Tax Estimator/Form 1040 screen, turn on your printer and press Shift-PrtSc. Your printout of the Form 1040 screen represents your starting point in the planning process.

Adding an IRA Deduction

Take a $2,000 IRA deduction for Paul and one for Amy in 1987. The IRA deduction is classified under Adjustments in the left column of Form 1040.

To take two IRA deductions for the couple:

1. On the Form 1040 screen, move the cursor to Adjustments.

2. Type **4000** (for $4,000).

3. Press Enter.

4. Press F1 to recalculate the tax (see fig. 10.20).

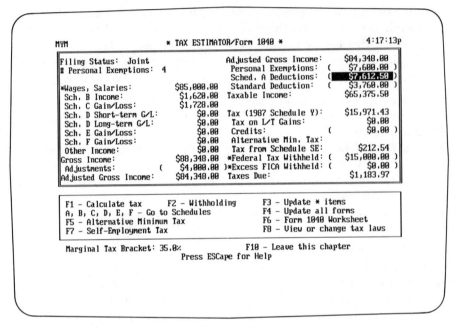

```
MYM                         * TAX ESTIMATOR/Form 1040 *                4:17:13p

Filing Status: Joint                     Adjusted Gross Income:    $84,348.00
# Personal Exemptions: 4                    Personal Exemptions: (   $7,600.00 )
                                            Sched. A Deductions: (   $7,612.50 )
*Wages, Salaries:        $85,000.00         Standard Deduction:  (   $3,760.00 )
 Sch. B Income:           $1,620.00      Taxable Income:            $65,375.50
 Sch. C Gain/Loss:        $1,728.00
 Sch. D Short-term G/L:       $0.00      Tax (1987 Schedule Y):     $15,971.43
 Sch. D Long-term G/L:        $0.00         Tax on L/T Gains:            $0.00
 Sch. E Gain/Loss:            $0.00         Credits:             (       $0.00 )
 Sch. F Gain/Loss:            $0.00         Alternative Min. Tax:
 Other Income:                $0.00         Tax from Schedule SE:      $212.54
Gross Income:            $88,348.00      *Federal Tax Withheld:  (  $15,000.00 )
 Adjustments:        (    $4,000.00 )    )*Excess FICA Withheld: (       $0.00 )
Adjusted Gross Income:   $84,348.00      Taxes Due:                  $1,183.97

  F1 - Calculate tax       F2 - Withholding      F3 - Update * items
  A, B, C, D, E, F - Go to Schedules            F4 - Update all forms
  F5 - Alternative Minimum Tax                  F6 - Form 1040 Worksheet
  F7 - Self-Employment Tax                      F8 - View or change tax laws

  Marginal Tax Bracket: 35.0%               F10 - Leave this chapter
                        Press ESCape for Help
```

Fig. 10.20. Form 1040 after the adjustment for IRAs.

The amounts for Adjusted Gross Income, Taxable Income, Tax, and Taxes Due all were adjusted based on this change. The Smiths still are in the 35 percent marginal tax bracket.

5. Press Shift-PrtSc to make a printout of this screen. Label it "1987 Tax Liability with IRA Deductions."

Selling Some Capital Assets

You may remember that the Smiths bought 50 shares of IBM stock in 1976 for $52 per share. The stock now sells for $142 per share and will yield a $4,500 long-term capital gain. They also own 200 shares of Apple Computer that they bought on January 23, 1986, for $22 per share. That stock now sells for $39 per share and will yield a $3,400 long-term capital gain. Although the Smiths have decided not to sell any of their capital assets in 1987, you still should experiment with this important section of the program so that you will be prepared to handle such sales.

The Smiths possess $7,900 in unrealized long-term capital gains. In 1987, although ordinary income tax rates go up as high as 38.5 percent, the maximum long-term capital gains rate is 28 percent. Because the Smiths already are in the 35 percent marginal tax bracket, their $7,900 would be taxed at a 28 percent rate. To calculate the additional tax that the Smiths would owe if they sold all their stock in 1987, from the Form 1040 screen press **D** to access Schedule D – Capital Gains and Losses (see fig. 10.21).

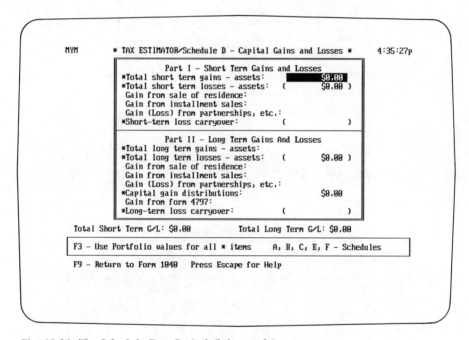

Fig. 10.21. The Schedule D – Capital Gains and Losses screen.

Move the cursor down to Part II – Long Term Gains and Losses. Type **7900** in the Total long term gains blank, and press Enter. Your screen should look like figure 10.22.

Press F9 to return to Form 1040. In the righthand column, notice that the tax on long-term gains is $2,212 (see fig. 10.23).

Now press **D** to return to Schedule D. Because the Smiths have decided not to sell any stocks, zero out the long-term gain. Then press F9 to return to Form 1040.

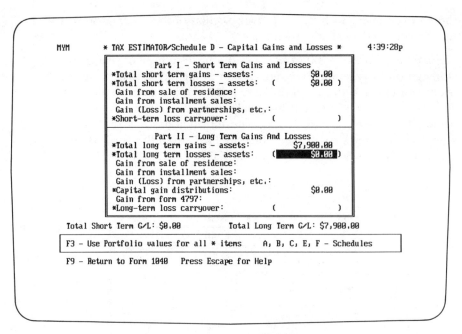

Fig. 10.22. The Capital Gains and Losses screen filled in.

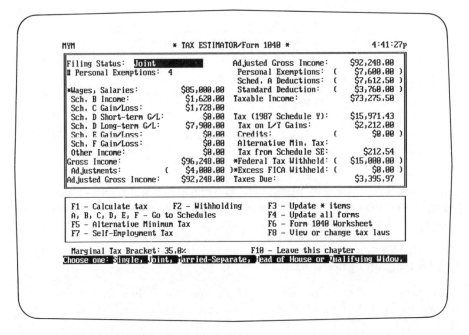

Fig. 10.23. The Form 1040 with Capital Gains.

Deferring State Income Tax Deductions

Determine whether the Smiths should pay their state income taxes in 1987 or in 1988. To keep this example simple, assume that all of the Smiths' other income and expense amounts for 1988 will be the same as for 1987. You can make your personal analyses a little more sophisticated later.

To begin, find a starting point for the 1988 projected income tax liability by retaining the figures that are currently on the Form 1040 screen and entering the 1988 tax laws. The 1987 tax laws should be loaded into the program already. To load the 1988 tax laws, press F8-View or Change Tax Laws from the Form 1040 screen. Then press F3-Load 1988. The 1988 tax laws are loaded automatically into the program. Press F9 to return to the Form 1040 screen, shown in figure 10.24. Notice that the program has calculated the Smiths' 1988 tax liability based on the 1987 income and expense figures.

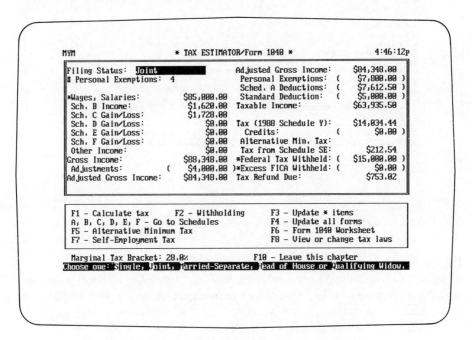

Fig. 10.24. The Form 1040 screen with 1988 tax laws loaded.

Before continuing, you must update Schedule A for differences in the tax law between 1987 and 1988.

To update Schedule A:

1. Type **A** (for Schedule A).

2. Press F9 to return to the Form 1040.

   Notice that the amount in the Schedule A blank has changed.

3. Press F1-Calculate Tax (see fig. 10.25).

4. Make a printout of your latest Form 1040 screen by pressing Shift-PrtSc. Label the printout "1988 Tax Liability with IRA Deductions."

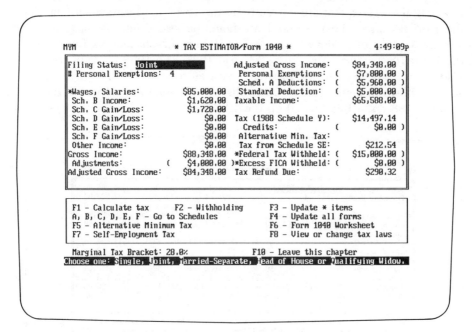

```
MYM                     * TAX ESTIMATOR/Form 1040 *              4:49:09p

Filing Status: Joint               Adjusted Gross Income:    $84,348.00
# Personal Exemptions:   4             Personal Exemptions: (  $7,800.00 )
                                       Sched. A Deductions: (  $5,960.00 )
*Wages, Salaries:       $85,000.00     Standard Deduction:  (  $5,000.00 )
 Sch. B Income:          $1,620.00  Taxable Income:            $65,588.00
 Sch. C Gain/Loss:       $1,728.00
 Sch. D Gain/Loss:          $0.00   Tax (1988 Schedule Y):     $14,497.14
 Sch. E Gain/Loss:          $0.00      Credits:             (     $0.00 )
 Sch. F Gain/Loss:          $0.00   Alternative Min. Tax:
 Other Income:              $0.00   Tax from Schedule SE:         $212.54
Gross Income:           $88,348.00 *Federal Tax Withheld: (  $15,000.00 )
 Adjustments:        (   $4,000.00 )*Excess FICA Withheld: (      $0.00 )
Adjusted Gross Income:  $84,348.00  Tax Refund Due:               $290.32


 F1 - Calculate tax      F2 - Withholding      F3 - Update * items
 A, B, C, D, E, F - Go to Schedules            F4 - Update all forms
 F5 - Alternative Minimum Tax                  F6 - Form 1040 Worksheet
 F7 - Self-Employment Tax                      F8 - View or change tax laws

 Marginal Tax Bracket: 28.0%             F10 - Leave this chapter
Choose one: Single, Joint, Married-Separate, Head of House or Qualifying Widow.
```

Fig. 10.25. The Smiths' 1988 tax liability with IRA deductions.

The income and expense amounts that you entered into the program are identical to those shown in the printout labeled "1987 Tax Liability with IRA Deductions," except for the Schedule A deductions. However, the tax liability is different. All the amounts are the same until the amount after the Adjusted Gross Income. Then the differences in the tax law for 1987 and 1988 are evident.

Although the number of personal exemptions is the same for both years, the Smiths' deduction increases by $200. The Schedule A deductions differ based on the decreased allowance of consumer interest deductions in 1988. The standard deduction also increases from $3,760 to $5,000. Finally, the 1988 tax decreases because of the larger deductions and the lower marginal tax rate. The 1987 marginal tax bracket of 35 percent becomes 28 percent in

1988. Remember that the income and expense amounts have not changed from one year to the next.

You can draw some preliminary conclusions now. First, with the same level of income, the marginal tax bracket is lower in 1988 than in 1987. Although you have not yet considered all the income levels, the Smiths probably should defer income from 1987 to 1988 (given the lower rates in 1988) and take deductions in 1987 rather than in 1988.

The analysis is simplified somewhat based on the time value of money. A dollar today is worth more than a dollar tomorrow; therefore, cost is involved in deferring income. Because of the large reduction in the tax rates from 1987 to 1988, deferring income probably will be advantageous still, even considering the time value of money. Furthermore, the money (a bonus, for example) often can be deferred for only a month or less. Continue reading to see whether your preliminary conclusion about deferring income and accelerating deductions remains true in practice.

Determine the impact of paying the $1,500 in state income taxes both in 1988 and in 1987. Because the 1988 tax laws currently are loaded into the program, you can determine the 1988 effect first. State income taxes are classified as itemized deductions, so they are included in Schedule A of your tax return. You can enter the $1,500 state income tax deduction either directly in the Sched. A Deductions blank on Form 1040 or in Schedule A where the amount is brought to Form 1040 automatically.

To enter state income taxes into Schedule A for 1988:

1. From the Form 1040 screen, type **A** (for Schedule A).

2. Move the cursor to the State and Local Taxes blank.

   The $3,700 amount is in the blank. If you add $1,500, then the State and Local Taxes total is $5,200.

3. Type **5200** (for $5,200) and press Enter.

   Your screen should look like figure 10.26.

4. Press F9 to return to Form 1040.

5. Press F1 to calculate the tax with the additional deduction.

   Because of the extra deduction, the Smiths' tax refund (see fig. 10.27) has increased compared to the refund shown in figure 10.25.

6. Make a printout of Form 1040 with the state tax deduction taken in 1988 by pressing Shift-PrtSc. Label the printout "1988 Tax Liability with IRA and State Tax Deduction."

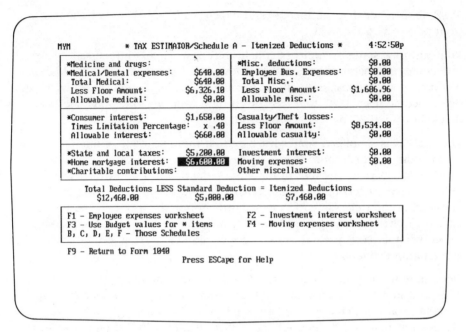

Fig. 10.26. Schedule A with state income tax amount updated.

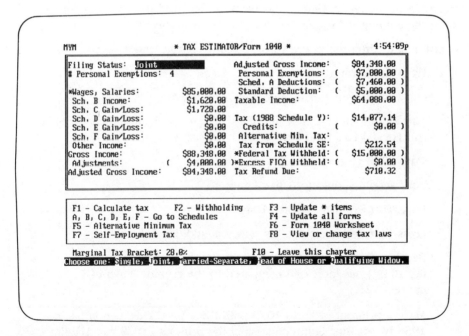

Fig. 10.27. The Smiths' 1988 tax liability with IRA and state tax deduction.

Without changing any figures, determine the impact that the state tax deduction has on 1987 taxes by reloading the 1987 tax laws. From the Form 1040 screen, press F8-View or Change Tax Laws. Then press F2-Load 1987 Tax Schedules and Parameters. Press F9 to return to the Form 1040 screen.

To update the amounts in Schedule A for the 1987 tax laws:

1. From the Form 1040 screen, type **A** (for Schedule A).

2. Press F9 to return to Form 1040.

   This step automatically updates the amount deductible from Schedule A.

3. Press F1 to recalculate the taxes with the 1987 tax laws.

   The marginal tax bracket, shown in figure 10.28, is 35 percent—the same as it was before the additional $1,500 deduction.

4. Make a printout of the Form 1040 screen by pressing Shift-PrtSc. Label the printout "1987 Tax Liability with IRA and State Tax Deduction."

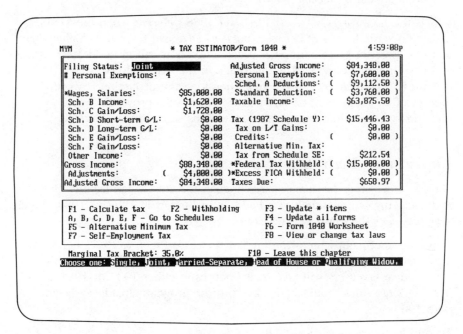

Fig. 10.28. The Smiths' 1987 tax liability with IRA and state tax deduction.

Compare your printouts to determine whether you will realize a greater tax savings by claiming your state tax deduction in 1987 or in 1988. Do not compare the 1987 tax liability with the 1988 tax liability, but compare the 1988 tax liability before and after the $1,500 state tax deduction is taken, and then compare the 1987 tax liability before and after the state tax deduction.

For 1988, Form 1040 indicates that without the state tax deduction, the Smiths get a $290.32 refund. With the state tax deduction, they get a $710.32 refund. The $420 tax decrease represents the tax benefit gained in 1988 by taking the state tax deduction that year.

Now determine the tax savings to be gained by taking the state tax deduction in 1987. Form 1040 indicates that without the state tax deduction, the Smiths owe $1,183.97 in taxes. With the state tax deduction, they owe $658.97 in taxes. Therefore, the tax savings is $525 if the state tax deduction is taken in 1987.

Apparently, therefore, if all other factors are equal, the state taxes that are owed should be paid before the end of the 1987 calendar year. The state tax deduction should be taken in 1987.

Why is the tax savings between 1987 and 1988 different when the $1,500 deduction stays the same? Because the 1987 marginal tax rate is higher than in 1988. Therefore, the same $1,500 deduction is worth more in 1987 than in 1988. How much more? The difference in the marginal tax rates is 7 percent (35 percent vs. 28 percent). Therefore, the deduction is worth 7 percent of an additional $1,500, or $105. The results prove that your preliminary conclusion was correct: deductions should be accelerated.

Deferring Year-End Bonuses

Look at some other tax items that can affect the Smiths' tax liability. Both Paul and Amy can take their year-end bonuses either in 1987 or 1988. Which year produces the lower tax increase?

You can experiment later with different scenarios (such as Paul's bonus in 1987 and Amy's in 1988, or vice versa), but for now, suppose that both hypothetical taxpayers will take their bonuses in either 1987 or 1988. The 1987 tax rules should be loaded into the program already, so begin with 1987.

To add bonuses and recalculate taxes for 1987:

1. On the Form 1040 screen, move the cursor to the Salary blank.

The sum of the Smiths' salaries ($85,000) should be displayed. Because Paul expects a bonus of $5,500, and Amy expects $7,000, you need to add their $12,500 bonus total to $85,000.

2. Type **97500** (for $97,500) and press Enter.

3. Press F1 to recalculate the taxes owed (see fig. 10.29).

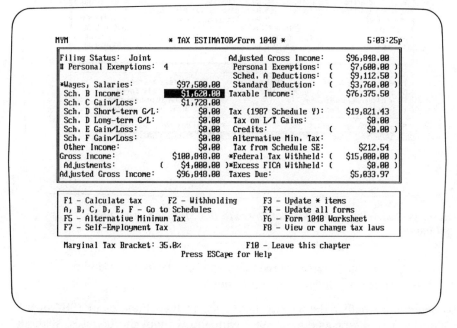

```
MYM                    * TAX ESTIMATOR/Form 1040 *              5:03:25p

Filing Status:  Joint              Adjusted Gross Income:     $96,848.00
# Personal Exemptions:  4            Personal Exemptions:  (   $7,600.00 )
                                     Sched. A Deductions:  (   $9,112.50 )
*Wages, Salaries:       $97,500.00   Standard Deduction:   (   $3,760.00 )
Sch. B Income:           $1,620.00   Taxable Income:           $76,375.50
Sch. C Gain/Loss:        $1,728.00
Sch. D Short-term G/L:       $0.00   Tax (1987 Schedule Y):    $19,821.43
Sch. D Long-term G/L:        $0.00   Tax on L/T Gains:              $0.00
Sch. E Gain/Loss:            $0.00   Credits:              (        $0.00 )
Sch. F Gain/Loss:            $0.00   Alternative Min. Tax:
Other Income:                $0.00   Tax from Schedule SE:        $212.54
Gross Income:          $100,848.00  *Federal Tax Withheld: (  $15,000.00 )
Adjustments:       (     $4,000.00 )*Excess FICA Withheld: (        $0.00 )
Adjusted Gross Income:  $96,848.00   Taxes Due:                 $5,833.97

  F1 - Calculate tax       F2 - Withholding      F3 - Update * items
  A, B, C, D, E, F - Go to Schedules             F4 - Update all forms
  F5 - Alternative Minimum Tax                   F6 - Form 1040 Worksheet
  F7 - Self-Employment Tax                       F8 - View or change tax laws

  Marginal Tax Bracket: 35.0%              F10 - Leave this chapter
                          Press ESCape for Help
```

Fig. 10.29. The Smiths' 1987 tax liability with IRA, state tax deduction, and bonus.

4. Make a printout of the screen and label it "1987 Tax Liability with IRA, State Tax Deduction, and Bonus."

Now you can reload the 1988 tax rules and recalculate for 1988. To reload the 1988 tax rules, press F8-View or Change Tax Laws. Then press F3-Load 1988. Now press F9 to return to Form 1040.

To update the Schedule A amounts to reflect the 1988 tax laws:

1. From the Form 1040 screen, type **A** (for Schedule A).

2. Press F9 to return to Form 1040.

3. Press F1 to recalculate the tax for the 1988 tax laws (see fig. 10.30).

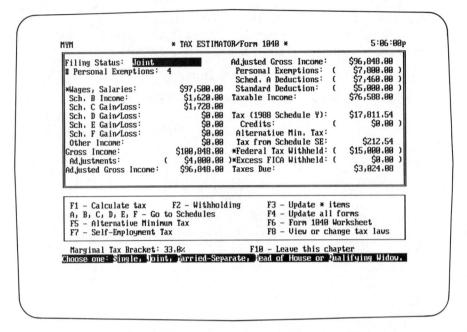

```
MYM                    * TAX ESTIMATOR/Form 1040 *              5:06:00p

Filing Status: Joint             Adjusted Gross Income:    $96,848.00
# Personal Exemptions:  4           Personal Exemptions:  (  $7,800.00 )
                                    Sched. A Deductions:  (  $7,460.00 )
*Wages, Salaries:        $97,500.00 Standard Deduction:   (  $5,000.00 )
Sch. B Income:            $1,620.00 Taxable Income:          $76,588.00
Sch. C Gain/Loss:         $1,728.00
Sch. D Gain/Loss:             $0.00 Tax (1988 Schedule Y):   $17,811.54
Sch. E Gain/Loss:             $0.00    Credits:           (      $0.00 )
Sch. F Gain/Loss:             $0.00 Alternative Min. Tax:
Other Income:                 $0.00 Tax from Schedule SE:       $212.54
Gross Income:           $100,848.00 *Federal Tax Withheld: ( $15,000.00 )
Adjustments:         (    $4,000.00 )*Excess FICA Withheld: (      $0.00 )
Adjusted Gross Income:   $96,848.00 Taxes Due:                $3,024.08


F1 - Calculate tax      F2 - Withholding    F3 - Update * items
A, B, C, D, E, F - Go to Schedules          F4 - Update all forms
F5 - Alternative Minimum Tax                F6 - Form 1040 Worksheet
F7 - Self-Employment Tax                    F8 - View or change tax laws

Marginal Tax Bracket: 33.0%                 F10 - Leave this chapter
Choose one: Single, Joint, Married-Separate, Head of House or Qualifying Widow.
```

Fig. 10.30. The Smiths' 1988 tax liability with IRA, state tax deduction, and bonus.

4. Make a printout of the screen and label it "1988 Tax Liability with IRA, State Tax Deduction, and Bonus."

To determine whether the Smiths should accept their bonuses in 1987 or in 1988, compare the taxes due in 1987 with and without the bonuses. Without the bonuses, the taxes due are $658.97. With the bonuses, the taxes due increase to $5,033.97. Because of the bonuses, the 1987 increase in taxes is $4,375. In 1988, the Smiths get a tax refund of $710.32 without the bonuses. The taxes due are $3,024.08 with the bonuses. The tax liability increases by $3,734.40.

Based on these figures, the Smiths probably should take their bonuses in 1988, because the tax liability increases by a smaller amount. In fact, they can save $640.60 in taxes simply by deferring the bonuses to 1988. (The bonuses can be taken January 1, 1988, instead of December 31, 1987.) The results are consistent with the earlier conclusion that income should be deferred until 1988.

Refinancing a House Mortgage

As discussed earlier, the Tax Reform Act of 1986 significantly changed the deduction of interest expense. Forty percent of the interest expense on consumer debt is deductible in 1988. By 1991, none of it will be deductible. On the other hand, with certain limitations, interest on debt from a personal residence will be fully deductible.

Complete the Income Tax Estimator tutorial by determining the Smiths' 1988 savings if they refinance their home mortgage to pay off their miscellaneous consumer debts. Suppose that it is too late in the year to be concerned about possible 1987 tax savings but that the Smiths may be able to save money in 1988 by refinancing their house mortgage. For this tutorial, ignore the fact that the Smiths should realize a nontax savings by refinancing, because the interest on their home mortgage will probably be lower than the rate that they pay on their credit card loans. That is an added benefit of refinancing. Instead, focus strictly on the tax savings for 1988.

First make sure that the 1988 tax laws are loaded into the program. From the Form 1040 screen, press F8-View or Change Tax Laws. Then press F3-Load 1988. Now press F9 to return to the Form 1040 (see fig. 10.31).

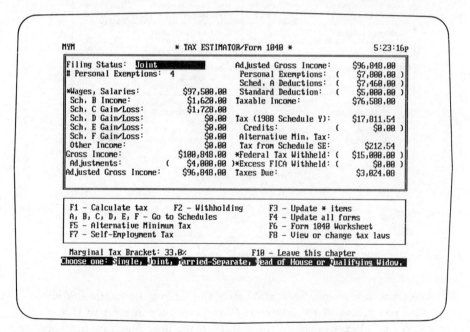

Fig. 10.31. The 1988 Form 1040 screen before reclassifying interest deductions.

To reclassify interest deductions:

1. Type **A** (for Schedule A).

   Suppose that the $1,650 in Other Interest is replaced by an equal amount of Home Mortgage Interest Paid by paying off the consumer debt and borrowing an equal amount with the taxpayers' house as security.

2. Position the cursor at the Consumer Interest blank, and press the space bar to wipe out the $1,650.

3. Move the cursor to Home Mortgage Interest, which contains a $6,600 amount. Because you want to add $1,650 to $6,600, type **8250** (for $8,250) in the blank.

4. Press Enter (see fig. 10.32).

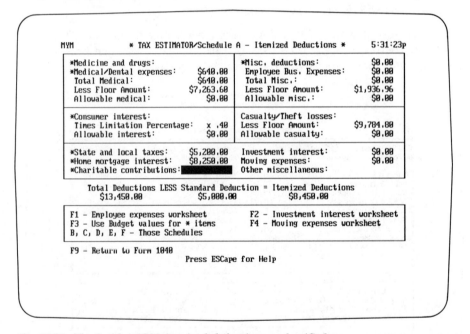

Fig. 10.32. The Smiths' 1988 itemized deductions reclassified.

You have not changed the amount of the interest deductions. You have just reclassified the interest from Consumer Interest to Home Mortgage Interest. Look at the results to see how much money you have saved.

5. Press F9 to return to Form 1040 (see fig. 10.33).

6. Make a printout of the screen, and label it "1988 Tax Liability with IRA, State Tax Deduction, Bonus, and Reclassification of Other Interest."

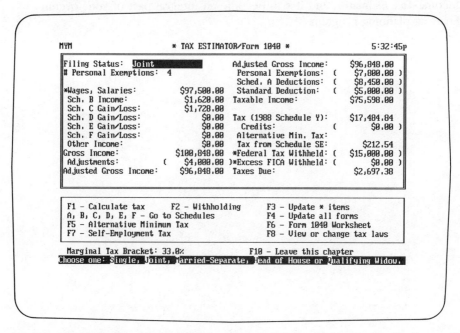

Fig. 10.33. The Smiths' 1988 tax liability with IRA, state tax deduction, bonus, and reclassification of other interest.

Compare this printout with the printout labeled "1988 Tax Liability with IRA, State Tax Deduction, and Bonus" in order to determine the tax savings from the reclassification. Without the reclassification, the amount of tax owed is $3,024.08. With the reclassification, the amount of tax owed is $2,697.38. The hypothetical taxpayers save $326.70 by paying off the old debt with money from refinancing their home mortgage. The savings will increase in 1989, 1990, and 1991 as the deduction for other interest is completely phased out. Furthermore, as mentioned earlier, the interest rate on the home mortgage debt should be lower than that on the consumer debt, which will result in additional savings.

By now, you should have a good grasp of the tax planning opportunities available in the Income Tax Estimator module of Managing Your Money. A key to effective planning is organization. Methodically consider the possibilities. Print and label the results of each scenario. Remember that the possibilities are countless. Although you may have wanted to take a bonus in 1988 because of its tax advantages, be sure you have sufficient cash in 1987 to make an IRA contribution. The Tax Estimator provides the tools to calculate each of the possibilities in a relatively short time. As in the other modules of the program, eventually you will become proficient at using the Income Tax Estimator, and it will become an integral part of your overall financial planning program.

## Chapter 11

Using the Card File

The Card File module is a useful tool for keeping track of large numbers of people, from business customers to friends of the family. You can keep detailed records about people you know, dial telephone numbers automatically, locate a record in the file (even if you remember only a person's first or last name or some information about the person), print lists or mailing labels for all or only a few of the people listed in the file, and perform a mailmerge of a document file with a record contained in the Card File.

From the Main Menu, press F9 to enter the Card File and to display the summary screen shown in figure 11.1. If you have not yet deleted the sample records from this module, the displayed records should be identical to those shown in the figure.

Viewing or Editing a Record

To display a sample record:

1. Position the cursor over the record that you want to see.

2. Press F2-View/Edit Record Pointed To (see fig. 11.2).

   Look at the information you can keep in the Card File. To change any of the information, you position the cursor at the blank and enter your own information.

3. Press F9 to back up to the summary screen of the Card File.

From the summary screen of the card file (see fig. 11.1), you can add a new record, look at the details of a certain record, delete a record, print a record

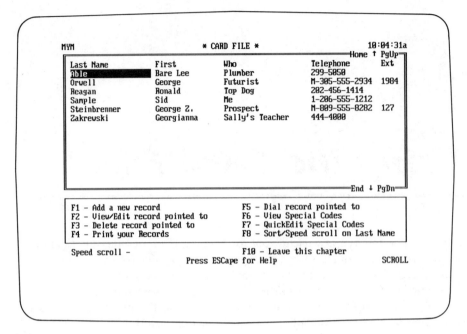

Fig. 11.1. The summary screen of the Card File module.

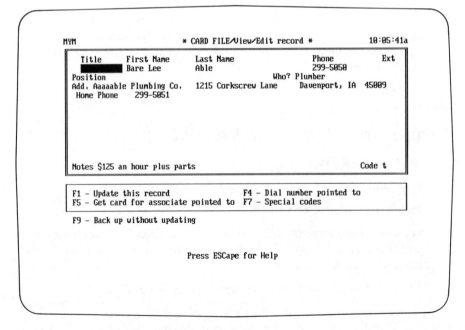

Fig. 11.2. A sample record displayed.

in any of the available formats, dial a record, look at special codes you have assigned to your records, edit the special codes, and search for a record that is on file based on the last name, first name, or who that person is.

Deleting a Record

To delete the sample records:

1. On the summary screen, position the cursor at the first record to be deleted.

2. Press F3.

3. Press F1.

   The program asks you to verify your instructions to delete the material.

4. Position the cursor at each of the remaining sample records and delete them.

   After you finish, your screen should look like figure 11.3.

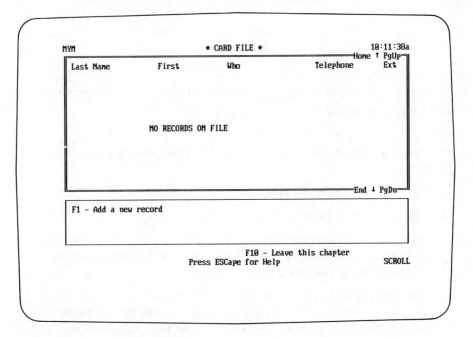

Fig. 11.3. Sample records deleted.

Adding a Record

To add a record:

1. From the Card File screen, press F1-Add a New Record to display the screen shown in figure 11.4.

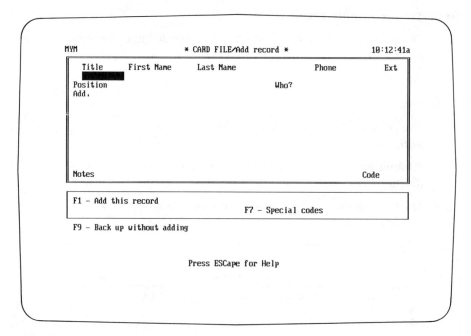

```
MYM                        * CARD FILE/Add record *              10:12:41a

   Title      First Name    Last Name                Phone         Ext
   ▓▓▓▓▓▓▓
   Position                              Who?
   Add.




   Notes                                              Code


   F1 - Add this record
                              F7 - Special codes

   F9 - Back up without adding


                     Press ESCape for Help
```

Fig. 11.4. The Add Record screen.

2. Type the person's title, if any, in the Title blank and then press Enter.

3. Type a first name in the First Name blank and press Enter.

4. Type a last name in the appropriate blank and press Enter.

5. Fill as many of the other blanks as you want. If you plan to use your modem and the Managing Your Money auto-dial function, then fill in the telephone number for this record.

6. Move the cursor to the Who? blank. Is the person your doctor, your lawyer, or your barber? Although you don't have to fill this blank, the information may later be valuable to you. For example, if you enter the occupations of people who perform work for you, you

can later direct the computer to search the file for a particular
person whose occupation you remember but whose name you
forget.

7. Fill in the three address lines, if you plan to print mailing labels
   later (see fig. 11.5).

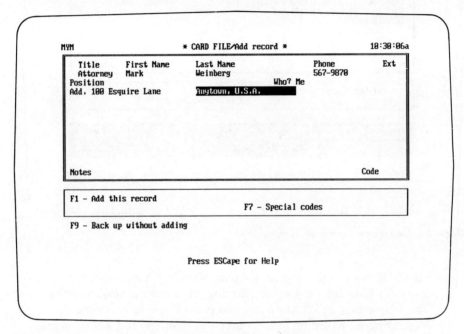

```
MYM                          * CARD FILE/Add record *              10:30:06a

     Title       First Name      Last Name              Phone            Ext
     Attorney    Mark            Weinberg               567-9870
   Position                                     Who? Me
   Add. 100 Esquire Lane        Anytown, U.S.A.




   Notes                                                        Code


   F1 - Add this record
                                        F7 - Special codes

   F9 - Back up without adding



                      Press ESCape for Help
```

Fig. 11.5. Name, occupation, address, and phone number entered.

8. Fill in the blanks located below the address lines, as follows:

   To complete any of the smaller blanks, select a descriptive item
   from the list at the bottom of the screen. Although the name and
   phone number are sufficient, you can include more descriptive
   information simply by typing the first letter or two of your choice.

   In the larger blanks, enter specific information about this record.
   For example, if you selected birthday to complete a smaller blank,
   then you would enter the person's birthday in the larger blank.

   After you finish, your screen should look similar to figure 11.6.

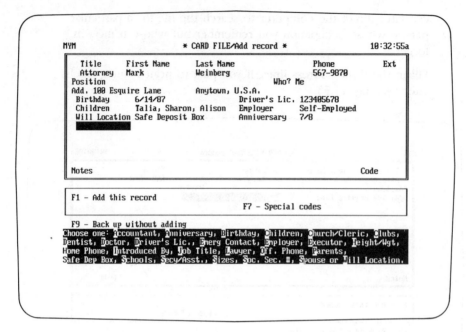

Fig. 11.6. Descriptive information added.

9. At the bottom of the screen, you can include a note about the person whose record you are entering. To enter the note, position the cursor over the Notes blank and press Ctrl-E to enter the Wordprocessor (see fig. 11.7). After you have entered a note, press F2 to return to the Card File screen.

10. In the Code blank, in the bottom right corner of the screen, you can type characters to identify the specific record or class of records.

Suppose, for example, that you have both personal and business records. You might type **P** in the Code blank for all your personal records and **B** on the blank for all your business records. Later, when you use the printing function of the Card File, you can simply instruct the program to print only the personal records or only the business records.

The program is flexible. You can use as many codes as you want, or you even can leave the Code blank empty.

11. Press F1-Add This Record (see fig. 11.8).

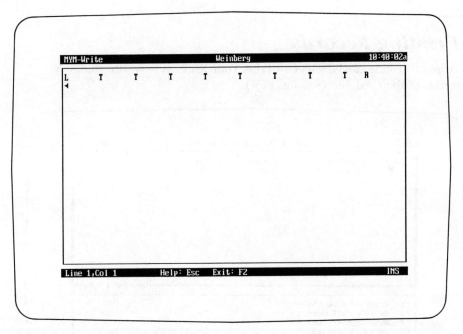

Fig. 11.7. The Wordprocessor screen.

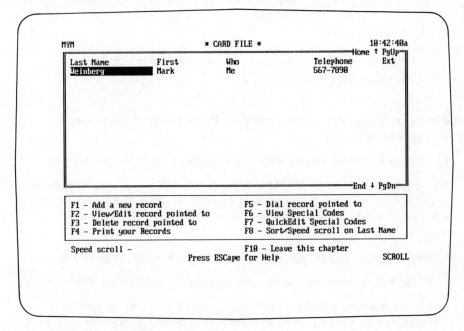

Fig. 11.8. A record added.

Printing Records

To print mailing labels, select F4-Print Your Records from the summary
screen of the Card File (see fig. 11.9).

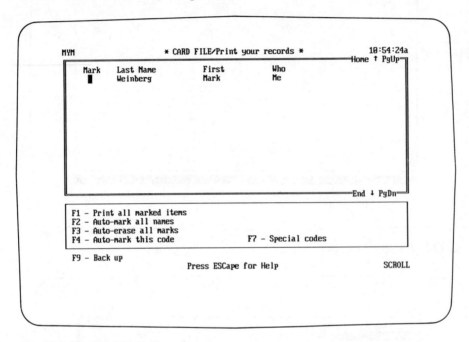

Fig. 11.9. The Print Your Records screen.

The menu at the bottom of the Print Your Records screen offers the
following options:

F1-Print All Marked Items: Allows you to print the selected records.

When you press F1-Print All Marked Items you will see the options shown
at the bottom of the screen in figure 11.10. You can perform a brief print,
a full print, print mailing labels and, new to Version 4.0, you can perform
a mailmerge.

B-Brief Print: Prints only certain data for each of the marked records.

F-Full Print: Prints all the data for each of the marked records.

L-Print Mailing Labels: Prints mailing labels that can be applied to
envelopes for mailing. (You may have to experiment in order to

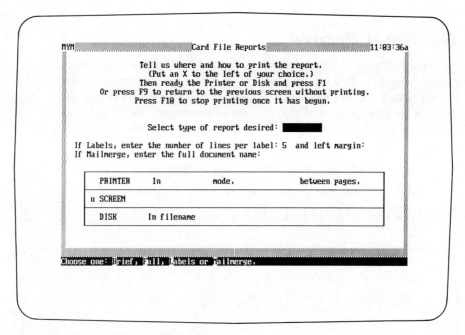

Fig. 11.10. The Card File Reports screen.

determine the number of lines on your mailing label and the left margin.)

M-Mailmerge: Allows you to print form letters and send them to anyone listed in the Card File. The program will substitute the appropriate name, address, phone number, etc. for each document printed.

F2-Auto-Mark All Names: Marks all the records that are on file.

F3-Auto-Erase All Marks: Erases the marks from every record on file.

F4-Auto-Mark This Code: Automatically marks all records that possess an assigned code. Suppose, for example, as you enter data into your records, that you type **C** in the Code blank for each of your clients. When you are ready to print, type **C** in the Auto-mark this code blank and press F4. All the records labeled with a C are marked for printing automatically. You can then print mailing labels for those records that are auto-marked.

F7-Special Codes: Displays the special codes you have used.

Take time to experiment with the print capabilities. When you are finished, press F9 to return to the previous screen.

Dialing a Record

To operate Managing Your Money's auto-dial function, you must connect a modem to your computer. In addition, you must specify that you are using a modem when you run the Setup program. (The program does not work with all modems.) Keep in mind that the auto-dialer works only if you have included a telephone number in the record of the person you have selected to call.

To configure Managing Your Money for a modem:

1. From the Main Menu, press Alt-F6.

   Your screen should look similar to figure 11.11.

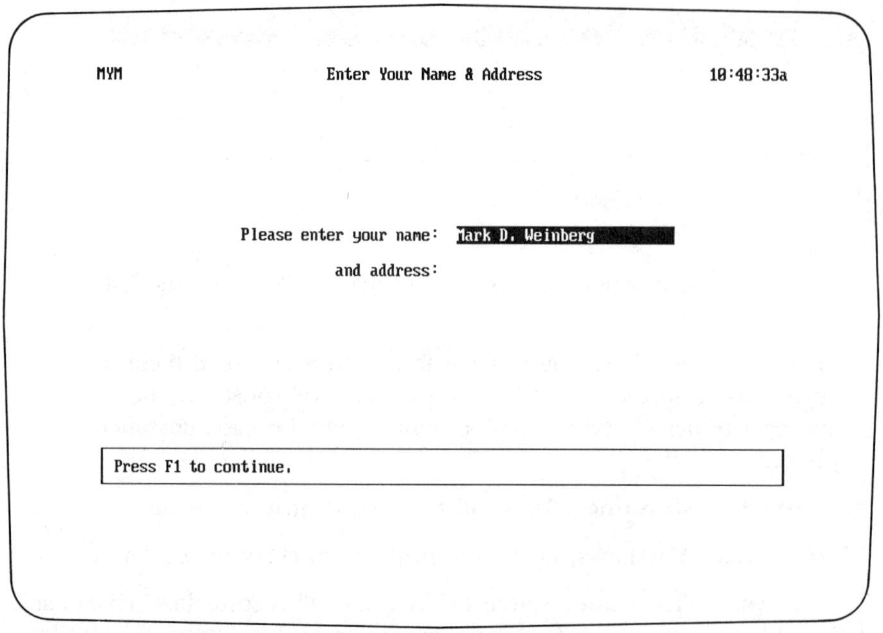

```
  MYM                    Enter Your Name & Address              10:48:33a




                Please enter your name:  Mark D. Weinberg
                          and address:






      Press F1 to continue.
```

Fig. 11.11. The Enter Name and Address screen.

2. Assuming that you don't have to change any of the system configurations other than the modem, press F1 four times to access the Modem Configuration screen (see fig. 11.12).

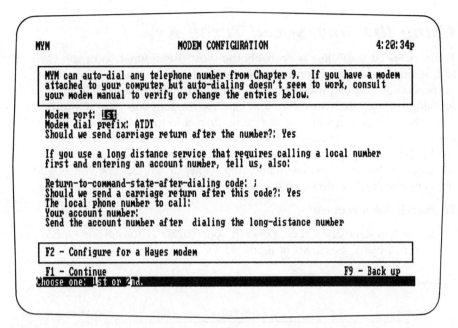

Fig. 11.12. The Modem Configuration screen.

3. Most modems are either manufactured by Hayes, or they are Hayes compatible. Try pressing F2 to see whether this configuration works for your modem. If the configuration doesn't work, you can always go back and reconfigure the system.

4. If you are using a long-distance telephone service (such as MCI or Sprint) that requires you to call a local telephone number before you dial a long-distance number, fill in the bottom portion of the screen as well.

5. Press F1 four times to save the new information and to return to the Main Menu. Press F9 to reenter the Card File.

To use the auto-dial function:

1. On the Card File summary screen, position the cursor at the record you want to dial.

2. Press F5-Dial Record Pointed To.

3. After the dialing stops, pick up the telephone receiver.

4. Press any key.

Using the Sort/Speed Scroll Key

The Sort/Speed Scroll key is probably the most useful function of the Card File, assuming that you have a large number of records on file. If you have many records, you can use this function to find a record quickly instead of scrolling through the entire file. You can use the function even if you don't remember the person's first or last name. If you forget the person's first and last name, you can search by "who" the person is, such as your plumber or lawyer. New to Version 4.0 is the Speed Scroll function. You can simply type the first few letters of the last name, first name, or who the person is, and the cursor will scroll down to the record.

To search for a record:

1. On the summary screen, position your cursor at the F8-Sort/Speed scroll blank, as shown in figure 11.13.

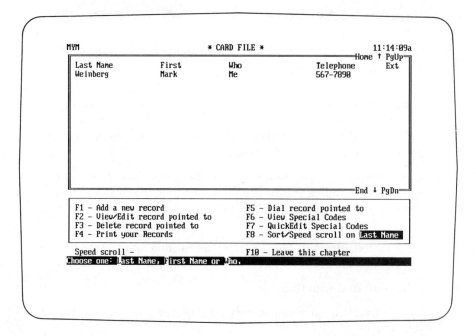

Fig. 11.13. Search specifications being entered.

2. In this blank, indicate whether you want the program to search through the records by last name, first name, or who the person is.

3. Press F8 to move the cursor to the appropriate column.

4. Now type the first few letters of the first name, the last name, or who the person is. The cursor will move automatically to the appropriate record.

Other Card File Features

Managing Your Money can display on your screen the special codes you have assigned to your records. From the summary screen, press F6-View Special Codes.

There is also the timesaving F7-QuickEdit Special Codes function. From the summary screen, press F7 to edit the special codes you have assigned to your records, without displaying the detail for each record.

Press F10 to exit the Card File. You can either save your changes or exit without saving the changes you made in the file.

Versions 3.0 and 4.0 have the function key F7-Save and Export Birthdays and Anniversaries to Chapter 2. Use this function to transfer to the Reminder Pad module all the files in which you have included either a birthday or an anniversary. You can select the number of days in advance that you want to be reminded of the upcoming date.

## Part III

Creating Graphs and Reports

## Chapter 12

Creating Graphs

Managing Your Money has impressive graphing capabilities. If you have a color monitor, you should be able to use all the graphing features. If you have a monochrome monitor, you may not be able to see the graphing options, depending on the way your system is configured.

Loading the Graphics Program

If your computer is set up to display graphs, you can print graphs to your printer by using the PrtSc (PrintScreen) key. First, however, you must load a graphics program (either the DOS graphics program or a different one) into the working memory of your computer. This step is not as complicated as it sounds. Instructions for loading the DOS graphics program follow. Separate instructions are given for floppy disk and hard disk systems. You must load the graphics program before you load the Managing Your Money program into memory.

To load the graphics program on a floppy disk system:

1. Insert your DOS disk (Version 2.0 or later) into drive A and then turn on your computer. (If your computer is already on, then with the DOS disk in drive A, press Ctrl-Alt-Del to reboot the system.)

2. After the A> prompt appears, type **GRAPHICS**.

3. Press Enter.

4. Start the Managing Your Money program in the usual manner. The graphics program remains in the working memory of the computer until you either turn off or reboot the computer.

5. Make sure that your printer is turned on and that it is properly connected to your computer.

6. To print a graph, display on the screen the graph you want printed, and then press Shift-PrtSc.

To load the graphics program on a hard disk system:

1. Turn on your computer and allow it to boot up automatically. (If your computer is already on, press Ctrl-Alt-Del to reboot the system.)

2. After the C> prompt appears, type **CD\DOS** and press Enter to move into the DOS subdirectory.

3. Type **GRAPHICS** and press Enter.

4. Start the Managing Your Money program in the usual manner. The graphics program remains in the working memory of the computer until you either turn off or reboot the computer.

5. Make sure that your printer is turned on and that it is properly connected to your computer.

6. To print a graph, display on the screen the graph you want printed, and then press Shift-PrtSc.

Accessing the Graphs

Graphs are available in modules 3 (Budget and Checkbook), 6 (Financial Calculator), 7 (Portfolio Manager), and 8 (Your Net Worth). Table 12.1 indicates the graphs that are available in Managing Your Money and the key sequence to press from the Main Menu in order to access them.

Some of the available graphs are discussed in this chapter. In addition, the text explains how you can use the graphs to help you in your personal financial analysis. The graphs displayed in this chapter's figures are based on either the program's sample data or data that was entered by the author.

Before you print any of the graphs, be sure to load the graphics program into your computer, using the steps given earlier in this chapter. Remember that you must load the graphics program *before* you load Managing Your Money into your computer's memory.

Table 12.1
Types of Graphs and How To Access Them

Name of Graph	Module	Function Keys
Cash Flow Analysis		
Monthly Cash Forecasting	3	F3, F3, F2
Budget and Actuals	3	F3, F1, F2, F6
Five-Year Cash Forecasting	3	F3, F3, F1, F1
All Budget Categories	3	F3, F1, F6
Retirement Planning		
Retirement Assets by Type	6	F6, F2, F1, F1, F2, F1
IRA/Keogh Fund Analysis	6	F6, F2, F1, F1, F2, F2
Contributions vs. Appreciation	6	F6, F2, F1, F1, F2, F3
Asset Distribution in Portfolio		
Assets by Risk	7	F7, F2, F1, F1, F6, F1
Assets by Tax Status	7	F7, F2, F1, F1, F6, F2
Assets by Liquidity	7	F7, F2, F1, F1, F6, F3
Assets by Industry Group	7	F7, F2, F1, F1, F6, F4
Assets by Recommendor	7	F7, F2, F1, F1, F6, F5
Assets by Type	7	F7, F2, F1, F1, F6, F6
Graph of Assets or Liabilities	8	F8, (F7-Level), F6

Cash Flow Analysis

Cash flow analysis, which is the focus of every good business plan, is an often ignored, but key component of effective personal financial planning as well. To achieve personal investment and retirement objectives, you must have cash available to set aside. By monitoring your current inflow and outflow of cash and projecting those amounts for the year ahead, you can determine (before it's too late) whether you should make changes and whether your projected budget will allow you to achieve your financial goals. The next four graphs should help you with your analysis.

Monthly Cash Forecasting

To access the monthly cash forecasting graph, as indicated in table 12.1, return to the Main Menu and press the F3, F3 and then F2 function keys in succession until you find the graph (see fig. 12.1). This graph plots the amount of cash you will have at the end of each of the next 12 months based on your budgeted and actual income and expenses.

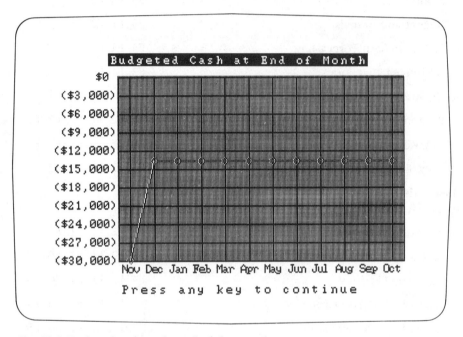

Fig. 12.1. Budgeted cash at the end of the month.

You can use the monthly cash forecasting graph as the basis for your cash flow analysis. You must, however, believe the graph. If your cash situation based on your current budget is not desirable for the next few months, then you must make a change. If you cannot increase your income level, you must find ways to decrease your expenses.

Five-Year Cash Forecasting

The five-year cash forecasting capabilities of Managing Your Money are available only after you have activated the optional Five-Year Planning feature of the Budget and Checkbook module. You may have activated this simple option already if you have completed the Budget and Checkbook tutorial presented in Chapter 5. If you haven't, the following steps will take you through the procedure.

To activate the Five-Year Planning option:

1. From the Main Menu, press F3-Budget and Checkbook to return to the Budget and Checkbook's Mini Menu.

2. Press F6-Optional Features.

3. Move the cursor to the Five-Year Planning option.

4. Type **Y** (for Yes).

5. Press F1-Activate/Deactivate These Options to record the status change of the optional feature and to return to the Budget and Checkbook's Mini Menu.

After the Five-Year Planning option is activated, you can access the five-year cash forecasting graph by pressing F3 from the Budget and Checkbook's Mini Menu, and then by pressing F1. If your five-year budgeted income and expenses have been been entered, press F1 to graph (see fig. 12.2).

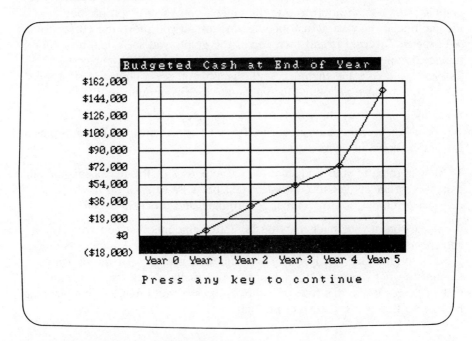

Fig. 12.2. Budgeted cash at the end of the year.

Planning five years ahead is a little more difficult than planning for only the coming year, but both are essential. Successful businesses often are not the ones with the best product or the lowest costs, but the ones that are best able to predict and plan for their financial needs. Likewise, individuals who are the most successful at planning their own financial future are not necessarily the ones who make the most money or spend the least.

Although the budgeting process must begin in the current month and continue through an entire year's budget, planning further into the future is essential for proper financial planning. Many people avoid long-term financial budgeting because of the greater degree of uncertainty involved. If you can accept that uncertainty and the likelihood that a five-year budget will change eventually, you will be more likely to achieve your financial goals.

Budget and Actuals

The budget and actuals graph lets you compare your budgeted income and expenses for the current year with the actual amounts that you earned and spent. From the Main Menu, press F3. Then press F1. The Budget and Checkbook/Budget Categories screen should be displayed.

Position the cursor over the words All Income Categories. If you access the graphing function without moving the cursor, you see a graph of your income budget vs. your actual income amounts. If you move the cursor to All Expense Categories and then access the graph, you see a graph of your budgeted expenses vs. your actual expenses. If you move the cursor to All Categories Netted and then access the graph, you see a comparison of the net of your budget and actual income and expense amounts.

Leave the cursor over the words All Income Categories so that you can look at a graph of your income categories. Press F2 and then press F1 to display the graph shown in figure 12.3.

To view a graph of your budget vs. actual expenses or the net of income and expenses, press any key to continue. Then press F9 to back up to the category level, position the cursor accordingly, and proceed as before.

A comparison of your budgets with the actual amounts that you are earning and spending is crucial to your financial planning process. A budget is only as good as the numbers used in it. If you find after a while that the budgeted amounts do not represent the amounts you actually spend, then you must make changes. Make this type of comparison early and often in your planning process so that you can correct problems.

All Budget Categories

To generate a pie graph that shows the breakdown of your income and expense categories, press F3 from the Main Menu. Then press F1 and F6 in succession. Your screen should display a graph that looks similar to the one shown in figure 12.4. Press any key to display a pie graph of the distribution of your expense categories (see fig. 12.5).

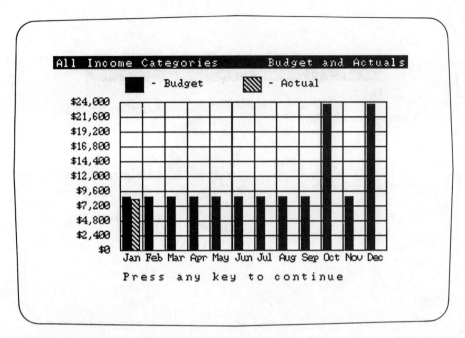

Fig. 12.3. All income categories: budgets and actuals.

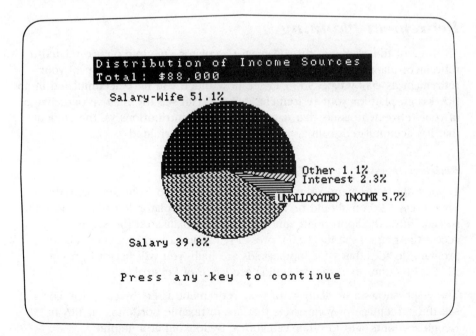

Fig. 12.4. The distribution of income sources.

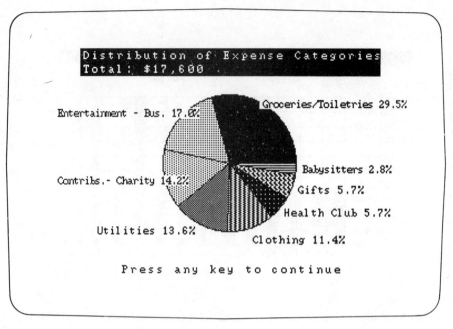

Fig. 12.5. The distribution of expense categories.

Retirement Planning

All three of the graphs in the Financial Calculator (module 6) are related to retirement planning. Using these graphs, you can see a breakdown of your retirement assets by type; you can see how much you have accumulated in an IRA/Keogh plan for your retirement, and you can see the relative percentage of your retirement assets that came from your contributions vs. the amount that has accumulated from appreciation of the contributed assets.

Retirement Assets by Type

To view the retirement assets by type graph, press F6 from the Main Menu. Then press F2. You should be at the Financial Calculator/Retirement Planning screen. Enter the appropriate amounts into the blanks on the screen. To access the graph (see fig. 12.6), press F1, F2, and F1 in sequence. (If the program decides that your input yields are high, you will have to press F1, F1, F2, F1 rather than the preceding sequence of keystrokes.)

The graph shows a breakdown of your retirement assets by category. You can see the percentage of your assets that are in taxable portfolios, in IRA or Keogh accounts, and in other categories. By looking at a graphic representation of the figures, you should better understand the distribution of

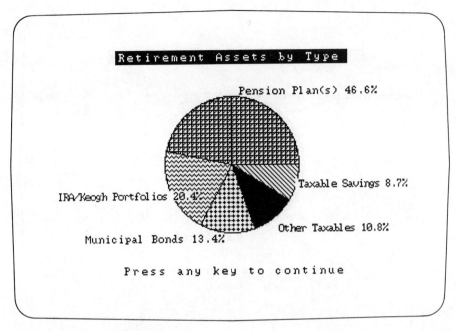

Fig. 12.6. Retirement assets by type.

your assets and be able to decide whether a realignment would better suit your objectives.

IRA/Keogh Fund Analysis

Access the pie graph that shows a breakdown of your retirement assets according to how much you have accumulated in an IRA/Keogh plan for retirement in almost the same way you accessed the preceding graph. From the Main Menu, press F6, then F2. After you have entered the appropriate figures in the Financial Calculator/Retirement Planning screen, press F1, F2, F2 (see fig. 12.7) or press F1, F1, F2, F2 if required.

The extra amount that you were able to accumulate by investing in a retirement plan such as an IRA or Keogh is displayed on this screen. You may be surprised at how much more quickly assets grow in an IRA than in a taxable portfolio. The reason for the drastic difference in the rate of appreciation is that taxes are deferred on a tax-free portfolio until the assets are withdrawn. Deferring taxes allows both the principal and the full amount of your earnings to provide earning power in future years. In a taxable portfolio, only the principal invested and the after-tax amount of the earnings remain in the portfolio to appreciate.

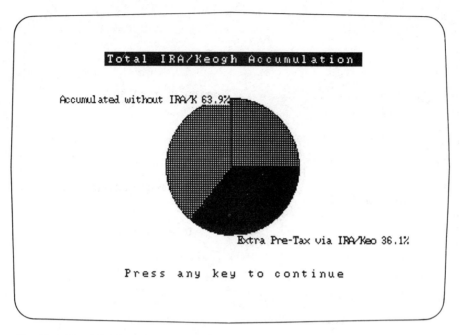

Fig. 12.7. Total IRA/Keogh accumulation.

Retirement Contributions Versus Appreciation

Access the retirement contributions vs. appreciation graph with the same screens and in the same manner as the preceding two retirement planning graphs. From the Main Menu press in succession F6, F2, F1, F2, and F3 (see fig. 12.8) or F6, F2, F1, F1, F2, F3, if required. The screen displays the percentage of your total retirement assets derived from contributions to your retirement fund and the percentage of the assets that came from the appreciation of your contributed assets.

Portfolio Analysis

The next six graphs that the program offers use certain criteria to display the breakdown of assets in your portfolio or in portfolios that you set up in the Portfolio Manager (module 7). You can select certain portfolios and selected assets from the portfolios and then graph the specified assets by risk, tax status, liquidity, industry group, recommendor, and type. The Portfolio Manager tutorial, presented in Chapter 8, explains the selection criteria.

To access each of the six asset distribution graphs, you first press the same sequence of five function keys. Then you press a sixth function key that

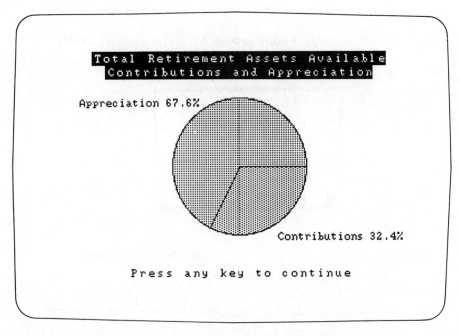

Fig. 12.8. Total retirement assets: contributions vs. appreciation in IRA/ Keogh.

differs for each graph. To access any of the portfolio graphs from the Main Menu, you press in succession F7, F2, F1, F1, and F6.

Whichever graph you are attempting to access, after pressing F2-Analyze Assets, you must select the portfolios and the assets listed in them. After pressing F1 the first time, you may want to enter some selection criteria in order to further narrow down the assets included in your graph. Finally, after pressing F6, your screen should look like figure 12.9. From this screen, you have the option to select and display any of the six portfolio graphs. Each of these graphs is described and illustrated in the text that follows.

Assets by Risk

Press F1 to display the distribution by risk graph shown in figure 12.10. By viewing the percentage of selected assets you have categorized as either speculative, moderate, or low risk, you may determine that the risk distribution of your assets is inconsistent with your long-term goals. If you are nearing retirement age and feel that you have sufficient accumulated assets for those years, then you would not place a large percentage of your assets in speculative investments. On the other hand, if your career is just

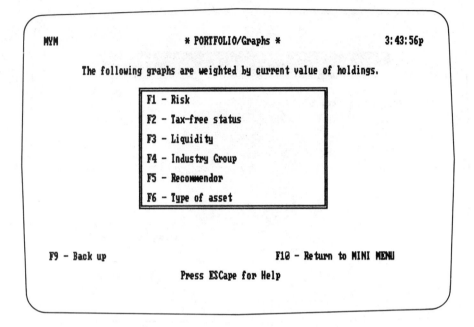

Fig. 12.9. The Portfolio Graphs screen.

beginning and you want to take a few chances with your accumulated amount in more than just low risk (and probably low return) assets, then a graph often puts these considerations in perspective and helps you make better decisions about your financial future.

Assets by Tax Status

Press F2 to display the distribution by tax-free status graph shown in figure 12.11. The graph shows the percentage of selected assets that are tax-free and the percentage that are taxable. Depending on your individual tax rate, you may be wise to make tax-free investments rather than taxable investments.

Assets by Liquidity

Press F3 to display the distribution by liquidity graph shown in figure 12.12. *Liquidity* measures how easily your investments can be converted into cash. Stocks that are traded on the stock exchange generally are referred to as *liquid* investments, and investments in a limited partnership are typically called *illiquid* investments. You can place certain assets in illiquid investments, but be sure to leave enough in liquid investments to meet financial emergencies. If you try to convert an illiquid investment into cash

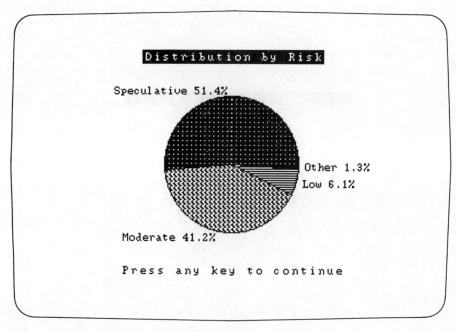

Fig. 12.10. The distribution of assets by risk.

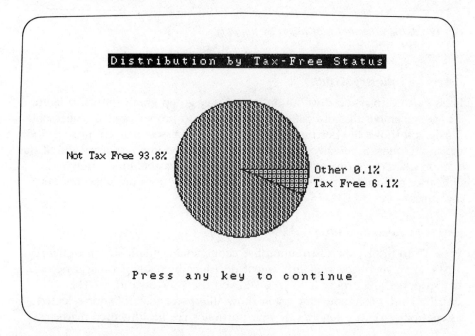

Fig. 12.11. The distribution of assets by tax-free status.

on short notice, you will probably receive an amount far below the market value of the investment (if you are even able to sell the investment).

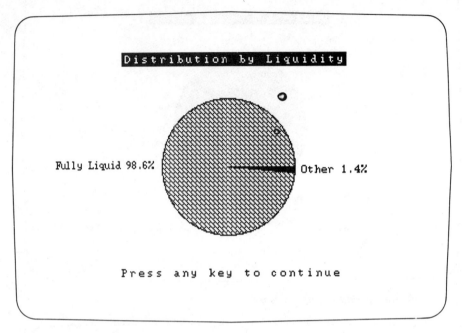

Fig. 12.12. The distribution of assets by liquidity.

Assets by Industry Group

Press F4 to display the distribution by industry group graph shown in figure 12.13. Remember that diversification is the key to proper asset management. This graph shows the percentage of your selected assets that are in specified industry groups. Eventually, you may be overinvested in an industry and, if the economy falters, you would be hit hard. Keep your assets in a variety of industries so that a downturn in any single industry does not wipe out your investment.

Assets by Recommendor

Press F5 to display the distribution by recommendor graph shown in figure 12.14. Have you made your investment decisions by reading a magazine or a newspaper? Did a broker help you? Did you use your own ideas? The distribution by recommendor graph shows the percentage of your selected assets from various categories. If your portfolios are healthy, then maybe you

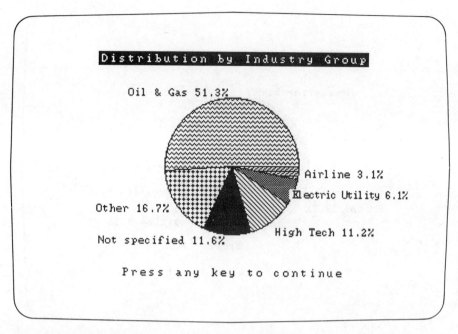

Fig. 12.13. The distribution of assets by industry group.

should continue the methods you have used in the past. If your investments are performing poorly, then the graph can help you identify the reasons.

Assets by Type

Press F6 to display the distribution by type of asset graph shown in figure 12.15. The percentage of your selected assets that are invested in common stocks, preferred stocks, mutual funds, bonds, or other type of investment is displayed on the screen. If you have been very successful with mutual funds, but the graph reveals that a large percentage of your assets are in low yielding bonds, then maybe you should make a change. Look at the graph, analyze the situation, and try to draw some conclusions. Then take action, if necessary. Believe the graphs. They don't lie.

Graph of Assets or Liabilities

The last graph presented here is in the Your Net Worth module (module 8). To access it, press F8 from the Main Menu. Move down to the level that you want to graph by pressing F7 until you see the F6-Graph This Level Option. When you get to this level, press F6 to display the graph shown in figure

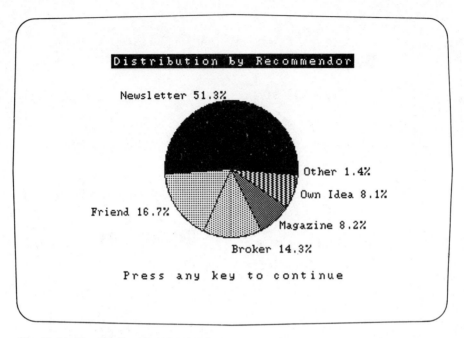

Fig. 12.14. The distribution of assets by recommendor.

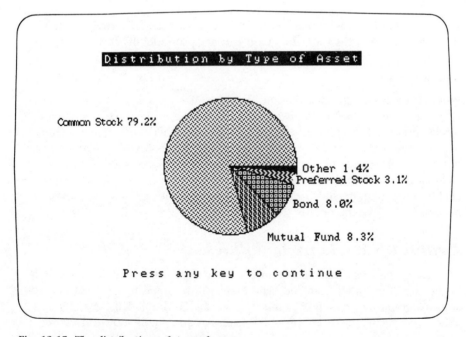

Fig. 12.15. The distribution of assets by type.

12.16. By showing you the various components in your net worth, this graph lets you see the makeup of your assets or your liabilities so that you can determine whether changes should be made.

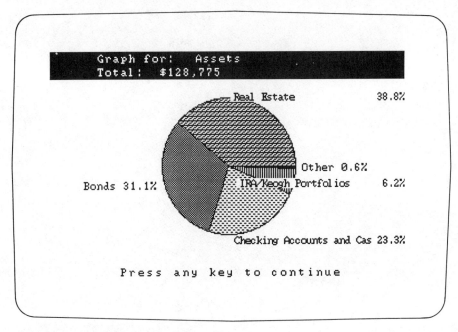

Fig. 12.16. The distribution of personal assets.

## Chapter 13

Creating Reports

With Managing Your Money, you can print many reports that you can keep either for a session or as part of your permanent record keeping. Some reports are as simple as a listing of your daily appointments. Others are as complex as an entire year's expenses grouped by tax category. (The latter report will certainly please your accountant.) If you need a certain report, or if you just want to know what is available, this chapter is for you.

Managing Your Money has three basic categories of reports:

- The *standard reports* help you keep track of such matters as your appointments, your budgeted and actual expenses, and the assets in or sold from your portfolio during the year.

- The *budget archive reports* allow you to view the archived transactions from the Budget and Checkbook module of the program and combine those archived transactions with the current transactions in a report.

- The *portfolio archive reports* allow you to view your archived transactions from the Portfolio Manager module of the program and combine those archived transactions with the current transactions in a report.

Accessing the Standard Reports

Table 13.1 lists the standard reports that are available in Managing Your Money and the key sequences to press from the Main Menu in order to access the reports.

The reports classified as the standard reports can be found in the Reminder Pad (module 2), the Budget and Checkbook (module 3), Insurance Planning (module 5), the Financial Calculator (module 6), the Portfolio Manager (module 7), Your Net Worth (module 8), and the Card File (module 9).

Table 13.1
Standard Reports and How To Access Them

Report	Module	Function Keys
Reminder Pad		
Hour-by-Hour Report	2	F2, F3, F1
Overview Report	2	F2, F4, F1
List of Appointments	2	F2, F5, F4, F1, F1
List of Reminders	2	F2, F6, F4, F1, F1
List of To-Dos	2	F2, F7, F4, F1, F1
Budget and Checkbook		
Budget Reports		
Annual Totals	3	F3, F1, F5, A, F1
Budget vs. Actual	3	F3, F1, F5, B, F1
Comprehensive	3	F3, F1, F5, C, F1
Check Register	3	F3, F2, F1, Alt-F4, F1
Print Checks	3	F3, F2, F1, F4, F1 or F3
*Amortization of Mortgage Loan	3	F3, F4, F2, F2, F1
**Aged Payables Report	3	F3, F2, F6, F5, F1
**Aged Receivables Report	3	F3, F2, F7, F5, F1
Print Invoices	3	F3, F2, F7, F6, F1
Insurance Planning		
Insurance Policy List	5	F5, F4, F4, F1
Financial Calculator		
College Planning Report	6	F6, F3, F1, F4, F1
General Investment Analysis	6	F6, F4, F4, F1
Rental Property Report	6	F6, F5, F1, F4, (D, S, or I), F1

Portfolio Manager

Financial Reminders	7	F7, F4, F4, F1

Asset Analyzer Reports

Appreciation	7	F7, F2, F1, F1, F4, A, F1
Yield	7	F7, F2, F1, F1, F4, Y, F1
Both	7	F7, F2, F1, F1, F4, B, F1

Aggregate Portfolio Display	7	F7, F2, F1, F1, F1, F2, F4, F1
Dividends	7	F7, F8, F4, F1
rint All Assets All Portfolios	7	F7, F3, F4, F1
Print Unsold Assets	7	F7, F3, F2, F4, F1
Print Sold Assets	7	F7, F3, F2, SO, F6, F4, F1
Print Short Assets	7	F7, F3, F2, SH, F6, F4, F1
Good-Til-Canceleds	7	F7, F3, F7, F4, F1

Your Net Worth

Personal Balance Sheet

Bank Style	8	F8, F4, B, F1
Corporate Style	8	F8, F4, C, F1
Level of Detail	8	F8, F4, 1–4 or all, F1

Card File

Telephone Listing	9	F9, F4, F1, B, F1
Detailed Card File	9	F9, F4, F1, F, F1
Mailing Labels	9	F9, F4, F1, L, F1
Mail Merge	9	F9, F4, F1, M, F1

*Available only for mortgage type loans.
**Available only if optional features of Accounts Payable and Accounts Receivable are activated.

The standard reports can include only data from active files. In contrast, the budget archive and portfolio archive reports can include archived data as well as data from active files.

You may print some of the standard reports, such as the list of appointments in the Reminder Pad, on a daily basis. You may need other reports only for special events. For instance, you may want to print a personal balance sheet to illustrate for your banker that the personal loan you requested should be approved.

You may print other reports on a regular, but less frequent basis, such as once a month. After updating the prices of the stocks and bonds in your portfolio at the end of the month, you may want to print a report of all your assets in all your portfolios so that you can see whether your investments are performing as well as they should be.

In time, you will find what is best for you and which reports provide you with the information you require. Begin by experimenting with all of the reports.

Versions 3.0 and 4.0 of Managing Your Money have the capability to print reports to your screen, to your printer, or to a disk. Print to your screen first in order to see what the report will look like, and then print a hard copy to your printer.

After you print a report to disk, you can use your own word-processing program or the one included with Managing Your Money to modify the report.

In addition to the list of reports discussed in this chapter, you can print any screen to your printer just by pressing Shift-PrtSc.

Designing Budget Archive Reports

The three budget archive reports listed in table 13.2 are the standard report formats provided by the program. If no further changes are made, then your standard report includes all your accounts and all your budget categories.

You can design your own reports including only some of your accounts and some of your budget categories.

To design your own budget archive report:

1. From the Main Menu, press Alt-F3.

2. Type **Y** or **N**.

Table 13.2
Budget Archive Reports and How To Access Them

Report	Function Keys
Listing by Account	Alt-F3, Y or N, Enter, Enter, F4, F5, F9, F5, F5
Listing by Tax Category	Alt-F3, Y or N, Enter, Enter, F4, F6, F9, F5, F5
Listing by Payee	Alt-F3, Y or N, Enter, Enter, F4, F7, F9, F5, F5

3. Press Enter twice.

Your screen should display the Budget Archive Report Generator (see fig. 13.1).

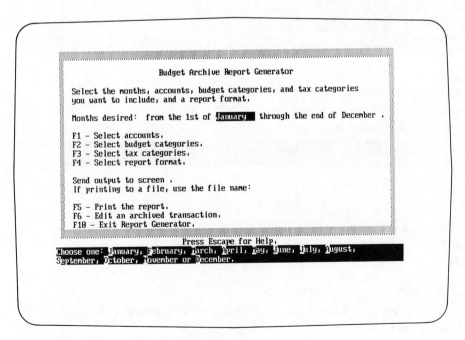

Fig. 13.1. *The Budget Archive Report Generator.*

You can press F⁴ to select accounts; F2 to select budget categories; F3 to select tax categories; or F4 either to select a standard report or to design your own report. As discussed in the "Archiving Temporarily" section of Chapter 5, "Using the Budget and Checkbook," a specified transaction will not be included in a report unless it is in a selected account, a selected budget category, and a selected tax category.

4. Press F4-Select Report Format to display the Sorting and Print Order screen (see fig. 13.2).

   From this screen, you can create your own customized report.

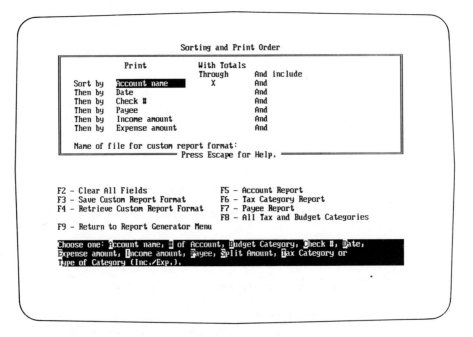

Fig. 13.2. The Budget Archive Sorting and Print Order screen.

5. Make any changes you want until you are satisfied with the design of your report.

6. To save the customized report, press F3-Save Custom Report Format.

When you later return to the Budget Archives, your customized
report will be there.

Designing Portfolio Archive Reports

Managing Your Money's portfolio archive reports are listed in table 13.3.
These reports can be modified in a manner similar to the way you modify the
budget archive reports.

Table 13.3
Portfolio Archive Reports and How To Access Them

Report	Function Keys
Listing by Portfolio	Alt-F7, Y or N , Enter, Enter, F4, F5, F9, F5, F5
Listing by Asset Name	Alt-F7, Y or N, Enter, Enter, F4, F6, F9, F5, F5
Schedule D (Capital gains or losses)	Alt-F7, Y or N, Enter, Enter, F6, F6, F6, F5

To design your own portfolio archive report:

1. From the Main Menu, press Alt-F7.

2. Press **Y** or **N**.

3. Press Enter twice.

   Your screen should display the Portfolio Archive Report Generator
   (see fig. 13.3).

   Now you can select the portfolios, the asset names, and the asset
   types that you want to include in your report. To be included in a
   report, a portfolio transaction must be in one of the selected
   portfolios, it must have one of the selected names, and it must be
   one of the selected asset types. Select the report format only after
   you have selected the transactions that you want to include in the
   report.

4. Press F4-Select Report Format to display the Sorting and Print Order
   screen (see fig. 13.4).

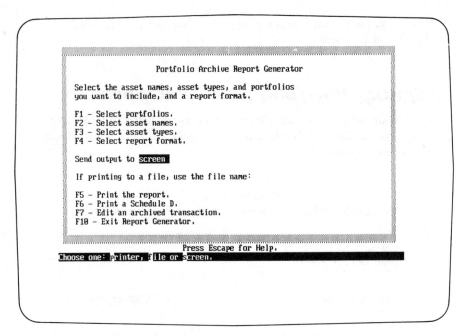

Fig. 13.3. The Portfolio Archive Report Generator.

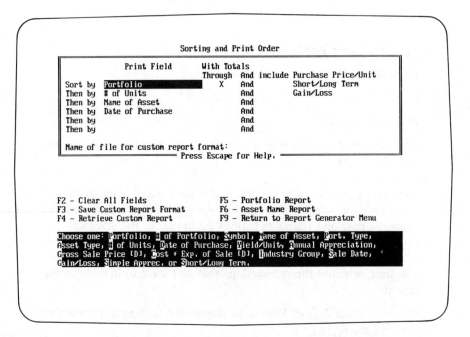

Fig. 13.4. The Portfolio Archive Sorting and Print Order screen.

5. Make any modifications that you want to your report.

6. To save the customized report, press F3-Save Custom Report Format.

   When you later return to the Portfolio Archives, your customized report will be there.

Menu Maps

Menu Overview*

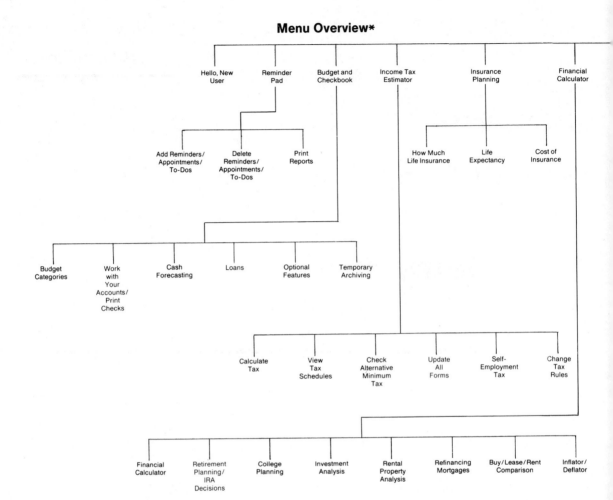

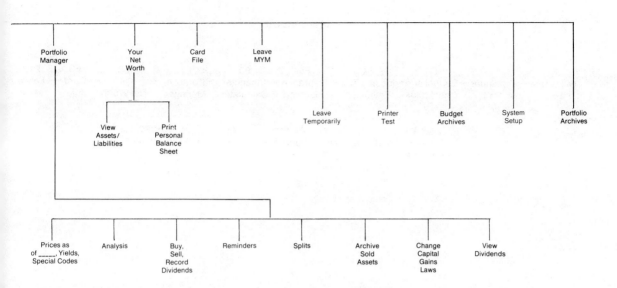

* This overview summarizes the features of the program. For exact menu options, see the maps that follow.

Main Menu

F1	F2	F3	F4	F5	F6	F7	F8	F9	F10
Hello, New User	Reminder Pad	Budget and Checkbook	Income Tax Estimator	Insurance Planning	Financial Calculator	Portfolio Manager	Your Net Worth	Card File	Leave MYM

Alt-F1	Alt-F2	Alt-F3	Alt-F6	Alt-F7
Leave Temporarily	Printer Test	Budget Archives	System Setup	Portfolio Archives

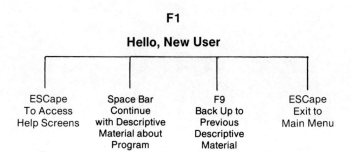

F1

Hello, New User

ESCape	Space Bar	F9	ESCape
To Access	Continue	Back Up to	Exit to
Help Screens	with Descriptive	Previous	Main Menu
	Material about	Descriptive	
	Program	Material	

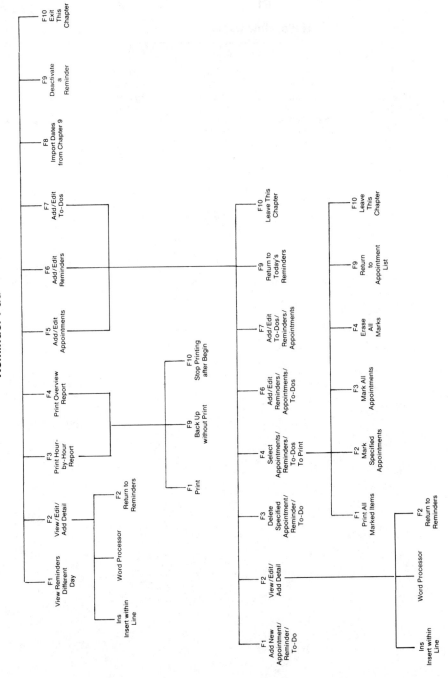

F2

Reminder Pad

F3

Budget and Checkbook

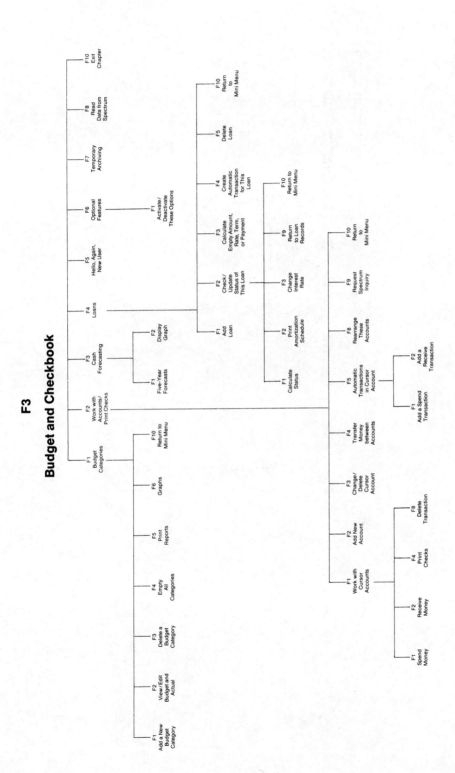

F4

Income Tax Estimator

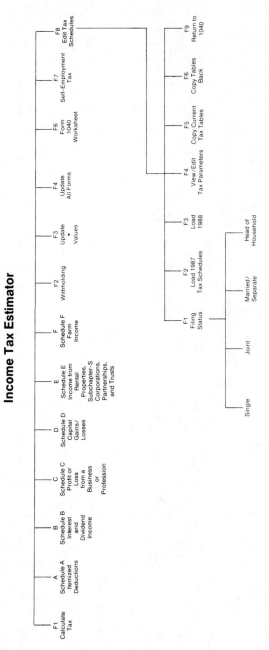

F5

Insurance Planning

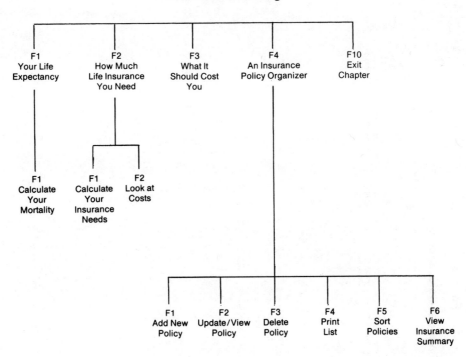

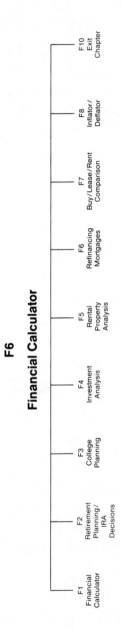

F6
Financial Calculator

F1
Financial
Calculator

F2
Retirement
Planning/
IRA
Decisions

F3
College
Planning

F4
Investment
Analysis

F5
Rental
Property
Analysis

F6
Refinancing
Mortgages

F7
Buy/Lease/Rent
Comparison

F8
Inflator/
Deflator

F10
Exit
Chapter

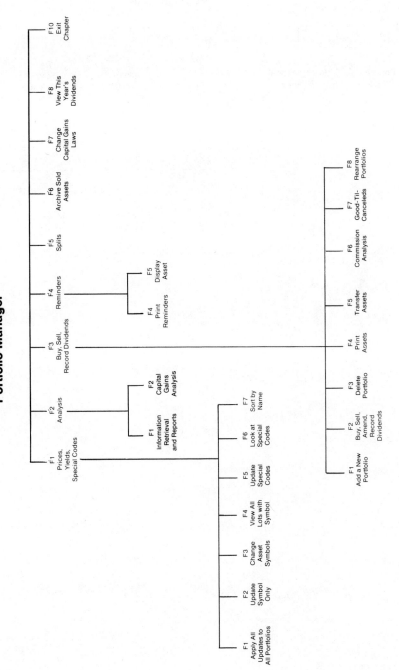

F7

Portfolio Manager

F8

Your Net Worth

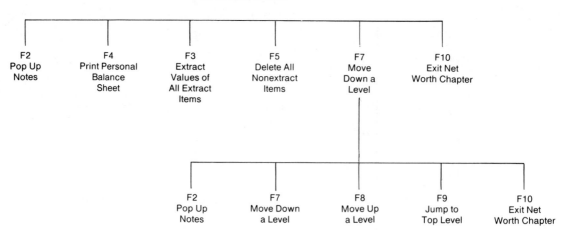

F2
Pop Up
Notes

F4
Print Personal
Balance
Sheet

F3
Extract
Values of
All Extract
Items

F5
Delete All
Nonextract
Items

F7
Move
Down a
Level

F10
Exit Net
Worth Chapter

F2
Pop Up
Notes

F7
Move Down
a Level

F8
Move Up
a Level

F9
Jump to
Top Level

F10
Exit Net
Worth Chapter

F9

Card File

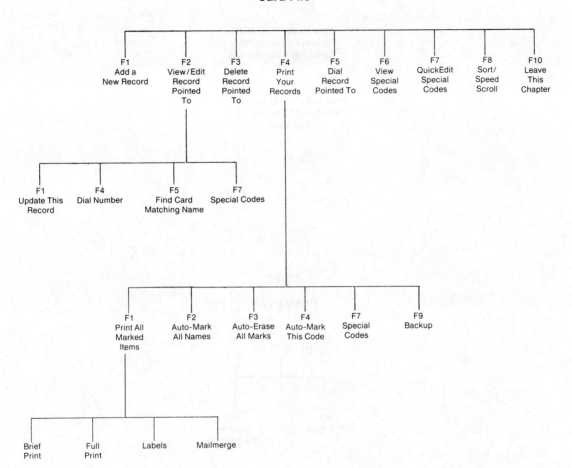

Alt-F1

Leave Temporarily

Enter **Exit** at the DOS
prompt (to return to
Managing Your Money)

Press any key to resume
Managing Your Money
operation

Alt-F2

Printer Test

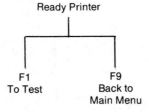

Ready Printer

F1
To Test

F9
Back to
Main Menu

Alt-F3

Budget Archives

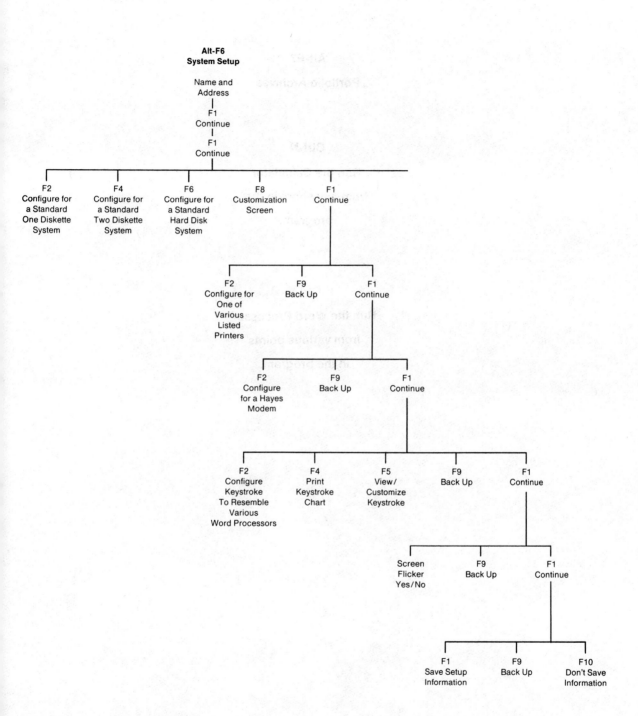

Alt-F6
System Setup

Name and
Address

F1
Continue

F1
Continue

F2
Configure for
a Standard
One Diskette
System

F4
Configure for
a Standard
Two Diskette
System

F6
Configure for
a Standard
Hard Disk
System

F8
Customization
Screen

F1
Continue

F2
Configure for
One of
Various
Listed
Printers

F9
Back Up

F1
Continue

F2
Configure
for a Hayes
Modem

F9
Back Up

F1
Continue

F2
Configure
Keystroke
To Resemble
Various
Word Processors

F4
Print
Keystroke
Chart

F5
View /
Customize
Keystroke

F9
Back Up

F1
Continue

Screen
Flicker
Yes / No

F9
Back Up

F1
Continue

F1
Save Setup
Information

F9
Back Up

F10
Don't Save
Information

Alt-F7

Portfolio Archives

Ctrl-N

Run the Calculator

from anywhere in the

program.

Ctrl-E

Run the Word Processor

from various points

in the program.

Glossary

Account

A grouping of financial transactions. Examples include a savings account, a checking account, and a credit card account.

Account Payable

An amount you owe to a creditor for goods purchased or services provided.

Account Receivable

An amount that is owed to you for goods sold or services provided.

Actuarial Table

A table that contains information on life expectancy or other similar information. An actuarial table is used by insurance companies to determine the premium to be charged for a given risk. The information in the table is compiled from actual data on large numbers of previous cases.

Adjusted Gross Income

A taxpayer's gross income less certain allowable deductions other than itemized deductions.

Alternative Minimum Tax

A tax designed to ensure that all individuals pay at least some income tax. Beginning in 1987, this tax is 21 percent of alternative minimum taxable income over an exemption amount. Alternative minimum taxable income is calculated by adding back certain otherwise allowable deductions to a taxpayer's adjusted gross income.

Amortization Schedule

A schedule that displays the split between interest and principal for each payment on a loan and the current loan balance.

Annual After-Tax Yield

The after-tax amount earned on an investment on an annual basis as a percentage of the cost of the investment.

Annual Appreciation

The percentage increase in the value of an asset or a group of assets during a one-year period.

Annual Depreciation

The percentage decrease in the value of an asset or a group of assets during a one-year period.

Annuity

A stream of payments that you receive for a period of years or indefinitely. The payments, which may be based on amounts that you paid into a fund during your period of employment, may serve as retirement income. The payments also could represent life insurance proceeds that were not paid out in a lump sum.

Archive File

A storage file that contains personal financial data that is no longer needed in the active files.

Archiving

The process of transferring data no longer necessary for current purposes from an active file to a storage file in order to free up memory on the computer.

Asset

Something that you own, such as a car or a house or even the money in your bank account.

Automatic Transaction

A receipt or disbursement of cash programmed into Managing Your Money because it occurs on a regular basis. After the amount is programmed, it can be recorded with just a few keystrokes.

Backing Up

The process of making duplicate copies of your program or your data files in order to minimize loss if your original files are damaged.

Balance

The current dollar amount in an account.

Balance Sheet

A list of assets, liabilities, and ownership equity at a specific point in time. In the case of an individual's balance sheet, the difference between assets and liabilities generally is called net worth instead of ownership equity.

Bond

A financial instrument that represents money owed to a holder by a company or other entity (known as the issuer).

Bond Discount

The amount, below the face amount, that is paid for a bond.

Bond Premium

The amount, exceeding the face amount, that is paid for a bond.

Budget

A plan for future income and expenses.

Budget Archives

Data that has been archived from the Budget and Checkbook module of Managing Your Money.

Capital Gain

The gain that results from the sale of certain assets by an individual. Such gain may be long term or short term depending on the length of time that the asset is held. (More than 6 months is long term.) Beginning in 1987, if the asset was held for more than 6 months, the gain is taxed at 28 percent. Beginning in 1988, the gain, whether long or short term, will be taxed at the same rate as ordinary income.

Capital Loss

The loss that results from the sale of certain assets by an individual. Such loss may be long term or short term depending on the length of time that the asset is held. (More than 6 months is long term.) Capital losses may be offset against capital gains in full, and the remainder, if any, may be deducted against ordinary income of up to $3,000 per year.

Cash Flow

An analysis of your actual or projected inflow and outflow of cash that is used to determine (after all your expenditures are made) whether you will have money left over for savings or investment or whether you will have to borrow or withdraw money from savings in order to meet your obligations.

Cash Management Account (CMA)

A combination brokerage account to hold stocks, bonds, and other similar investments and a money market account to ensure that cash balances remain productive.

Commission

The fee paid to a broker for buying or selling an asset for you.

Common Stock

An ownership interest in a company. A holder of common stock generally possesses voting rights in the company. Common stock is subordinate, in terms of dividend and liquidation preference, to any preferred stock that may be outstanding.

Compounding of Interest

Earning interest on your interest.

Copy Protection

The method used by the developers of computer software packages to prevent unauthorized copying of the program.

Coupon Rate of Bond

The stated interest rate that the issuer of a bond is obligated to pay as a percentage of the bond's face amount.

Current Yield of Bond

The coupon interest rate of a bond divided by the price paid for the bond.

Data File

A file that contains personal financial data.

Day Order

An order that is placed with a broker to buy or sell an asset at a specified price. The price expires at the end of the day if not executed.

Diversification

The spreading out of investments among various industry groups and types of investment in an effort to reduce risk.

Dividend

An amount paid by a company or other entity to the holder of shares of the company's stock. A dividend generally represents a distribution of the company's earnings.

DOS

Stands for disk operating system. DOS is a set of commands that helps you run programs on your computer.

Effective Annual Yield

The stated interest rate as adjusted for the effects of compounding.

Expense

An outflow of cash that may represent payment for a service performed or for the purchase of an asset.

Face Amount of Bond

The amount that the issuer of a bond is obligated to repay to the bondholder when the bond matures.

Fee-Only Planners

Financial planners who charge a fee for their services, but who don't make any additional amount on the sale of investments that they recommend.

FICA

Social Security tax.

Form 1040

The basic federal tax form that individuals file annually.

Function Keys

The F1 through F10 and Alt-F1 through Alt-F7 keys that are used to move within the program and to perform program functions.

Future Value

The dollar amount that the present sum will reach at a specified interest rate and after a certain number of years or other period of time.

Good-Til-Canceled Order

An order that a broker receives to buy or sell an asset at a specified price. The price remains in effect until the transaction is executed at the specified price or until the order is canceled.

Graph

A pictorial representation of certain financial data showing a breakdown by designated category.

Help Screens

Certain screens in Managing Your Money that are designed to answer questions about each program function. You can access the screens from anywhere in the program by pressing the ESCape key.

Home Banking

A program function that allows you to transfer money between accounts and pay certain bills by telephone if you have a modem attached to your computer and you bank at Chase Manhattan Bank.

Income

Any inflow of cash that represents wages, interest, or even a loan repayment.

Internal Rate of Return

The annual after-tax rate of interest you would have to earn in order to equal the results obtained from a particular investment.

IRA

Stands for individual retirement account. An IRA, a creation of the Internal Revenue Code (the tax laws), allows qualified individuals to save for retirement without current taxation on earnings in the account and, in certain cases, with a deduction for amounts paid into the account.

Itemized Deductions

Certain specified expenses that can be deducted on an individual's federal tax return (Form 1040). Examples of itemized deductions are interest, state and local income and property taxes, and contributions to charity.

Liability

An amount that you owe. Examples of liabilities are bank loans and unpaid amounts charged on your credit cards.

Life Expectancy

The age to which an individual is expected to live. Life expectancy is based on such factors as family longevity, overall health, and marital status and is calculated by entering these factors into actuarial tables.

Liquidity

The ease with which you can convert an asset to cash. A fully liquid asset is one that can be converted to cash immediately (a publicly traded stock, for example). An illiquid asset is one that may take a long time to convert to cash (a house in an economically depressed area, for example).

Main Menu

The control center of Managing Your Money. You must use the Main Menu in order to access the program's functions.

Mini Menu

The control center of certain program modules. You must use the Mini Menu within certain modules in order to access a module's functions.

Modem

A device that can be attached to your computer so that you can transmit information over telephone lines.

Mortgage Points

The up-front fee charged by a bank or other lending institution when making a mortgage loan.

Mutual Fund

An investment vehicle that takes the money received from investors and purchases a variety of stocks or bonds. A mutual fund allows investors to gain wider diversification of their investments and to obtain the services of professional money managers.

Net Worth

The difference between total assets and total liabilities.

Personal Exemption Amount

The amount that taxpayers are allowed to deduct from gross income on their tax returns for each dependent claimed. In 1986, the amount was $1,080 for each exemption; in 1987 and 1988, the amount is $1,900; and in 1989, the amount is $2,000.

Portfolio

Any collection of assets that you group together. A portfolio can consists of a coin collection, baseball cards, or more typically, stocks and bonds.

Portfolio Archives

Data that has been archived from the Portfolio Manager module of the program.

Preference Items

Certain specified deductions, allowed by the tax code, that must be added back to adjusted gross income in order to calculate the alternative minimum tax. Examples of preference items are depreciation and money made on certain stock options.

Preferred Stock

An ownership interest in a company. A holder of preferred stock generally does not possess voting rights in the company. Preferred stock is superior, in terms of dividends and liquidation preference, to the company's common stock.

Present Value

The dollar amount that you begin with in financial calculations.

Program File

A file containing the commands that make Managing Your Money work.

Reconciliation of Checkbook

The process of comparing the balance listed in your checkbook (the book balance) with the ending balance that the bank has listed (the bank balance) and then accounting for the difference between the two balances.

Reversionary Term Insurance

A type of term life insurance which requires that you requalify every certain number of years in order to be covered by the policy. The requalification procedure may involve a physical exam, and, if your health has deteriorated, you may be rejected for coverage.

Risk

The measurable likelihood of losing the principal you invest.

Self-Employment Tax

The Social Security tax that must be paid on net earnings from self-employment.

Settlement Date

The date that the money is due for the purchase or sale of an asset. For stocks traded on a public market, the settlement date generally is seven days after the trade date.

Source Disk

The disk that contains material to be copied to a target disk.

Stock

An ownership interest in a company.

Stock Dividend

A small stock split in which shareholders receive dividends in the form of additional shares. Instead of doubling or tripling the number of shares outstanding, the number of shares may increase by a smaller amount. For example, in a 10 percent stock dividend, a shareholder would receive 1 share for every 10 shares of stock owned. The stock price drops accordingly, as in a stock split.

Stock Multiple

A figure that indicates the current price of a stock as compared to the earnings per share of the stock. For example, a stock that is selling for $30 per share and that had $1.50 per share of earning for the latest year, is selling at a multiple of 20.

Stock Option

A stockholder's right, but not an obligation, to buy a given number of shares of stock at a stated price for a stated period of time, without regard to the stock's market price on the date that the option is exercised.

Stock Split

An increase in the number of outstanding shares of stock, which results in a decrease in the stock price. Typically, stocks split two-for-one or three-for-two. The number of shares you hold increases, but the value of your holdings does not change, nor does your percentage of holdings in the company.

Target Disk

The disk onto which material from a source disk is copied.

Tax Shelters

Investments in which taxpayers were able to take deductions (arising out of their investments) against their ordinary income, thereby reducing their tax liabilities. Beginning in 1987, the new tax law curtails the use of tax shelters.

Taxable Portfolio

A portfolio in which the gains and losses from the sale of assets in the portfolio are taxable.

Temporary Archiving

The temporary combining of unarchived data with archived data so that an entire year's data can be analyzed at one time.

Term Life Insurance

Life insurance that is purchased for a stated period of time. If the insured dies during the period that the policy is in force, then the policy will pay off.

Trade Date

The date that an asset is actually purchased or sold.

Turbo-Search Key

A Managing Your Money program function, in the Budget and Checkbook module, that allows you to allocate to a budget category amounts that are spent or received.

Whole Life Insurance

Life insurance that, once purchased, covers the insured for his or her entire life. Whole life insurance contains both a life insurance component and an investment component. This type of insurance generally can be cashed in prior to the death of the insured.

Yield to Maturity of Bond

The total return on a bond investment. Yield to maturity takes into account the coupon rate of interest paid on the bond, the premium or discount paid for the bond, and the length of time until the bond matures.

Index

distribution of assets by
 industry group, 362
 liquidity, 360, 362
 recommendor, 362, 364
 risk, 359-361
 tax status, 360-361
 type, 363-364
IRA/Keogh fund, 357-358
loading a program, 349-350
portfolio analysis, 358-363
printing, 350
retirement
 assets by type, 356-357
 contributions versus appreciation, 358
 planning, 356-363

H

hard disk system
 installing Managing Your Money on, 36-37
 loading DOS graphics program on, 350
 making backup copies on, 50
Hello New User module, 16, 40-47
Help mode, 28
Help screens, 212, 259
 accessing, 28
 Reminder Pad module, 77
home banking, 19, 152
Home key, 94
hypothetical portfolio, 216-218

I

income, 93-102
 rental, 290
 shifting, 290
 tax, 286-331
  calculating, 312-331
  dividend income, 301
  filing status, 300
  interest income, 301
  personal exemptions, 301
  salaries, 301
  Schedule A
   deductions, 308-310
   updating, 321-328

  Schedule B, 301-306
  Schedule C, 302, 304-306
  Schedule D, 319-320
  Schedule E, 307
  Schedule F, 307
  state and local, 288
Income Tax Estimator module, 20-21, 69, 285-298
 accessing, 20
 entering data into, 299-312
 Investment Interest worksheet, 311
 Moving Expenses worksheet, 311
individual tax rates, 286-287
inflation (effects of), 196
Inflator/Deflator, 156, 196-197
installing
 Managing Your Money, 35, 41-49
  hard disk system, 36-37
  single floppy disk system, 39-40
  two floppy disk system, 37-39
insurance
 analysis, 21
 costs, 21
 organizing policies, 21
 reversionary, 206
 review, 64, 68-69
 term life, 206-207
 whole life, 206
Insurance Planning module, 21, 70, 199-207
 accessing, 21
 determining life insurance needs, 202-205
 estimating cost of life insurance, 205-207
 life expectancy, 200-202
integrated system, 19
interest
 deductions (reclassifying), 330-331
 rate, 165
  versus yield, 155, 166-167
 tax deductible, 288-298
internal rate of return, 155
 rental property investment, 184-185
Internal Revenue Service (IRS), 288, 293, 296
inventories, 24
investment(s)
 analysis, 64, 68-69, 180-183
 diversification, 362

portfolio archiving
    temporarily, 264-267
    Portfolio Manager module, 263-267
portfolio graphs
    accessing, 359-360, 362-363
Portfolio Manager module, 23-24, 209-270
    accessing, 23
    adding assets to portfolios, 221-228
    aggregation of assets, 250-252
    analyzing
      assets, 241
      capital gains, 256-258
    archiving data in, 33
    commission analysis, 218-219
    comparing assets to index, 252-253
    creating new portfolio, 216-218
    deleting sample data, 215-216
    designing reports, 267-268
    displaying and analyzing yield, 248-254
    displaying appreciation, 248
    financial reminders, 258-261
    good-til-canceled orders, 219-221
    graphing portfolio holdings, 254-255
    portfolio archiving, 263-267
    printing
      lists of assets, 228
      unsold assets, 233-234
    selecting
      portfolios for analysis, 241-248
      shares to sell, 239-241
    Sell, Record Dividends, 214
    selling stocks, 234-239
    setting up portfolios, 216
    sorting assets, 240
    stock splits, 261-263
    unsold assets, 232-241
    updating
      capital gains laws, 268-269
      prices, 229-231
    viewing this year's dividends, 269
portfolios
    hypothetical, 216-218
    IRA/Keogh, 216
    taxable, 216

preference items
    extracting from Schedules A, B, and E, 315
    tax deductions, 289
premium, 165
present balance, 168
present value, 158, 160-162
    future expense, 160-162
printer
    configuration, 44-45
    doesn't work, 45
    testing (Alt-F2), 27
printing
    amortization schedule, 134-136
    appointments, 81-82
    balance sheets, 281-283
    checks, 127-129
    customizing, 44-45
    form letters, 341
    graphs, 350
    keystroke chart, 47
    lists of assets, 228
    loan records, 134-136
    mailing labels, 340-341
    records, 340-341
    reminders, 86
    reports, 146-148, 370
      to screen, 179
    screens, 370
    tax schedules, 293
    unsold assets, 233-234
profit or loss (business), 302, 304-306
program disks, 35
    copying, 36
property management
    active, 186
    passive, 186

R

rate of return, 210
rearranging accounts, 104
reconciling checking account, 19, 124-127

V

values
    future, 158-160
    present, 158, 160-162
verifying tax rate schedules, 296
viewing
    assets in Your Net Worth module, 274-275
    keystroke chart, 47
    liabilities in Your Net Worth module, 275-276
    records in Card File module, 333-335
    this year's dividends, 269

W

Warning Days in reminders, 83-84
"what if" analysis, 69, 291, 317
"what if" calculations, 20-21
whole life insurance, 206
word processor, 25, 30, 338-339
    accessing, 31
    in Reminder Pad, 78, 81
    Keystroke Chart, 46-47
    setting up, 31
    WRITE ON THE MONEY, 46-47
working disks, 35-36
writing checks, 108-110

Y

year-end bonuses (deferring), 326-328
yield(s)
    after tax, 177
    to maturity, 165-166
Your Net Worth module, 24, 67, 271-283
    accessing, 24
    adding assets or liabilities, 277-280
    deleting sample data, 277
    graphs, 363, 365
    printing balance sheets, 281-283
    viewing
        assets, 274-275
        liabilities, 275-276

More Computer Knowledge from Que

LOTUS SOFTWARE TITLES

DATABASE TITLES

MACINTOSH AND APPLE II TITLES

APPLICATIONS SOFTWARE TITLES

WORD-PROCESSING AND DESKTOP PUBLISHING TITLES

HARDWARE AND SYSTEMS TITLES

PROGRAMMING AND TECHNICAL TITLES

Que Order Line: **1-800-428-5331**

All prices subject to change without notice. Prices and charges are for domestic orders only.
Non-U.S. prices might be higher.

MORE COMPUTER KNOWLEDGE FROM QUE

Place
Stamp
Here

Que Corporation
P.O. Box 90
Carmel, IN 46032

REGISTRATION CARD

Register your copy of *Using Managing Your Money* and receive information about Que's newest products. Complete this registration card and return it to Que Corporation, P.O. Box 90, Carmel, IN 46032.

Name _____Phone _____

Company _____Title _____

Address _____

City _____ST _____ZIP _____

Please check the appropriate answers:

Where did you buy *Using Managing Your Money* ?
- ☐ Bookstore (name: _____)
- ☐ Computer store (name: _____)
- ☐ Catalog (name: _____)
- ☐ Direct from Que
- ☐ Other: _____

How many Que books do you own?
- ☐ 1 or less
- ☐ 2-5
- ☐ 6-10
- ☐ More than 10

How long have you been using Managing Your Money?
- ☐ Less than six months
- ☐ Six months to one year
- ☐ 1–3 years
- ☐ More than 3 years

What influenced your purchase of *Using Managing Your Money*?
- ☐ Personal recommendation
- ☐ Advertisement
- ☐ In-store display
- ☐ Price
- ☐ Que catalog
- ☐ Que postcard
- ☐ Que's reputation
- ☐ Other:_____

How would you rate the overall content of *Using Managing Your Money*?
- ☐ Very good
- ☐ Good
- ☐ Not useful
- ☐ Poor

How would you rate *PART I: An Introduction to Managing Your Money and Financial Planning*?
- ☐ Very good
- ☐ Good
- ☐ Not useful
- ☐ Poor

How would you rate *PART II: Managing Your Money Tutorial*?
- ☐ Very good
- ☐ Good
- ☐ Not useful
- ☐ Poor

How would you rate *PART III: Creating Graphs and Reports*?
- ☐ Very good
- ☐ Good
- ☐ Not useful
- ☐ Poor

What do you like *best* about *Using Managing Your Money*?

What do you like *least* about *Using Managing Your Money*?

How do you use *Using Managing Your Money*?

What other Que products do you own?

What other software do you own?

Please feel free to list any other comments you may have about *Using Managing Your Money*.

_____

_____

_____

_____

_____

_____

FOLD HERE

—————————————————————
—————————————————————
—————————————————————
—————————————————————

Place
Stamp
Here

Que Corporation
P.O. Box 90
Carmel, IN 46032